fourth edition

ESSENTIALS OF EDUCATIONAL MEASUREMENT

Robert L. Ebel

David A. Frisbie
University of Iowa

PRENTICE-HALL, INC., Englewood Cliffs, New Jersey 07632

Library of Congress Cataloging-in-Publication Data

EBEL, ROBERT L.
   Essentials of educational measurement.

   Bibliography: p.
   Includes index.
   1. Educational tests and measurements.
2. Examinations—Evaluation. 3. Examinations—
Design and construction. 4. Examinations—
Interpretation. I. Frisbie, David A. II. Title.
LB3051.E22   1986   371.2′6   85-12036
ISBN 0-13-286006-6

Editorial/production supervision: *Edith Riker*
Cover design: *Ben Santora*
Manufacturing buyer: *Barbara Kittle*

Essentials of Educational Measurement
is the fourth edition of the book
formerly titled *Measuring Educational Achievement.*

Printed in the United States of America

10 9 8 7 6 5 4 3 2 1

ISBN   0-13-286006-6   01

Prentice-Hall International (UK) Limited, *London*
Prentice-Hall of Australia Pty. Limited, *Sydney*
Prentice-Hall Canada Inc., *Toronto*
Prentice-Hall Hispanoamericana, S.A., *Mexico*
Prentice-Hall of India Private Limited, *New Delhi*
Prentice-Hall of Japan, Inc., *Tokyo*
Prentice-Hall of Southeast Asia Pte. Ltd., *Singapore*
Editora Prentice-Hall do Brasil, Ltda., *Rio de Janeiro*
Whitehall Books Limited, *Wellington, New Zealand*

CONTENTS

PREFACE

Essentials of Educational Measurement was designed originally to serve as a textbook for introductory educational measurement courses and to provide a useful reference for practicing teachers and those responsible for test development in business, government, and the professions. The revisions in this Fourth Edition have been made with these purposes and audiences in mind. A major theme of this book is that individuals who are responsible for making and using tests of cognitive abilities must have a grasp of the fundamental concepts, principles, and understandings of measurement to perform their tasks competently. Though practical utility has been emphasized, theoretical background has been introduced where it appeared to be essential for providing a complete background for the applications discussed. However, it is assumed that the reader has no previous coursework in either educational measurement or statistics.

This edition has not benefited directly from the cumulative wisdom and experience that Bob Ebel brought to the first three editions. His sudden death in November 1982 came at the time when he had just begun to finalize his plans for this revision. Unfortunately for me, I did not have an opportunity to discuss his plans with him or to obtain his reactions to the revisions I have made. I have tried to retain the philosophical positions and viewpoints that we shared, but have not been reluctant to express opinions or to use approaches we may not have held jointly. Consequently, whatever virtues these pages may hold are ours, but whatever shortcomings remain are my sole responsibility.

A major organizational change in this Fourth Edition is the reordering of the chapters on statistical concepts, reliability, and validity. All have been placed before the chapters on test development, item writing, and test analysis because of the prerequisites they provide for the content presented in these latter chapters. This change is intended to highlight the notion that all the methods we employ and all the judgments we make in developing a test are geared to producing reliable measures and maximizing valid score use.

The first three chapters deal with fundamental issues and concepts in educational measurement. Chapter 1 focuses on the current uses of tests, some of the alleged abuses, and recent litigation involving tests. The second chapter introduces the Basic Teaching Model as a conceptual tool for describing the role of evaluation in the teaching process. In addition, one section is devoted to distinguishing norm-referenced, domain-referenced, and criterion-referenced score interpretations. Chapter 3 contains expanded sections on the cognitive outcomes of education and the role of instructional objectives in evaluation.

The fourth chapter stresses conceptual understanding of statistical topics that are important prerequisites for understanding measurement concepts and for interpreting test scores skillfully. Statistical computation is emphasized only to the extent that it may facilitate understanding of relationships and abstract ideas. Chapter 5, "The Reliability of Educational Tests," has been revised only slightly, but the validity chapter that follows it has been rewritten. Even greater weight is given to the idea that, for tests of cognitive ability, validation and test development are essentially simultaneous processes.

Chapter 7 gives an overview of test planning, including a preview of each of the item forms for which separate chapters follow. It has been reorganized, and a section on performance testing has been added. The content on essay testing (Chapter 8), writing true-false items (Chapter 9), and writing short-answer items (Chapter 11) remains essentially unchanged. However, Chapter 10 has been reorganized substantially to describe detailed aspects of writing multiple-choice items, and sections on alternate-choice and multiple true-false items have been added.

Topics related to test administration and scoring have been updated, and a section on computer-assisted test administration has been added in Chapter 12. Chapter 13 deals with test-evaluation considerations and item-analysis procedures for content-referenced tests, in addition to the item-analysis topics included in the previous edition. The chapter on grading has less emphasis on institutional grading procedures and more discussion of methods of assigning course grades and procedures for grading assignments.

Chapters 15–18 deal with standardized measures of achievement, intelligence, aptitude, and other aspects of personality. The first of these combines topics on score interpretations, norms, and methods of setting the passing score with new sections on sources of information about tests and criteria for selecting standardized tests.

Finally, a new chapter has been written on recent developments in the field of educational testing. Sections on the impact of computers, mandated assessment, National Assessment of Educational Progress, and item-response theory are intended to introduce these topics and stimulate the reader's interest to pursue current literature related to each.

Three other changes are noteworthy. The glossary of terms has been updated and reference citations have been changed from footnote format to a reference-list format keyed to author and date of publication. The projects and problems that follow most chapters have been reviewed. Some have been modified, others have been added, and still others have been left unchanged. Answers or sample responses for each are included in a revised Instructor's Manual.

I am most grateful for the encouragement, patience, and many forms of support given to me by my family, friends, and colleagues during the process of this revision. I thank Anne Cleary for her assistance in obtaining time and resources for me to complete this work. I thank Steve Dunbar, Dick Ferguson, Bob Forsyth, Dave Lohman, and Russ Noyes for providing useful comments on some of the earlier chapter drafts. I thank Jay Curran and Clare Kreiter for their research assistance, and Jan Bream for many hours of typing drafts and redrafts of each chapter. I thank Hazel Ebel for her encouragement, trust, and friendship. To Bob Ebel—my teacher, colleague, and friend—I will always be grateful.

D. A. F.
Iowa City, Iowa

1

THE STATUS OF EDUCATIONAL TESTING

THE PREVALENCE OF TESTING

Testing of achievements in learning and of aptitude for learning is widespread in the United States and throughout the world. Teachers give classroom tests to motivate student efforts to learn and to assess the outcomes of those efforts. Schools develop testing programs to inform the public of the success of the schools' instructional programs. State lawmakers legislate the use of tests that will provide evidence of the educational accomplishments and educational needs of the schools. Civil service divisions in federal, state, and local governments make and use tests to aid in the selection and placement of employees of the highest merit. Personnel directors in business and industry use tests for similar purposes. Professional associations use tests to certify competence to practice. Counseling psychologists use tests to diagnose difficulties and design remedial treatments for their clients. The list of individuals and agencies that use tests, and of the purposes for which tests are used, seems almost endless.

Some of these tests, unfortunately, are not of the highest quality. Too many of them are produced hurriedly by persons with no special training in test construction and no special aptitude for the task. Test scores are not always interpreted correctly or used wisely. Testing is not universally popular despite its widespread use. Some teachers, seeking to avoid the labor and the stress of testing their students, belittle the value of test scores. Students whose egos have been bruised by low test scores cry out against testing. But if we want to motivate and reward efforts to learn, if we want effective and productive schools, if we want to deal fairly with individuals on the basis of their capabilities, we need more testing, not less. Despite the current prevalence of testing, we are far from receiving the full benefits that could be gained from the wise use of good tests.

CRITICISMS OF TESTS AND TESTING

No one who is well acquainted with the tests currently used to assess educational achievement is likely to claim that they are above criticism. The process of assessing achievement in learning is much more complicated than it may seem to be at first glance. The naive view is that all one has to do is to give a test. Each student either passes or fails. The proportion who pass indicates the effectiveness of the educational program. Where the test comes from, what it actually measures, how good it is, what the scores mean, how the passing score is determined—these and many other hard questions that trouble test specialists a great deal trouble the general public hardly at all.

In fact, very little of the criticism of tests and testing comes from the general public. Most of it comes from members of three special interest groups:

1. Professional educators who are uneasy about the accountability associated with standardized tests and external testing in general.
2. Reformers who regard testing as part of an unsuccessful and outmoded instructional process.
3. Free-lance writers whose best sellers purport to expose scandals in important human institutions.

From none of these groups of critics is one likely to get a constructive criticism of tests and testing. What they want is not to improve the tests, to correct their faults, to make them more useful educational tools—it is rather to discredit tests, to minimize their influence, or to get rid of them altogether.

Nonetheless, the criticisms need to be taken seriously. If they are repeated often enough and loudly enough with no response, they will come to be accepted as true, no matter how little evidence there is to support them.

Here are some of the most frequently mentioned criticisms of tests and testing.

1. That the tests are *invalid*, measuring only superficial, unimportant aspects of achievement.
2. That *objective tests* are used mainly because they can be easily scored, regardless of serious shortcomings of triviality, ambiguity, and guessing.
3. That IQ *testing* has led to the labeling of particular pupils as bright or dull, in both cases distorting their expectations and diminishing their efforts.
4. That external testing programs impose *external controls* on the curriculum and lead teachers to give up sound, long-range instruction in order to "teach to the test."

5. That testing places students under harmful *stress* and exposes them to unnecessary experiences of failure, destroying their self-confidence and killing the joy of learning.
6. That the tests carry a white, middle-class *bias*, misrepresenting the achievements and the potential of cultural minorities.
7. That the testing environment is too *highly controlled*, causing students to lose their individuality and creating measures of artificial behavior.

RESPONSES TO THE CRITICISMS

The matter of test validity is dealt with extensively in the chapters on what educational tests should measure and on test validity. Here it need only be said that tests provide the best information teachers and students can get on the success of efforts to teach and to learn.

The values and limitations of objective tests are dealt with in the chapters on test planning, on essay testing, and on types of objective test items. With very few exceptions, whatever can be tested at all can be tested with objective tests, usually with greater precision and often with greater convenience than with other types of tests.

Some of the sharpest attacks on the tests used in education have been directed at intelligence, or IQ, tests. The focus of recent controversy has been on whether or not there are racial differences in intelligence. This is part of the larger question of the extent to which a person's mental abilities are the result of heredity. This issue will be examined in some detail in the chapter on intelligence testing.

Two observations may suffice for present purposes. The first is that IQ testing is probably more vulnerable to informed criticism than are most other forms of educational testing. The nature of intelligence is commonly misunderstood, and IQs are commonly misinterpreted. They can be and have been used to discourage some pupils from trying to learn, and to excuse teachers from trying to teach them.

The second observation is that there are important differences between intelligence tests and standardized tests of achievement in what is to be measured, how well it can be measured, and what effect its measurement will have on the progress of learning. Thus it is not true, as critics of testing sometimes imply, that the deficiencies and abuses of the one are necessarily also characteristic of the other.

External Control of the Curricula

Standardized tests of achievement are sometimes attacked because of their supposed effect on the curricula of local schools. It is charged that they enforce curricular conformity, that they fail to test what local schools or particular teachers have been trying to teach, that they hamper curricular innovations or the use of open curricula. There is substance to these charges, but the effects are neither so overpowering nor so harmful as the critics imply.

If a school wants its students to score highly on certain tests, it must of course see to it that they receive instruction in those achievements sampled by the tests. Yet these are areas that panels of expert teachers from various regions of the nation have identified as important for most students to learn. Local schools or individual teachers who decide to concentrate on achievements other than these should be prepared to do two things: (1) to argue convincingly to the public that what they are trying to teach is indeed more important than the things the standardized test is testing; and (2) to prepare, give, and report the results on a local test that does measure what they have been trying to teach. Few of those who complain about the curricular restrictions of standardized testing are prepared to do either of these things.

A school that focuses instruction on what the tests measure surely will teach other things as well. Even in the basic skill or core areas that the test does sample, there will be class time and teacher time to venture into interesting and useful areas of learning not covered by the standardized tests. Standardized tests can dominate local curricula only to the extent that school administrators and school teachers permit.

Teaching to the Test

If the effectiveness of instruction is to be assessed on the basis of student performance on a test, the temptation may be strong for the teacher to prepare students to handle the specific questions that will be included in the test. This is often called *teaching to the test*. Obviously, it is not an educationally beneficial procedure. It also tends to spoil the test as a measure of general achievement in the subject area. But if the test is a readily available, published test, an insecure or short sighted teacher might undertake to teach to the test. Even a test specifically constructed for a particular assessment task is, in effect, a "published" test once it has been used. If teachers are so inclined, they can find out a great deal about the particular questions included in it.

Several things can be done to lessen the likelihood of teaching to the test. Teachers can be warned against it and informed that their supervisors will be alert to notice if it occurs. Students can be advised about its undesirability and asked to report its occurrence. Of course, the surest but most expensive way to forestall it is to prepare a new test form for each new assessment effort.

Before leaving this topic, let us make an important distinction between teaching to the test (attempting to fix in students' minds the answers to particular test questions) and teaching material *covered* by the test (attempting to give students the capability to answer questions *like* those in the test on topics covered by the test). The first is thoroughly reprehensible. The second reflects purposeful teaching. Just as there is no warrant for giving away the answers to particular questions, so there is no warrant for testing performance on tasks students were never taught to perform. A teacher or school whose work is to be assessed is entitled to know what the students will be expected to do. This calls for close cooperation and clear communication between teachers on the one hand and test constructors on the other. An assessment test must be thoroughly relevant to the instruction it is intended to assess. Since a test can never elicit more than a sample of performance, usually much more will be taught than can be tested. However, the test never should go beyond what has been taught.

Stress, Failure, and Discouragement

Claims that testing is harmful to students have taken many forms: tests threaten and upset students; some students even break down and cry when faced with a test; if students get a low score on a test, they will become discouraged and quit trying; students' self-concepts will be damaged seriously; and testing is incompatible with educational procedures designed to be supportive of students.

There is undoubtedly anecdotal evidence to support some of these claims. Common sense suggests, however, that the majority of students are not harmed by testing. There are no substantial survey data that would contradict common sense on this matter. Teachers seem much more often concerned with students who don't care enough how well or how poorly they do on tests, than with the relatively exceptional instances of students who seem to care too much.

It is normal and biologically helpful to be somewhat anxious when facing any real test of performance in life. But it is also a necessary part of growing up to learn to cope with the kind of tests that life inevitably brings. Of the many challenges to a child's peace of mind caused by such things as angry parents, playground bullies, bad dogs, shots from the doctor, and things that go bump in the night, tests surely must be among the least fearsome for most youngsters. Unwise parental pressure can in some cases elevate anxiety to harmful levels. But usually the child who breaks down in tears at the prospect of a test has problems of security, adjustment, and maturity that testing did not create, and that cannot be solved by eliminating tests. Indeed, more frequent testing might help to solve the problem.

A student who consistently gets low test scores on material that the student has tried hard to learn is indeed likely to be discouraged. If this does happen, the school cannot claim to be offering a good educational program, and the teacher cannot claim to be doing a good job of teaching. Most low test scores, however, go to students who, for whatever reason, have not tried very hard to learn. In the opinion of the teachers of such students, it is the trying rather than the testing that is most in need of correction.

The Problem of Test Bias

Standardized tests of educational achievement have been attacked for their alleged bias against cultural minorities and against students with poor reading skills. The reason for the attack, at least in part, is that such students tend to score lower on standardized tests than their agemates. But surely lower scores alone do not signify bias. If they did, every spelling test would be biased against poor spellers, and every typing test against persons who never learned to type. A test is biased only if it yields measures that are consistently lower than they should be.

That students who do poorly on a particular test written in English might do better if the test were in Spanish, or if the questions were presented orally, does not mean that the original test is biased against them. It simply means that they have not learned enough of what that particular test measures. Its linguistic context is part of the test. The particularity of what the test measures does not constitute bias.

The score of a student on an achievement test indicates how successfully the test questions were answered under the conditions of the test. The reasonable assumption usually is made that the student would be equally successful with other tasks requiring the same knowledge or ability. Consequently, if a test score is judged to be an inaccurate indication of the student's level of achievement in the domain covered by the test, bias is not the likely explanation. It is more likely that the conditions for testing were undesirable or that a reasonably good test was chosen for a purpose other than the one for which it was intended originally.

The possibility of bias in intelligence tests is much greater than it is in achievement tests. Scores on a test of general intelligence are supposed to indicate a person's ability to learn many different kinds of things from success in having learned a few other things. If the examinees all had nearly equal opportunity to learn what the intelligence test requires, the indications of general intelligence may be reasonably accurate. If not, the test may yield seriously biased indications of intelligence.

The Effect of Controlled Conditions

Precise measurement requires careful control, or standardization, of the conditions surrounding it. Obviously this control renders the behavior being measured to some degree artificial, but artificiality is a price that scientists and engineers, as well as psychologists and teachers, have usually found worth paying to achieve precision. For tests intended to measure typical behavior, such as personality, attitude, or interest, the price may sometimes be too high. That is, the behavior in the artificial test situation may be so different from typical behavior in a natural situation that precise measurement is wasted effort. But for tests of educational aptitude or achievement, the gain in precision resulting from the controlled conditions that formal testing can afford usually far outweighs the slight loss in relevance of behavior.

Perhaps an illustration from physical ability testing may be helpful. Judges watching a group of children at play (the natural situation) could make rough estimates of the relative abilities of the students to run fast, jump high, or throw some object far. But the precision of the estimates obtained in such an uncontrolled, unstandardized situation would probably be quite low. Individual judges would not be likely to agree with each other, or even with themselves on different occasions, in the estimates they would report. If precise estimates are desired, the judges, the children, and everyone else concerned would probably prefer to see them made under the standardized and controlled conditions of a regular track meet. No one would worry much about the possibility that the ones who performed best in the track and field events might perform less well on the playground.

Because all students in a class usually take the same test of achievement under the same conditions, some critics have concluded that uniform written tests, particularly objective tests, disregard individual differences and even tend to suppress individuality. The fact that some classroom tests are scored by machines has served to strengthen this misconception. Mass testing and machine scoring suggest a standardized uniformity in education that seems inconsistent with concern for individual students and their unique needs and potentials.

However, although the tests and the processes of testing are as nearly alike for all students of a given class as we can make them, test scores differ markedly. Those who score high on one test reflect superior ability and achievement in that area. Those who score low reveal deficiencies. Tests tend to reveal differences among students, not to suppress or conceal them. In fact, uniformity in the conditions of testing is a prerequisite to unequivocal indication of individual differences. If the tests are not identical for all students, not all of the differences in their scores can be attributed to differences among them in ability or achievement. The kind of information about individual differences that uniform tests reveal so clearly is essential to identifying and meeting the unique needs of individual students.

The emphasis in this chapter on the value of written tests is not intended to suggest that tests should be the sole means used in judging students' educational achievement. Sometimes teachers are concerned mainly with the development of physical skills or social behavior, in which case direct observation is a much better basis for assessment. Nor should teachers and professors ignore their own direct observations, in the classroom or elsewhere, of a student's level of understanding or ability to use knowledge. The broader the basis of observations on which evaluation rests, the better, provided only that each observation carries no more weight in determining the final result than its appropriateness and accuracy warrant.

TESTING AND THE LAW

The criticisms of tests and testing have not been limited to philosophical bantering in scholarly publications or to eye-catching articles in popular magazines. The use of test scores to make critical decisions about people has led some to seek legal opinions related to the social and economic consequences of testing. Following

World War II, and especially since the Supreme Court decision in the case of *Brown* v. *Board of Education* (1954), the impact of testing on the opportunities for education and employment of blacks and other minorities has come under increasing scrutiny in the courts. Here are a few of the more noteworthy cases.

1. *Stell* v. *Savannah* (1964). Attorneys for two white children argued that desegregation of the Savannah, Georgia, schools would be harmful to all children because of the disparity in tested ability between black and white students. The lower court accepted this argument, but a U.S. Court of Appeals rejected it and required the Savannah school district to desegregate.

2. *Hobson* v. *Hansen* (1967). Judge Skelly Wright ruled against the use of ability test scores to place District of Columbia students on different instructional tracks: honors, regular, general, and basic. Because the ability-test scores were influenced by the cultural backgrounds of the students, blacks were disproportionately assigned to lower tracks that led to lower-income jobs.

3. *Griggs* v. *Duke Power Company* (1971). The court ruled that requirements for employment such as a high school diploma or a passing score on a test must be shown to be relevant to some specific criterion of success on the job.

4. *Larry P.* v. *Wilson Riles* (1979). Judge Robert Peckham decided that the use of intelligence-test scores to place children in classes for the educably mentally handicapped was illegal because it had a disproportionate effect on black children in the California districts in which it occurred. Peckham's decision was upheld by a federal appeals court in 1984.

5. *Debra P.* v. *Turlington* (1979). The court agreed that the use of tests of minimum competence as a basis for awarding a high school diploma was legal. However, it suspended use of the test by the state of Florida for four years. By that time all students who had any part of their education in previously segregated schools would have had the opportunity to be graduated from high school.

6. *Bakke* v. *California* (1978). When Alan Bakke, who had been denied admission to the medical school of the University of California at Davis, discovered that minority applicants with test scores lower than his had been admitted, he sued the university. The Supreme Court ruled that the university should admit Bakke, and implied that the use of different standards for applicants of different races was inappropriate. However, the Court also suggested that it was proper for the race of an applicant to be considered when admissions decisions were being made.

While all these cases involved the use of tests, the crucial issue in many of them was a matter of social policy. Is desegregation in school important enough to justify some apparent sacrifice of optimum conditions for learning (*Stell, Hobson*)? Is it proper for employers to specify employee qualifications that are not directly related to specific job requirements (*Griggs*)? Should an otherwise valid selection procedure be disqualified because of adverse impact on minorities (*Larry P.*)? In attempting to right old wrongs, should selection procedures discriminate to the advantage of minorities (*Debra P., Bakke*)?

These are hard questions. It is not surprising that the courts have not been wholly consistent in the answers they have given. As decisions are handed down, social policy is gradually formed. It is important to note that test makers are seldom the defendants in cases such as these. Test users often are the defendants, but the charges against them have to do more with the social consequences of their testing than with the technical adequacy of their tests. The tests themselves are not on trial.

Truth in Testing

The so-called Truth-in-Testing Law, enacted in New York State in 1979, required any company offering testing services in the state to do three things:

1. to provide on request to anyone who took the test a copy of the test questions, the correct answers, and the examinee's answers, and
2. to explain fully how the test score was calculated and what it means, and
3. to identify all studies of the validity of the test and its uses.

Similar bills have been introduced in several other state legislatures and in the Congress of the United States.

It is the first of these requirements that has troubled testing companies such as the Educational Testing Service, the Psychological Corporation, and American College Testing Programs. Many of the tests they offer are confidential so that items from the tests can be reused in other tests or, on some occasions, in the same test. Public disclosure of the items limits or prevents reuse and requires that new items be written for each new testing. It also hampers the equating procedures test makers use to make scores comparable from one test form to another. The stipulations of the Truth-in-Testing Law have increased the costs of testing and have reduced testing opportunities for special groups, particularly handicapped examinees. Because of the law, some organizations that administer testing programs stopped offering their tests in New York State temporarily, forcing applicants from New York to travel to surrounding states to take those tests.

The testing companies always have been perfectly willing to comply with the second and third requirements of the New York law. They typically provide more information on these subjects than most examinees want or can use. If they have not always explained fully the derivation of the scores reported, or disclosed all the details of their validity studies, it is because these often involve complex and sophisticated statistical techniques that are difficult to describe and explain simply.

Truth-in-testing laws have been promoted by various public interest research groups, for which Ralph Nader, a consumer advocate, is a leading spokesman. The primary target of Nader's investigation has been the Educational Testing Service (ETS). Results of a six-year "investigation" of ETS were published in 1980 under the title *The Reign of ETS: The Corporation That Makes Up Minds.* Written responses by ETS to charges leveled by the report have been circulated widely (Educational Testing Service, 1980a, 1980b).

There has been and continues to be a great deal of truth in the testing done by the major testing companies. The so-called truth-in-testing laws have added little to that truth. On balance, in fact, those laws probably have harmed good testing more than they have helped it. The existing laws are likely to be modified to make them more reasonable and helpful. The basis of support for similar laws in other states and at the national level seems to be small.

THE POTENTIAL VALUE OF TESTING IN EDUCATION

There is currently much testing in education, but tests seldom contribute as much as they could to effective instruction. How much is learned in any particular course of instruction depends largely on how much the students want to learn and on how hard the teacher works to help them to learn it. These efforts by students and by teachers depend, in turn, on the immediate and ultimate rewards that seem likely to result from their efforts. Tests can be used to provide recognitions and rewards for success in learning. They can be used to motivate and direct efforts to learn. They can be used, in short, to contribute substantially to effective instruction.

Tests have sometimes been used very successfully to stimulate efforts to learn. For example, in the Iowa Academic Contest (Lindquist, 1960) that began in 1929, high school students were offered tests in each of the major subjects of study: English, history, geometry, physics, and so on. Those who received highest scores in the local test were invited to a district contest, where a similar but somewhat more difficult test was given. Those who scored highest in the district tests were invited to the state contest, where they took a third level of tests. Those who scored highest on these tests were offered scholarships to the State University.

This academic contest was used by some high school principals to provide incentives for both students and teachers to work hard at learning. In one school the local contest winners were recognized at a school assembly and in news stories. In conferences with teachers whose students had done well on the tests, the principal offered congratulations and support for continued efforts to teach effectively. In conferences with teachers whose students had not done well, the principal tried to identify things that the principal or the teacher might do to make students more successful the next year. Thus the whole school was led to believe that learning was important, and that successful efforts to learn would be rewarded. A good environment for learning was created in the school, and every student, not just the contest winners, benefited from it.

In many schools, unfortunately, tests are not used so effectively to stimulate and facilitate learning. Test scores do not matter very much, and unless they matter they cannot contribute much to effective instruction. There are several reasons, none of them very good, why many teachers and school administrators depreciate testing and do as little of it as possible. The tests are criticized as having little value or as being actually harmful. Doing a good job of testing demands skills that many educators know that they lack, and requires work that their lives are more comfortable without. Testing involves comparison and competition. Even though these are facts of life, some teachers believe that schools should protect their students from competition as much as possible. Unless all students can win, none should be allowed to win. Thus some schools are content with a comfortable mediocrity so long as the public will tolerate it.

In many states and in many communities, heavily taxed citizens are no longer willing to tolerate mediocrity in their schools. They are asking for evidence that their tax dollars are buying excellence in education. They are asking that the schools do something, or demanding that communities do something, to correct the conditions that educators blame for low achievement in learning. Public school teachers and administrators are public employees. It is entirely proper for the public to hold the schools accountable for doing the best job possible under the circumstances.

There are two things, both involving the use of tests, that teachers and schools can do, and ought to do, to justify their stewardship to the community. Each teacher ought to present evidence periodically to the school administration that the students he or she has been teaching have made substantial progress in learning. Each school ought to present evidence periodically to the community that the students in the school are making substantial progress in learning. It is not sufficient for teachers and schools to describe their processes of instruction and to claim that they know how to do a good job of educating children. The public is more interested in the product than in the process, and it would like to see evidence to support the claims.

It is possible to use tests effectively to promote learning. Current obstacles need to be removed and objections need to be addressed. But effective test use demands teachers and school administrators who are skilled in the use of educational tests. The remainder of this book is devoted to the presentation of information and ideas that will contribute to the development of some of these essential skills.

SUMMARY

The main ideas of this chapter can be summarized in the following propositions:

1. The increase in test use in recent years has not been accompanied by a proportionate increase in overall test quality or improved test-score interpretation.
2. Most criticisms of educational testing are intended to discredit tests and reduce their use, rather than to make the tests better.
3. Tests provide the best information teachers and students ordinarily can get about the success of their efforts to teach and learn.
4. Objective tests can provide valid, precise, and convenient measures of the most important outcomes of education.
5. Criticisms of intelligence testing have some justification but should not be generalized to apply equally to standardized achievement tests.
6. The influence standardized tests have on local

school curricula is likely to be more beneficial than harmful.

7. "Teaching to the test" is deplorable if it means giving students answers to the particular questions on a test; it is commendable if it means helping students to learn what they must know to answer questions like those on the test.

8. Claims that testing harms students tend to be exaggerated and are seldom based on substantial evidence.

9. Achievement tests are given under specially devised and carefully controlled conditions to improve the precision of measurement without seriously impairing test validity.

10. Test bias may exist to some degree, but it cannot account for substantial differences in test scores between different cultural groups.

11. Recent court cases that involve testing have focused almost exclusively on the social consequences of testing and fair test use rather than on the tests themselves.

12. The anticipated benefits to examinees of the truth-in-testing laws have not been realized, particularly when compared to the costs to examinees and test publishers.

13. Tests could be used to promote learning better if both teachers and schools systematically presented test results to administrators and to the community as evidence of the educational progress of their students.

2

MEASUREMENT AND THE PROCESS OF EDUCATION

EVALUATION, MEASUREMENT, AND TESTING

The purpose of evaluation is to make judgments about the quality or worth of something—an educational program, worker performance or proficiency, or student attainments. That is what we attempt to do when we evaluate students' achievements, employees' productivity, or prospective practitioners' competencies. In each case the goal is not simply to describe what the students, employees, or other personnel can do. Instead we seek answers to such questions as: How good is the level of achievement? How good is the performance? Have they learned enough? Is their work good enough? These are questions of value that require the exercise of judgement. Evaluation is the process of making such judgments. In addition, the term is used to refer to the product of that process. That is, we might, for example, submit our evaluation (the product) of Scott's school performance to his parents following our evaluation (the process) of his accomplishments. In this respect evaluation has a dual connotation.

Formative and Summative Evaluation

The terms *formative* and *summative* were introduced by Scriven (1967) to describe the various roles of evaluation in curriculum development and instruction. Formative evaluation is conducted to monitor the instructional process, to determine whether learning is taking place as planned. Summative evaluation is conducted at the end of an instructional segment to determine if learning is sufficiently complete to warrant moving the learner to the next segment of instruction. The distinctions between these two types of evaluation have implications for test development and test use in the classroom. As will be noted later, information gathered primarily for summative purposes may be used on occasion for formative purposes as well.

The major function of formative evaluation in the classroom is to provide feedback to the teacher and to the student about how things are going. Such feedback provides an opportunity for the teacher to modify instructional methods or materials to facilitate learning when feedback indicates things are not going well. Formative evaluation requires the gathering of fairly detailed information on frequent occasions. Information is obtained through teacher observation, classroom questioning, homework assignments, and short tests or quizzes. Only in highly systematized programs of individualized instruction are tests used prominently for formative evaluation.

However, formal classroom tests, such as unit tests or final examinations, are the most frequently used tools in summative evaluation. The major function of summative evaluation in the classroom is to determine the status of achievement at the end of an instructional segment, to determine how well things went. Relative to formative evaluation, there is greater finality associated with summative evaluation. The information gathered is less detailed in nature but broader in the scope of content or skills assessed.

Obviously both types of evaluation are necessary components of classroom instruction. In some cases information gathered for summative purposes may be useful in a formative sense. For example, the scores on a unit test may be used to evaluate achievement at the end of that unit. At the same time the scores reflect progress in the course and in the broader instructional program. In such circumstances the tests should be designed to yield useful information for summative evaluation purposes, but the scores might be used incidentally as gross indicators of progress in the broader context.

What Is Measurement?

Measurement is the process of assigning numbers to individuals or their characteristics according to specified rules. Measurement requires the use of numbers but does not require that value judgments be made about the numbers obtained from the process. We measure achievement with a test by counting the number of test items a student answers correctly, and we use exactly the same rule to assign a number to the achievement of each student in the class. Measurements are useful for describing the amount of certain abilities that individuals have. For that reason, they represent useful information for the evaluation process. But can we measure all the important outcomes of our instructional efforts?

Can Achievement Be Measured?

Education is an extensive, diverse, complex enterprise, not only in terms of the achievements it seeks to develop, but also in terms of the means by which it seeks to develop them. Our understanding of the nature and process of education is far from perfect. Hence it is easy to agree that we do not now know how to measure all important educational outcomes. But in principle, all important outcomes of education are measurable. They may not be measurable with the tests currently available. They may not even be measurable in principle, using only paper-and-pencil tests. But if they are known to be important, they must be measurable.

To be important, an outcome of education must make an observable difference. That is, at some time, under some circumstances, a person who has more of it must behave differently from a person who has less of it. If different degrees or amounts of an educational achievement never make any observable difference, what evidence can be found to show that it is in fact important?

But if such differences can be observed, then the achievement is measurable, for all measurement requires is verifiable observation of a more-less relationship. Can integrity be measured? It can if verifiable differences in integrity can be observed among individuals. Can mother love be measured? If observers can agree that a hen shows more mother love than a female trout, or that Mrs. A shows more love for her children than Mrs. B, then mother love can be measured.

The argument, then, is this: *To be important an educational outcome must make a difference. If it makes a difference, the basis for measurement exists.*

To say that A shows more of trait X than B may not seem like much of a measurement. Where are the numbers? Yet out of a series of such more-less comparisons, a scale for measuring the trait or property can be constructed. The Ayres scale for measuring the quality of handwriting is a familiar example of this (Ayres, 1912). If a sequence of numbers is assigned to the sequence of steps or intervals that make up the scale, then the scale can yield quantitative measurements. If used carefully by a skilled judge, it yields measurements that are reasonably objective (that is, free from errors associated with specific judges) and reliable (that is, free from errors associated with use of a particular set of test items or tasks).

Are some outcomes of education essentially qualitative rather than quantitative? If so, is it reasonable to expect that these qualitative outcomes can be measured?

It is certainly true that some differences between persons are not usually thought of as more-less differences. This person is a man; that one is a woman. This person has blue eyes; that one has brown. This person speaks only French; that one speaks only German. But we can express these qualitative differences in quantitative terms. This person has more of the characteristics of a man;

that one has less. This person has more eye-blueness; that one has less. This person has more ability to speak French; that one has less.

We may think of the weight of a man, his age, or the size of his bank account as quantities, while regarding his health, his friendliness, or his honesty as qualities. But it is also possible to regard all of them—weight, age, savings, health, friendliness, and honesty—as qualities. And if they serve to differentiate him from other men because he exhibits more or less of them than other men, they become quantitative qualities. It is difficult to think of any quality that interests us that cannot also be quantified. "Whatever exists at all exists in some amount," said E. L. Thorndike (1918, p. 16). And William A. McCall (1939) has added, "Anything that exists in amount can be measured" (p. 18).

Relating Testing to Evaluation and Measurement

Tests represent one particular measurement technique. A *test* is a set of questions, each of which has a correct answer, that examinees usually answer orally or in writing. Test questions differ from those used in measures of attitudes, interest, or preference or certain other aspects of personality. The questions in tests of achievement or many tests of intelligence have answers that content experts can agree are correct; correctness is not determined by the particular values, preferences, or dislikes of a group of judges.

All tests are a subset of the quantitative tools or techniques that are classified as measurements. And all measurement techniques are a subset of the quantitative *and* qualitative techniques used in evaluation. A major concern in this text, but certainly not the only one, will be with the development of tests that can contribute to summative evaluation of student learning. Other measurement and evaluation techniques are useful for other evaluation purposes, but tests that measure relevant school learning with precision are the most useful tools available to teachers for most classroom summative evaluation needs.

EVALUATION AND TEACHING: THE BASIC TEACHING MODEL

Evaluation takes place in a context, which influences the purposes for evaluating as well as the procedures and the uses that are made of the outcomes. The instructional context and the relationship of evaluation to it must be understood as prerequisites to understanding educational measurement. To that end, the role of evaluation in instruction can be described by using a model that explains how the teaching process works. There are many models that describe the variety of approaches to teaching found in our schools, but the Basic Teaching Model (BTM), introduced by Glaser (1962), accounts for the fundamental components of most specific teaching models such as the Socratic approach, the individualized instruction approach, or the computer-dominated instruction approach (Joyce et al., 1980). Few teachers probably follow the BTM explicitly to guide their instructional activities. And though we do not specifically endorse the use of the BTM or any other particular model, we do advocate instructional approaches, by whatever name, that include the basic functions represented in the BTM as described below.

The main purposes of the BTM are to identify the major activities of the teacher and to describe the relationships among them. Figure 2-1 is a diagram of the model. Our primary interest is in the Performance Assessment component, but we cannot understand completely the role of evaluation without understanding how Performance Assessment relates to other teaching activities. *Instructional Objectives*, the first component of the BTM, represents the teacher's starting point in providing instruction. What should students learn? What skills and knowledge should be the focus of instruction? The second component, *Entering Behavior*, indicates that the teacher must try to assess the students' levels of achievement and readiness to learn prior to beginning instruction. What do the students know already? How receptive to learning are they?

Once the teacher has decided what will be taught and to whom the teaching is to be directed, the "How?" must be determined. The *Instructional Procedures* component includes the materials and methods of instruction the teacher selects or develops to facilitate student learning. At this point instruction could begin, and often it does. But unless the teacher makes plans to evaluate students' performances, the students and teacher will not be sure when learning is complete. The *Performance Assessment* component helps to answer the question, "Did we accomplish what we set out to do?" Tests, quizzes, teacher observations, projects, and demonstrations are evaluation tools that help to answer this question. Thus evaluation should be a significant aspect of the teaching process.

The model shows a fifth component, the *Feedback Loop*, that can be used by the teacher as both a management and a diagnostic procedure. If the results of evaluation indicate that sufficient learning has occurred, the loop takes the teacher back to each component, in succession, so that plans for

Figure 2-1 The Basic Teaching Model (DeCecco and Crawford, 1974).

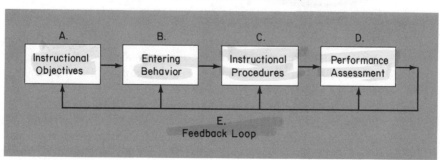

beginning the next instructional unit can be developed. But when evaluation results are not so positive, the Feedback Loop is a mechanism for identifying possible explanations. Were the objectives too vaguely specified? Did students lack essential prerequisite skills or knowledge? Was the film or text relatively ineffective? Was there insufficient practice opportunity? Such questions need to be asked, and often they are. However, other questions need to be asked, perhaps more often than they are. Were the test questions appropriate? Were enough observations made? Were relevant criteria used in grading the projects? Were directions clear to students? The Feedback Loop returns to the Performance Assessment component to indicate that we must review our evaluation procedures, after the fact, to assess the appropriateness of the procedures and the accuracy of the scores. Unless the tools of evaluation are developed with care, inadequate learning may go undetected or ample learning may be misinterpreted as inadequate.

In sum, good teaching requires planning for and using good evaluation tools. And evaluation does not take place in a vacuum. The BTM shows that other components of the teaching process provide cues about what to evaluate, when to evaluate, and how to evaluate. Our purpose is to identify such cues and to take advantage of them in building tests that measure achievement as precisely as possible.

THE PRINCIPAL TASK OF THE SCHOOL

When one considers the reasons why schools were built, the reasons why children and adults attend them, and the activities that go on inside them, it seems clear that the principal task of the school is to facilitate cognitive learning. However, this thesis has been challenged by some who argue that schools should be concerned primarily with one of the following:

a. moral character (Ligon, 1961)
b. adjustment to life (U.S. Office of Education, 1951)
c. reconstruction of society (Counts, 1932)
d. self-confidence (Kelley, 1962)

Clearly all these things are good. Since learning can contribute to each of them, they are not so much alternatives to learning as they are reasons for learning. But should they be given primary emphasis in defining the task of the school? Do they not have more to do with the ends of living than with the means the school should use to help pupils toward those ends?

Those who define the task of the school in terms of character, adjustment, self-confidence, or the good society tend to be critical of emphasis on learning in conventional schools. Loving does more than learning to make people happy, they say, and faith is better than reason as a guide to the good life. They tend to oppose structured learning situations, the setting of specific goals, the objective assessment of attainments, and the use of grades to report and record those attainments. They say that a teacher's primary concern should be to send students home in the afternoon thinking better of themselves than when they came to school in the morning. A child's happiness, they say, is more important to society than the ability to read. By thus denying the central role of learning in the activity of the school, they find it easy to excuse themselves from teaching, or their students from learning, anything very specific.

Many teachers, however, do not agree with those who set "higher" goals than learning for education. While they acknowledge the ultimate importance of character, adjustment, self-confidence, and the good society, they cite at least two reasons why none of them should replace learning as the school's primary focus of attention.

The first reason is that the school is a special-purpose social institution. It was designed and developed to do a specific task: that is, to facilitate learning. Other agencies are responsible for other parts of the complex task of helping people to live good lives together. There are families and churches, legislative assemblies and courts, publishers and libraries, factories and unions, markets and moneylenders. To believe that the whole responsibility for ethical character, life adjustment, social reconstruction, or happiness must rest on the schools is as presumptuous as it is foolish.

Let us never doubt the power of education for human betterment. But let us not make the mistake, either, of assuming that the schools can and should undertake to solve directly all the world's problems—war, oppression, poverty, exploitation, inflation, unemployment, anxiety, despair, underdevelopment, or overpopulation. If the schools take the burdens of the world on their shoulders, they are likely to neglect the specific tasks of training, instruction, and education that are their special responsibility. The task of facilitating learning is challenging enough, and important enough, to occupy all of a school's time and to consume all of its energy and resources.

The second reason for believing that the schools should continue to emphasize learning is the basic, instrumental importance of learning to all human affairs. With their gift of language, human beings are specially equipped for learning. Cognitive excellence is their unique excellence. The more they know and understand, the better, more effective, and happier they are likely to be.

How better can school help children toward happiness than by increasing their knowledge and understanding of themselves and the world in which they live? By what other means can adjustment be facilitated, character developed, or ability to contribute to society increased? Is not cognitive learning effective in reaching all these goals? And is there any other means?

Yes, there is one. It is the psychological process called conditioning (DeCecco and Crawford, 1974). It makes use of rewards and punishments to establish specific, habitual responses to certain specific conditions. Much of our behavior was molded, especially during our first years of life, by processes of conditioning. Even as adults we are still subject to its influences. If the school is concerned solely with training, if its sole mission is to establish certain specific, unvarying responses or behavior patterns; then it should depend heavily on conditioning, for conditioning can probably get that job done faster and more effectively than cognitive learning. But what conditioning cannot do is give a person flexibility and freedom. Conditioning is better suited to the training of horses or dogs than to the education of human beings to live happy, useful lives as free men and women.

Those who object to emphasis on learning as the school's primary task may do so because they think of learning as academic specialization, designed mainly to prepare a person for further learning, and remote from the practical concerns of living. No doubt some of what all schools have taught warrants this judgment. But learning need not be, and ought not be, the learning of useless things. It can and should be the student's main road to effective living. When it is, it merits recognition as the primary task of the school.

THE FUNCTIONS OF ACHIEVEMENT TESTS

There are good reasons to believe that the measurement of educational achievement is essential to effective formal education. Formal education is a complex process, requiring a great deal of time and money and the cooperative efforts of many people. Efforts must be directed toward the attainment of specific goals. Education is not automatically or uniformly successful. Some methods are more effective than others. Efficient use of learning resources often requires special motivation, guidance, and assistance. All of those concerned with the process of education—students, teachers, parents, and school officials—need to know periodically how successful their efforts have been, so that they can decide which practices to continue and which to change. It is the function of educational measurement to provide them with this knowledge.

To teach without evaluating the results of teaching would be foolish. Those who suggest that schools do not need tests, or might even do a better job of educating students if tests were prohibited, seldom go so far as to argue that evaluation is not needed. They seldom suggest that learning can be promoted effectively by teachers and students who have no particular goals in view, and who pay no attention to the results of their efforts. If tests were abandoned, some other means of assessing educational achievement would have to be used in their place. No other means that is as efficient, as dependable, and as beneficial to the process of education has yet been discovered.

The major function of a classroom test is to measure student achievement and thus to contribute to the evaluation of educational progress and attainments. This is a matter of considerable importance. To say, as some critics of testing have said, that what students know and can do is more important than their scores on a test or grades in a course implies, quite incorrectly in most cases, that knowledge and scores are independent or unrelated. To say that testing solely to measure achievement has no educational value also implies, and again quite incorrectly in most cases, that test scores are unrelated to educational efforts, that they do not reward and reinforce effective study, that they do not penalize unproductive efforts, or that they do not tend to discourage lack of effort.

Tests can, and often do, help teachers and professors to give more valid, reliable grades. Because these grades are intended to summarize concisely a comprehensive evaluation of student achievement, because they are reported to the students and their parents to indicate the effectiveness of their efforts, because they are entered in the school record and may help to determine honors and opportunities for further education or future employment, it is important that teachers and professors take seriously their responsibilities for assigning accurate, meaningful grades. Students are urged, quite properly, not to study *merely* to earn high grades. But, in terms of the students' present self-perceptions and future opportunities, there is nothing "mere" about the grades they receive.

A second major function of classroom tests is to motivate and direct student learning. The experience of almost all students and teachers supports the view that students do tend to study harder when they expect an examination than when they do not, and that they emphasize in studying those things on which they expect to be tested. If the students know in advance they will be tested, if they know what the test will require, and if the test does a good job of measuring the achievement of essential course objectives, then its motivating and guiding influence will be most wholesome.

Anticipated tests are sometimes regarded as extrinsic motivators of learning efforts, less desirable or effective than intrinsic motivators would be. Learning should be its own reward, it is said. Fortunately, no choice need be made between extrinsic and intrinsic motivation. Both contribute to learning. Withdrawal of either would be likely to lessen the learning of most students. For a fortunate few, intrinsic motivation may be strong enough to stimulate all the effort to learn that the student ought to put forth. For the great majority, however, the motivation provided by tests and other influential factors is indispensable.

Classroom tests have other useful educational functions. Constructing them should cause instructors to think carefully about the goals of instruction in a course. It should lead them to define those goals operationally in terms of the kind of tasks a student must be able to handle to demonstrate achievement of the goals. On the students' part, the process of taking a classroom test and discussing the scoring of it afterward can be a richly rewarding learning experience. As Stroud (1946) has said,

> It is probably not extravagant to say that the contribution made to a student's store of knowledge by the taking of an examination is as great, minute for minute, as any other enterprise he engages in. (p. 476)

Hence, testing and teaching need not be considered as mutually exclusive, as competitors for valuable class time. They are intimately related parts of the total educational process, as the BTM illustrates.

LIMITATIONS OF ACHIEVEMENT TESTS

It is easy to show that mental measurement falls far short of the standards of logical soundness that have been set for physical measurement. Ordinarily the best it can do is provide an approximate rank ordering of individuals in terms of their ability to perform a more or less well defined set of tasks. The units used in measuring this ability cannot be shown to be equal. The zero point on the ability scale is not clearly defined.

Because of these limitations, some of the things we often do with test scores, such as finding means, standard deviations, and correlation coefficients, ought not to be done if strict mathematical logic holds sway. Nonetheless we often find it practically useful to do them. When strict logic conflicts with practical utility, it is the utility that usually wins, as it probably should.

On the other hand, the logical limitations of test scores mean that they are unlikely to contribute to the formulation of psychological laws that can compare in precision with, say, the laws of motion. But then, development of precise laws of human behavior is unlikely on other, more fundamental grounds. Deficiencies in the scales of measurement are not the only, nor the most serious, problems in this area.

It is well for us to recognize the logical limitations of the units and scales used in educational measurement. But it is also important not to be so impressed by these limitations that we stop doing the useful things we can legitimately do. One of those useful things is to measure educational achievement.

Are some outcomes of education too intangible to be measured? No doubt there are some that we speak of often, like critical thinking or good citizenship, that are so difficult to define satisfactorily that we have given up trying. To this extent they are intangible, hard to measure, and hard to teach purposefully. We may feel intuitively that critical thinking and good citizenship are immensely important. But if we are unable to state objectively what they consist of, it is hard to show that the concepts they might stand for are, in fact, important.

The processes of education that a particular student experiences probably have subtle and wholly unforeseen effects on that individual, and possibly on no one else. Some of these effects may not become apparent until long after the student has left school. These, too, could be regarded as intangible outcomes. It is unlikely that any current tests, or any that could conceivably be built, would measure these intangibles satisfactorily. In individual instances they might be crucially important. But since they may be largely accidental, subtle, and quite possibly long delayed in their influence, the practical need to measure them may be no greater than the practical possibility of measuring them.

The belief that certain important outcomes of education are difficult to measure may stem in part from a confusion between measurement and prediction. For example, most people agree that it is quite difficult at present to measure motivation or creativity. But those who want to measure motivation or creativity are interested mainly in future prospects, not in present status or past achievements. They are less interested in the motivation or the creative achievements individuals have shown in the past than in how hard they will work and how successfully they will create in the future.

Difficult as the problems of measuring some complex human traits are, they are much simpler than the problems of predicting future success, especially if that success requires a fortunate coincidence of many influences. To help keep our thinking straight, we probably should not charge those difficulties to the limitations of educational measurement. We might charge them in part to the somewhat indefinite generality of the concepts (motivation, creativity, and so on), in part to the complexity of human behavior, and in part to our cherished, if partly imaginary, freedom of choice and action.

Finally, it should be recognized that paper-and-pencil tests do have some limitations. They are well adapted to testing verbal knowledge and understanding and ability to solve verbal and numerical problems. These are important educational outcomes, but they are not all. One would not expect to get far using a paper-and-pencil test to measure children's physical development. Perhaps such a test could be made to yield somewhat better measures of the social effectiveness of adults, but even here the paper-and-pencil test is likely to be seriously limited. Both performance tests of physical development and controlled observations of behavior in social situations would be expected to offer more promise than a paper-and-pencil test.

However, it is important to remember that the use of alternative measures of achievement does not in any way lessen the need for objectivity, relevance, reliability, and validity. To achieve these qualities of excellence in measurement may well be even more difficult in performance testing and observational rating than it is in paper-and-pencil testing. But the usefulness of the measurements depends on them.

ALTERNATIVES TO TESTS

Teachers obtain information about the educational achievements of their students from many sources other than tests (Dorr-Bremme, 1983). They observe informally, and almost constantly, what students do and say. Some of these observations are written down to form anecdotal records. Check lists and participation charts help teachers to observe and record behavior comprehensively and systematically. Sociograms provide graphic representations of the structure of personal relations—friendships, preferences, evaluations, and so on—among the students in a class. Evaluations of performances and products can be defined and quantified with the help of rating scales. A more detailed description of some of these other sources of information about students is found in Chapter 9 of Mehrens and Lehmann (1984) or in Chapter 14 of Noll et al. (1979).

In many cases information obtained from nontest sources is essentially descriptive and provides no direct measurement of ability or achievement in learning. If the information does not result in numbers, it does not constitute a measurement. As noted earlier, measurement consists of the assignment of numbers to persons or things so that the larger numbers indicate greater amounts of some characteristic of the person or thing. Assessments of student abilities can be made on the basis of descriptive information. These assessments are bound to be qualitative, but they are covertly, casually, and only quite roughly quantitative. They provide only limited and very imperfect measures of achievement. Observations of behavior, however specific and objective, may have some value in assessing achievement, but they are no adequate replacement for good classroom achievement tests.

Ratings of performances or products, on the other hand, do involve assigning numbers to things, and hence do constitute measurements. But these alternatives to tests tend to be specific to particular aspects of achievement. While they can rarely replace tests, they can be useful supplements to the information tests provide. Most teachers use ratings of a student's performance in class, and of the student's written work, as part of the basis for assessing the student's achievement in learning. It is important to note at this point that the value of ratings, as well as of a test or any other measurement of educational achievement, depends on the objectivity, the reliability, the validity, and the utility of the measures they yield. Imperfect as tests may be, they are typically much more objective, reliable, and valid than the alternatives to tests tend to be. Assessments of achievement in learning should not be limited to tests, but the alternatives should be used with care and with full realization of their limitations and pitfalls.

KINDS OF ACHIEVEMENT TESTS

Tests are sometimes differentiated by the type of score interpretation they most readily yield: norm-referenced, criterion-referenced, or domain-referenced. Though these terms aptly describe types of test-score interpretations, they are used frequently by teachers, writers, and measurement specialists to refer to kinds of tests. That is, a norm-referenced test is one that permits us to make norm-referenced interpretations of the scores obtained from it. It is important to distinguish between the types of score interpretations that can be made, because it is possible to apply more than one type to the scores from a single test. Despite this possibility, it is seldom advantageous to interpret a set of scores in more than one way; good tests tend to be built to optimize the user's ability to make a single type of interpretation. Hence, there are important variations in the procedures adopted for constructing tests that will yield one type of score interpretation rather than another. These types of test-score interpretations can be categorized broadly as content-referenced, group-referenced, or criterion-referenced. Each is listed in Figure 2-2 along with terms that represent variations of each type.

Content-Referenced

A *content-referenced* interpretation is made when the performance level of an individual is compared with (or referenced to) an explicit content area. That is, the individual's achievement level is described in terms of some specifically defined set of skills or sphere of knowledge. Nitko (1970) defined a criterion-referenced test in these same terms when he indicated that it "is deliberately constructed to give scores that tell what kinds of behaviors individuals with those scores can demonstrate" (p. 37). Glaser (1963) had previously stated that the term "criterion," as used in criterion-referenced test, does not mean a predictive criterion and should not be used synonymously with "cutoff score." The meaning of a score is derived from test content without regard for how other examinees may have scored. Thus content-referenced is used here as a broad term that encompasses the meaning originally attached to criterion-referenced by Glaser, Nitko, and others.

Both Hively (1974) and Millman (1974b) recognized the ambiguity associated with the term criterion-referenced and offered the term *domain-referenced* as a more exact descriptor of a test designed primarily to optimize content-referenced interpretations. "(Criterion) carries surplus associations to mastery learning that are best avoided by using the more general term 'domain' instead" (Hively, 1974, p. 6). A domain can be broadly conceived as (a) a large number of related but separate skills or behaviors, (b) several somewhat related but separate skills or behaviors, (c) several somewhat related clusters of homogeneous skills or behaviors, or (d) one single skill or behavior. This broad definition is consistent with Millman's definition of a domain-referenced test as "any test consisting of a random or stratified random sample of items selected from a well-defined set or class of tasks (a domain)" (1974b, p. 315). A single instructional objective or a cluster of instructional objectives that defines a unit of instruction could both be considered domains. In the latter case, each objective might be referred to as a subdomain.

The use of instructional objectives gives rise to a special type of content-referenced interpretation called *objectives-referenced*. When the items in a test adequately correspond to all of the instructional objectives of interest to the

Figure 2-2 Categories of Test-Score Interpretation.

I. Content-referenced	II. Group-referenced	III. Criterion-referenced
A. Domain-referenced	A. Norm-referenced	A. Content-referenced base
B. Objectives-referenced	B. Treatment-referenced	B. Norm-referenced base

test user, scores can be interpreted in terms of mastery of those objectives. When the domain is a single objective, the interpretation is mastery or nonmastery. If the domain is a cluster of instructional objectives, the interpretation may center either on the proportion of objectives mastered or on mastery versus nonmastery of each objective in the domain. The original score reports from the National Assessment of Educational Progress (1970) are examples of objectives-referenced interpretation.

The major difference between domain-referenced and objectives-referenced interpretations is in the amount of inference that must be made about what examinees have mastered. Domain-referenced interpretations are made when test items represent only a (random) sample of the behaviors or skills of interest. Some behaviors included in the domain definition may not be included among or may be under-represented by the items in the test. Inferences must be made on the basis of both sampled *and* unsampled behaviors. Course final examinations, course proficiency tests, "chapter" achievement tests, and commercially prepared achievement batteries are likely applications for domain-referenced interpretations. However, when all behaviors in the domain of interest are represented completely by the test items, inferences about other behaviors are unnecessary. Score interpretations can be made in reference to only the cluster of behaviors (objectives) or to each single behavior for which items are included in the test. Unit pretests, curriculum-embedded tests, and unit achievement tests in a course are possible applications for objectives-referenced interpretations.

Group-Referenced

A *group-referenced* interpretation is made when an individual's score is compared with the scores of other individuals in a specific group. Norm-referenced interpretation of scores is the most widely used type of group-referenced interpretation. A *norm-referenced* test is "one whose scores get their meaning by reference to a table of norms, that is, a table of percentile ranks or similarly derived scores" (Millman, 1974a, p. 189).

The user of norm-referenced tests generally is interested in identifying individual differences in achievement levels within the examined group. Such tests are constructed so that test-score variability and test discrimination are maximized. The behaviors or skills being measured usually are defined by broad content categories, but they also may be defined quite explicitly. Test items may, but seldom do, represent a "random" sample of items from some well-defined population of items. Typically items are written to discriminate; they must be content relevant, but need not conform to the same rigid content definition and sampling requirements associated with domain-referenced measures.

Treatment-referenced interpretations (Millman, 1974a), another form of group-referenced interpretation, are made in certain research or program evaluation contexts. When two or more groups are each exposed to a different instructional treatment or strategy, the usual goal of summative evaluation is to compare the achievement scores of the groups. Thus, group scores (means) are compared rather than individual scores. Treatment-referenced interpretations are made when the score of one group is compared with the scores of other groups that have experienced the same, rival, or no instructional treatment. Tests designed to yield such interpretations contain items that are sensitive to instruction. That is, they are much easier when answered by students who have been instructed than by those who have not (Millman, 1974a). Interpretations are made in reference to varying methodological treatments or instructional levels. The mean score of a given group takes on significance only when compared with the mean of some other relevant group. No direct reference is made to item content or subject matter to derive meaning from the scores. Treatment-referenced interpretations can be made to judge the impact of a particular program, instructional sequence, or method of instruction. Achievement scores obtained through most of the "methods" research reported in the education literature are interpreted in a treatment-referenced fashion.

Criterion-Referenced

The meaning Glaser (1963) and others originally attached to the term *criterion-referenced* has become more closely associated with domain-referenced in recent years. For example, Popham and Husek (1969) defined criterion-referenced measures as

> those which are used to ascertain an individual's status with respect to some criterion; i.e., performance standard. It is because the individual is compared with some established criterion, rather than other individuals, that these measures are described as criterion-referenced. The meaningfulness of an individual score is not dependent on comparison with other testees. We want to know what the individual can do, not how he stands in comparison to others. (p. 2)

Definitions of criterion-referenced tests offered by Glaser and Nitko (1971), Jackson (1970), and others are variants of that cited above. The historical "evolution" of the term is well documented by Nitko (1983).

In many situations test users are not particularly interested in domain scores (content-referenced) or in norms (group-referenced scores). A minimally acceptable standard of performance is sometimes the single most logical basis for deriving meaning from a test score. Criterion-referenced seems to be a logical label for describing such interpretations. A *criterion-referenced interpretation* is made when an individual's score is compared with a cutoff score that represents a performance standard. Each person who exceeds the criterion score is judged as "acceptable," "passing," or "admitted"; each examinee who scores below the criterion score is "unacceptable," "failed," or "rejected." No attempt is made to compare the performances of individuals with one another, and no attempt is made to determine specifically what portion of a content domain an individual has mastered. The operational definitions of mastery associated with pretesting, formative testing in individualized instructional settings, and course proficiency testing are based on criterion-referenced interpretations using either a single cutoff score or multiple cutoff scores.

Criterion-referenced interpretations are not necessarily domain-referenced interpretations that require a cutoff score. Criterion-referenced interpretations are related to either content-referenced or group-referenced interpretations, depending on the method used to determine the criterion score(s). The method selected to establish a criterion score (cutoff) relates to the purpose for testing and to the type of decision to be made about the examinees. For example, a test might be given to identify the most talented mathematics students in an entering college freshman class. Those in the top 10 percent might be placed in an honors calculus sequence. The cutoff score might be established by examining the performance of an entering group on the mathematics test and locating the score separating the top 10 percent from the bottom 90 percent. The criterion-referenced interpretation of the scores of this and subsequent entering groups would have essentially a group-referenced basis.

Cutoff scores also can be set so that the criterion-referenced interpretation would have a content-referenced base. Suppose the mathematics department had no quota for their honors sequence but, instead, wished to identify individuals who had command of certain basic mathematical skills and concepts. A group of instructors might examine the test item-by-item to determine how many items they think a student must answer correctly to satisfy the prerequisites of the honors calculus sequence. A cutoff score might be set using the average judgment of the instructors. This method of establishing a criterion score is content-referenced and can be implemented without administering the test to any group of individuals.

Figure 2-2 depicts the relationships among the types of score interpretations discussed above. More will be said about these types of interpretations as we consider the various stages of test development and the procedures for evaluating the quality of achievement tests. It will become more apparent as we progress that a single test can be developed to yield all these types of score interpretations, but the value of doing so is quite small.

Finally, it should be noted that the terms shown in Figure 2-2, and the relationships depicted among them, are not used in uniform fashion by measurement specialists. In particular, the term criterion-referenced is used by some synonymously with domain-referenced or objectives-referenced. We have attempted to use domain-referenced as it is used conventionally in education but have distinguished between it and criterion-referenced. We have done so in an attempt to highlight and to eradicate the popular misconception that the mere use of cutoff scores assures absolute score interpretation. The fact that cutoff scores may be established with either a group-referenced or a content-referenced basis seems to be overlooked too frequently. It is true that a cutoff score can be set for any test, but it also is true that we cannot satisfactorily interpret the scores from such a test unless the basis for establishing the cutoff score is known.

SUMMARY

The principal ideas developed in this chapter can be summarized by these 21 statements:

1. Evaluation is a judgmental process used to determine the quality or worth of a performance, product, process, or activity.
2. The results of formative evaluation are used primarily to monitor and improve the instructional process, but the results of summative evaluation are used primarily to make "final judgments" about the quality of the results of instruction.
3. Measures are tools of evaluation that require a quantification of information.
4. Any important outcome of education is necessarily measurable, but not necessarily by means of a paper-and-pencil test.
5. It is a mistake to believe that qualities cannot be measured.
6. All tests are measures, and all measures are included in the set of qualitative and quantitative techniques of evaluation.
7. The Basic Teaching Model is a conceptual description of the essential ingredients of the teaching process. Its components—instructional objectives, entering behavior, instructional procedures, performance assessment, and feedback loop—represent the general activities one would expect to find among the procedures of successful teachers, regardless of the specific teaching model they employ.
8. The relationship of evaluation activities to the other essential aspects of teaching can be described with the Basic Teaching Model.
9. There are good reasons for believing that the primary task of the school is to facilitate cognitive learning.
10. Among the limited means that schools can use to help students become effective and happy adults, cultivating their cognitive abilities is the most appropriate and desirable.
11. The measurement of educational achievement is essential to effective formal education.
12. The primary function of a classroom test is to measure student achievement accurately.
13. Classroom tests can help motivate and direct student achievement and can contribute to learning directly.
14. The development of a good classroom test requires the instructor to define the course objectives in specific terms.
15. The fact that educational measurements fail to meet high standards of mathematical soundness does not destroy their educational value.
16. Educational outcomes that are said to be intangible because they are not clearly defined are as difficult to attain through purposeful teaching as they are to measure.
17. The imperfect tests we now use serve us far better than we would be served by the use of qualitative assessments alone.
18. Content-referenced and group-referenced more precisely describe kinds of test-score interpretations than types of tests.
19. Domain-referenced and objectives-referenced, both types of content-referenced interpretations, are applied in situations where the test content is either a sample of interest or the entire universe of interest, respectively.
20. Norm-referenced interpretations involve comparing one person's score with the scores of other individuals, but treatment-referenced interpretations compare the score of one group with the scores of other groups.
21. Criterion-referenced interpretations require a cutoff score that may be determined with either a content-referenced basis or a group-referenced basis.

3

WHAT ACHIEVEMENT TESTS SHOULD MEASURE

THE COGNITIVE OUTCOMES OF EDUCATION

If we look at what actually goes on in our school and college classrooms, labs, libraries, and lecture halls, it is reasonable to conclude that the major goal of education is to develop in students a *command of substantive knowledge*. Achievement of this kind of cognitive mastery is certainly not the only concern of educators, parents, and students, but it is, and ought to be, the central concern. What is this knowledge and how does it relate to understanding, thinking, and performing? We need answers to these questions before we can decide which achievements our educational tests should measure.

The Source of Knowledge

Knowledge originates in information that can be received directly from observation or indirectly from reports of observations. Anything we hear, read, see, or otherwise experience can become part of our knowledge. If it is remembered, it does become knowledge. But if it is only remembered, without being thought about, it remains mere information, the most elementary and least useful form of knowledge. If, on the other hand, information becomes the subject of our reflective thought—if we ask ourselves, "What does it mean?" "How do we know?" "Why is it so?"—we may come to understand the information. It can be integrated into a system of relations among concepts and ideas that constitutes a structure of knowledge. This process of encoding is essential to later retrieval; observations that are not encoded cannot be recalled (Anderson, 1972). Information that is stored in our memory by semantic encoding, by associating its meaning with information already stored, is powerful, useful, and satisfying relative to information stored by episodic encoding (Anderson, 1983). In the latter case, information is stored by associating it with other information related to our personal experience. Telephone numbers, what we wore two days ago, and what we plan to do next weekend are examples of information that is episodic. We may not remember that we learned the meaning of "prognosticator" in seventh grade (episodic encoding), but we likely still remember what it means (semantic encoding). Information that has been assimilated into our structure of knowledge is likely to be a more permanent possession than information that is simply remembered (Boulding, 1967).

The source of our verbal knowledge exists in our minds in the form of tacit knowledge (Polanyi, 1964) and as such is a purely private possession. But if concepts can be abstracted from these images and expressed in words, and if the relations among the concepts can be expressed in sentences, then the information imagery is converted into verbal knowledge. This can be communicated, made public. It can be recorded and stored for future reference and it can be manipulated in the process of reflective thinking. Thus verbal knowledge is a very powerful form of knowledge. The peculiar excellence of humans among all other earthly creatures is their ability to produce and use verbal knowledge.

If a structure of verbal knowledge consists entirely of a system of articulated relations among concepts and ideas, can it be described *completely* by listing the elements (propositions) that compose it? Might not a complex structure involve relations or dimensions that are not expressed by the constituent elements of the structure? Certainly a listing of the elements of a structure may lack some that have not been perceived or expressed in words. But to cite an example of such an unperceived and unexpressed element, one would have to perceive and express it. It could then be added to the list. The conclusion that a structure of verbal knowledge can be described by listing the concepts and propositions that compose it appears to be logical. The whole in this case appears to be precisely equal to the sum of *all* the parts.

The Role of Propositions in Testing

If the primary goal of education is to help students develop and build structures of verbal knowledge, it follows logically that tests designed to measure achievement be composed of items that help to determine the extent to which these structures of verbal knowledge exist. Cohen and Nagel (1934) have made two comments that seem particularly useful in this context: (1) knowledge is of propositions and (2) a proposition is a statement that can be said to be true or false. (Our use of the term here is not limited to the basic if-then statements used in logical analysis in the field of philosophy.) Propositions are expressed in sentences, but not all sentences are propositions. Those expressing questions or commands cannot be said to be true or false, nor can those that report purely subjective wishes or feelings. Propositions are always declarative statements about objects or events in the external world. For example:

The earth is a planet in the solar system.
A body immersed in a fluid is buoyed up by a force equal to the weight of the fluid displaced.
As we consume or acquire additional units of any commodity, the satisfaction derived from each additional installment tends to diminish.
William J. Bryan failed in his bid for election to the presidency of the U.S. in the campaign of 1896.

The relation of propositions such as these to objective test items of the true-false variety is direct and simple. Less obvious is the fact that such propositions are implicit in most other types of objective items—multiple-choice, matching, short-answer, or completion. What we test in each case, beyond students' ability to understand the language used in the test item, is their knowledge of the proposition that makes one answer correct and others incorrect. All the propositions cited above probably deserve to be preserved and passed on to future generations. Contrast them with these propositions:

Rain fell in New York City on December 1, 1984.
The cost of living in Canada increased by two-fifths of a point during October, 1985.
Work-limit tests are mentioned on page 136 of *Educational Measurement*, edited by E. F. Lindquist.

Objective-test items ought not to be based on propositions such as these, but sometimes, unfortunately, they are.

Despite the fact that the major goal of education is to develop in students a command of substantive knowledge, and despite the fact that all knowledge is knowledge of propositions, it is not easy to discover ready-made propositions that are suitable as bases for objective test items. To be suitable, propositions need to meet at least four criteria:

1. They must be concise, worded as accurately and unambiguously as the precision of knowledge and language permit.
2. They must be true, as established by a preponderance of experts in the field.
3. They must be among those most worthy of remembering, as judged by experts in the field.
4. They must represent knowledge unique to the field, principles and concepts not generally known by those who have not studied the subject matter.

The difficulty of finding or creating propositions that meet these standards in some areas of study may raise questions about the value of study in that field.

If relevant test items are too difficult to prepare, it may be because the structure of substantive knowledge is too weak.

Knowledge and Thinking

Thinking, understanding, and performing are among the significant goals of education, but none of these behaviors can be produced or nurtured without a substantive knowledge base. Thinking is a process and knowledge is a product, but the two are intimately related (Aaron, 1971, p. 103). New knowledge cannot be produced internally or used without thinking, and thinking always involves knowledge. Thought processes are wholly dependent on the knowledge being processed. Knowing how to think can be distinguished from knowing what is so but cannot be separated from it. Acquiring knowledge and learning how to think thus would seem to be interdependent goals. To say that schools should teach students how to think instead of teaching them knowledge is to urge the impossible (Hirst, 1972, p. 397–99). In sum, the best way to teach people how to think is to help them acquire useful knowledge; the ability to think is necessarily dependent on having something to think about.

Knowledge and Understanding

To assimilate new information learners must incorporate it into their own structure of knowledge. They must relate it to what they already know. Relating is understanding. Thunder is understood better when it is related to lightning. Fermentation is understood better when it is related to bacteria. In general, the understanding of any separate thing involves seeing its relations to other known things. And knowledge that is understood is more useful than knowledge that is only information.

Teachers can give students information. They cannot give them understanding, for a person's understanding is a private, personal possession created by the one who seeks it. We earn for ourselves the right to say "I understand." How much we know about a subject depends not only on how much information we have obtained from others or from our experiences. It depends also on how much we have thought about that information, related it to and tested it against other elements of information we have received. This is a primary purpose of study. We ask students to study because we expect such activities will cause them to think about relationships between what they know and what we want them to learn. New information that can be associated with present knowledge by elaborate means will be remembered and understood; information that enters the structure of knowledge with superficial associations likely will not be understood, but it may be remembered. Learning activities and homework that do not foster understanding are correctly perceived as "busy work."

To be understood, information must become part of a coherent structure of knowledge. When occasion for its use arises, we must be able to remember it and see its relevance. When all of this is true, we can say we have *command* of the knowledge. Possession of knowledge is not enough. The bad name knowledge learning has in some educational circles has resulted from too much emphasis on possession and not enough emphasis on command.

Finally, what we know probably is known with widely varying degrees of understanding. At the low end of the scale are things that are simply known, like the middle name of an acquaintance, or like the formula Einstein proposed to express the relation of energy to matter. Understanding may be absent either because there is little to be understood, as in the case of the middle name, or because too little is known on the subject or too little time has been spent in thoughtful attempts to understand, as in the case of the Einstein formula. The possibility of finding new relations and thus gaining more understanding always exists. However, most of us settle for understanding less about most subjects than we actually could understand; the cost of learning more seems greater than the knowledge would be worth to us. No doubt the presence of such sentiments provides one of the greatest challenges to teachers as they attempt to facilitate student learning. How do we increase the worth of knowing something or decrease the "cost" of learning it?

Knowledge and Cognitive Ability

Our concern here is with the measurement of the cognitive outcomes of education. The term "cognitive ability" will be used narrowly and specifically to refer to whatever particular kind of task can be done using the mind. Intelligence or general mental ability, general numerical ability, verbal fluency, and ability to reason are examples of *general* abilities outside the realm of the meaning of cognitive ability as used here. Contrast them with these examples of cognitive ability:

> Ability to tell the story of the Pilgrim voyage
> Ability to calculate the square root of a number
> Ability to outline the economic theories of J. M. Keynes
> Ability to trace the circulation of blood
> Ability to describe the origins of the Industrial Revolution
> Ability to identify the parts of a flower by name
> Ability to describe a method for removing tarnish from copper

These abilities indicate what a person can do. They require applications of knowledge to perform specific tasks or to answer particular questions. They can be taught specifically and are learned specifically.

Most written tests used to measure school achievement, professional capabilities, or qualifications for effective performance on the job are tests of specific cognitive abilities like those listed above. To acquire any such cognitive ability a person must learn how to do it. That learning requires the acquisition of knowledge. To perform a cognitive task one must know how to do it. The basis of any cognitive ability is knowledge. Experience and practice may develop and perfect the ability, enabling the person to perform the tasks more efficiently and accurately. But the basic requirement is that the person know how the task is to be done. To suggest that a person might lack the ability to do something the person knows perfectly well how to do is hardly reasonable. Knowledge is the key.

It is sometimes said that persons may possess knowledge they do not know how to use. They may indeed. From this fact the inference is sometimes drawn that knowledge alone is not enough; something more is necessary. Such an inference is open to question. It may be a lack of sufficient knowledge of the right kind. Those who cannot apply knowledge they possess may simply lack the knowledge of how to apply it. The problem may not be the inadequacy of knowledge per se, but inadequacies in the specific knowledge possessed.

Knowledge and Performance

The contribution of knowledge to effective human behavior is sometimes questioned. Knowledge alone is not enough, says the businessman. It does not guarantee financial success. Knowledge alone is not enough, says the college president. It does not guarantee scholarly achievement. Knowledge alone is not enough, says the religious leader. It does not guarantee virtue. Knowledge alone is not enough, says the philosopher. It does not guarantee wisdom.

They are all right, of course. Knowledge alone is not enough. But in our complex world of chance and change, no one thing or combination of things will ever be enough to guarantee financial success or scholarly achievement or virtue or wisdom. Although this is true, few would deny that the command of substantive knowledge does contribute greatly to the attainment of these and other ultimate goals.

Some have argued that knowing *how* does not always require knowing *that* (Ryle, 1949). But are the two really so distinct and unrelated? For cognitive tasks, would not a sufficient amount of relevant knowing *that* enable a person to know *how*? If one knows *that* to find the quotient of two common fractions one must invert the divisor and multiply, and all that those words mean, does one not know *how* to divide common fractions? In general, if we wish to teach someone *how* to do something, is there any better way than to teach them *that* this, this, and this must be done?

Surely knowing is not the same as doing. If the doing involves physical manipulation, it may require psychomotor skills that knowing cannot supply. Even in the realm of pure mental tasks, practice may increase facility. But facility aside, can doing any mental task require more than knowing perfectly well how to do it? If so, what is that "something more"? The best way to prepare learners to complete a cognitive task is to help them acquire the knowledge of how to complete it. The basis of that knowledge is necessarily verbal knowledge. Given sufficient motivation to attempt to complete a task, sufficient verbal knowledge about how to complete it should enable learners to do so successfully.

THE ROLE OF INSTRUCTIONAL OBJECTIVES

The knowledge and understanding that is the focus of instructional efforts in our schools and on our campuses is the same knowledge and understanding that tests of achievement ought to measure. The specific knowledge we expect students to learn is represented in the Instructional Objectives component of the Basic Teaching Model described in Chapter 2. The teacher's job is to define the structures of knowledge, the concepts and relationships that should be the basis for instruction. Statements of instructional objectives can be useful for instructional planning, for promoting intentional learning, and for developing the tools for performance assessment. What are instructional objectives and where do they come from? How can they be used to enhance our evaluation efforts?

The Derivation of Instructional Objectives

Instructional objectives are statements that describe the abilities students should be able to display to demonstrate that important concepts and principles have been incorporated into their own structures of knowledge. These statements indicate what the learner should be able to do at the end of an instructional sequence. Because the development of cognitive abilities ought to be the primary concern of our schools, the delineation of these important abilities is no trivial matter. Particularly at the elementary and secondary school levels, the job of deciding what students should learn, what they should know, should not be left to the classroom teacher alone. Most purposeful formal learning is organized in the context of a curriculum defined in terms of grade levels and subject matters. For example, the instructional objectives of a seventh-grade mathematics class must fit into the entire organizational plan; they should not be decided solely by the personal preferences, interests, or capabilities of each different seventh-grade mathematics teacher in the school district.

The derivation of instructional objectives in an organized curriculum is outlined in Figure 3-1. The pyramid develops from a small set of educational goals that indicate the purpose of the instructional program. These goals are broad, general statements that are the foundation of the educational program. Parents, teachers, school board members, and administrators decide jointly what the educational goals of the schools should be. For example, "To develop the skills necessary to live as an independent adult" may be a goal specified for the middle school curriculum. To accomplish this goal, level objectives are

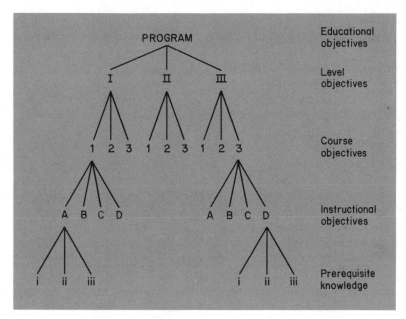

Figure 3-1 The Source of Instructional Objectives—The Pyramid Effect.

prepared for each of the middle school grade levels. A level objective for grade seven might be: "To use basic mathematical concepts and processes to solve problems encountered in daily living."

The level objective for the seventh grade, one of several, suggests the need for a mathematics course. The purpose of the course is to address all of the level objectives related to mathematics content. Another tier of objectives is needed to define in more detail the mathematics curriculum for grade seven. One course objective might be to "compute with ratios and proportions to solve practical word problems." Once course objectives such as this have been specified, teachers must organize them logically and sequentially. Typically such activities result in the formation of instructional units, defined by yet more detailed descriptions of the abilities students should attain—instructional objectives. An example from a unit on ratios and proportions might be: "To compute the price per ounce of several comparable grocery commodities to determine the least expensive." The final tier, prerequisite knowledge, suggests that new learning builds on prior learning and that students' entering behaviors must be considered in planning the instructional procedures for a particular unit.

The pyramid illustrates that instructional objectives are derived from a few broad educational goals through successive stages in hierarchical fashion. Each stage yields more statements, collectively, than the prior stage, and the statements generated at any one stage are more precise than those in the prior stage in indicating the nature of the ability to be achieved. In fact, the writing of instructional objectives can become a seemingly endless task if the writer attempts to separate cognitive abilities into increasingly finer components.

Statements of Instructional Objectives

In contrast to educational goals and level objectives, instructional objectives should be prepared primarily by those who will do the teaching. The statements should be written in a form and at a level of specificity that will make them most useful for their intended purposes. These purposes can be broadly categorized as instructional planning, learner information, and evaluation planning.

Instructional Planning.   Objectives can be used to determine prerequisite knowledge learners need to enable them to benefit from instruction. (Such prerequisites are sometimes called *enabling objectives*.) The most appropriate materials and instructional methods to use depend on the nature of the instructional objectives and how these objectives relate to prior learning. How to apportion time in an instructional unit and how much time to allocate to practice both depend on the nature of the cognitive abilities learners are expected to achieve.

Learner Information.   Students need to know what is expected of them. Particularly beyond the primary grades, academic expectations can be communicated by providing the learners with statements of instructional objectives. Such communications promote intentional learning rather than incidental learning (Klauer, 1984). It seems inefficient for students to have to guess what the purposes of various assignments or activities are. Certainly a list of instructional objectives should not be a set of questions begging for memorized responses. Yet statements that highlight the important information, concepts, and principles within a content domain can be a motivating tool to direct students' energy or to manage students' efforts in learning. Clear expectations contribute to producing a level of attention and stimulation that is necessary to foster maximum performance.

Evaluation Planning.   Statements of objectives represent a key element in developing the tools of performance assessment. The cognitive abilities indicated by instructional objectives dictate the type of measure to use (observation, objective test, paper, or project) to assess achievement. If a test seems most appropriate, the objectives suggest what types of test items (essay, multiple-choice, problem-type) are most appropriate. The nature of the objectives also may suggest how frequently evaluation should occur and, perhaps, how much formative evaluation is needed.

Though there is general agreement among educators about the need for and the role of instructional objectives, there remains less agreement about how such statements should be prepared. Some have advocated the use of behavioral objectives that require considerable detail, resulting in a multitude of statements for a relatively short instructional unit (Mager, 1962). Ebel (1972) has examined the shortcomings of behavioral objectives and has advocated the use of relatively general statements of learning outcomes. Gronlund's (1981) approach draws on both of these extremes in that it incorporates both implicit statements of general learning outcomes and explicit statements of specific learning outcomes.

How instructional objectives should be prepared for a specific situation may be dictated by the teaching model adopted. For example, individualized approaches to instruction (Bloom, 1968; Glaser, 1968; Keller, 1968) require explicit statements of objectives to define and organize the curriculum, to plan instructional activities, to monitor learner progress, and to advance the learner through the curriculum. Domain-referenced or objectives-referenced tests are essential measures of achievement in these teaching models. Regardless of the teaching model, instructional objectives are useful to test constructors as guides to the nature of test content and to the differential emphasis of topics within a test. Highly specific statements may even be useful in suggesting particular questions or types of questions to ask.

The Taxonomies of Educational Objectives

A number of educators have devoted considerable effort to reducing the ambiguity associated with stating instructional objectives and translating these objectives into relevant test items. In doing so, they divided learning outcomes into three nonoverlapping domains: cognitive, affective, and psychomotor. The first document stemming from this work, *Handbook I: The Cognitive Domain* (Bloom et al., 1956), provides six categories for classifying cognitive behaviors: knowledge, comprehension, application, analysis, synthesis, and evaluation. The categories are intended to be hierarchical in terms of the intellectual demand placed on the learner. That is, knowledge, the remembering of information, is less demanding than comprehension, the relating of concepts or the translation of ideas from one form to another. Evaluation, the most demanding, requires judgments using criteria remembered or formulated by the learner. Each major category is further subdivided, and test items are presented to illustrate how achievement can be measured at each taxonomic level.

Handbook II: The Affective Domain (Krathwohl et al., 1964) is similar in purpose to Handbook I but relates to interests, values, and attitudes. The five categories are arranged hierarchically in terms of increasing level of involvement: receiving, responding, valuing, organization, and characterization by a value. A taxonomy for the psychomotor domain has been proposed by several educational psychologists (Harrow, 1972; Kibler et al., 1981). The categories of each vary, but they generally relate to gross bodily movements, finely coordinated bodily movements, nonverbal communications, and speech behaviors.

The cognitive taxonomy has received the most attention from test constructors because it has been available the longest and because it describes the kinds of abilities test constructors are most interested in measuring. A major contribution of the taxonomy is the awareness it has created regarding the intellectual level at which instructional objectives and test items are written. That is, teachers who may have written most of their objectives to require simple remembering or recall of information have come to realize that they actually intended for students to understand and apply knowledge. By using the taxonomy to classify objectives teachers can see more readily whether their expectations are appropriate.

Though the cognitive taxonomy can be somewhat useful for classifying objectives in terms of the level of behavior required, it is not very useful for classifying test items. Unfortunately some teachers and test constructors have failed to realize this shortcoming. The problem can be illustrated with the following test item. To which category of the taxonomy does this item relate most directly?

1. **Why is a fusible alloy better than its constituents for use in automatic fire sprinkling systems?**
   *a. **The alloy generally has a lower melting point.**
   b. **The alloy generally can accommodate greater water pressure.**
   c. **The alloy generally has a higher melting point.**
   d. **Each of the constituents is a better conductor of electricity than the alloy.**

On the surface this item appears to measure achievement beyond the recall level, perhaps comprehension or even application of principles. However, a full assessment cannot be made without knowing what events transpired during instruction. If the fire-sprinkler illustration was used as an example in class or in a text, the item is a measure of recall of that information. Only if the item presents a new or novel situation can it be categorized as an application item in terms of Bloom's cognitive taxonomy. It is very difficult to pinpoint the mental processes involved in answering a particular test question, even when we know what took place during instruction.

PROBLEMS IN MEASURING COGNITIVE KNOWLEDGE

Rote Learning

Do objective tests encourage rote learning? Do they reward students for memorizing pat answers to a few standard questions? Do they require little more than recognition or recall of isolated factual details? No doubt the answers to all of these questions could be "Yes." However, it is quite possible to construct tests that do not encourage or reward rote learning.

The phrase *rote learning* refers to both a process and a product. The process is one of repetition of the same sequence of words, as in learning a poem, the lines of a play, or the basic facts of addition or multiplication. The product is a ready recall of the exact words or number sequences that were learned.

Clearly rote learning is sometimes useful and necessary, as in the examples just given. It is an effective means of storing information. But just as clearly it has little to do with knowledge as defined in this chapter, or with understanding and application. It is mostly meaningless and mechanical learning. A tape recorder can beat the human mind hands-down at rote learning.

Hence rote learning has only limited and special applications in an instructional program. Good instruction in most areas will not encourage it. Good achievement tests in most subjects will award low scores to students who have depended on it as their primary means of learning. All the test constructor need do to combat the rote learner is to ask questions that the examinee has never seen before, questions with answers that cannot be learned by rote, questions that require reflective thought. If a test rewards or encourages rote learning, it is not because of the form of the test item (multiple-choice, true-false, or whatever) but because it includes questions to which pat answers were or could have been learned by rote.

From the point of view of the learner, rote learning is seldom a very attractive pastime. It is dull, hard work, with no promise of any long-term value. A student may engage in it out of desperation, in the hope of getting by on a quiz or examination, but it seldom leaves any sense of permanent achievement. Because rote learning may be far less common than our fears of it imply and because it is generally unattractive and ineffective, the danger that tests of factual knowledge will reward and encourage rote learning may not be serious.

Meaningless Verbalization

There is a related danger that deserves to be taken more seriously. It is the danger of mistaking verbal facility and fluency for command of substantive knowledge. To the degree that test items demand only acquaintance with verbal stereotypes, with familiar word sequences or associations, and to the degree that they may be answered successfully on the basis of word-word associations alone, without clear perceptions of word-thing relationships, to that degree the tests may be measuring superficial verbal facility rather than command of substantive knowledge.

It is possible, and perhaps not uncommon, for speakers or writers to use words with more concern for fluency and grace in expression than for the accuracy of the ideas being expressed. Most of us recognize and use more words, phrases, and stereotyped expressions than we understand clearly. One of the main responsibilities of test makers in working with words in test items or with students' verbal responses is to make sure that mere verbal facility does not pass for substantive knowledge. To do this they must seek original expressions for ideas, simple and accurate but unconventional. If they use familiar textbook language, it should be done in such a way that a student who merely recognizes the phrase but does not understand it will be attracted to a wrong answer. Test makers must invent novel questions and problem situations so that recognition alone will not lead to the correct answer.

AFFECTIVE OUTCOMES AS EDUCATIONAL GOALS

Those who teach and those who develop tests are sometimes accused of over-emphasizing cognitive learning, with consequent neglect of the affective determiners of behavior. Some say teachers are preoccupied with what their students know or do not know; students, on the other hand, are most concerned with what they like or dislike, and how they feel. Further, say the critics, the most profound challenges in our society are not cognitive. They are challenges to our social unity and to our individual righteousness, to our ethical standards and to our moral values, to our courage and to our compassion. If our schools dwell too much on cognitive outcomes, they will fail to contribute as they should to meeting these other important challenges (Tyler, 1974).

These charges and criticisms are not without foundation. Feeling is as real and as important a part of human nature as is knowing. How we feel is almost always more important to us than what we know, and how we behave is a paramount concern of those whose lives we share. And since behavior is sometimes determined more by how we feel about a situation than by what we know about it, clearly the affective dimension will play a most important role in meeting the challenges of society.

Perhaps, then, schools should transfer some of their concerns for cognitive outcomes to affective outcomes? There are two reasons why such a reemphasis should not occur. The first is that many affective goals can be reached, at least in part, through cognitive means. Affect and cognition are not independent aspects of the personality: How we feel about a problem or an event depends in part on what we know about it. Wisdom does not guarantee happiness, but the lack of it often entails great unhappiness. The affective failures among students—the alienated, the dropouts, even the bright revolutionaries—can almost always be traced to some prior cognitive failure of theirs or ours. Psychologists who try to help people with problems of affect usually use cognitive means. The psychotherapy they practice is essentially a cognitive process of fostering self-knowledge in the patient. Training sessions and courses in human relations focus on the cognitive aspects of bias and prejudice and attempt to create a new awareness of interpersonal relationships by expanding the knowledge structures of participants.

The second reason why our schools should not put more stress on affective outcomes is that, other than modeling, the only noncognitive means a school can use to attain such ends is the process of conditioning. When a school adopts and enforces (with rewards and punishments) certain roles of behavior, it conditions students to exhibit those kinds of behavior regularly.

What students initially accept as "the way things are done around here" is gradually transformed into the belief that things ought to be done that way.

No teacher can afford to ignore the affective side effects of efforts to promote cognitive learning. In fact, the affective disposition to learn must be considered by teachers in assessing the entering behavior of their students for each instructional unit. But teachers should not use their concern for affect as an excuse for paying less attention to cognitive outcomes.

Our schools and colleges were established primarily to develop cognitive competence, in the well-founded belief that this was the best society could do to help young people become effective and happy men and women. Other social institutions such as the family, church, and government may share this responsibility, but like the school, each of these social organizations has other primary purposes that establish them as unique institutions in our society.

SUMMARY

Some of the main ideas developed in this chapter may be summarized in the following statements:

1. A major goal of education is to develop in the students a command of substantive knowledge.
2. Knowledge is information that has been integrated into a structure of relations between ideas.
3. A structure of verbal knowledge can be described by listing the concepts and relationships of which it is composed.
4. All verbal knowledge can be expressed in propositions.
5. Propositions provide the basis for most good objective achievement-test items.
6. Thinking necessarily produces knowledge, but knowledge must be present for a being to have something to think about.
7. Understanding is a strictly internal process that involves the meaningful attachment of new ideas to an already existent structure of knowledge.
8. The prerequisites for performing a cognitive task are the desire to do it and the knowledge of how to do it.

9. The major source of the instructional objectives that describe student outcomes is a series of statements of objectives derived from a set of educational goals.
10. Instructional objectives can be prepared in such a way that they will be useful to teachers for instructional and evaluation planning and to students for guiding intentional learning.
11. The taxonomies of educational objectives are more useful to teachers for instructional planning than for evaluation planning or test development.
12. Rote learning is a process of information storage that has little to contribute to the cultivation of knowledge.
13. Few students make extensive use of rote learning, in part because it cannot lead to command of knowledge.
14. Uncritical acceptance by learners of words of vague or uncertain meaning interferes with the development of command of knowledge.
15. Schools should seek to attain affective ends only through cognitive means.

PROJECTS AND PROBLEMS

Project: Article Report

Read and report on five recent journal articles on testing. Choose articles that interest you and that you can understand. Locate the articles by consulting the *Education Index* or *Current Index to Journals in Education (CIJE)*. Write a report on each article, following the form and style of the example on page 44. Limit your report to a single page.

Sample Article Report

AUTHOR: Betts, Gilbert L.

POSITION: Editor, Educational Test Bureau, Minneapolis, Minnesota.

TITLE OF ARTICLE: "Suggestions for a Better Interpretation and Use of Standardized Achievement Tests."

REFERENCE: *Education,* vol. 71 (December 1950), 217–21.

THESIS: In order to get a meaningful measurement, achievement should be graded in relation to ability to achieve.

DEVELOPMENT: The intelligence test should be used as a measure of ability to achieve, and the achievement test score should be used as a measure of achievement. The two scores should then be compared for purposes of judging achievement. The use of grade norms leads to mediocrity because the more capable students are not motivated. If they are rated against themselves, they will receive more equal motivation. Improved use of tests begins with selection. Each test should be selected to cover the area the tester desires to cover and to measure what he desires to measure.

CONCLUSION: Achievement and intelligence should be compared by percentile ranks to see if the students are working up to their ability. All students should learn at their own rates but each should receive proper motivation in regard to his or her abilities.

EVALUATION: The author presents a very good argument in that good students are not properly motivated when achievement is judged solely on the basis of grade norms, as is many times done. One trouble with his suggested remedy is that when the poor students are motivated on the basis of their own intelligence scores, which correlate very highly with achievement scores, they will tend to become somewhat more satisfied with their performances as they are.

Project: Data on a Measurement Problem

Using a reference located through the *Education Index, Current Index to Journals in Education, Psychological Abstracts, Review of Educational Research,* or simply by leafing through issues of *Educational and Psychological Measurement, The Journal of Educational Measurement,* or other periodicals, find an article that presents solid data on a measurement problem that interests you. Data of this kind are almost certain to be numerical: numbers, proportions, averages, ratios, differences, standard deviations, correlation coefficients, significance levels, and so forth.

Write a brief summary of the study reported in the article, following the form illustrated on page 45.

Here are some measurement problems for which you might want to collect data:
  I. Functions
    A. Measurement of motivation
    B. Measurement of vocabulary
    C. Measurement of writing ability
    D. Prediction of success in college
    E. Credit by examinations
    F. Wide-scale testing programs
  II. Construction
    A. Types of objective-test items

Guessing on Objective Tests

Problem:

How much guessing do students do on objective tests?

Procedure:

College students taking true-false tests in a course on educational testing were asked to check any questions on their test copies to which their answers were no better than blind guesses. The answers they gave to these questions were then marked on a separate "Guesses" answer sheet. The inducement to report these guesses and to report them accurately was the promise that the students would be given credit for as many right answers as the laws of chance would predict, even if their actual guesses were not that good.

Data:

		Midterm	Final	Midterm	Final
1.	Test	Midterm	Final	Midterm	Final
2.	Date	7-7-67	7-25-67	10-23-67	12-4-67
3.	Number of items	98	89	108	116
4.	Number of students	158	158	121	121
5.	Responses	15,484	14,062	13,068	14,036
6.	Percent correct	76	72	76	71
7.	Guesses	486	905	620	1,108
8.	Percent of responses	3.1	6.4	4.7	7.9
9.	Guesses correct	271	494	336	575
10.	Percent correct	56	55	54	52
11.	Test reliability	0.79	0.89	0.79	0.81

Conclusion:

Students like these taking tests like these do relatively little blind guessing.

Reference:

Ebel, Robert L. "Blind Guessing on Objective Achievement Tests," *Journal of Educational Measurement,* vol. 5 (Winter 1968), 321–25.

      B. Free-response vs. choice-type tests
      C. Number of multiple-choice options
      D. Effects of position of correct response among multiple-choice options.
      E. Specific determiners
      F. Negative suggestion effects of true-false test items
   III. Administration
      A. Methods of presenting test items
      B. Open-book examinations
      C. Extent of cheating on examinations
      D. Testwiseness
      E. Effects of practice
      F. Effects of special coaching
      G. Response sets and objective-test responses
      H. Test anxiety
      I. Persistence on objective tests
      J. Correctness of first impressions on objective-test answers

K . Test time limits
L . Rate of work scores
M. Correction for guessing
N. Accuracy of objective-test scoring
IV. Evaluation
   A . Determination of the difficulty of objective-test items
   B . Item difficulty distributions
   C . Indices of item discrimination
   D. Reliability of essay-test grades
   E . Validity of the Spearman-Brown formula
   F . Methods of scaling test scores.

4

DESCRIBING AND SUMMARIZING TEST SCORES

The score on a test is usually the sum of the scores on the separate items that comprise the test. For an objective test the score may be simply the number of questions answered correctly. For an essay test the reader may assign points to each answer indicating a subjective judgment of its adequacy. The size of an examinee's score in relation to the maximum possible score provides a domain-referenced interpretation and some indication of the quality of performance. In other circumstances it may be more useful to make group-referenced interpretations, to compare one student's score with scores of other examinees. It may be helpful to examine the relationship of scores on one test with scores from the same group of students on other tests or to investigate the intrinsic quality of the test. To obtain these kinds of information, we need the help of statistical methods. The purpose of this chapter is not to duplicate the content of a good statistics text, but to describe statistical ideas that are a foundation for measurement concepts to be considered in subsequent chapters.

FREQUENCY DISTRIBUTIONS

A *frequency distribution* is a two-column list that describes a set of scores in a concise and systematic manner. One column lists all scores in the set from highest to lowest; the other column, the frequency column, shows the number of examinees that obtained each score. Table 4-1 shows the scores of a class

Table 4-1   Scores of 25 Students on Two Spelling
Tests

Student	List A—Monday	List B—Friday
Aaron	65	67
Barbara	75	72
Ben	66	72
Bud	88	92
Clyde	71	76
Donald	72	72
Dorothy	91	90
Eugene	82	80
Fay	84	80
Frank	76	81
Gary	69	64
Gladys	67	70
Jack	74	78
Jeff	80	77
Jerry	87	90
Joan	65	68
Marcy	91	85
Nadine	77	78
Nathaniel	96	94
Patricia	93	87
Peggy	79	78
Perry	84	89
Richard	76	75
Scott	73	78
Wendy	61	69

of 25 students on two spelling tests of 100 words. The first test, List A, was given on Monday; the second test, List B, contained different words and was dictated on Friday. A frequency distribution for the scores on List A is shown in Table 4-2. This distribution of scores is a useful visual aid for identifying the relative position in the group of any one student and for obtaining a picture of overall group performance at a glance. Note that there is a number in the score column for every possible score from highest to lowest. If the scores with zero frequencies (scores that no students obtained) were omitted from the frequency distribution, a somewhat distorted picture of overall group performance might be conveyed.

Frequency Polygons and Histograms

The information summarized by a frequency distribution also can be represented pictorially by a *frequency polygon* or a *histogram*. The frequency polygon also is known as a *line graph*. Figure 4-1 is an example of a frequency polygon using the scores of 14 examinees obtained on a 15-item quiz. The

Table 4-2   Frequency Distribution of 25 Scores on
List A

Score	Frequency	Score	Frequency
96	1	78	0
95	0	77	1
94	0	76	2
93	1	75	1
92	0	74	1
91	2	73	1
90	0	72	1
89	0	71	1
88	1	70	0
87	1	69	1
86	0	68	0
85	0	67	1
84	2	66	1
83	0	65	2
82	1	64	0
81	0	63	0
80	1	62	0
79	1	61	1

score scale is depicted along the horizontal line and the frequency scale is on the vertical line. An alternative representation is the histogram or bar graph, shown in Figure 4-2.

Frequency polygons and histograms are equally useful for describing a set of test scores efficiently. Detailed procedures for constructing both types

Figure 4-1   Sample Frequency Polygon.

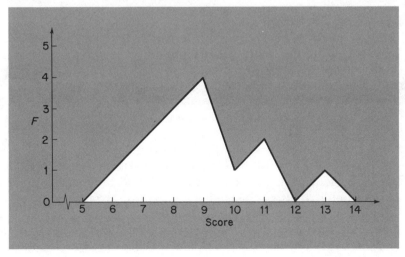

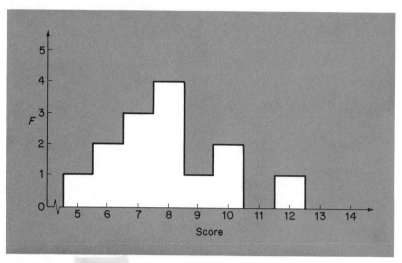

Figure 4-2 Sample Histogram.

of graphs can be found in most introductory statistics textbooks. (See, for example, Minium and Clarke, 1982 or Spence et al., 1983.)

Characteristics of Frequency Polygons

That frequency polygons come in all shapes and sizes can be verified from the variety shown in Figure 4-3. These curves are line graphs like the one in Figure 4-1 except that they have been smoothed, the jagged lines have been replaced by a smooth curved line, and the vertical line used to determine frequencies has been omitted. Such modifications usually indicate that the polygons do not represent any one set of data precisely, but a general distribution having certain dominant characteristics.

Considerable economy is associated with describing or sketching the frequency polygon that represents a set of test scores rather than enumerating each score or even preparing a frequency distribution. But to communicate such information, the characteristics that distinguish frequency polygons from one another must be known and understood. Four of these important characteristics are illustrated in Figure 4-3, and others will be noted in subsequent sections of this chapter.

A *symmetric* curve is one that has two halves, each a mirror image of the other. It is possible to draw a straight line through each of the top two polygons in Figure 4-3 so that, if we were to fold the figure on that line, the two halves would appear as one. Nonsymmetric or asymmetric curves are those that do not have this property. Such curves are said to be *skewed*. In part (b) of Figure 4-3, each skewed curve has a large "hump" and one long tail extending in one direction. The curve on the right is negatively skewed and the one on

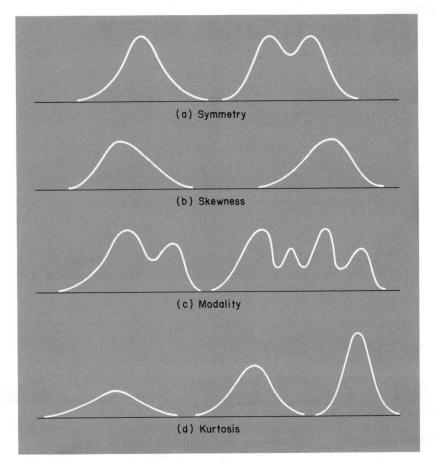

Figure 4-3 Frequency Polygons Illustrating Varying Characteristics.

the left is positively skewed. Note that the direction in which the tail extends on the score scale indicates whether the curve is skewed positively (to the right where positive numbers are found) or negatively (to the left where negative numbers might be found).

Since polygons can differ in the number of humps or peaks they contain, modality is another distinguishing characteristic. The *mode* of a score distribution is the most frequently occurring score.[1] (Can you verify that the mode of the scores in Figure 4-1 is 9?) A curve is *uni*modal if it has one mode, *bi*modal if it has two modes, and *multi*modal if it has many modes. When a frequency polygon has more than one peak, we must look to the tallest to describe the

[1] Some statistics textbooks refer to all identifiable peaks of a curve as modes, and some distinguish between major and minor modes based on differences in height. For simplicity we will retain the meaning "most frequently occurring score" throughout this book.

modality. Part (c) of Figure 4-3 shows a unimodal curve and a bimodal curve. Note that the curve with four peaks has two that are taller than the others, and those two are equally tall.

The last row of Figure 4-3 illustrates the kurtosis property of frequency polygons. *Kurtosis* relates to the relative flatness or peakedness of the curve. The names describing these curves (platykurtic, mesokurtic, and leptokurtic) can be remembered by associating the prefix of the term with a visual image of the shape of the curve.

To test your understanding of the properties of frequency polygons and their interrelationships, try to draw a figure to verify that each of the following statements is true:

1. Not all skewed distributions are unimodal.
2. Some leptokurtic distributions are not symmetric.
3. A rectangular distribution is multimodal.
4. Not all bimodal distributions are symmetric.
5. A single distribution can be symmetric, unimodal, and mesokurtic.
6. Some platykurtic distributions are skewed.

DESCRIBING SCORE DISTRIBUTIONS

Two particularly important characteristics of a distribution of scores are (1) the typical or average score and (2) the amount of dispersion or variability of the scores. The statistics used to report the typical score, measures of central tendency, are the mode, median, and mean. To report dispersion, one is likely to use the range or the standard deviation as a measure of variability.[2]

Measures of Central Tendency

The *mode* was defined previously in considering modality as a property of a frequency polygon. It is the most frequently occurring score. The *median* is the score above which and below which exactly half of the scores are found: the middlemost score. For the scores 5, 4, 3, 2, 1 the median is 3; for the scores 8, 7, 5, 2 the median is 6, halfway between 7 and 5. If the distribution contains an even number of scores, the median is the average of the two middle scores. Thus the mode must be a score actually obtained by an examinee, but the median need not be. When the score distribution is large and there are several people with tied scores in the vicinity of the median, the computational procedures are slightly more complicated. Because the median also is the 50th percentile,

---

[2] Another measure of dispersion, the semi-interquartile range, is used so infrequently to describe test scores that we have not discussed it here. Most introductory statistics textbooks describe its computation and use.

the procedures described later in this chapter for computing percentiles can be used for finding the median.

The *mean* is the average score, obtained by summing all the scores and dividing the sum by the number of scores. For the scores 5, 4, 3, 2, 1 the sum is 15 and the mean is 3. These operations are represented by the formula:

$$\overline{X} = \frac{\Sigma X}{n} = \frac{15}{5} = 3 \qquad\qquad 4.1$$

where

$\overline{X}$ is the mean,
ΣX is the sum of the scores, and
n is the number of test scores.

Ordinarily the median is easier to determine than the mean, especially when the number of scores is small. If the score distribution is skewed, the median usually gives a more reasonable indication of the typical score than does the mean. Consider, for example, the set of scores: 8, 9, 10, 11, 22. What are the values of the median and mean? Notice that the median (10) is more indicative of the typical score and that the magnitude of the mean (12) is influenced in the direction of the extreme score. Note also that four of the five scores are below the mean but only two are below the median.

Because the value of each score in a set affects the value of the mean, it tends to be a more stable indicator of central tendency than does the median. That is, the value of the mean is likely to change less from one set of scores to another set of the same kind. Furthermore, the mean is used, directly or indirectly, in calculating other important statistics. For this reason the mean generally is regarded by statisticians as a more precise and useful measure of central tendency than the median. However, we will find the median very useful for certain test-evaluation and test-score-interpretation purposes.

So why have three different ways to indicate central tendency? Why not just use the mean and forget the rest? The mode is easy to determine but not always unique. There may be two or more modes in a score distribution. The median generally is easier to determine than the mean but is less stable than the mean. Different situations suggest a preference for one measure over the other, but in many situations it matters little which is used. For what kind of score distribution are the mean and median the same value? Is there any circumstance in which all three measures are equal?

Measures of Variability

The *range* of a distribution is a number that indicates how many score points the distribution covers. For the scores 8, 7, 3, 2, 1 the range is 8. Note that this is *one more than the difference between the highest and lowest scores*. The range is a relatively unstable indicator of the amount of dispersion in a set of scores because its value depends on only two scores, the most extreme scores in the entire distribution of scores.

The most common and useful measure of variability is the *standard deviation*. A conceptual understanding of the standard deviation can be gained by learning how this statistic is computed. The distribution of scores 5, 4, 3, 2, 1 is used again for simplicity to illustrate. Calculating the standard deviation involves four steps:

1. Compute each person's *deviation score* by subtracting the mean from each person's test score.
2. Square each deviation score (multiply each deviation score by itself) and sum all the squared deviation scores.
3. Divide the sum by the number of test scores.[3] This yields a quantity called the *variance*.
4. Find the square root of the variance. This value is the standard deviation. (Remember to verify that your answer makes sense, that it is not larger or smaller than it should be, logically.)

These steps can be represented by this formula for finding the standard deviation:

$$s = \sqrt{\frac{\Sigma (X - \bar{X})^2}{n}} \qquad\qquad 4.2$$

where

> s is the standard deviation,
> Σ is the symbol meaning "the sum of," and
> X is an individual's test score.

The calculation of the standard deviation is illustrated in Table 4-3. The scores are listed in column 1 and their sum is used to determine the mean. The deviation scores are calculated and listed in column 2. The squared deviation scores are shown in column 3 along with their sum. The sum, 10, divided by the number of scores, 5, yields the variance. The standard deviation, 1.41, is the square root of the variance. Is 1.41 a reasonable value for the standard deviation of these 5 scores? What does it mean?

Conceptually, the standard deviation is a number that indicates, on the average, how much the scores in a distribution differ from the mean by. If the scores are all very close together near the mean, the standard deviation should be a relatively small number. However, if the scores are spread out over a large

---

[3] Statistically speaking, this division yields a "biased" estimate of the variance. An unbiased estimate would be obtained by dividing by $(n - 1)$, one less than the total number of scores. Since most electronic calculators that are programmed to yield the variance or standard deviation use $(n - 1)$ as the divisor, the value they yield should be slightly larger than that obtained with equation 4.2.

Table 4-3 Calculating Standard Deviation

(1) X	(2) $X - \bar{X}$	(3) $(X - \bar{X})^2$
5	2	4
4	1	1
3	0	0
2	−1	1
1	−2	4
Sum 15	0	10

$$s = \sqrt{\frac{10}{5}} = \sqrt{2} = 1.41$$

range, the standard deviation should be a relatively large number. In Table 4-3 some scores differ from the mean by two points, some by one point, and one does not differ from the mean. Our answer, 1.41, seems reasonable as an average amount by which these scores differ from their mean.

The conceptual definition given above is not the *statistical* definition exactly. Some students ask why it is necessary to go through all the squaring and "unsquaring" business. The answer to this question requires more statistics than we should concern ourselves with here. But notice that to calculate the *average deviation score,* we would obtain zero, no matter what set of scores we used. The sum of the deviations from the mean is always zero. (This is how the mean is defined statistically.) The squaring and square-root operations overcome this difficulty to yield a unique value for the standard deviation.[4]

Standard deviations are used in defining standard test scores such as College Board or ACT scores, in determining comparable or equivalent scores on two tests, in expressing the accuracy of a test score, and in controlling the weights of quizzes, project scores, and test scores in determining course grades. Variances, which so far have been used only to calculate standard deviations, will help in understanding some aspects of test reliability. Knowing a little about variances and standard deviations is a prerequisite to understanding important concepts about test scores, test characteristics, and other kinds of measures.

THE NORMAL DISTRIBUTION

Distributions of test scores frequently approximate a *normal distribution*—that is, a symmetric, bell-shaped curve. For this reason, and because it is convenient to have a standard model as a point of reference when describing the characteristics

[4] A formula that is equivalent to equation 4.2 and that is simpler computationally is

$$s = \sqrt{\frac{n \sum X^2 - (\sum X)^2}{n^2}}$$

of any given score distribution, the characteristics of the normal curve are important to know about.

Some of the essential characteristics of the normal distribution are illustrated in Figure 4-4. The curve is unimodal, symmetric, and mesokurtic. All three measures of central tendency have the same value. The horizontal scale along the base is marked in standard-deviation units with pluses and minuses corresponding to points above and below the mean, respectively.

The percentages shown in each area indicate how much of the total area under the curve lies within that area. In terms of the test scores in the distribution, the percentages indicate what portion of all the scores are between the values shown on the base line. For example, about 34 percent of all scores are between the mean score and the score that is one standard deviation above the mean. It is useful to remember that about 68 percent of the scores are between $-1s$ and $+1s$, about 95 percent of the scores are between $-2s$ and $+2s$, and about 2.5 percent of the scores are in each tail beyond $\pm 2s$. These rounded percentage values are sufficiently accurate for our purposes; more exact decimal values can be found in tables in a basic statistics book.

The normal distribution is a theoretical curve based on an unlimited number of scores or observations. Therefore, it extends without limit on either side of the mean well beyond $\pm 3s$. In practice and for convenience, it is often considered to extend from about three standard deviations below to three standard deviations above the mean. (Actually 99.72 percent of all scores comprising the distribution are within those limits.) But the distribution of scores from a class of, say, 30 students typically will not show a range of scores encompassing six standard-deviation units. Hoel's (1947) figures indicate that the following ratio of score range to standard deviation can be expected for groups of the size shown here.

Sample Size	Typical Range in Standard-Deviation Units
10	3.0
50	4.5
100	5.0
1000	6.5

The typical values shown are averages. For example, we should expect a set of ten scores that approximate a normal distribution to range from about $-1.5s$ to about $+1.5s$. There are too few scores in the distribution to *expect* that any one would be as far as three standard deviations above the mean, for example. It would be a useful computational check for a teacher to realize that in a distribution of 25 test scores, the highest score is more apt to be two than three standard deviations above the mean.

While it is true that many test-score distributions approximate the shape of the normal curve, there is no compelling reason why they ought to. In fact,

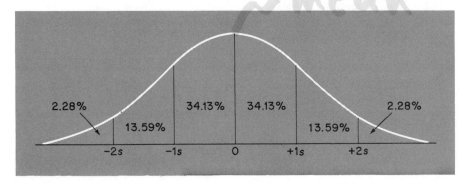

Figure 4-4   The Normal Distribution.

to achieve highest test-score reliability (minimal error of measurement) with a
given number of test items, a somewhat flatter, less mesokurtic, score distribution
is advantageous (Rummel, 1950). Test constructors who point with pride to
the beautifully normal distribution of scores that their tests yield may be using
a somewhat inaccurate standard of quality.

PERCENTILES AND PERCENTILE RANKS

Since the scores on different tests, when taken by different groups, can have
widely different means, standard deviations, and distributions, it is useful to
have some standard scale to which they all can be referred for comparison
purposes. One such scale is *percentile ranks*. This scale will be discussed in some
detail because it is so useful in interpreting and working with scores from both
teacher-made and standardized achievement tests.

Computing Percentile Ranks

The percentile rank of a given test score can be defined in three similar
but significantly different ways. It is the percentage of scores in a distribution
of scores that:

1. falls below the given score, or
2. falls at or below the given score, or
3. falls below the midpoint of the given score interval.

Table 4-4 shows the effects of these different definitions on the percentile ranks
of five hypothetical scores. The highest score gets a percentile rank of only 80
under definition 1. The lowest score gets a percentile rank of 20 under definition
2. The median score gets a percentile rank of 40 under definition 1 and of 60
under definition 2. But under definition 3 the median score gets a percentile

Table 4-4 Effect of Different Definitions of Percentile Ranks

	PERCENTILE RANK UNDER DEFINITION		
Score	1	2	3
5	80	100	90
4	60	80	70
3	40	60	50
2	20	40	30
1	0	20	10

rank of 50, as it should in a symmetric distribution of scores. In addition, the highest and lowest scores are both the same distance from the extremes of the percentile rank scale, as they also should be. For these reasons definition 3 is preferred.

There are three steps in the process of computing the percentile ranks of the scores in a particular distribution using definition 3.

1. Prepare a frequency distribution.
2. Add successive frequency values, beginning with the lowest score, to obtain a column of cumulative frequencies. Note that for any one score, this requires taking half of the frequencies associated with that score and adding to it all frequencies below that score.
3. Convert each cumulative-frequency value into a percentage based on the total number of scores (the last cumulative-frequency value).

Table 4-5 illustrates the computation of percentile ranks for the List A spelling scores taken from Table 4-1. Notice that the score scale extends from one score below the lowest score obtained to one score above the highest score obtained. And the scale includes all possible scores between the extremes, even though no student actually obtained some of those scores. The number of students who received each of the scores is shown in the second column of the table.

The third column gives a cumulative frequency for each score. It is calculated by counting the number of scores lower than the given score and adding half the number of scores at that score point. Consider the score 75, for example. There are ten scores lower than 75, and one score of 75. So, we take the 10, and one-half of the one, and get a cumulative frequency of 10.5.

The fourth column of percentile ranks is obtained by dividing each cumulative-frequency value by the total number of scores and multiplying the result by 100. Thus to find the percentile rank of any score in a distribution of scores you must know three things:

Table 4-5 Computation of Percentile Ranks

Score Scale	Score Frequencies	Cumulative Frequency	Percentile Rank	Score Scale	Score Frequencies	Cumulative Frequency	Percentile Rank
97	0	25.0	100	79	1	14.5	58
96	1	24.5	98	78	0	14.0	56
95	0	24.0	96	77	1	13.5	54
				76	2	12.0	48
				75	1	10.5	42
94	0	24.0	96				
93	1	23.5	94	74	1	9.5	38
92	0	23.0	92	73	1	8.5	34
91	2	22.0	88	72	1	7.5	30
90	0	21.0	84	71	1	6.5	26
				70	0	6.0	24
89	0	21.0	84				
88	1	20.5	82	69	1	5.5	22
87	1	19.5	78	68	0	5.0	20
86	0	19.0	76	67	1	4.5	18
85	0	19.0	76	66	1	3.5	14
				65	2	2.0	8
84	2	18.0	72	64	0	1.0	4
83	0	17.0	68	63	0	1.0	4
82	1	16.5	66	62	0	1.0	4
81	0	16.0	64	61	1	0.5	2
80	1	15.5	62	60	0	0.0	0

1. How many scores there are altogether.
2. How many scores were lower than the given score.
3. How many students obtained the given score.

Consider a set of 38 scores in which there is one score of 52 and there are nine scores below 52. What is the percentile rank of 52? Well, the cumulative frequency for 52 is 9.5 (9 plus ½). When 9.5 is divided by 38 and multiplied by 100, the result is 25. So the percentile rank of 52 is 25; 25 percent of the scores in this distribution are below the midpoint (52) of the score interval 51.5–52.5.

Percentile and *percentile rank* are used interchangeably by some, but these are really different terms. We say that the percentile rank of 52 is 25, but the 25th percentile is 52. A percentile rank must be a number between 0 and 100, but a percentile is a score value in the distribution of scores. When we want to know what score has 72 percent of the scores below the midpoint of its interval, we seek the 72nd percentile. To find this score in Table 4-5, we first determine how many scores are represented by 72 percent of 25, the total number of scores. The answer is 18. Then we scan the cumulative-frequency column to find the score below which 18 scores are found. The corresponding score from the first column is 84. The 72nd percentile is a score of 84. But the percentile rank of 84 is 72.

Interpreting Percentile Ranks

Test scores expressed as percentile ranks are sometimes confused with test scores expressed as percent correct. They are, of course, quite different. A *percent correct score* is determined by an examinee's performance relative to the content of the test. It expresses the relation between the number of points awarded to a specific examinee's paper and the maximum possible number of points for any paper. Usually the expectation is that few examinees in a group will receive percent correct scores less than some value near 70 percent, which is often set arbitrarily as the passing score. If the group as a whole does well on an examination, the percent correct scores will run higher than if the group as a whole does poorly.

A percentile rank, on the other hand, is determined solely by the relation between a specific examinee's score and the scores of other examinees in the group tested. Percentile ranks must necessarily range from near 0 to near 100, regardless of whether the group as a whole does well or poorly on the examination.

Percentile ranks differ from the original or raw test scores, and many other types of scores derived from them, in another respect. They are rectangularly distributed. Raw-score distributions, and those of many other types of scores, generally approximate a normal distribution, in which the scores are concentrated near the middle, with decreasing score frequencies as one moves out to the high and low extremes. In a rectangular distribution the score frequencies are uniform all along the scale. The relation between a normal distribution and a rectangular distribution is illustrated in Figure 4-5.

It is clear from this figure that percentile ranks magnify raw-score differences near the middle of the distribution but reduce raw-score differences toward the extremes. Stated in other words, a difference of 10 percentile rank units near the extremes corresponds to a much larger raw-score difference than does the same difference in percentile ranks near the mean. For example, for a set of 100 scores that form a normal distribution, the number of scores between the 50th percentile and the 55th percentile is *the same as* the number of scores between the 90th and 95th percentiles. But the raw-score difference between the 50th and 55th percentiles is smaller than the raw-score difference between the 90th and 95th percentiles. The score differences in standard-deviation units are 0.13 and 0.37, respectively. (This can be verified using a normal distribution table, found in most statistics books.)

STANDARD SCORES

Like percentile ranks, standard scores provide a standard scale, a common yardstick, by which scores on different tests by different groups may be compared

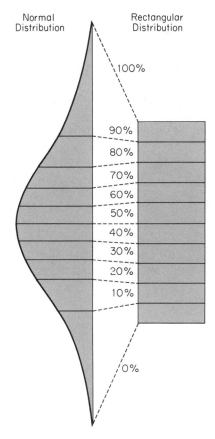

Figure 4-5
Relation Between Normal
and Rectangular Distributions.

reasonably. And like percentile ranks, standard scores inherently yield group-referenced score interpretations. Standard scores typically are used to interpret the results from standardized tests. They are considered in this chapter because they can be related well to both the normal curve and percentile ranks and because they are useful in the procedures for determining grades.

Linear Standard Scores

Raw scores are transformed into standard scores using the raw-score mean and standard deviation. The effect of this transformation is to create a new score scale that has a predetermined mean and standard deviation. One basic type of standard score, the z-score, is found using this formula:

$$z = \frac{X - \overline{X}}{s} \qquad\qquad 4.3$$

where X is the student's raw score, $\overline{X}$ is the mean of the raw scores, and s is the standard deviation of the raw scores. Notice that the numerator in this formula is the person's deviation score. The z-score indicates how many standard deviations from the mean (plus or minus) the person has scored. A student who scores at the mean has a z-score of 0. If the student has a raw score that is exactly one standard deviation *above* the mean, the z-score is +1.0. A $z = -1.5$ indicates the student scored one and one-half standard deviations *below* the mean. The z-score is seldom used itself to make score interpretations, but it is needed in further computation to yield some commonly used standard scores.

The *T*-score, for example, is computed using this formula:

$$T = 10(z) + 50 \hspace{4cm} 4.4$$

and standard scores on the College Board's achievement tests or Scholastic Aptitude Test (SAT) were established with this formula:

$$\text{CEEB Score} = 100(z) + 500 \hspace{3cm} 4.5$$

The original standard scores used to report the results from the Iowa Test of Educational Development (ITED) come from this formula:

$$\text{ITED Score} = 5(z) + 15 \hspace{3.5cm} 4.6$$

Finally, stanines are computed with the formula:

$$\text{Stanine} = 2(z) + 5 \hspace{4cm} 4.7$$

Stanine values are rounded to the nearest whole number.

Table 4-6 shows the characteristics of these linear standard scores and the relationships between them and percentile ranks in a normal distribution. To say that the transformation from raw scores to standard scores is *linear* means that if the corresponding pairs of scores, raw score and standard score, are plotted on a graph, they will form a single straight line. This also means that the shape of the frequency polygon of the transformed standard scores is the same as the shape of the raw-score frequency polygon. The *T*-score distribution will be negatively skewed if the raw-score distribution was, the CEEB-score distribution will be leptokurtic if the raw-score distribution was, and a bimodal, symmetric raw-score distribution will yield an ITED-score distribution with those same properties.

Notice that the mean and standard deviation of each standard score scale as shown in Table 4-6 are readily apparent in the corresponding formula for computing each. To create a new standard score scale, we simply multiply the z-score by the standard deviation desired for the new scale and then add the value of the mean desired for the new scale. For example, if we wanted a *J*-score scale that would have a mean of 40 and a standard deviation of 12, the formula needed would be:

$$J = 12(z) + 40 \hspace{4cm} 4.8$$

Table 4-6 Characteristics of Standard Scores in a Normal Distribution

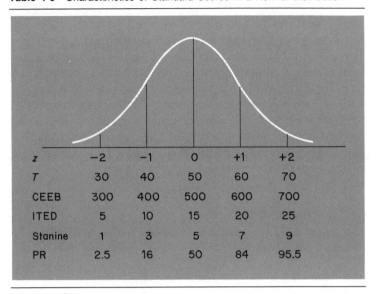

z	−2	−1	0	+1	+2
T	30	40	50	60	70
CEEB	300	400	500	600	700
ITED	5	10	15	20	25
Stanine	1	3	5	7	9
PR	2.5	16	50	84	95.5

Normalized Standard Scores

If one wishes to assume that the trait being measured by a test is normally distributed, it is possible to transform the raw scores in a *nonlinear* fashion so that the new distribution will be normal. Obviously it is not desirable to perform such a transformation on a distribution of scores that does not resemble the shape of a normal distribution. The main reason for normalizing a set of scores is to permit interpretations that take advantage of the properties of the normal curve. Stanines and other standard scores reported by publishers of standardized tests typically are normalized. The procedures for computing normalized standard scores are described in most introductory statistics textbooks.

The *Normal Curve Equivalent (NCE),* a type of normalized standard score, has been made popular recently through its use in reporting evaluation results from Title I programs of the Elementary and Secondary Education Act (ESEA). NCEs are computed with this equation:

$$NCE = 21.06(z) + 50 \qquad\qquad 4.9$$

where the z is a normalized z. The computed NCE value is rounded to the nearest whole number, and only values from 1 to 99 are used. NCEs resemble *T*-scores in that both have means of 50, but the possible range of NCEs is the same as that for percentile ranks.

COEFFICIENTS OF CORRELATION

Correlation coefficients are statistics that show the extent to which scores from one measure are related to scores from the same individuals on a second measure. For example, there is a need for an index of the relation between sets of test scores when estimating some kinds of test reliability. If a single test is given to the same group on different occasions, if two equivalent test forms are given to the same group, or if a single test is split into two equivalent halves that are separately scored, we use a correlation coefficient to estimate the degree of agreement between the pairs of scores on the two measures for each person.

Computing Correlation Coefficients

There is a wide variety of correlation coefficients, each appropriate for certain conditions and each computed in a somewhat different manner. The most common type, the *Pearson product-moment correlation,* will be illustrated here. Suppose five basketball players are being "tested" on their ability to shoot free throws. Each is allowed ten attempts at the beginning of a practice session and ten attempts at the end. The results are shown in the first two columns of Table 4-7. What relation is there between the number of shots made (out of ten) before practicing and the number made after practicing? How well does this short free-throw shooting test distinguish between the better and poorer shooters?

The correlation is computed using the formula:

$$r_{XY} = \frac{n \sum XY - (\sum X)(\sum Y)}{\sqrt{[n \sum X^2 - (\sum X)^2][n \sum Y^2 - (\sum Y)^2]}}$$

4.10

where

n is the number of pairs of scores,
$\sum$ is the symbol meaning "the sum of,"
X is the score of a person on one variable,
Y is the score of the person on a second variable.

Table 4-7   Data for Computing Correlation

| Player | SCORES | | X^2 | Y^2 | XY |
	Before (X)	After (Y)			
Carolyn	5	5	25	25	25
Jessica	6	8	36	64	48
Kelly	9	7	81	49	63
Lori	5	7	25	49	35
Marcy	8	9	64	81	72
Sum	33	36	231	268	243

The various sums required to compute the correlation coefficient are shown at the bottom of each column in Table 4-7. We can substitute these values in equation 4.10 to complete the computation:

$$r_{XY} = \frac{(5)(243) - (33)(36)}{\sqrt{[5(231) - (33)^2][5(268) - (36)^2]}}$$

$$r_{XY} = \frac{27}{\sqrt{(66)(44)}} = \frac{27}{54} = 0.50$$

The example used here is extremely simple, intended only to show what a correlation coefficient is and how it is calculated. Most situations in which a correlation coefficient is desired involve at least 30 pairs of scores and larger numbers or decimal values. Surely electronic calculators and computers can provide greater efficiency and accuracy than the hand computations illustrated above. Finally, the raw-score formula (equation 4.10) can be modified to produce equivalent results when either deviation scores or z-scores are readily available:

$$r_{XY} = \frac{\Sigma(X - \overline{X})(Y - \overline{Y})}{n s_X s_Y} \qquad\qquad 4.11$$

$$r_{XY} = \frac{\Sigma z_X z_Y}{n} \qquad\qquad 4.12$$

Note that subscripts are used with s and z to distinguish between scores from the two measures (X and Y) for which the correlation is to be estimated.

Interpreting Correlation Coefficients

A correlation coefficient is a number that may range from $+1.00$, through zero, to -1.00 and that indicates two things. The sign (plus or minus) shows the direction of the relationship, and the magnitude of the number indicates the extent of the relationship. Perfect correlations, $+1.00$ or -1.00, rarely exist in practice, but both represent the *highest* possible correlation between two variables. A correlation of 0.00 means there is no relationship between the two variables.

A graphical representation of the pairs of scores for which a correlation coefficient is computed can be useful for two reasons. First, we can tell from a graph if the points tend to cluster about a single straight line. If they do *not*, a more complex method of computation is required. Second, we can estimate both the direction and magnitude of the relationship from a visual inspection of the graph. The graph provides a means of checking the accuracy of calculations when the correlation coefficient is computed.

Four scatterplots are shown in Figure 4-6 to illustrate the graphical representation of the correlation of two sets of scores. Each point in a graph

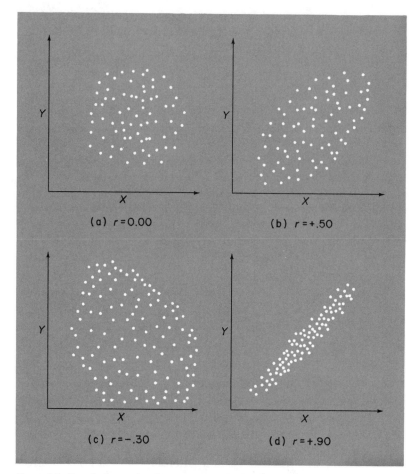

Figure 4-6 Sample Scatterplots Showing Varying Relationships Between Two Sets of Scores.

represents a pair of scores, X and Y, for each person. In diagram (a), lower scores on Test X are associated with low, moderate, and high scores on Test Y. Higher scores on Test X have the same kind of relationship with scores on Test Y. Therefore, we can conclude there is little or no relationship between the two sets of scores. A similar analysis can be made of each of the other three diagrams to verify the value of the correlation coefficient given. Another approach to interpreting the scatterplot is to ask how accurately we could predict someone's Y score when we know their score on Test X. The data in diagram (d) permit the most accurate prediction of Test Y scores, while the data in diagram (a) suggest that our prediction would be a mere guess. Finally, we might observe the rank orders of individual scores on X and compare with those on Y. If the rankings are similar on both, the correlation is high and positive, but if the rankings are more nearly opposite on the two, the correlation is high and negative.

It is helpful in interpreting a correlation coefficient to relate it to the coefficients obtained in other more-or-less familiar situations. For example, scores on equivalent forms of a well-constructed achievement test, administered separately within a few days of each other to the same group, should show correlations of 0.90 or higher. Scores on good tests intended to predict future educational achievement correlate with a subsequent good measure of achievement at levels averaging about 0.50 and ranging from about 0.30 to about 0.70. Correlations between scores on individual objective test items average about 0.10 but often range from about -0.30 to about 0.50.

Coefficients of correlation are widely used to study test scores. If calculated accurately they provide precise estimates of the degree of relationship among the data on which they are based. Two cautions are in order, however. First, the relationship expressed by a correlation coefficient is not necessarily a causal one. Other factors, each related to X and Y, may help to explain why X and Y are related so highly. For example, if the grades of algebra students correlate -0.60 with number of hours of television watched in a typical week, this does not mean that frequent television watching directly causes low grades. But both variables may relate to number of hours spent on homework in the typical week, a variable that may explain why the correlation is moderately high and negative. Second, when a coefficient obtained from one sample of individuals is used to estimate the correlation either for another sample from the same population, or for the entire population, due note should be taken of the sample size. In general, small samples give inexact estimates of the correlation that would be obtained from other samples, or from the entire population.

SUMMARY

Some of the principal ideas developed in this chapter are summarized in the following statements:

1. To do an adequate job of interpreting a set of test scores, it is necessary to understand and use a variety of statistical tools: frequency distributions, percentile ranks, standard scores, and measures of central tendency, variability, and correlation.
2. A frequency distribution of scores is an ordered listing of score values that shows how many individuals obtained each of the scores in the list.
3. A frequency polygon or histogram provides a graphic means of representing the same information displayed by a frequency distribution.
4. Knowledge of the physical characteristics of a frequency polygon—symmetry, skewness, modality, and kurtosis—is helpful in supplying a general verbal description of a set of scores.
5. The median is either the middle score (if the number of scores is odd) or a point midway between the two middle scores (if the number of scores is even).
6. The mean of a set of scores is found by adding all the scores and dividing the sum by the total number of scores.
7. A few extremely high or extremely low scores tend to pull the value of the mean away from the median and in the direction of the extreme scores.
8. The variance of a set of scores is the sum of the squared deviations of the scores (from the mean) divided by the number of scores.
9. The standard deviation is the square root of the variance.
10. Conceptually, the standard deviation is a number that shows the average amount by which the scores in a distribution deviate from the mean.

11. The normal curve is a theoretical, symmetric, bell-shaped frequency polygon that has become a relative standard for describing certain types of test data.

12. The larger the number of scores in a group, the greater the expected range of scores in standard deviation units.

13. One can give scores in any set a standard, relative meaning by converting them into percentile ranks.

14. The percentile rank of a score is most appropriately defined as the percent of scores in a group that fall below the midpoint of the given score interval.

15. A complete set of percentile ranks yields a frequency polygon that is rectangular in shape.

16. Percentile ranks are percent values between 0 and 100; percentiles are raw scores that may have any value on a given raw-score scale.

17. Conversion of normally distributed scores to percentile ranks increases apparent score differences near the center of the distribution and decreases them near either of the extremes of the raw-score distribution.

18. A z-score indicates the number of standard-deviation units an individual has scored above (+) or below (−) the mean.

19. Normalized standard scores are provided by many test publishers, so that the useful properties of the normal curve can be incorporated in the interpretation of the scores.

20. The correlation coefficient is a measure of the degree of correspondence between two variables, based on paired values of the variables obtained from each of a number of persons or things.

21. Possible values of the correlation coefficient range from 1.00, expressing perfect positive (direct) relationship, through 0, expressing absence of relationship, to −1.00, expressing perfect negative (indirect) relationship.

22. Scatter diagrams are graphs that can be used to estimate the correlation, magnitude, and direction between the variables used in plotting it.

23. A relatively high correlation between two variables is not sufficient evidence for concluding that one variable can predict the other in a causal relationship.

24. Correlation coefficents obtained from small samples are subject to large sampling errors.

PROJECTS AND PROBLEMS

Problem: Calculating the Mean and the Standard Deviation

This exercise is based on the two lists of spelling-test scores presented in Table 4-1. The frequency distribution for the List A scores was given in Table 4-2 and the median, mean, variance, and standard deviation have been calculated and shown below. Your task is to prepare a similar display—frequency distribution and each of the statistics—for the List B scores. You need not show details of your calculations, but do make your calculated values as accurate as those shown here. Show some concern for the neatness of your work and check each of your answers for reasonableness.

I.	Median	76
II.	Mean	
	ΣX	1942
	$\overline{X}$	77.68
III.	Variance	
	Σx^2	2275.44
	ΣX^2	153,130
	s_X^2	91.0176
IV.	Standard Deviation	9.54

Problem: Calculating Percentile Ranks

Prepare a table like that shown in Table 4-5 for computing the percentile ranks of the List B spelling-test scores. Use the same method as was used with the List A scores.

Problem: Calculating a Correlation Coefficient

Compute the product-moment correlation coefficient (equation 4.10) using the first ten pairs of scores (Aaron-Frank) in Table 4-1. Draw a scatterplot to verify that your computation is a reasonable one for these data.

5

THE RELIABILITY OF EDUCATIONAL TESTS

THE IMPORTANCE OF RELIABILITY

For most tests of educational achievement, the reliability coefficient provides the most revealing statistical index of quality that is ordinarily available.[1] If the scores yielded by any educational achievement test were all perfectly accurate, true scores with no errors attributable to the particular sample of questions used, to alertness, anxiety, fatigue, or other factors that might affect examinee performances, to lucky guesses or unlucky slips, and with no errors caused by the mistakes or biases of the person scoring the test, then the test would have perfect reliability, reflected by a reliability coefficient of 1.00. No educational achievement test, no other type of mental test, and indeed no physical measurement has ever achieved this degree of perfection. Error is unavoidably involved in any measurement, but the goal of measurement specialists in all fields is to reduce these inevitable errors of measurement to a reasonable minimum.

Expertly constructed educational achievement tests often yield reliability coefficients of 0.90 or higher on a scale of 0.00–1.00. In contrast, the achievement tests used in many elementary, secondary, and college classrooms often show reliability coefficients of 0.50 or lower. One of the ways of making test scores more reliable is to lengthen the test on which they are based, that is, to include

[1] Much of this discussion of reliability relates directly to tests designed to yield norm-referenced test-score interpretations. A separate section deals with the reliability of content-referenced measures and the implications of reliability for criterion-referenced measures.

more questions or items in it. But a test having a reliability coefficient of 0.50 would need to be increased to nine times its original length to bring its reliability up to 0.90. (The basis for this statement is provided by equation 5.5 in this chapter.) Hence, from this point of view, a test having a reliability coefficient of 0.90 is nine times as good as a test having a reliability coefficient of 0.50.

Reliability is a necessary but not a sufficient condition for quality in an educational achievement test. The author of a test that yields highly reliable scores may only have succeeded in measuring something irrelevant or trivial with very great precision. On the other hand, the author of a test that yields only unreliable scores has clearly not succeeded in measuring anything very precisely. If a test does not yield reliable scores, whatever other potential merits it may have are blurred and may be largely lost. Only to the degree that test scores are reliable can they be useful for any purpose whatsoever (Ebel, 1968a).

Reliability is important to students whose grades are often heavily dependent on the scores they make on educational achievement tests. If they were clearly aware of the importance of test reliability to them, it is likely that they would ask for evidence that the tests used to measure their achievement are not only fair in terms of the purposes of the course, but also are of sufficient technical quality to yield reliable scores.

Reliability is important also to teachers who are aware that their examinations have shortcomings and who seek to improve them. Estimates of the reliabilities of teacher-made tests would provide the essential information for judging their technical quality and for motivating efforts to improve them. Lengthening an unreliable test is not the only way, and may not be the best way, to improve its reliability. If modern knowledge and techniques of test construction are applied, most educational achievement tests can be made to yield scores having reliability coefficients that at least approach 0.90.

Definitions of Test Reliability

The reliability coefficient for a set of scores from a group of examinees is the coefficient of correlation between that set of scores and another set of scores on an equivalent test obtained independently from the members of the same group.

Three aspects of this definition deserve comment. First, it implies that reliability is not a property of a test in itself but rather when that instrument is applied to a particular group of examinees. The more appropriate a test is to the level of abilities in the group, the higher the reliability of the scores it will yield. The wider the range of talent in a group, the higher the reliability of the scores yielded by a test of that talent.

Second, the operational definition specifies the use of a correlation coefficient as a measure of reliability. One of the properties of the correlation coefficient is that it provides a relative, rather than an absolute, measure of agreement between pairs of scores for the same persons. If the differences between scores for the same person are small relative to the differences between scores for different persons, then the test will tend to show a high reliability. Conversely, if the differences between scores for the same person are large relative to the differences between persons, then the scores will show low reliability.

Third, the operational definition calls for two or more independent measures, obtained from equivalent tests of the same trait for each member of the group. This is the heart of the definition. From this it follows that the various means of obtaining independent measurements of the same achievement will provide the basis for several distinct methods for estimating test reliability.

A Theoretical Definition

For theoretical purposes we assume that a test score can be partitioned into two components: a true score and an error score. The hypothetical true score of an individual is the average of the scores the person would obtain if tested on many occasions with the same test. The relationship between these scores is simply

$$X = T + E \tag{5.1}$$

As an example, if we could separate test scores into their true and error components, we might have these values for two students

	X	T	E
Scott	31	28	+3
Mike	25	27	−2

Note that the true scores are nearly identical, but Scott's observed score is enough higher than Mike's that the two might be assigned different test grades. Since we never can determine the size of an examinee's error score, we would like to estimate how large the error score is, on the average, for the group that was tested. To do so, we take the theoretical situation one step further.

The variance of the observed test scores can be written as

$$s_X^2 = s_T^2 + s_E^2 \tag{5.2}$$

The variance is the square of the standard deviation of the scores, s_X^2, an indication of the amount of dispersion present in the score distribution. Equation 5.2 depends on the assumptions that the errors are random, uncorrelated with the true scores, and that the errors within a group cancel each other out, so that the average error score is zero. The equation says that the observed scores of a group differ because individuals have different true scores and because error scores vary from person to person. The reliability of a set of scores can be expressed as the ratio of the variance of true scores to the variance of observed scores:

$$r = \frac{s_T^2}{s_X^2}$$

5.3

The reliability coefficient is an expression of how much of the variability that we see in observed scores is due to variability in true scores within the group tested. When the ratio is large (near 1.00), it means that the variability in observed scores can be explained mainly by the fact that the examinees truly differ in the trait the test measures. A relatively small ratio means that random errors, rather than true differences, are the major reasons why examinees obtain different scores.

Sources of Score Variability

A major goal of test makers is to maximize the true variance and minimize the error variance in the scores on their tests. What are the factors that influence each type of variance? What are the many reasons that explain why individuals in a group achieve different scores when they take a test that is appropriate for the ability level of the group?

Thorndike (1951) classified the possible sources of variance in scores in an attempt to identify those that contribute to the two types of variance. His categorization scheme is reproduced in Figure 5-1. Some factors explain why an individual might obtain different scores on the same test on two occasions, and some explain why examinees tested on the same occasion might obtain scores that differ from one another. A detailed discussion of each category can be found in Stanley (1971). For our purposes, several generalizations can be drawn from the listing in Figure 5-1 (see page 74):

1. All the sources of variance do not necessarily operate in every testing situation.
2. Some factors contribute to error scores in some testing situations but contribute to true scores in other situations.
3. Reliability is not simply an intrinsic trait of a test; its value depends on the nature of the group tested, the test content, and the conditions of testing.

METHODS OF ESTIMATING RELIABILITY

There is a need to estimate test-score reliability so that we know how much measurement errors might interfere with the interpretability of the scores. Because reliability is influenced by the group tested, the test content, and testing conditions, it is not possible to settle for a single method for estimating reliability

I. *Lasting and general characteristics of the individual*
    A. Level of ability on one or more general traits, which operate in a number of tests
    B. General skills and techniques of taking tests
    C. General ability to comprehend instructions

II. *Lasting but specific characteristics of the individual*
    A. Specific to the test as a whole (and to parallel forms of it)
        1. Individual level of ability on traits required in this test but not in others
        2. Knowledge and skills specific to a particular form of test items
    B. Specific to particular test items
        1. The "chance" element determining whether the individual does or does not know a particular fact (sampling variance in a finite number of items, not the probability of guessing the answer)

III. *Temporary but general characteristics of the individual* (Factors affecting performance on many or all tests at a particular time)
    A. Health
    B. Fatigue
    C. Motivation
    D. Emotional strain
    E. General testwiseness
    F. Understanding of mechanics of testing
    G. External conditions of heat, light, ventilation, etc.

IV. *Temporary and specific characteristics of the individual*
    A. Specific to the test as a whole
        1. Comprehension of the specific test task
        2. Specific tricks or techniques of dealing with the particular test materials
        3. Level of practice on the specific skills involved (especially in psychomotor tests)
        4. Momentary "set" for a particular test
    B. Specific to particular test items
        1. Fluctuations and idiosyncrasies of human memory
        2. Unpredictable fluctuations in attention or accuracy, superimposed upon the general level of performance characteristic of the individual

V. *Systematic or chance factors affecting the administration of the test or the appraisal of test performance*
    A. Conditions of testing—adherence to time limits, freedom from distractions, clarity of instructions, etc.
    B. Unreliability or bias in subjective rating of traits or performances

VI. *Variance not otherwise accounted for (chance)*
    A. "Luck" in selection of answers by "guessing"

Figure 5-1 Possible Sources of Variance in Score on a Particular Test (Thorndike, 1951).

in all testing situations. At least five methods are used in practice to obtain the independent measurements necessary for estimating reliability. These methods yield test-retest, equivalent-forms, internal-analysis, reader-reliability, and analysis-of-variance coefficients.

Test-Retest

The test-retest method is essentially a measure of examinee reliability, an indication of how consistently examinees perform on the same set of tasks. The simplest and most obvious method of obtaining repeated measures of the same ability for the same individuals is to give the same test twice. This would provide two scores for each individual tested. The correlation between the set of scores obtained on the first administration of the test and that obtained on the second administration yields a test-retest reliability coefficient. Note that such temporary characteristics listed in Figure 5-1 as health, fatigue, memory fluctuations, and comprehension of the specific test task are likely to contribute to the error score when this method is used. The test-retest method is particularly useful in situations where the trait being measured is expected to be stable over time. Then if the scores on the two occasions yield different rank orderings of the examinees, measurement error is the single most likely explanation for such differences.

A number of objections to the test-retest method have been raised. One is that exactly the same test items are used in both sets. Since this set of items represents only one sample from what is ordinarily a very large population of possible test items, the scores on the retest provide no evidence on how much the scores might change if a different sample of questions was used (category II.B.1 from Figure 5-1). Another objection is that students' answers to the second test are not independent of their answers to the first. Their responses on the retest undoubtedly are influenced to some degree by recall and possibly also by student discussion and individual or joint effort to learn the material in the interval between tests. A third objection is that if the interval between the test and the retest is long, errors of measurement may get confused with real changes in student ability as a result of learning. Finally, readministration of the same test simply to determine how reliable it is does not appeal to most students and teachers as a very efficient use of educational time. Lack of interest on the students' part sometimes may make the second test a much poorer measure than the first, even though the actual test is the same in both cases. The test-retest method is not recommended for estimating the reliability of scores from classroom achievement tests.

Equivalent Forms

If multiple forms of a test have been produced in such a way that it seems likely that the scores on these alternate forms will be equivalent, and if each student in the group is given two forms of the test, then the correlation between scores on the two forms provides an estimate of their reliability. A high reliability estimate is evidence that the test forms can be used interchangeably as measures of the same trait. The major drawback to this approach is that teachers ordinarily do not prepare alternate forms of educational achievement tests, particularly those designed for classroom use. Some of us have enough trouble building one good test for each testing occasion. However, many widely used standardized achievement tests do provide alternate test forms at each of several levels. When equivalent forms are used to measure progress or growth within a school year or to assess the effects of experimental treatments, evidence of high equivalent-forms reliability is essential so that educational gains are not masked or artificially elevated due to measurement errors.

Methods of Internal Analysis

The difficulties associated with the determination of test-retest and equivalent-forms reliability coefficients encouraged the search for more practical methods. The methods described in this section are based on the administration of a single test and on the use of component subtests—information internal to the test—to estimate test-score reliability.

Split halves. A common approach is to split a test into two reasonably equivalent halves. These independent subtests are then used as a source of the two independent scores needed for reliability estimation. One standard method of splitting a test has been to score the odd-numbered items and the even-numbered items separately. Then the correlation between scores on the odd- and even-numbered items is calculated. Of course, splitting a test in this way means that the scores on which the reliability is based are from half-length tests. To obtain an estimate of the reliability of the full-length test it is necessary to correct, or step up, the half-test correlation to the full-length correlation. This is done with the help of the Spearman-Brown formula.

When we need to predict the reliability of a test twice as long as a given test, as in the split-halves method, the formula is:

$$r_2 = \frac{2(r)}{r + 1} \qquad\qquad 5.4$$

where r is the reliability of the original test. For example, if the odd-even correlation for a particular test is 0.82, the reliability of the total test is 1.64 divided by 1.82, which is approximately 0.90.

The general Spearman-Brown formula is used to predict the new reliability expected from increasing (decreasing) the length of a test of known reliability by adding (subtracting) items similar to the original ones. The formula is:

$$r_n = \frac{n(r)}{(n - 1)r + 1} \qquad\qquad 5.5$$

where r_n is the reliability of the new, lengthened test, n is the number of times the original test is lengthened, and r is the reliability of the original test.

Suppose a given test has a reliability of 0.50 and we wish to increase the original length of the test by nine times, adding new items equivalent in content and difficulty to the original items. The reliability of the new test is predicted to be:

$$r_n = \frac{9(0.50)}{(9-1)(0.50)+1} = \frac{4.50}{5.00} = 0.90$$

If the original test contained 20 test items, the new test would need 180 equivalent items to yield a reliability of 0.90. Of course for this prediction to hold, students should be expected to respond to 180 items without getting more bored or fatigued than they would get by responding to the original 20.

Kuder-Richardson. Two of the most widely accepted methods for estimating test reliability were developed by Kuder and Richardson (1937). Their formula 20, abbreviated "K-R20," is:

$$r = \frac{k}{k-1}\left[1 - \frac{\sum pq}{s^2}\right] \qquad\qquad 5.6$$

where

> k is the number of test items,
> Σ is the symbol for "the sum of,"
> p is the proportion of correct responses to a particular item,
> q is the proportion of incorrect responses to that item (so that p plus q always equals 1), and
> s^2 is the variance of the scores on the test.

This formula is applicable only to tests scored dichotomously—one point for each correct answer and no points for an incorrect answer. If the scores from a test are corrected for guessing or if some other form of weighted scoring is used, more complex variations of the formula must be used.

The Kuder-Richardson estimate for reliability will not necessarily yield the same result as the split-halves method.[2] Conceptually, K-R20 is the average correlation achieved by computing all possible split-halves correlations for a test. There are many ways to split a test into two halves; some splits will yield two fairly equivalent halves while others will yield somewhat nonequivalent halves. Since the K-R20 can be thought of as the average of all possible splits, its value will be larger relative to nonequivalent splits and smaller relative to fairly equivalent splits. This idea is particularly important to consider when evaluating standardized tests to select for a school testing program. The technical

[2] An illustration of the computations of K-R20 can be found in Ebel (1979).

manual for a given test may report split-halves reliability estimates, while the manual for another may report Kuder-Richardson estimates.

The computation of K-R20 requires information on the difficulty (proportion of correct responses) of each item in the test. If the test items do not vary widely in difficulty, a reasonably good approximation of the quantity pq can be obtained from information about the test mean and the number of items. This formula, K-R21, estimates the value of K-R20:

$$r = \frac{k}{k-1}\left[1 - \frac{\overline{X}(k-\overline{X})}{ks^2}\right]$$

5.7

Can you verify that K-R21 is 0.32 for a six-item test that has $\overline{X} = 3.3$ and $s^2 = 2.01$? For this same test K-R20 was computed to be 0.40. One limitation of the K-R21 is that it always gives an underestimate of the reliability coefficient when the items vary in difficulty, as they almost always do. If a test includes many items on which the average score is either near perfect (1.0) or near zero, this underestimate could be quite large. If most of the items have average scores of more than 30 percent but less than 70 percent, the underestimate is much smaller. A formula for correcting some of this underestimation was developed by Wilson and others (1977).

Coefficient alpha. Coefficient alpha provides a reliability estimate for a measure composed of items scored with values other than 0 and 1 (Cronbach, 1951). Such is the case with essay tests having items of varying point values or attitude scales that provide responses such as strongly agree and strongly disagree with intermediate response options. The formula resembles that for K-R20, because K-R20 is actually a special case of the alpha procedure. The formula is:

$$\alpha = \frac{k}{k-1}\left[1 - \frac{\sum s_i^2}{s^2}\right]$$

5.8

where s_i^2 is the variance of a single test item. When alpha is used to estimate the reliability of a test that is scored dichotomously (1 or 0), the result will be exactly the same as that calculated using K-R20.

Reader Reliability

Essay tests, whose scores depend appreciably on the expert judgment of a reader, are sometimes scored independently by two or more readers. The correlation between or among the multiple sets of ratings for a single set of student test papers provides a measure of the reliability with which the papers were read (Ebel, 1951).

However, these coefficients of *reader* reliability should not be confused with coefficients of *examinee* reliability or coefficients of *test* reliability. A coefficient of reader reliability simply indicates how closely two or more readers agreed in rating the same set of examination papers. A coefficient of examinee reliability indicates how consistently examinees perform on the same set of tasks. The test-retest reliability coefficient is essentially a measure of examinee reliability. A coefficient of test reliability, on the other hand, indicates how similarly the examinees perform on different, but supposedly equivalent tasks. Equivalent-forms and internal-analysis methods estimate test reliability. Sometimes reader reliability for an essay test can be quite high, though its test reliability might be quite low.

Reliability of Essay Scores or Ratings

A method for estimating the reliability of essay-test scores or ratings from multiple judges uses the basic coefficient alpha formula given in equation 5.8. The formula is:

$$r = \frac{k}{k-1}\left[1 - \frac{\sum s_i^2}{s_t^2}\right]$$ 5.9

where

k is the number of separately scored essay-test questions or independent ratings of a performance,

s_i^2 is the variance of students' scores on a particular item or from a particular rater,

$\sum s_i^2$ is the sum of these items or rater variances for all test items or all raters, and

s_t^2 is the variance of either the total essay scores or the sums of the ratings from all raters.

This method of estimating reliability of scores or ratings employs concepts from the statistical procedure called *analysis-of-variance*. A high reliability coefficient results when the total essay scores for examinees are quite variable *and* the item scores for individuals across the items are quite similar. In such circumstances the separate essay items are consistent in identifying individual differences in the achievement measured by the essay test as a whole.[3]

RELIABILITY AND ERRORS OF MEASUREMENT

A reliability coefficient, as has been said, is an estimate of the coefficient of correlation between one set of scores on a particular test for a particular group

---

[3] An application of this method to a simple case is illustrated in Ebel (1979).

of examinees and an independent set of scores on an equivalent test for the same examinees. The higher this coefficient, the more consistently the test is measuring whatever it does measure. Perfect reliability, never actually obtained in practice, would be represented by a coefficient of 1.00. Although reliability coefficients of 0.96 or higher are sometimes reported, most test constructors are reasonably well satisfied if their tests yield reliability coefficients in the vicinity of 0.90. The reliability coefficients ordinarily obtained for teacher-made tests tend to fall considerably short of this goal.

The reliability coefficient is a useful indicator of the extent to which a set of test scores is error-free or error-ladden, but it furnishes no direct assistance in estimating the true scores of examinees. In almost all practical measurement situations, the only information available is the set of observed scores of the persons measured. Their true scores and error scores are both unknown. However, given the standard deviation of the distribution of observed scores and the reliability coefficient of those scores, the standard deviation of the hypothetical error scores can be estimated. This quantity is called the *standard error of measurement*. The formula, derived from equations 5.2 and 5.3, is

$$s_E = s_X\sqrt{1 - r} \qquad\qquad 5.10$$

The relationship of the standard error of measurement to true scores, error scores, and observed scores can be seen using the hypothetical test scores in Table 5-1. Note that for each of the five students the observed score equals the true score plus the error of measurement. The mean of the true scores is 15, and the mean of the errors of measurement is zero, which makes the observed score mean 15, also. The variances of each of the three types of scores are given in the next line of the table. The ratio of the true-score variance to the observed-score variance is 0.865, which is the reliability of this set of observed scores. The standard deviation of the errors of measurement is $\sqrt{2.8}$ or 1.67. When the values of s_X and r are substituted in equation 5.10, the value $s_E = 1.67$ is obtained. This shows that an estimate of the standard deviation of the errors of measurement can be obtained with the standard deviation of the observed scores and the reliability coefficient, without any information about the individual errors of measurement.

The standard error of measurement provides an indication of the absolute accuracy of the test scores using the observed-score scale. For example, if the standard error of measurement for a set of scores is 3, then for slightly more than two-thirds of the observed scores (about 68 percent of them) the errors of measurement will be three or less score points. For the remainder of the scores, of course, the errors of measurement will be greater. For individual score-interpretation purposes the standard error of measurement is used to create a range of scores within which the person's true score is expected to be. Using the values from Table 5-1, we could be about 68 percent sure that Dan's true score is in the interval 10 ± 1.67 or 8.33–11.67. To be 95 percent sure,

Table 5-1 Reliability and Errors of Measurement

Students	True Scores	Errors of Measurement	Obtained Scores
Arline	18	−2	16
Dan	9	+1	10
Jean	15	+2	17
John	21	+1	22
Victor	12	−2	10
Mean	15	0	15
Variance	18	2.8	20.8

$$\text{Reliability} = \frac{18}{20.8} = 0.865$$

$$s_E = \sqrt{2.8} = 1.67 \quad \text{(direct calculation)}$$

$$s_E = \sqrt{20.8\,(1 - 0.865)}$$

$$= 4.56 \times 0.367$$

$$= 1.67 \quad \text{(from formula)}$$

we would say Dan's true score is within the interval $10 \pm (2)1.67$ or 6.66–13.34. Note that the percentages 68 and 95 correspond to the percentages under the normal curve within one and two standard deviations, respectively, of the mean.

THE RELIABILITY OF CONTENT-REFERENCED TESTS

Reliability is as important for content-referenced and criterion-referenced tests as it is for norm-referenced tests, and it can be determined in much the same way. The notion that "classical" test theory and "traditional" methods of test analysis are inappropriate for content-referenced or criterion-referenced tests is based on a misconception—namely, that scores on such tests show no variability because all who take these tests tend to make perfect scores, answering all questions correctly. While this is a theoretical possibility, it almost never actually happens. One could "rig" a test to make it happen, but such a test would serve no useful educational purpose. The only reason for giving an objectives-referenced test, for example, is to identify who has and who has not achieved certain instructional objectives (Shavelson et al., 1972). Even on these tests we should expect score variability if there is variability in how much or how well students have learned.

The procedures that are used to estimate the reliability of norm-referenced tests also can be used to estimate the reliability of content- or criterion-referenced tests. For example, domain-referenced scores obtained from statewide testing in mathematics are more likely to form a skewed distribution than a symmetric one, but there is likely to be considerable score variability. There is, of course, one important difference for objectives-referenced tests: the reliabilities of interest are for scores from each of several small clusters of items, each cluster being related to a separate instructional objective. The use of multiple reliabilities for objectives-referenced tests seems to be the most plausible approach to assessing the accuracy of scores obtained from them.

In many objectives-referenced tests, the clusters intended to measure the attainment of a particular objective include only a few items. We expect the reliabilities of such short tests to be quite low, but in practice they usually turn out to be surprisingly high. The explanation is found in the homogeneity of the item clusters. Since each item in a cluster is intended to measure the same ability, correlations between items tend to be high, which indicates highly reliable cluster scores. As the level of specificity of the objective decreases, however, the item cluster will be less homogeneous in content, and, consequently, the correlations between items in the cluster will be lower and the cluster scores will be less reliable.

Because criterion-referenced tests serve to categorize individuals on the basis of their scores—mastery vs. no mastery, pass vs. fail, satisfactory vs. unsatisfactory—we are just as concerned with the reliability of the decision as with the reliability of the scores. For example, if we retest with an equivalent form, will we assign each examinee to the same category on the two occasions? Do the odd-numbered and even-numbered scores categorize individuals to support the same decisions? When the number of classification categories is greater than two, it seems reasonable to be concerned with traditional reliability estimates and score variability. In the case of assigning letter grades to test scores, for example, decision consistency is not likely to be high if scores tend to cluster within a small range on the score scale. A second testing with an equivalent form probably would yield a large number of grade assignments that would differ from those obtained from the first testing. Kane and Brennan (1980) have reviewed a variety of indices that have been proposed to estimate decision consistency or agreement for domain-referenced tests.

FACTORS INFLUENCING TEST RELIABILITY

The coefficient of reliability of a set of test scores is related to a number of other characteristics of the test and of the group tested. Typically the reliability coefficient will be greater for scores:

1. from a longer test than from a shorter test
2. from a test composed of more homogeneous items than from a more heterogeneous test

3. from a test composed of more discriminating items than from a test composed of less discriminating items
4. from a test whose items are of middle difficulty than from a test composed mainly of quite difficult or quite easy items
5. from a group having a wide range of ability than from a group more homogeneous in ability
6. from a speeded test than from one all examinees can complete in the time available

The Spearman-Brown formula (equation 5.5) indicates the theoretical relation between test reliability and test length. The effect of successive doublings of the length of an original five-item test, the reliability of which was assumed to be 0.20, is shown in Table 5-2. The same data are shown graphically in Figure 5-2.

As the table and the figure indicate, the higher the reliability of the test, the smaller the increase in reliability with added test length. Adding 60 items to a 20-item test could increase its reliability from 0.50 to 0.80. But adding 80 more items to the 80-item test would raise its reliability only from 0.80 to 0.89. To achieve perfect reliability, an infinite number of items would have to be used, which of course means that perfect reliability cannot be attained by lengthening any unreliable test.

Two assumptions, one statistical, the other psychological, are involved in the use of the Spearman-Brown formula. The statistical assumption is that the material added to the original test to increase its length has the same statistical properties as the original test. That is, the added items should have the same average difficulty as the original items, and their addition to the test should not change the average intercorrelation among the test items. The psychological assumption involved is that lengthening the test should not change the way in which the examinees respond to it. If practice on items like those in the test facilitates correct response, if fatigue or boredom inhibits it, or if any other factors make the examinees respond quite differently to the lengthened test, reliability predictions based on the Spearman-Brown formula could be erroneous.

Table 5-2   Relation of Test Length
to Test Reliability

Items	Reliability
5	0.20
10	0.33
20	0.50
40	0.67
80	0.80
160	0.89
320	0.94
640	0.97
∞	1.00

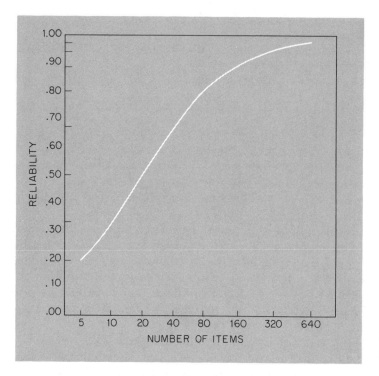

Figure 5-2
Relation of Test Length to
Test Reliability.

Homogeneity of test content also tends to enhance test reliability. A 100-item test in American history is likely to be more reliable than a 100-item test covering all aspects of achievement in high school. Also the subject matter in some courses, such as mathematics and foreign languages, is more tightly organized, with greater interdependence of facts, principles, abilities, and achievements, than is the subject matter of literature or history. This is another aspect of test content homogeneity that makes high reliability easier to achieve in tests of mathematics and foreign languages than in some other tests of educational achievement.

The items in homogeneous tests also tend to have higher indices of discrimination than items in tests covering more diverse content and abilities. But item discrimination is also heavily dependent on the technical quality of the item—on the soundness of the idea underlying the item, the clarity of its expression, and—in the case of multiple-choice items—the adequacy of the correct response and the attractiveness of the distracters to examinees of lower ability. The nature and determination of indices of discrimination and their relation to test reliability will be discussed in greater detail in Chapter 13. For the present it will be sufficient to say that the relation is close and important. Working to improve the discrimination of the individual items in most classroom tests is probably the most effective means of improving test reliability and, hence, test quality.

The difficulty of a test item affects its contribution to test reliability. An item that all examinees answer correctly, or all miss, contributes nothing to test reliability. An item that just about half of the examinees answer correctly is potentially capable of contributing more to test reliability than an item that is either extremely easy or extremely difficult. Of course, such an item could also be totally nondiscriminating. Items of intermediate difficulty, that is, from 30 to 80 percent correct responses, are all capable of contributing much to test reliability. Items that more than 90 percent or fewer than 10 percent of the examinees answer correctly cannot possibly contribute as much. Contrary to popular belief, a good test seldom needs to include items that vary widely in difficulty.

The reliability coefficient for a set of test scores depends also on the range of talent in the group tested. If an achievement test suitable for use in the middle grades of an elementary school is given to pupils in the fourth, fifth, and sixth grades, the reliability of the complete set of scores will almost certainly be higher than the reliability of any subset of scores for a single grade.

The reliability coefficient, as we have said, reflects the ratio of true score variance to observed score variance. The wider the range of talent, the greater the true score variance. If the variance of the errors of measurement is unaffected by the range of talent, as should be expected, then the observed score variance will not increase as fast (that is, in the same proportion) as the true score variance. Thus increasing the range of talent, and hence the true score variance, tends to increase the reliability coefficient.

Classroom tests are sometimes constructed and scored so that the range of scores obtained is much less than that which is theoretically available. For example, an essay test with a 100-point maximum score may be graded with a view to making 75 a reasonable passing score. This usually limits the effective range of scores to about 30 points. A true-false test, scored only for the number of items answered correctly, has a useful score range of only about half the number of items. A multiple-choice test, on the other hand, may have a useful score range of three-fourths or more of the number of items in the test. Hence a 100-item multiple-choice test is usually more reliable than a 100-item true-false test. But students generally can respond to three true-false items in the time required to respond to a pair of content-parallel multiple-choice items (Frisbie 1973, 1974). With testing time held constant, a 150-item true-false test is likely to be about as reliable as a 100-item multiple-choice test.

The dependence of test reliability on score variability is illustrated by the hypothetical data in Table 5-3. The essay test was assumed to consist of ten questions, each worth a maximum of 10 points, with a score of 75 on the entire test set in advance as the minimum passing score. The other two tests are scored by giving one point for each correct answer; no "correction for guessing" is used. Each multiple-choice item is assumed to offer four alternative choices, so that the expected chance score on that test is 25. The expected chance score on the true-false test is 75, half of the 150 items.

Table 5-3 Hypothetical Test Statistics for Three Tests

Statistic	TEST TYPE		
	Essay	True-False	Multiple Choice
Number of items	100	150	100
Expected mean	87.5	112.5	62.5
Expected standard deviation	5	15	15
Effective score range	(75–100)	(75–150)	(25–100)
Estimated reliability	.57	.88	.91

Notice that the expected variability of the true-false and multiple-choice tests, as reflected by the effective score range, is the same and the reliabilities are nearly the same. However, the relatively small amount of variability expected in the essay scores would produce a reliability coefficient of only about 0.57. But this phenomenon is not simply a function of the difference between essay and objective tests. If we equate test lengths rather than testing time, a 100-item true-false test would yield an effective score range of 50 (100 − 50) and a corresponding reliability estimate of 0.76. While these are hypothetical data, based on deductions from certain assumptions, they are reasonably representative of the results we could expect teachers to achieve in using tests of these types.

It is possible to construct a 100-item multiple-choice test whose reliability coefficient will be above 0.90, but it is not easy to do and relatively few instructors succeed in doing it. Again, 100-point essay tests can be handled so that their reliability will be as satisfactory as that of a 100-item multiple-choice test. But this also is not easy to do, and few of those who prepare and score classroom tests succeed in doing it without taking special pains.

Scores from a test given to a group under highly speeded conditions will ordinarily show a higher reliability coefficient than would be obtained for scores from the same test given to the same group with time limits generous enough to permit all examinees to finish. But most of the increased reliability of speeded test scores is spurious, an artifact of the method of estimating reliability. If, instead of estimating reliability from a single administration of the speeded test, we were to administer separately timed equivalent forms of the test under equally speeded conditions, the correlation between scores on these equivalent forms would be less than that estimated from a single administration. Hence the apparent increase in reliability that results from speeding a test is usually regarded as a spurious increase.

Here is what causes the trouble. Scores on a speeded test depend not only on how many items examinees can answer, but also on how fast they can work to answer them. Thus to estimate the reliability of scores on a speeded test one must estimate both ability and speed. By splitting a test into halves or into individual items, one can get two independent estimates of ability. But there is no way of getting independent estimates of speed, short of timing separately the responses to individual items or parts of the test. When this is not done, the estimates of speed are not only dependent, they are forced to appear almost identical. The apparent reliability of the measurements of speed is very high. When this is combined with a valid estimate of the reliability of the measurements of ability, the composite is spuriously inflated. The implication of this is that dependable estimates of test score reliability can be obtained from a single administration of a test only if the speed at which examinees work is not an important factor in determining their scores.

In this chapter, we have stressed the importance of test reliability as a factor in test quality. How can test constructors make more reliable tests? By taking advantage of the factors affecting reliability that are under their control. This means writing, revising, and selecting test items so that they will discriminate as clearly as possible between relatively greater versus less achievement of those things the test is intended to measure. Choosing items of high discrimination will result automatically in choosing items of middle difficulty—that is, items that 30 to 80 percent of the examinees can answer correctly. Test builders will also include as many items as possible in the test, so as to make the test as long as possible. When the time available for testing is limited, as it usually is, test constructors should favor items that are least time-consuming individually.

SUMMARY

The main conclusions to be drawn from the ideas developed in this chapter can be summarized in the following propositions:

1. Educational tests always are less than perfectly reliable because of item sampling errors, examinee performance errors, and scoring errors.
2. Test reliability can be defined operationally as the correlation between scores on two equivalent forms of a test for a specified group of examinees.
3. Reliability can be defined theoretically as the proportion of observed-score variance due to true-score variance.
4. The reliability of scores for a given test may vary considerably depending on the group tested and the conditions of testing on different occasions.
5. Separate estimates of test reliability, examinee reliability, and scoring reliability may be obtained.
6. Neither test-retest nor equivalent-forms methods are practically useful for estimating the reliability of a classroom test.

7. The Spearman-Brown prophecy formula is useful for estimating the reliability of a lengthened or shortened test.
8. The Kuder-Richardson formulas yield estimates of test reliability from data on the variability of the test scores, variability of the item scores, and the number of test items.
9. Coefficient alpha may be used in place of the Kuder-Richardson formulas for estimating the reliability of tests not scored dichotomously.
10. The more widely the items in a test vary in difficulty, the more seriously the Kuder-Richardson formula 21 may underestimate reliability.
11. The standard error of measurement is an estimate of the general magnitude of errors, expressed in test-score units.
12. The standard error of measurement can be estimated by multiplying the standard deviation of the scores by the square root of the difference, 1 minus the reliability coefficient.
13. The reliability of scores from content-referenced

measures can be estimated appropriately with the methods used for group-referenced measures.

14. It may be more important to estimate decision consistency than score reliability for tests used to make mastery decisions.

15. Longer tests composed of more discriminating items are likely to yield more reliable scores than shorter tests composed of less discriminating items.

16. Tests composed of homogeneous content are likely to be more reliable than those containing heterogeneous content.

17. The more variable the scores obtained from a test, the higher its reliability is likely to be.

18. Scores obtained from groups heterogeneous in achievement are likely to be more reliable than those obtained from homogeneous groups.

PROJECTS AND PROBLEMS

Problem: Calculation of a Reliability Coefficient

Using the data given below, calculate a split-halves, a Kuder-Richardson 20, and a Kuder-Richardson 21 reliability coefficient.

Note: The easiest and most accurate way to get the quantity $\Sigma\, pq$ needed for K-R20 is to multiply the number of right answers to an item by the number of wrong answers. Add these products for all items and divide by the number of students squared. In this problem,

$$p = \frac{R}{15}, \quad q = \frac{W}{15} \quad \text{so} \quad \Sigma\, pq = \frac{R \times W}{225}$$

Table A

Item	Key	A	B	C	D	E	F	G	H	I	J	K	L	M	N	O
									STUDENT							
1	2	4	2	2	2	2	2	4	2	2	2	4	2	2	1	1
2	2	2	2	2	2	2	1	4	2	2	4	0	0	0	3	4
3	2	2	2	1	3	1	2	1	2	1	2	2	1	2	1	1
4	2	3	2	2	2	2	2	2	4	4	3	1	1	4	4	1
5	4	4	4	4	4	2	4	4	4	2	1	4	0	1	2	1
6	3	4	2	2	3	3	3	3	3	3	2	3	3	3	3	3
7	1	1	3	1	2	3	1	1	3	2	3	0	0	3	0	1
8	3	3	3	3	3	3	3	3	4	3	3	3	1	1	1	3
9	2	1	2	2	3	2	2	2	2	1	2	1	2	2	4	2
10	2	2	2	4	2	2	1	1	2	1	2	1	1	2	1	1

6

THE VALIDITY OF
EDUCATIONAL TESTS

One of the most frequent charges laid against tests used to assess achievement, to select personnel, or to certify competence to practice is that they lack validity. Surely some tests deserve to be found guilty as charged. However, in some cases the claim that a test lacks validity simply helps an examinee to explain away his or her poor test performance. In other cases the charges express a general dislike for or mistrust of all tests. Often those who make such charges cannot say clearly just what is wrong with the tests or what could be done to correct the alleged defects. Perhaps they should not be criticized too strongly on this account, however. Even test specialists have difficulty in coming to agreement on what validity means and how it should be demonstrated (Kane, 1982). One aim of this chapter is to provide some sensible, practical bases for answering the kinds of questions about validity that are most frequently asked in relation to educational tests.

THE MEANING OF VALIDITY

The term *validity*, when applied to a test, refers to the precision with which the test measures some cognitive ability. There are thus two aspects to validity: what is measured and how precisely it is measured. The cognitive abilities referred to are abilities to perform observable tasks, abilities that have as their bases a command of substantive knowledge. How precisely a test measures an ability is indicated by the reliability of the scores. Reliability is a necessary condition for validity. It is not a sufficient condition, though. Unless the test scores measure what the test user intends to measure, no matter how reliably, the test scores will not be very valid.

Validity traditionally has been regarded as a test characteristic, generally the most important quality of a test. But the current thinking of measurement experts is that validity should be associated with the use to be made of the scores from a test (Joint Technical Standards for Educational and Psychological Testing, 1984). In particular, validity refers to the appropriateness of making specific inferences or of making certain decisions on the basis of scores from a test. The question, then, is not "Is this test valid?" but "Is it valid to use the scores from this test to make these kinds of interpretations about these examinees?"

A group of English and language arts teachers might agree that a particular test measures important language-usage skills, and does so quite reliably. That the test is "good" may not be debatable, but its validity for each of several different uses may be. The scores from it might be used to decide who is ready for advanced writing, who is in need of remedial assistance, and who should be encouraged to enroll in foreign language study. The test may be shown to be valid for the first two purposes, but not the third. Certainly the quality or goodness of a test cannot be ignored when making judgments about validity, but it is the use to be made of the scores that should be the focus of such judgments. At times we might refer to a test as being valid, but this is logical only when the intended use is obvious, and when it is obvious that what the test measures is consistent with the intended use.

The appropriateness of using test scores for making particular interpretations is judged from evidence gathered by the test user. A variety of evidence might be presented to demonstrate valid test use, and most could be grouped into one of three categories: content, criterion-related, and construct. *These are not types of validity but are types of validity evidence.* The content type concerns how well the test content represents some defined domain of abilities that the user intends to measure. The criterion-related aspect concerns the relationship, usually the correlation, between the test scores and the scores on some practical criterion measure of the relevant abilities. Finally, the construct type is concerned with the overall meaning of the scores—what the collection of items in a test measures. For a specific test use, one type of evidence may be more important than the other two, or it may be the only relevant kind of evidence to provide to establish the validity of that test use (Joint Technical Standards for Educational and Psychological Testing, 1984).

EVIDENCE USED TO SUPPORT VALIDITY

The meaning of validity and the types of evidence used to support it can be illustrated by considering the validity of scores obtained from the written examination required by most states of those who seek a driver's license. Typically scores from the written test, a practical driving test, and a vision test are combined to make a judgment about who is eligible to obtain a license. The primary purpose of licensing drivers is to protect the public from those who might endanger the property and lives of others through unsafe use of a motor vehicle. For the written test, the validity question is: "Is it appropriate to infer that high scorers will be safer and more responsible drivers than low scorers?" What kind of evidence could be supplied to support the validity of the written-test scores? Content validation involves showing that the content of the test measures the same knowledge and understanding possessed by those who we label as "safe and responsible drivers." However, someone must define "safe driver" and "responsible driver" and specify the knowledge such drivers must possess. Validity would be supported if driving experts agreed that the test-item content was representative of the content specified by the domain definition.

Criterion-related validation requires evidence that the written-test scores are positively related to some criterion measure, a measure of "knowledge of safe driving rules and driving laws or regulations." What measure could be used as a criterion? Perhaps a driving test. But a driving test requires more than knowledge of the laws and rules of the road. Performance behind the wheel also requires psychomotor abilities, physical ability to see and judge distance, and mental alertness and concentration. The driving test appears not to be a very suitable criterion, nor does the vision test. What else measures the same abilities as the written test and measures it as well? If we could identify such a criterion measure, perhaps *it* should be used in place of the written test for licensing purposes. Maybe criterion-related evidence cannot be found and perhaps it is not needed.

What about construct validation? To furnish construct evidence we must show that the total test score is a measure of the overall ability defined by the collection of abilities supposedly measured by the separate items. In addition, we should demonstrate that abilities irrelevant to the construct, safe and responsible driver, are not being measured by the test. This is essentially the same evidence furnished by content validation in this case. If the test items are found to be representative of the domain definition, and if the items are judged to be measures of relevant abilities, then the scores from those items represent a measure of achievement in the desired domain. No additional evidence appears necessary; the meaning of the test scores is derived from the nature of the tasks examinees are asked to perform.

The written driver's test is an achievement test, much like the standardized and teacher-made tests used in schools, the tests used by professional associations to certify competence to practice, and many of the tests used by business and government to assist in personnel selection. The role of content, criterion-related, and construct validation in assessing the appropriate use of scores from such tests needs a closer look. Though the validation of such tests may involve more than one type of evidence, the foundation for the validity of scores from them is content validation.

Content Validation

All tests provide scores that require an inference in interpretation. Tests contain only a sample of all possible items that could be used to measure the attainment of knowledge in the domain of interest. The score interpretations, whether group-referenced, content-referenced, or criterion-referenced, are based on the population of items, not just the sample used in the test. We *infer* that a student who answers correctly 75 percent of the test items would likely answer 75 percent of the items in the population. For tests of cognitive ability, are such inferences appropriate? To the extent we can be confident in making such inferences, we have support for reliability because we are in effect saying that 75 percent is an accurate estimate. On another different but similar set of items from that population, we would expect the student to answer about 75 percent of the test items correctly.

Another type of inference must be made that relates to the essence of validity directly. In the case of the written driver's test, we want to infer that those who score high on the test will be safer and more responsible drivers than those who score low. To do so, the test content must be based on an explicit definition of "safe driving ability," a delineation of the knowledge, skills, and understandings of which safe drivers must have command. A sample of some of the statements that might be offered to develop the safe driver definition are:

1. Distinguish the meanings of road signs of different colors.
2. Describe the function of a carburetor.
3. Describe the procedure for gaining control of a car that begins to skid on ice or snow.
4. Find the shortest distance between two cities using a highway map.
5. Identify the meaning associated with signs of varying geometric shape.
6. Describe the procedures for changing a flat tire.

Some statements could be excluded from the definition because they represent useful skills but skills not essential for safe driving. The even-numbered statements probably fit in this category. On the other hand, the definition likely would be considered incomplete without including statements such as "Differentiate between the meanings of solid and broken lines that define driving lanes." Once the definition has been made explicit, it is possible to compare test items with the definition to assess the relevance of the items. If the items have been written to match the domain definition precisely, the inferences we wish to make about safe and responsible driving will be valid. From this point of view, the answer to the validity question is inherent in the test-development process. There is no additional need to validate the test or test scores. Only when the ability to be measured has *not* been defined unambiguously need the question of validation arise. But under such circumstances it would be foolish for the test developer to create a test; there would be no clear basis for deciding what kinds of tasks would be appropriate to include.

Those who develop tests of cognitive ability produce validity evidence in the process if they:

1. Define explicitly the ability to be measured.
2. Describe in detail the tasks to be included in the test.
3. Explain the reasons for using such tasks to measure the ability in question.

A written document that contains these components provides an explicit rationale indicating what the test measures and is evidence for *intrinsic rational validity* (Ebel, 1983). The evidence is intrinsic because it is built into the test. It is rational "because it is derived from rational inferences about the kind of tasks that will measure the intended ability" (p. 7). When the test maker is also the test user, the evidence for appropriate score use is in the work; that is, both the specifications for test construction and the items themselves are necessary and sufficient. No separate validation process is needed.

Most test makers, including teachers, aim to produce tests that have intrinsic rational validity, but they seldom acknowledge this goal explicitly. They seldom regard the process of test construction as a process of validation; they seldom document in writing the reasons for particular decisions in test development. Those who do prepare written documentation to support intrinsic rational validity provide answers to these questions:

1. *About what set of abilities are inferences to be made?* As part of this description it is sometimes useful to note certain extraneous abilities that should be excluded intentionally from the major ability of interest. For example, in tests of mathematics problem solving, reading ability should be minimized.
2. *What domain of knowledge, skills, or tasks provides a basis for such inferences?* A content outline that describes the tasks of interest is needed. The outline should cover the entire universe of content to be measured, not just the content reflected by the specific test items that might be developed. Sometimes chapter headings in a text are a good starting point for defining the domain.
3. *What is the relative importance of the subdomains that comprise the domain definition?* Are there sets of related tasks that are more important than others? If so, the test-development plan should reflect the differences, so that more test items will be included for the more important subdomains. One subdomain might receive a weight of 10 percent, for example, while a more important one is assigned 25 percent.
4. *What kinds of test items have properties that will permit the testing of achievement of the domain elements?* For example, in view of the tasks outlined above in step 2, are either essay or short-answer items more appropriate than multiple-choice items? Why?
5. *Do the test items adequately reflect the domain knowledge, skills, and tasks?* This question relates to the match between test-item content and the content specified in the domain outline. How well did the item writer translate the task descriptions into test items?

6. *Do the subsets of test items adequately represent the domain in terms of the relative importance of the subdomains?* Is the content weighting in the test consistent with the decisions made in step 3?

7. *What domains or subdomains outside of the domain of interest are present in the test?* Are there extraneous factors that could interfere with the score interpretations the user wishes to make? Is reading ability, vocabulary level, or computational skill, beyond that intended, required to answer items correctly?

These seven guidelines emphasize what the test measures or is intended to measure. Cronbach (1983, p. 11) has argued that what the test measures is less vital than what the test *should* measure. However, these two concerns are identical when the test maker and test user are one in the same and when evidence for intrinsic rational validity is at hand. But the "should" question is significant to ask when selecting a test that was developed by others or when interpreting scores from tests developed by others. Again the evidence of intrinsic rational validity is fundamental, but two additional questions must be addressed by the potential test user: (1) How does *my* domain definition compare with that of the existing test? and (2) How does *my* set of relative weights for subdomains compare with that of the existing test?

We have long known that validity depends on the purposes for which a test is used, the group with which it is used, and the circumstances in which it is used. Validity depends not only on the quality of the test but on how the test was used and on how decisions were reached on the basis of the test scores. Choosing a valid test is less important than using it validly. The responsibility of the test developer is to be as clear as possible about what is being measured and to produce a test that measures as accurately as possible. The responsibility of the test user is to make valid decisions using the test scores and all other available relevant information.

Criterion-Related Validation

The correlation between test scores and criterion measures has been regarded by many as the best kind of evidence to support valid test use. It seems to provide an independent, objective validation of the subjective judgments and decisions made during test development. But few widely used tests of cognitive abilities have been supported with impressive criterion-related evidence of validity. This could mean that the tests are simply poor tests. But a more plausible explanation is that the extent to which the test measures what it is intended to measure cannot be conveyed by the correlation between test scores and scores on the criterion measure.

In some cases appropriate criterion measures are simply unavailable (Ebel, 1961a). What should be used as a criterion measure for a test of ability in fifth-grade arithmetic or a test of ability to understand contemporary affairs? The tests themselves are usually intended to be the best measures of these abilities that can be devised. If better measures were available, the tests would not be needed. That many test developers have failed to present convincing empirical evidence of the validity of their tests is not for want of concern, effort, or skill. It is because correlational evidence for the validity of most educational tests is essentially unproducible. The same can be said with respect to professional licensure examinations (Kane, 1982).

In other cases appropriate criteria turn out to be difficult or nearly impossible to measure accurately. On-the-job performance ought to be an appropriate criterion for an employee selection test. But for any except the simplest jobs, what constitutes satisfactory performance is hard to define, expensive to assess, and difficult to measure impartially. The relevance of performance ratings as criteria for the validity of a written test is open to question, also. A written test cannot possibly measure many of the characteristics that contribute to high ratings for job performance. Such a test, however, can measure desirable characteristics that are unlikely to show up clearly on a performance rating. In situations like these, there is little justification for presenting evidence on correlation with a criterion as the primary evidence of validity.

A major problem with empirical test validation is the imperfect or uncertain validity of the criterion scores. Criterion scores themselves should be highly valid measures of the ability being tested. This also means the criterion scores should be reliable and their reliability coefficient should be included as validity evidence. A standard used for judging the validity of test scores certainly ought to be at least as valid as the scores being judged against that standard.

Correlational procedures hold little promise for providing primary evidence of validity, but they may be useful in providing secondary, confirming evidence. If ability A is related in some degree to abilities B, C, and D, then scores from a test of A should correlate to some degree with scores from B, C, and D. If they do, the confidence that test A measures ability A is increased.

It is important to note that such secondary evidence of validity cannot take the place of intrinsic rational validity evidence. What test A measures is determined by the tasks included in it. One cannot discover what test A measures by studying the correlation of scores from test A with scores from tests B, C, and D. How do we know what these other tests measure? We must examine the tasks included in them. If that is the basis for the meaning of scores from tests B, C, and D, why not use it as the basis for the meaning of scores from test A as well?

Criterion-related evidence for validity has been classified traditionally as either *predictive* or *concurrent* evidence. When test scores are used to predict criterion scores at some future time, the required evidence has been regarded as predictive. Concurrent evidence has been sought to show that a given set of test scores "concurrently" measures the same abilities as a specified set of criterion scores. Both situations call for correlational evidence, and both suffer from the problems identified above that plague criterion measures. The prediction of college freshman grade-point average using college admission test scores illustrates the dilemma. Both measures reflect the ability to do college-level work, but certainly the criterion measure, grade-point average, is influenced by many other important factors—nature of the coursework, student effort and motivation, grading policies in the courses, and ability to establish supportive social relationships among peers. Correlations between test scores and grade-point averages tend to be around 0.50: there is much these two measures do *not* have in common. As secondary evidence of validity for the test scores, the correlations are supportive. But content validation is the only logical process for supplying evidence that the scores measure important cognitive abilities required of beginning undergraduate students.

Construct Validation

The term *construct* refers to psychological constructs, each a theoretical conceptualization about an aspect of human behavior that cannot be measured or observed directly. Examples of constructs are intelligence, achievement motivation, anxiety, dominance, and reading comprehension. As originally conceived, construct validity was concerned with the validity of a hypothetical construct as measured by a particular test (Cronbach & Meehl, 1955). The validity of the construct, and of the test used to measure it, was to be demonstrated by the degree to which scores from the test of the construct correlated with scores from tests of other constructs in ways that a personality theory would predict. This is a useful abstract conception, but it has not shown much practical utility. Personality theories tend not to be precisely quantitative, so that within broad limits, almost any observed correlation can be said to be consistent with the theory.

Concern for construct-validation evidence usually is expressed when there appears to be a discrepancy between what a test is supposed to measure and what it appears to measure. Is this a test of understanding of scientific principles, as the title suggests, or is it really an intelligence test? Is that a test of intelligence, or is it really a measure of verbal facility? Some test makers name their tests and describe what their tests are measuring, not in terms of the tasks they include, but in terms of the traits they presumably measure. That is why we have tests of rigidity, intelligence, persistence, creativity, tolerance, spatial relations, and many other traits. For tests like these, the question of whether the test really measures what it claims to measure does arise, as it should. Does the task of completing a figure analogy measure intelligence? Does ability to list unconventional uses for a brick measure creativity?

Most of what we teach in educational institutions are skills, knowledge, and abilities. These can be defined operationally. They are not hypothetical constructs. Ability to type, spell, solve algebra problems, or extract meaning from a poem are not the kind of latent traits Cronbach and Meehl had in mind. In sum, measures of school achievements and employee or professional competence should not require any special construct evidence of validity for the test user to make appropriate or meaningful inferences on the basis of scores derived from them. Validity evidence is incorporated in the test-development process by rational statements about what abilities are measured and why the test tasks are appropriate for measuring those abilities.

QUESTIONS ABOUT VALIDITY

What do test developers and test users need to know about validity? They need to know enough to be able to make wise decisions when defining test content and preparing relevant test items. They need to know what questions to ask and what judgments to make when selecting between alternative tests to use for a particular purpose. They need to be aware of factors that might tarnish the traditional interpretations that might be made with test scores. And they need to be able to give informative answers to questions likely to be asked by examinees and the public about the tests they use. Here are some common questions and appropriate answers that might be used by teachers to describe their classroom achievement tests.

Is This Test Valid?

If validity refers to goodness or test quality, the answer might very well be "yes." But more precisely, one can say that valid use is being made of a good test. It is good for two reasons. First, the kinds of tasks included in it and the types of knowledge they deal with have been defined clearly in the test specifications. Second, it yields reliable scores. In addition, it is being used appropriately, because what it requires the students to do is exactly what the instructional objectives and instructional procedures have been designed to help them do.

Has This Test Been Validated?

If validating the test means providing evidence of high correlation between these test scores and some other measure of the same ability (a criterion), the answer must be "No." Tests of this kind cannot be validated in that way because the necessary criterion measures do not exist and cannot be produced. The test scores themselves represent the best measure we know of to judge the attainment of the abilities we are trying to measure. These steps were taken to assess the quality of the test:

1. What the test was intended to measure was defined explicitly in the test specifications.
2. The test was prepared to conform strictly to the specifications.
3. Analysis of the test scores showed a very satisfactory level of reliability.

Thus this test was "validated" by building relevance into the test items and by demonstrating adequate reliability. Strictly speaking, the validity depends on how the scores are used. Even a good test, used inappropriately, likely will result in invalid interpretations and decisions.

Is This Test Biased?

Scores on this test indicate what any examinee, regardless of sex, race, or social condition, can do (or chooses to do) with tasks like these under test conditions. Some might do much better on a different test covering the same materials but expressed in another language. Some might do a little better if the tasks were part of a routine job rather than part of a test. This test measures achievement of particular knowledge and understandings. The scores reflect that achievement without giving advantage or disadvantage to any group of individuals. *If* this test is biased, it is biased against those who have not learned to perform the tasks required by the test items, those who have not achieved the knowledge and relationships that form the basis for testing. But it is such differences in actual achievement that the scores on this test are intended to discover.

Answers like these will not satisfy a critic intent on discrediting a test, but they are informative answers. They are honest answers as well, to the extent that the test was built with the care implied by the responses.

SUMMARY

Some of the principal ideas developed in this chapter are summarized in these eight statements:

1. Validity is much more a characteristic of test use than it is of the test itself.
2. Valid test use requires good tests, those that conform to a clear specification of test content and yield reliable scores.
3. What a test of abilities measures is defined more clearly by the tasks it requires than by the name of the trait it is supposed to measure.
4. Evidence of valid use of tests of cognitive abilities is inherent in the test-construction process, in the definition of the abilities and in the rationales for including each of the test tasks.
5. The value of correlational evidence to support the valid use of a test is secondary to the value of direct judgmental evidence.
6. No adequate criterion measure exists with which to compare educational tests for the purpose of providing evidence of valid test use.
7. No special evidence of construct validity is needed to defend the valid use of educational tests of abilities.
8. Validation is a process intertwined with test-construction procedures rather than a process that immediately follows test construction.

PROJECTS AND PROBLEMS

Project: Assessing Valid Test Use

The situations below provide the context for using a particular test for a specified purpose. In each case outline the specific information the user should gather to provide evidence for the validity of their intended use of the scores. Your response should describe the inference(s) to be made with the scores and an explanation of why the evidence you outline supports making the inference.

1. The Thomasville School District is planning a summer enrichment program for creative middle-school students. The curriculum coordinator plans to administer the Fisher Creativity Test to students in grades 6 and 7 and to select the top-scoring ten students in each grade for participation.

2. The instructor of the introductory psychology course at the University of West Dakota has written a 100-item multiple-choice proficiency examination for her course. Any student who earns a score of at least 83 on the test will be given credit for the course and need not register for it.

3. The Fifth National Bank of Westby requires applicants for its teller positions to take a battery of tests for employment screening. Scores on the three tests—basic arithmetic, Norwegian grammar, and current events—are combined with equal weight to form a composite. Applicants with scores below a certain point are not scheduled for a final interview.

4. Students in a lifesaving class must take a final performance test to obtain certification as a life guard. The test contains such tasks as: entering the water fully clothed and disrobing in one minute, correctly performing two types of surface dives, and gaining control of a struggling victim before towing him or her at least 50 yards. Each task is rated by the instructor on a five-point scale, on which 3 is the passing score.

5. A 50-item multiple-choice mathematics placement test is administered to all new freshmen at a university. Students are advised to register in either college mathematics, pre-calculus, or calculus on the basis of their test score.

6. The State of Iowa wishes to license electricians to protect the public from individuals whose work may be unsafe or ineffective. Applicants for licensure must pass a written test that covers concepts and principles of electricity, interpretation of wiring diagrams, and knowledge of the state code for electrical installation and repair. Any individual who has not passed the test may work as an electrician only under direct supervision of a licensed electrician.

7

PLANNING ACHIEVEMENT-TEST DEVELOPMENT

ALTERNATIVE TYPES OF TESTS

The most commonly used types of tests are the essay, the objective (including short-answer), and the mathematical problem type. Performance tests as well as oral examinations are less common perhaps, but where they are used, circumstances often dictate their use over the other types. This section is devoted to a brief comparison of the characteristics of these various test types and to a description of the relative merits of each in situations where a choice is feasible.

First, some common misconceptions need to be addressed. It is not true that one type tests real understanding whereas another tests only superficial knowledge. As Richardson and Stalnaker (1935) said some time ago, "The form of a test gives no certain indication of the ability tested." It is not true that luck is a large element in scores on one type and nearly or totally absent in another. On the contrary, all types can require much the same kind and level of ability, and if handled carefully, can yield results of satisfactory reliability and validity (Stalnaker, 1937; Coffman, 1966; Dressel, 1978). A good essay test or a good objective test can be constructed so that it will rank a group of students in nearly the same order as that resulting from a good problem test. But this is not to say that the various types can be used interchangeably with equal ease and effectiveness.

Both essay and problem tests are easier to prepare than objective tests.

But the objective test generally can be scored more rapidly and more reliably than either of the other types, particularly the essay test. Where very large groups of students must be tested, the use of objective tests permits greater efficiency with no appreciable sacrifice in validity. But where classes are small, the efficiency advantage is in the opposite direction, and essay or problem tests often are preferred.

The problem type has the apparent advantage of greater intrinsic relevance—of greater identity with on-the-job requirements—than either of the other types. It is sometimes claimed that ability to choose an answer is different from, and less significant than, ability to produce an answer. But most of the evidence indicates that these abilities are highly related (Ward, 1982; Sax and Collet, 1968).

Because of the length and complexity of the answers they require and because the answers must be written by hand, neither essay nor problem-type tests can sample the content domain as widely as an objective test. Writing is a much slower process than the reading on which objective tests depend.

In objective tests and problem tests there is often a good deal more objectivity, particularly in scoring, than in essay tests. The student usually has a more definitive task, and the reasons for giving or withholding credit are more obvious to all concerned. But it is important to realize that even the objective test is based on many subjective decisions as to what to test and how to test it. For the problem test there is the additional element of subjectivity in scoring that is not present in the objective test. How much credit to give for an imperfect answer and which elements to consider in judging degree of perfection are often spur-of-the-moment, subjective decisions. In considering the relative merits of essay, problem, and objective tests, it is important to remember that the only useful component of any test score is the objectively verifiable component of it, regardless of the kind of test from which it was derived. To the degree that a test score reflects the private, subjective, unverifiable impressions and values of one particular scorer, it is deficient in meaning, and hence in usefulness, to the student who received it or to anyone else who is interested in using the score.

Whatever test form examiners use, they should seek to make measurements as objective as possible. A measurement is objective to the extent that it can be verified independently by other competent measurers. It is conceivable that measurements obtained from a good essay test could be more objective in this sense than measurements obtained from a poor multiple-choice test. But it is fair to say that those who use essay tests tend to worry less about the objectivity of their measurements and evaluations than those who use multiple-choice tests.

Most teachers probably choose the types of test items that seem most useful to them, or that they feel most competent to use effectively. However, it is possible that force of habit or misconceptions prevent some teachers from trying other types that could prove more advantageous to them. The classroom testing practices of many school and college faculties probably could be improved by a periodic review of the types of tests being used.

Performance Tests

For some instructional objectives, the most relevant tools of performance assessment require students to demonstrate their achievement through means other than paper and pencil. These situations frequently involve skill learning that contains one or more psychomotor components. Performance tests can be used to determine if students can apply the knowledge and skills they have practiced and learned. Methods of performance testing can be categorized broadly as identification tasks, work products, and simulations.

Identification tests may require students to name objects, differentiate between objects given their names, or identify objects according to their function or their relationship to other objects. Which of these rocks is limestone or granite or agate? Given a skeleton, what is the name of this bone? Where do the pectoral muscles connect? For what purposes is this saw (point to a coping saw) more useful than this one (point to a hack saw)? Which needle is most appropriate for administering a subcutaneous injection to a three-year-old?

Work-product tests can be used to evaluate procedures involved in accomplishing a task or to determine the quality of a product. Teachers can evaluate drawings and collages in art, buttonholes and soufflés in home economics, tuned-up engines and coffee tables in industrial education, and penmanship or paragraph cohesiveness in language arts. In each case the goal is summative evaluation, even if observations of process are made as the student progresses toward completion of the project.

Simulations are contrived situations established for the purpose of observing student behavior, assessing speed and accuracy, or determining if an appropriate outcome is achieved. Dance instructors watch their students do the swing or polka, music teachers listen for proper notes and cadence, and psychologists watch and listen to their counseling students in role-playing situations. Those who have been certified in CPR are aware that timing, position, and know-how are important, but the outcome is of paramount importance.

Performance tests can serve unique evaluation purposes, but they also present some unique measurement problems. Unless each student performs the same identification tasks and simulations or prepares the same work product, the tasks may not be comparable. Hence, the scores derived from them may not be comparable. Great care must be exercised by the test developer to ensure equivalent testing for all students in the class. The scoring of performance tests tends to be quite subjective, even when an explicit grading guide is prepared. Identification tests and simulations are time-consuming to prepare and administer, especially to large groups. On the whole, performance tests tend to be less efficient than objective tests. In many situations the validity of simulations is highly questionable; the most realistic simulations tend to be the most costly to develop and administer. Even when simulation scores yield high reliability, their cost is likely to be greater than their benefit.

Oral Examinations

In essence the oral examination involves two persons, examiner and examinee, face-to-face. The examiner asks questions. The examinee attempts to answer them. The examiner probes with further questions or accepts the answer. Finally he or she judges the quality of the answers and grades the examinee accordingly. Often the grade is either pass or fail.

Sometimes, to improve the objectivity of the examination, more than one examiner is present. Or to improve the efficiency of the process and the fairness of the judgments, several examinees might be interviewed simultaneously, giving each a chance to respond to the same questions and to comment on answers given by the other examinees. Sometimes the examinees are directed to question each other, with the examiners acting only as judges, or even with the judging left to the examinees themselves. Brody and Powell (1947) have described in detail some of these variations on the basic oral examination.

Employment interviews often include a kind of oral examination, and there is some similarity in the principles of good practice for both. The oral examination can be properly regarded as one kind of performance test, but since very special circumstances surround it—the stress of being under observation, the unequal status of the participants, the importance of what hangs in the balance—the performance can seldom be regarded as typical behavior.

Obviously the oral examination does involve direct contact and interaction between examiner and examinee. This makes it, if not less threatening, at least more personal, and possibly more humane than written examinations. Some even regard an oral examination as an enjoyable experience.

Personal characteristics that would be impossible to assess on a written test can be evaluated in the face-to-face situation—the candidate's appearance, manner, personality, alertness, forthrightness, stress tolerance, and speech pattern and quality. One can judge the impression the examinee would probably make on others.

When the purpose of the examination is to assess the examinee's knowledge or intellectual abilities, the oral approach permits a flexibility that the written examination usually lacks. The examinee can be asked to expand, clarify, or justify an answer. An important point can be probed in depth. A competent examiner may thus be able to get a clear picture of the examinee's abilities and limitations. Also, the problem of cheating can hardly arise in an oral examination; even bluffing may be harder to manage effectively in spur-of-the-moment responses to oral questions than on a written exam. Finally, like all good examinations, an oral examination can be a learning experience.

However, it is easy for oral examination enthusiasts to claim too much.

An oral examination does no better than a written one in assessing intangible, poorly defined traits such as character, creativity, or "general fitness." Those who claim it tests examinees' ability to think on their feet, that is, to think effectively under stress, ignore the fact that most people do their best thinking while not under stress. Resistance to "choking up" under stress is probably not a very good indicator of overall effectiveness. Above all, advocates of oral examinations should avoid claiming that they measure abilities such as loyalty to the organization, honesty, industry, integrity, or even ability to get along with others, for these are characteristics that examinees have little opportunity to show, or examiners to observe, in the oral examination situation.

Oral examinations are subject to serious limitations, which account for their virtual disappearance as tools for educational evaluation. Because the oral examination is essentially an individual process, it is very time-consuming. In fact, to yield a fair sample of the examinee's abilities, it should last at least 30 minutes, and often more than one examiner must be used to obtain an objective assessment. Obviously, these qualities make oral examinations costly and complex to administer.

The personal contact and interaction between examiner and examinee that is one of the assets of the oral examination is also a liability. It opens the door to prejudice, partiality, and discrimination on grounds other than the relevant traits and abilities. Other influences lower the validity of the examination. For some, as has been suggested above, the stress of the confrontation may upset normally effective mental processes. For others, glibness and pleasantness may help to conceal genuine deficiencies.

The major limitation of the oral examination is the difficulty of obtaining reasonably reliable scores in reasonable amounts of time. Scores can be both reliable and valid *if* several raters are used, *if* they are all looking for the same things, and *if* the examination is long enough and structured enough so that examinees can present a fair picture of their overall traits and abilities. Usually, however, this calls for more care, skill, and time than most examiners can dedicate to the task.

ESTABLISHING THE PURPOSE FOR TESTING

The stages of the test-development process begin with describing the purpose for testing. Why are we testing? What do we intend to measure? How will the test scores be used or what kinds of score interpretations do we want to make? These are important questions to answer, and often they are not answered easily. But the answers lay the foundation for subsequent decision making as the test-development or test-selection process proceeds.

A good test rarely serves multiple purposes equally well. Tests designed to measure achievement precisely probably are motivating to students and may be instructive as well. However, tests designed primarily to motivate students to study are not likely to be good summative assessments of student learning.

Most teacher-made tests are intended to provide precise measures of achievement that can be used to report school progress to students and to their parents. And this should be their primary function.

A part of establishing the purpose for testing is deciding how the scores should be interpreted. What referent will be used to obtain meaning from the scores? Content? Scores of a norm group? Statements of objectives? For classroom testing purposes, the answer should be tied closely to the grading system, to the referent used to give meaning to the course grades. For statewide competency testing, the scores are likely to be referenced to the content domain from which the test was developed. For personnel selection based on hiring the most qualified of those who are at least minimally qualified, criterion-referenced interpretations (with a norm-referenced basis) probably are needed. And testing for professional certification or licensure requires criterion-referenced interpretations with either a norm-referenced or content-referenced basis.

The implications for determining the type of score interpretation needed will become more apparent as we consider the separate aspects of test construction. The goal at each stage of construction is to do those things that will provide a distribution of valid scores, a distribution that has the characteristics that optimize our ability to make the type of interpretations we planned to make. A high degree of intrinsic rational validity cannot be achieved without making explicit, detailed statements about what the test measures.

ASPECTS OF ACHIEVEMENT

Educational achievement in most courses consists in acquiring command of a fund of usable knowledge and in developing the ability to perform certain tasks. Knowledge can be conveniently divided into verbal facility and practical know-how. Abilities usually include ability to explain and ability to apply knowledge to the taking of appropriate action in practical situations. Some courses aim to develop other abilities, such as ability to calculate or ability to predict.

Some of the words used to identify achievements are more impressionistic than objectively meaningful, however. Some categories of educational achievement are based on hypothetical mental functions, such as comprehension, analysis, synthesis, scientific thinking, or recognition, whose functional independence is open to question. Those who currently attempt to describe mental processes and functions may be a little, but not significantly, better off than sixteenth-century map makers (Swift, 1948).

> So geographers in Afric maps
> With savage pictures fill their gaps
> And o'er unhabitable downs
> Place elephants for want of towns. (p. 571)

Unless mental processes are directly related to obvious characteristics of different kinds of test questions, it is somewhat difficult to use them confidently in planning a test or analyzing its contents. As Thorndike (1918) put it, "We have faith also that the objective products produced, rather than the inner condition of the person whence they spring, are the proper point of attack for the measurer, at least in our day and generation" (p. 160). Occasionally, too, the specified areas of achievement are so closely related to specific units of instruction that it is difficult to regard them as pervasive educational goals.

Most of the questions used in many good classroom tests can be classified with reasonable ease and certainty into one or another of the following seven categories:

1. Understanding of terminology (or vocabulary)
2. Understanding of fact and principle (or generalization)
3. Ability to explain or illustrate (understanding of relationships)
4. Ability to calculate (numerical problems)
5. Ability to predict (what is likely to happen under specified conditions)
6. Ability to recommend appropriate action (in some specific practical problem situation)
7. Ability to make an evaluative judgment

Multiple-choice test items illustrating each of these categories are presented in Figure 7-1.

Items belonging to the first category always designate a term to be defined or otherwise identified. Items dealing with facts and principles are based on descriptive statements of the way things are. If the question asks, Who? What? When? or Where? it tests a person's factual information. Items testing explanations usually involve the words *why* or *because,* while items belonging to the fourth category require the student to use mathematical processes to get from the given to the required quantities. Items that belong in both categories 5 and 6 are based on descriptions of specific situations. "Prediction" items specify all of the conditions and ask for the future result, whereas "action" items specify some of the conditions and ask what other conditions (or actions) will lead to a specified result. In judgment items the response options are statements whose appropriateness or quality is to be judged on the basis of criteria specified in the item stem.

The usefulness of these categories in the classification of items testing various aspects of achievement depends on the fact that they are defined mainly in terms of overt item characteristics rather than in terms of presumed mental processes required for successful response. The appropriate proportion of questions in each category will vary from course to course, but the better tests tend to be those with heavier emphasis on application of knowledge than on mere ability to reproduce its verbal representations. But since it is more difficult to write good application questions than reproduction questions, unless test constructors decide in advance what proportion of the questions should relate to each specified aspect of achievement, and carry out this decision, they may produce unbalanced tests.

Figure 7-1 Multiple-Choice Items Intended to Test Various Aspects of Achievement.

I. *Understanding of terminology*
  A. The term *fringe benefits* has been used frequently in recent years in connection with labor contracts. What does the term mean?
    1. Incentive payments for above-average output
    2. Rights of employees to draw overtime pay at higher rates
    3. Rights of employers to share in the profits from inventions of their employees
    *4. Such considerations as paid vacations, retirement plans, and health insurance
  B. What is the technical definition of the term *production*?
    1. Any natural process producing food or other raw materials
    *2. The creation of economic values
    3. The manufacture of finished products
    4. The operation of a profit-making enterprise

II. *Knowledge of fact and principle*
  A. What principle is utilized in radar?
    1. Faint electronic radiations of far-off objects can be detected by supersensitive receivers.
    *2. High-frequency radio waves are reflected by distant objects.
    3. All objects emit infrared rays, even in darkness.
    4. High-frequency radio waves are not transmitted equally by all substances.
  B. The most frequent source of conflict between the western and eastern parts of the United States during the course of the nineteenth century was
    *1. the issue of currency inflation.
    2. the regulation of monopolies.
    3. internal improvements.
    4. isolation vs. internationalism.
    5. immigration.

III. *Ability to explain or illustrate*
  A. If a piece of lead suspended from one arm of a beam balance is balanced with a piece of wood suspended from the other arm, why is the balance lost if the system is placed in a vacuum?
    1. The mass of the wood exceeds the mass of the lead.
    2. The air exerts a greater buoyant force on the lead than on the wood.
    3. The attraction of gravity is greater for the lead than for the wood when both are in a vacuum.
    *4. The wood displaces more air than the lead.
  B. Should merchants and middlemen be classified as producers or nonproducers? Why?
    1. As nonproducers, because they make their living off producers and consumers
    2. As producers, because they are regulators and determiners of price
    *3. As producers, because they aid in the distribution of goods and bring producer and consumer together
    4. As producers, because they assist in the circulation of money

IV. *Ability to calculate*
  A. If the radius of the earth were increased by three feet, its circumference at the equator would be increased by about how much?
    1. 9 feet   *3. 19 feet
    2. 12 feet   4. 28 feet
  B. What is the standard deviation of this set of five measures—1, 2, 3, 4, 5?
    1. 1   4. $\sqrt{10}$
    *2. $\sqrt{2}$ 5. None of these
    3. 9

107

Figure 7-1 *(Continued)*

V. *Ability to predict*
  A. If an electric refrigerator is operated with the door open in a perfectly insulated sealed room, what will happen to the temperature of the room?
      *1. It will rise slowly.
       2. It will remain constant.
       3. It will drop slowly.
       4. It will drop rapidly.
  B. What would happen if the terminals of an ordinary household light bulb were connected to the terminals of an automobile storage battery?
       1. The bulb would light to its natural brilliance.
      *2. The bulb would not glow, though some current would flow through it.
       3. The bulb would explode.
       4. The battery would go dead in a few minutes.

VI. *Ability to recommend appropriate action*
  A. Which of these practices would probably contribute *least* to reliable grades from essay examinations?
      *1. Weighting the items so that the student receives more credit for answering correctly more difficult items.
       2. Advance preparation by the rater of a correct answer to each question.
       3. Correction of one question at a time through all papers.
       4. Concealment of student names from the rater.

  B. "None of these" is an appropriate response for a multiple-choice test item in cases where
       1. the number of possible responses is limited to two or three.
      *2. the responses provide absolutely correct or incorrect answers.
       3. a large variety of possible responses might be given.
       4. guessing is apt to be a serious problem.

VII. *Ability to make an evaluative judgment*
  A. Which one of the following sentences is most appropriately worded for inclusion in an impartial report resulting from an investigation of a wage policy in a certain locality?
       1. The wages of the working people are fixed by the one businessman who is the only large employer in the locality.
       2. Since one employer provides a livelihood for the entire population in the locality, he properly determines the wage policy for the locality.
       3. Since one employer controls the labor market in the locality, his policy may not be challenged.
      *4. In this locality, where there is only one large employer of labor, the wage policy of this employer is really the wage policy of the locality.
  B. Which of the following quotations has most of the characteristics of conventional poetry?
       1. "I never saw a purple cow;
            I never hope to see one."
      *2. "Announced by all the trumpets of the sky
            Arrives the snow and blasts his ramparts high."
       3. "Thou art blind and confined,
            While I am free for I can see."
       4. "In purple prose his passion he betrayed
            For verse was difficult.
            Here he never strayed."

108

TEST SPECIFICATIONS

The firmest basis for the construction of a good test is a set of explicit specifications that indicate the following:

> Forms of test items to be used
> Number of items of each form
> Kinds of tasks the items will present
> Number of tasks of each kind
> Areas of content to be sampled
> Number of items in each area
> Level and distribution of item difficulty

Test specifications of this kind are useful not only in guiding the constructor of the test, but also in informing students what they may expect to find on the examination and how they can best prepare to do well on it. That information is likely to enhance the value of the test as an incentive to learning. If it is not provided, the examinees may claim, with some justice, that the test was unfair.

One of the devices that has been used to outline the coverage of a test, as part of the test specifications, is the two-way grid, sometimes called a "test blueprint." The several major areas of content to be covered by the test are assigned to the several rows (or columns) of the grid. The several major kinds of abilities to be developed are assigned to the columns (or rows). Each item may then be classified in one of the cells of the grid. Various numbers of items are assigned to each of the rows and columns. Knowing the proportion of items specified for a particular row and for a particular column, one can ideally determine the proportion of items appropriate for the cell formed by that row and that column.

The two-way grid is a good first step toward balance in a test. But it has limitations. For some tests a one-dimensional classification of items may be entirely adequate. Others may require three or four. There is some tendency for content to be related to goals or abilities. Hence the assumption that every cell should be represented by at least one item can be unwarranted. Since the number of cells in the chart equals the number of content areas multiplied by the number of educational goals, there is often a fairly large number of such cells. This leads to a more refined classification of items and a more difficult task of classifying them than may actually be necessary to produce a balanced test.

Another problem in using this device arises from difficulty in providing clear definitions of the categories involved, particularly the goal or ability categories. Content categories, on the other hand, are usually simpler to deal with. In a test for a course in consumer mathematics, for example, it is quite easy to tell whether a given item deals mainly with insurance or with taxation. It is much more difficult to decide whether it deals more with the ability to weigh values than it does with the ability to spend money wisely. Experience suggests that the reliability of a classification of test items in the usual two-way grid may be quite low, especially along the goal or ability dimension.

One way of reducing this difficulty is to classify test items in terms of their overt characteristics as verbal objects instead of on the basis of educational goals to which they seem to relate or mental abilities they presumably require. Another step toward making the measurement of balance more workable is to forego the fine detail in classification demanded by the two-way grid. Instead, one could settle for separate specifications of the desired weighting on each basis for classifying the items, such as item type or content area.

To guide test construction effectively and to inform prospective examinees adequately, the specifications need to be fairly detailed. To answer the question, How detailed? we might pose another question: If they were followed exactly by a competent item writer, would they be likely to produce an acceptable test? Obviously, specifications should be detailed enough to indicate what kinds of items should be written on what general areas of learning; but they should not be so detailed as to give away the actual questions that will appear on the test.

Two examples of explicit specifications follow. Figure 7-2 specifies the item forms, kinds of tasks, areas of content, and item difficulties. Figure 7-3 illustrates the kinds of tasks that will make up the test. Each of these test characteristics will be discussed in greater detail in the pages that follow.

Content to Be Covered by the Test

An area of information or an ability is appropriate to use as the basis for an objective test item in a classroom test if it has been given specific attention

Figure 7-2 Specifications for a College-Level Test of Understanding of Educational Measurement.

Form of Item	Number	Content Areas	Items
Multiple choice	50	Nature of educational measurement	2
		History of educational measurement	2
Kinds of Tasks	*Items*	Statistical techniques	7
Terminology	5	Finding and selecting tests	3
Factual information	10	Tests and objectives	3
Generalization	10	Teacher-made tests	4
Explanation	10	Test tryout and analysis	2
Calculation	5	Elementary school testing	5
Prediction	5	Secondary school testing	4
Recommended action	5	Educational aptitude	5
	50	Personality and adjustment	2
Item Difficulty		Observational techniques	2
Intended average percent correct	70%	School testing programs	5
Range of percents correct	40%–90%	Using the results of measurement	4
			50

Figure 7-3 Examples of Kinds of Tasks.

(1) *Terminology* (statistical techniques)
What is meant by the term "error of measurement" as it is used by technically trained specialists?
  a. Any error in test construction, administration, scoring, or interpretation that causes a person to receive different scores on two tests of the same trait.
  b. A test score that is unreliable or invalid as a result of (1) sampling errors in test construction, (2) performance errors on the part of the examinee, or (3) evaluation errors on the part of the scorer.
  *c. The difference between a given measurement and an estimate of the theoretical true value of the quantity measured.
  d. The difference between the obtained score and the predicted score on a trait for a person.

(2) *Factual information* (educational aptitude)
How does one determine a child's mental age on the Stanford-Binet Scale?
  a. By dividing the number of tests passed by the child's age in years.
  *b. By giving a specified number of months of credit for each test passed.
  c. By noting the highest level at which the child answers all tests correctly.
  d. By noting the highest level at which the child answers *any* test correctly.

(3) *Generalization* (educational aptitude)
Expert opinion today assigns how much weight to heredity as a determiner of intelligence?
  *a. Less weight than in 1900   c. All of the weight
  b. More weight than in 1900   d. None of the weight

(4) *Explanation* (personality and adjustment)
Why is the Rorschach Test regarded as a projective test?
  a. Because scores on the test provide accurate projections of future performance.
  *b. Because the examinee unintentionally reveals aspects of his own personality in the responses he makes.
  c. Because the stimulus material is ordinarily carried on slides that must be projected for viewing.
  d. Because the test is still in an experimental, developmental phase.

(5) *Calculation* (educational aptitude)
What is the I.Q. of an eight-year-old child whose mental age is 10 years?
  a. 80
  b. 90
  *c. 125
  d. The answer cannot be determined from the data given.

(6) *Prediction* (test tryout and analysis)
If two forms of a 50-item, 30-minute test are combined to produce a single 100-item, 60-minute test, how variable and reliable will scores from the combined test be (in comparison with those from a single short form)?
  *a. More variable and more reliable
  b. More variable but less reliable
  c. Less variable but more reliable
  d. Less variable and less reliable

(7) *Recommended action* (teacher-made tests)
In drafting a multiple-choice test item which of these should be written *second*?
  a. The stem question   c. A good distracter
  *b. A good answer   d. An absurd distracter

111

in instruction. Emphasis in an achievement test on things that were not taught or assigned for learning is hard to justify.

One approach to defining the appropriate universe for sampling is to list as topics, in as much detail as seems reasonable, the areas of knowledge and abilities toward which instruction was directed. In the simplest case, where instruction is based on a single text, section headings in the textbook may provide a satisfactory list of such topics. If sections are regarded as about equal in importance, and if there are *n* times as many of them as of items needed for the test, the instructor might systematically sample every *n*th topic as the basis for a test item.

If the various sections of the text are not reasonably equal in importance or if no single text provided the basis for teaching, instructors may wish to create their own list of topics. Perhaps separate lists of vocabulary items, items of information, and topics involving explanation, applications, calculation, or prediction may be required. This last approach may make it easier to maintain the desired balance among the several aspects of achievement. Illustrative portions of lists of topics for various aspects of achievement are shown in Figure 7-4.

Figure 7-4 Illustrative Portions of Topic Lists for a Test on Classroom Testing.*

List A—Vocabulary

1. Aptitude test
2. Bimodal distribution
3. Composite score
4. Expectancy table
5. Factor analysis

List B—Knowledge

1. Achievement quotients
2. Types of test items
3. Essay tests
4. Kuder-Richardson formulas
5. Educational uses of tests

List C—Explanation

1. Correction for attenuation
2. Use of standard scores
3. Cross validation
4. Separate answer sheet
5. Guessing correction formula

List D—Application

1. Reporting scores
2. Test selection
3. Sources of information
4. Judging test quality
5. Item writing

List E—Calculation

1. Mean
2. Index of item difficulty
3. Index of item discrimination
4. Percentile rank
5. Reliability coefficient

* All of these lists are merely illustrative; each could include many more items.

FORMS OF OBJECTIVE-TEST ITEMS

The most commonly used kinds of objective items are multiple-choice, true-false, matching, classification, and short-answer. Many other varieties have been described in other treatments of objective test-item writing (Wesman, 1971). However, most of these special varieties have limited merit and applicability. Their unique features often do more to change the appearance of the item, and often to increase the difficulty of using it, than to improve the item as a measuring tool.

Two special item types that have achieved some popularity, the true-false with correction and the multiple-response variation of the multiple-choice item, are displayed in Figure 7-5. The disadvantages of both appear to outweigh their advantages. Presumably the corrected true-false item is less subject to guessing than the ordinary true-false item and tests recall as well as recognition. However, the added difficulty and uncertainty involved in scoring student responses to it seem to more than offset whatever slight reduction in guessing or slight increase in recall testing the item might produce. The multiple-response item, also called a "multiple multiple" or complex multiple-choice, is essentially a collection of true-false statements. If the statements were presented and scored like independent true-false items, they would yield more detailed and reliable information than they can in multiple-response form. The use of multiple true-false items, a more preferred item form, is described in greater detail in Chapter 10.

Figure 7-5 Some Special Item Types.

---

(1) **True-false with correction**
Directions: If the statement is true as given, write the word "true" on the blank following the item. If it is false, find a substitute for the underlined word or phrase that would make it true. Then, write the substitute on the blank following the item.

Example:	*Answer*
0. The use of steam revolutionized transportation in the <u>17th</u> century.	0. 19th

(2) **Multiple-response**
Directions: Choose the most nearly correct set of responses from among those listed.

Example: *Responses*

0. Our present constitution

    a. was the outgrowth of a previous failure.   1. *a*

    b. was drafted in Philadelphia during the summer (May to   2. *a, b*
        September) of 1787.   3. *a, b, c*

    c. was submitted by the Congress to the states for adoption.   4. *b, c, d*

    d. was adopted by the required number of states and put into   *5. *a, b, c, d*
        effect in 1789.

Those critics who urge test makers to abandon the "traditional" multiple-choice and true-false forms and to invent new forms to measure a more varied and more significant array of educational achievement have failed to grasp two important points:

1. *Any* aspect of cognitive educational achievement can be tested by either the multiple-choice or the true-false form.
2. What a multiple-choice or true-false item measures is determined much more by its content than by its form.

Multiple-choice and true-false test items are widely applicable to a great variety of tasks. Because of this, and because of the importance of developing skill in using each form effectively, separate chapters are devoted to true-false and multiple-choice item forms later in this text.

The multiple-choice form of test item is relatively high in ability to discriminate between better and poorer students. It is somewhat more difficult to write than some other item types, but its advantages seem so apparent that it has become the type most widely used in tests constructed by specialists. Theoretically, and this has been verified in practice, a multiple-choice test with a given number of items can be expected to show as much reliability in its scores as a typical true-false test with almost twice that number of items. Here is an example of the multiple-choice type.

Directions: Write the number of the best answer to the question on the line at the right of the question.

Example: Which is the most appropriate designation for a government in which control is in the hands of a few people?

1. **Autonomy**	3. **Feudalism**	<u>4</u>
2. **Bureaucracy**	4. **Oligarchy**	

The true-false item is the simplest to prepare and is also quite widely adaptable. It tends to be less discriminating, item for item, than the multiple-choice type, and somewhat more subject to ambiguity and misinterpretation. Although theoretically a high proportion of true-false items could be answered correctly by blind guessing, in practice the error introduced into true-false test scores by blind guessing tends to be small. This is true because well-motivated examinees taking a reasonable test do very little blind guessing. They almost always find it possible to give a rational answer and much more advantageous to do so than to guess blindly. The problem of guessing on true-false test questions will be discussed in greater detail in Chapter 9. Here is an example of the true-false form.

Directions: If the sentence is essentially true, encircle the letter "T" at the right of the sentence. If it is essentially false, encircle the letter "F."

Example: A substance that serves as a catalyst in a chemical reaction may be recovered unaltered at the end of the reaction.

Ⓣ   F

The matching type is efficient in that an entire set of responses can be used with a cluster of related stimulus words. But this is also a limitation since it is sometimes difficult to get clusters of questions or stimulus words that are sufficiently similar to make use of the same set of responses. Further, questions whose answers can be no more than a word or a phrase tend to be somewhat superficial and to place a premium on purely verbalistic learning. An example of the matching type is given here.

Directions: **On the blank before the title of each literary work place the letter that precedes the name of the person who wrote it.**

Literary Works	Authors
b___ 1. *Paradise Lost*	*a.* **Matthew Arnold**
	b. **John Milton**
e___ 2. *The Innocents Abroad*	*c.* **William Shakespeare**
	d. **Robert Louis Stevenson**
d___ 3. *Treasure Island*	*e.* **Mark Twain**

The classification type is less familiar than the matching type, but possibly more useful in certain situations. Like the matching type, it uses a single set of responses but applies these to a large number of stimulus situations. An example of the classification type is the following.

Directions: **In the following items you are to express the effects of exercise on various body processes and substances. Assume that the organism undergoes no change except those due to exercise. For each item blacken the appropriate answer space.**
1. **If the effect of exercise is to *increase* the quantity described in the item**
2. **If the effect of exercise is to *decrease* the quantity described in the item**
3. **If exercise should have no *appreciable effect,* or an *unpredictable effect* on quantity described in the item**

27.	**Rate of heart beat**	■ ☐2 ☐3
28.	**Blood pressure**	■ ☐2 ☐3
29.	**Amount of glucose in the blood**	☐1 ■ ☐3
30.	**Amount of residual air in the lungs**	☐1 ■ ☐3

The short-answer item, in which students must supply a word, phrase, number, or other symbol is inordinately popular and tends to be used excessively in classroom tests. It is easy to prepare. In the early grades, where emphasis is on the development of vocabulary and the formation of concepts, it can serve a useful function. It has the apparent advantage of requiring the examinee to think of the answer, but this advantage may be more apparent than real. Some studies have shown a very high correlation between scores on tests composed of parallel short-answer and multiple-choice items, when both members of each pair of parallel items are intended to test the same knowledge or ability (Eurich, 1931; Cook, 1955).

This means that students who are best at *producing* correct answers tend also to be best at *identifying* them among several alternatives. Accurate measures of how well students can identify correct answers tend to be somewhat easier to get than accurate measures of their ability to produce them. There may be special situations, of course, where the correlation would be much lower.

The disadvantages of the short answer form are that it is limited to questions that can be answered by a word, phrase, symbol, or number and that its scoring tends to be subjective and tedious. Item writers often find it difficult to phrase good questions on principles, explanations, applications, or predictions that can be answered by one specific word or phrase. Here are some examples of short-answer items.

Directions: On the blank following each of the following questions, partial statements, or words, write the word or number that seems most appropriate.

Examples:

What is the valence of oxygen? <u>−2</u>

The middle section of the body of an insect is called the <u>thorax.</u>

What major river flows through or near each of these cities?

Cairo	<u>Nile</u>
Calcutta	<u>Ganges</u>
New Orleans	<u>Mississippi</u>
Paris	<u>Seine</u>
Quebec	<u>St. Lawrence</u>

Some authorities suggest that a variety of item types be used in each examination in order to diversify the tasks presented to the examinee. They imply that this will improve the validity of the test or make it more interesting. Others suggest that test constructors should choose the particular item type that is best suited to the material they wish to examine. There is more merit in the second of these suggestions than in the first, but even suitability of item form should not be accepted as an absolute imperative. Several item forms are quite widely adaptable. A test constructor can safely decide to use primarily a single item type, such as multiple-choice, and to turn to one of the other forms only when it becomes clearly more efficient to do so. The quality of a classroom test depends much more on giving proper weight to various aspects of achievement, and on writing good items of whatever type, than on choice of this or that type of item.

Complexity versus Efficiency

In recent years some achievement tests have tended toward the use of complex tasks, often based on descriptions of real or imagined situations, or requiring the interpretation of data, diagrams, or background information. Illustrations of a variety of complex test items have been prepared by Educational

Figure 7-6 Descriptions of Complex Items.

---

(1) **The item begins with a description of a dispute among baseball players, team owners, and Social Security officials over off-season unemployment compensation for the players. Examinees are asked whether the players are justified in their demands, not justified, or whether they need more information before deciding. Then, they are asked whether each one of a series of statements about the case supports their judgment, opposes it, or leaves them unable to say.**

(Taxonomy, **pp. 196–97)**

(2) **An unusual chemical reaction is described. Examinees are asked to consider which of a series of possible hypotheses about the reaction is tenable and how the tenable hypotheses might be tested.**

(Taxonomy, **pp. 183–84)**

(3) **Examinees are given a chart on which the expenditures of a state for various purposes over a period of years have been graphed. Then, given a series of statements about the chart, they are asked to judge how much truth there is in each.**

(Taxonomy, **pp. 118–19)**

Testing Service (1963) and by Bloom and his colleagues (1956). Some examples of complex items of this type are shown in Figure 7-6.

There are several reasons for this trend. Since these tasks obviously call for the *use* of knowledge, they provide an answer to critics who assert that objective questions test only recognition of isolated factual details. Further, since the situations and background materials used in the tasks are complex, the items presumably require the examinee to use higher mental processes. Finally, the items are attractive to those who believe that education should be concerned with developing a student's ability to think rather than mere command of knowledge (as if knowledge and thinking were independent attainments!).

However, these complex tasks have some undesirable features as test items. Because they tend to be bulky and time-consuming, they limit the number of responses examinees can make per hour of testing time, that is, the size of the sample of observable behaviors. Hence, because of reduced reliability, tests composed of complex tasks tend to be inefficient in terms of accuracy of measurement per hour of testing.

Further, the more complex the situation, and the higher the level of mental process required to make some judgment about it, the more difficult it becomes to defend any one answer as the best answer. Complex test items tend to discriminate poorly. They also tend to be inordinately difficult, unless the examiner manages to ask a very easy question about a complex problem situation. Even the strongest advocates of complex situational or interpretive test items do not claim that good items of this type are easy to write.

The inefficiency of these items, the uncertainty of the best answer, and the difficulty of writing good ones could all be tolerated if the complex items did, in fact, measure more important aspects of achievement than can be measured by simpler types. However, there is no good evidence that this is the case. A simple question like, "Will you marry me?" can have the most profound consequences. It can provide a lifetime's crucial test of the wisdom of the man who asks it and of the woman who answers.

It would be a mistake in testing to pursue efficiency wherever it may lead, for it may lead to testing only vocabulary and simple word associations, and these are inadequate for testing all the dimensions of command of knowledge. It is equally a mistake to value the appearance of complexity for its own sake. If the complex item tests a genuinely important achievement that is within the grasp of most students and that cannot be tested in any simpler way, then retain it. If not, seek some other important achievement or seek to test it more simply.

THE NUMBER OF ITEMS

The number of questions to include in a test is determined largely by the amount of time available for it. Many tests are limited to 50 minutes, more or less, because that is the scheduled length of the class period. Special examination schedules may provide periods of two hours or longer. In general, the longer the period and the examination, the more reliable the scores obtained from it. However, it is seldom practical or desirable to prepare a classroom test that will require more than three hours.

For various reasons there is a growing trend to make tests include few enough questions so that most students have time to attempt all of them when working at their own normal rates. One reason for this is that speed of response is not a primary objective of instruction in most high school and college courses and hence is not a valid indication of achievement. In many areas of proficiency, speed and accuracy are not highly correlated. Consider the data in Table 7-1. The sum of the scores for the first ten students who finished the test was 965. The highest score in that group was 105. The lowest was 71. Thus, the range of scores in that group was 35 score units. Note that though the range of scores varies somewhat from group to group, there is no clear tendency for students to do better or worse depending on the amount of time spent. One can conclude from these data that on this test there was almost no relation between time spent in taking the test and the number of correct answers given.

A second reason for giving students ample time to work on a test is that examination anxiety, severe enough even in untimed tests, is accentuated when pressure to work rapidly as well as accurately is applied. A third is that efficient use of an instructor's painstakingly produced test requires that most students respond to all of it (Ebel, 1953). In some situations speed tests may be appropriate and valuable, but these situations seem to be the exception, not the rule.

Table 7-1 The Relation Between Rate of Work and Test
Scores*

Order of Finish	Sum of Scores	Range of Scores
1–10	965	35
11–20	956	32
21–30	940	31
31–40	964	32
41–50	948	52
51–60	955	25
61–70	965	27
71–80	1010	30
81–90	942	24
91–100	968	40

* Based on a test in educational measurement composed of 125 true-false test items taken by 100 students on November 3, 1969. The mean score on the test was 96.1. The tenth student finished the test after working on it for 50 minutes. The 100th student used 120 minutes.

The number of questions that an examinee can answer per minute depends on the kind of questions used, the complexity of the thought processes required to answer them, and the examinee's work habits. The fastest student in a class may finish a test in half the time required by the slowest. For these reasons it is difficult to specify precisely how many items to include in a given test. Experience with similar tests in similar classes is the best guide.

Sampling Errors in Test Scores

If the amount of time available for testing does not determine the length of a test, the accuracy desired in the scores should determine it. In general, the larger the number of items included in a test, the more reliable the scores will be as measures of achievement in the field. In statistical terminology, the items that make up a test constitute a *sample* from a much larger collection, or *population,* of items that might have been used in that test. A 100-word spelling test might be constructed by selecting every fifth word from a list of the 500 words studied during the term. The 500 words constitute the population from which the 100-word sample was selected.

Consider now a student who, asked to spell all 500 words, spells 325 (65 percent) of them correctly. Of the 100 words in the sample, he spells 69 (69 percent) correctly. The difference between the 65 percent for the population and the 69 percent for the sample is known as a *sampling error*. Statisticians refer to the population quantity, 65 percent in this case, as a parameter. The sample quantity, 69 percent in this case, they refer to as a statistic. A statistician, or anyone else for that matter, can use a statistic obtained from a sample to estimate the parameter of a population.

For example, if a teacher wishes to estimate the average weight of 30 students in a second grade, she or he might weigh five of them and find the average of their weights. That sample statistic would probably be close to but not identical with the average that would have been obtained if all 30 students had been weighed to find the population parameter. The difference would be a sampling error.

In the case of the spelling test just cited, the population of possible questions is real and definite. But for most tests it is not. That is, there is almost no limit to the number of problems that could be invented for use in an algebra test, or to the number of questions that could be formulated for a history test. Constructers of tests in these subjects, as in most other subjects, have no pre-determined, limited list from which to draw a representative sample of questions. But their tests are samples, nevertheless, because they include only a fraction of the questions that could be asked in each case. A major problem of test constructers is thus to make their samples fairly represent a theoretical total population of questions on the topic.

The more extensive the area of subject matter or abilities a test is intended to cover, the larger the population of potential questions. The size of this population places an upper limit on the size of the sample that can be drawn from it; that is, the sample cannot be larger than the population. But population size does not place a *lower* limit on the size of the sample. A population of 1000 potential items can be sampled by a test of ten, 50, or 100 items. So can a population of 100,000 potential items. The larger the population, the more likely it is to be heterogeneous, that is, to include diverse and semi-independent areas of knowledge or ability. To achieve equally accurate results, a somewhat larger sample is required in a heterogeneous than in a homogeneous field. And, as we have already noted, generally a larger sample will yield a sample statistic closer to the population parameter than a more limited sample.

Now since any test is a sample of tasks, every test score is subject to sampling errors. If test scores are expressed as percent correct, the larger the sample, the smaller the sampling errors are likely to be. Posey (1932) has shown that examinees' luck, or lack of it, in being asked what they happen to know is a much greater factor in the grade they receive in a ten-question test than in one of 100 questions. Sampling errors are present in practically all educational test scores. However, it is important to realize that such errors are not caused by mistakes in sampling. A perfectly chosen random sample will still be subject to sampling errors simply because it is a sample.

LEVEL AND DISTRIBUTION OF DIFFICULTY

There are two ways in which the problem of test difficulty can be approached. One is to include in the test only those items that any student who has studied successfully should be able to answer. If this is done, most of the students can be expected to answer the majority of the items correctly. Put somewhat differently, so many correct answers are likely to be given that many of the items will not be effective in discriminating among various levels of achievement—best, good, average, weak, and poor. The score distribution will be very homogeneous, as reflected by a small standard deviation. But if our goal is to make norm-referenced score interpretations, clearly such a test would yield disappointingly unreliable scores.

The other approach is to choose items on the basis of their ability to reveal different levels of achievement among the students tested. This requires preference for moderately difficult questions. The ideal difficulty of these items should be at a point on the difficulty scale midway between perfect (100 percent correct response) and the chance-level difficulty (50 percent correct for true-false items, 25 percent correct for four-alternative multiple-choice items). This means the proportion of correct responses should be about 75 percent correct for an ideal true-false item and about 62.5 percent correct for an ideal multiple-choice item. This second approach generally will yield more reliable scores for a constant amount of testing time.

Some instructors believe that a good test includes some difficult items to "test" the better students and some easy items to give poorer students a chance. But neither of these kinds of items tend to affect the rank-ordering of student scores appreciably. The higher-scoring students generally answer the harder items and, therefore, earn higher scores yet. Nearly everyone will answer the easy items. The effect of easy items is to add a constant amount to each examinee's score, to raise all scores, but without affecting the rank order of students' scores. For good norm-referenced achievement measures, items of moderate difficulty, not too hard and not too easy, contribute most to discriminating among students who have learned varying amounts of the content of instruction.

Tests designed to yield content-referenced score interpretations likely will be easier in difficulty level than their group-referenced counterparts. When testing for minimum competence or for mastery, the expectation is that most students have reached the minimum level or have achieved mastery. The items in these tests should be easy for most students but difficult for those who have not mastered the content the items represent. It should be clear that a test item in isolation is not easy or difficult. The difficulty of an item relates to the nature of the group and depends on the extent to which those in the group possess the ability presented by the task.

SOME REQUIREMENTS FOR EFFECTIVE TESTING

If all teachers and prospective teachers were skilled in the arts of test development and use, there would be little need for professional training in test construction. However, on their own testimony and on that of their sometimes suffering students—not to mention the reports of specialists called in to advise them on their testing problems—teachers do reveal shortcomings in their use of tests.

In order to ask significant, novel questions, to express them properly and plainly, and to provide acceptable model answers, test constructers must be thoroughly familiar with the material to be tested. They must be accurately aware of the examinees' level and range of understanding and ability so that they can choose problems of appropriate intrinsic difficulty and present them so that they will have appropriate functional difficulty. And only by understanding the thought processes of the students and the misconceptions the less capable ones are likely to have can test builders make wrong answers attractive to those of low achievement.

Skill in written expression is also required to communicate clearly and concisely the information and instructions that make up the test and the test items. A mastery of the techniques of item writing entails acquaintance with the most useful forms of test items, with their unique virtues, limitations, and pitfalls. And no less important is the desire to spend the time and make the effort necessary to do a competent, workmanlike job.

The traits just enumerated either contribute to good teaching as well as good testing, or contribute uniquely to good testing. More of the short-comings observed in classroom tests probably result from deficiencies in teaching technique rather than in testing procedure. But the correction of deficiencies in command of subject matter, and skill in teaching, is beyond the scope of this book. Nothing that can be said about the techniques of test construction and use will enable an incompetent teacher to make a good test. What a book on classroom testing may do is to help good teachers make better tests than they would otherwise.

A point worth mentioning in passing is that some instructors, outstanding in their scholarship and teaching ability, possess rather naive notions about the requirements for effective measurement of educational achievement. The nuclear physicist, the economic theorist, the Shakespearean scholar, and many of their expert colleagues may practice rather primitive and untrustworthy techniques of testing and grading.

The gap between what we know about how educational achievement ought to be measured and what we actually do is sometimes explained away as a failure in communication, which it almost certainly is. Test specialists are blamed for having developed highly abstruse concepts and highly technical jargon that place their special knowledge beyond the reach of the typical teacher. No doubt there is some justification for this charge. But some of the responsibility may also belong to the teachers. They may have expected that their own native good sense, plus some effortless sleight of hand, could qualify them as experts in educational measurement. The matter is not quite that simple, as Henry Dyer (1958) has pointed out.

> I don't think the business of educational measurement is inherently simple, and I don't think it is something that can be wrapped up in a do-it-yourself

kit. Any way you look at it, the measurement of human behavior is bound to be a terribly complex process, since the phenomena of human behavior are themselves as complex as anything in the universe.

Common Mistakes of Teachers in Testing

What are some of the mistakes that even expert teachers and eminent professors make in measuring educational achievement? What are some of their unsound practices in classroom testing?

First, they tend to rely too much on their own subjective judgments, on fortuitous observations, and on unverified inferences. The wide difference among different judges in their evaluations of the same evidence of student achievement—that is, the unreliability of those judgments—has been demonstrated over and over again, yet many teachers have never checked on the reliability of any of their tests and may not even have planned those tests purposely to make them as reliable as possible.

Second, both teachers and professors tend to put off test preparation to the last minute and then to do it on a catch-as-catch-can basis. A last minute test is likely to be a poor test. Further, such a test cannot possibly have the constructive influence in motivating and directing student learning that a good test of educational achievement ought to have and that a test planned and described to students early in the course would have.

Third, many teachers use tests that are too inefficient and too short to sample adequately the whole area of understanding and abilities that the course has attempted to develop. Essay tests have many virtues, but efficiency, adequacy of sampling, and reliability of scoring are not among them.

Fourth, teachers often overemphasize trivial or ephemeral details in their tests, to the neglect of understanding of basic principles and ability to make practical applications. To illustrate, it is probably far more important to understand the forces that brought Henry VIII into conflict with the pope than to know the name of his second wife. Yet some teachers are more inclined to ask about the specific, incidental details than about the important general principles.

Fifth, the test questions that teachers and professors write, both essay and objective, often suffer from lowered effectiveness due to unintentional ambiguity in the wording of the question or to inclusion of irrelevant clues to the correct response. Too few teachers avoid these hazards by asking a competent colleague to review the tests beforehand.

Sixth, the inevitable fact that test scores are affected by the questions or tasks included in them tends to be ignored, and the magnitude of the resulting errors (called *sampling errors*) tends to be underestimated. Many classroom teachers believe that a test score will be perfectly accurate and reliable if no error has been made in scoring the individual items or in adding these to get a total score. Differences as small as one score unit are often taken to indicate significant differences in attainment.

Finally, many teachers and professors do not use the relatively simple techniques of statistical analysis to check on the effectiveness of their tests. A mean score can show whether or not the general level of difficulty was appropriate for the group tested. A standard deviation can show how well or how poorly the test differentiated among students at different levels of attainment. A reliability coefficient can show how much or how little the scores on this test are likely to differ from those the same students would get on an independent, equivalent test.

An analysis of the responses of good and poor students to individual test items can show whether the items discriminate well or poorly and, if poorly, can suggest why and what needs to be done to improve the item. The calculation of these statistics is quite simple. There is no better way for teachers and professors to continue to improve their skill in testing, and the quality of the tests they use, than to analyze test results systematically and to compare the finding of these analyses with ideal standards of test quality, such as those discussed in Chapter 13.

SUMMARY

The principal ideas developed in this chapter may be summarized in these statements:

1. The form of a test gives no certain indication of the ability tested.
2. Whatever form of test is used, examiners should attempt to make their measurements as objective as possible. A measurement is objective to the extent that it can be verified by another independent measurer.
3. When a performance test and an objective test can be used to achieve essentially the same purpose, the objective test likely will be more efficient, be more relevant, and yield more reliable measures.
4. Oral examinations allow for flexibility in the examining process, but tend to be time-consuming, to be subject to personal bias, and to yield measurements of low reliability.
5. The most important function of classroom tests is to obtain precise measures of students' achievements.
6. All questions that ask Who? What? When? or Where? are properly classified as factual information questions.
7. Items intended to test various aspects of achievement ordinarily can be classified more reliably on the basis of overt item characteristics than on the basis of the mental processes they presumably require.
8. An outline of topics dealt with in instruction provides a useful basis for developing test items that will sample the desired achievement representatively.
9. Multiple-choice and true-false items can be used to measure any aspect of cognitive educational achievement.
10. Other item types have more limited usefulness but may be advantageous in certain circumstances.
11. Situational or interpretive test items tend to be inefficient, difficult to write, sometimes hard to defend, and unconvincing as measures of higher mental processes.
12. Most classroom achievement tests should be short enough, in relation to the time available, so that virtually all students have time to attempt all items.
13. The number of items to be included in a test should be influenced by the amount of time available, the accuracy desired in the scores, and the homogeneity of content to be sampled.
14. In most achievement tests, the items that contribute the greatest amount of useful information are those on which the proportion of correct response is halfway between 100 percent and the expected chance score.
15. Competence in teaching is necessary, but not a sufficient condition, for expert test construction.
16. Construction of a good objective test requires special knowledge of testing techniques and special skill in the use of language.

17. Some common weaknesses of teacher-made tests are attributable to: (a) reliance on subjective judgments, (b) hasty test preparation, (c) use of short, inefficient tests, (d) testing of trivial content, (e) careless wording of questions, (f) neglect of content sampling errors, and (g) failure to analyze the quality of the test.

PROJECTS AND PROBLEMS

Project: Development of a Test Plan

Draw up detailed plans for an important test, such as an hour-long final test, or an important series of shorter tests in elementary reading or arithmetic. Describe your plan in a paper of 1000–1500 words, organized around the following headings:

1. *Identity of the Test.* Give the proposed test title and indicate the subject, grade level, and type of test (for example, achievement, aptitude, diagnostic).
2. *Purpose of the Test.* State the purpose of the test and defend its educational value.
3. *Type and Number of Test Questions.* Identify the type or types of questions (essay, short-answer, true-false, multiple-choice, for example) to be used, and the number of each. Defend your choices on the basis of the purposes of the test and the time available.
4. *Abilities to Be Measured.* What will be your criteria of relevance for the test items? What item content will you include (understanding, problem solving, explanation, application, and so forth) or intentionally omit (rote memory, verbal recall, general intelligence, testwiseness). Defend your decisions. Provide one or two illustrations of each of the various kinds of items you plan to use.
5. *Content to Be Covered.* Present a content outline and a justification for it.

This assignment will be graded for completeness and quality. Instructors will not second-guess your decisions unless your judgments are clearly questionable. They are more interested in the value of this activity as a learning exercise—in the questions it causes you to ask and answer—than in its limited value as a measure of your competence. However, since it involves a substantial amount of work, do not let sloppy appearance reduce its apparent worth.

8

THE USE OF ESSAY TESTS

THE POPULARITY OF ESSAY TESTS

Essay tests continue to be a very popular form, especially among scholars and at the higher levels of education. Their history of usage dates back earlier than 2300 B.C. in ancient China, and until the turn of the century they were about the only form of written examination in wide use. Thus they have the sanction of tradition (Coffman, 1971).

However, there are other reasons for their popularity. One is convenience. In contrast with objective tests, essay tests are relatively easy to prepare—the difficult part of the job is usually grading students' answers. Another is the security they provide to the examiner. Writers of essay questions are seldom required, as are composers of objective test items, to defend the "correct" answer or to demonstrate that none of the "wrong" answers is as good as the correct answer. Essay questions require the student to create an explicit answer that the scorer can rate without describing the basis of any rating scale or without showing his or her own version of an ideal answer. Thus the deficiencies of an essay question are seldom so readily available for observation as are those of an objective test item.

It is also quite easy for the grader of an essay test to control the general level and distribution of scores. Whether the examiner allows no points, five points, or even seven points for a seriously inadequate answer is a matter of personal decision. Thus, no matter how inappropriate the level of difficulty of an essay test, the grader can adjust the standards so some—but not too many—will receive scores below some preset minimum passing score. The fact that test-item difficulty is not a crucial factor contributes in no small measure to the popularity of the essay test.

THE VALUE OF ESSAY TESTS

Those who argue for essay tests and against objective tests usually do so on the ground that essay tests provide a better indication of students' real achievements in learning. Students are not given ready-made answers but must have command of an ample store of knowledge that enables them to relate facts and principles, to organize them into a coherent and logical progression, and then to do justice to these ideas in written expression. Recall is, of course, involved in the composition of an answer to an essay-test question, but it would be a gross oversimplification to characterize an essay test as simply a measure of recall.

Further, the answers given to an essay-test question can often provide clues to the nature and quality of students' thought processes. Some writers of essay-test questions occasionally deliberately choose indeterminate issues as the basis for their questions. What the student concludes, they say, is unimportant. The evidence on which the examinee bases the conclusion and the cogency of his or her arguments in support of it are said to be all-important.

Many of the traits that essay tests have been said to measure, such as critical thinking, originality, and ability to organize and integrate, are not at all clearly defined. Those characteristics of the answers that serve to indicate which students have more and which have less of these traits are seldom set forth explicitly. When the scores awarded to essay-test answers are explained or defended, deductions from a maximum possible score are usually attributed to some combination of these deficiencies:

1. Incorrect statements were included in the answer.
2. Important ideas necessary to an adequate answer were omitted.
3. Correct statements having little or no relation to the question were included.
4. Unsound conclusions were reached, either because of mistakes in reasoning or because of misapplication of principles.
5. Bad writing obscured the development and exposition of the student's ideas.
6. There were flagrant errors in spelling and the mechanics of correct writing.

Mistakes in the first four categories can be attributed either to weaknesses in the student's command of knowledge or to lack of clarity and specificity in the examiner's question. Mistakes in the last two categories either indicate a weakness in written self-expression or reflect the difficulties of the hand in keeping up with a mind racing ahead under the pressure of a time limit. As essay tests are typically used, the unique functions they have that are beyond the scope of objective tests seem somewhat limited and indefinite. Odell's (1927) scales for rating essay-test answers suggest strongly that the length of a student's answer may be closely related to the score it receives. Longer answers tend to receive higher ratings.

Influence on Study

That the nature of the examination expected affects the preparation students make for it is attested by experience, reason, and research (Meyer, 1935; Terry, 1933). Surveys of student opinion conducted about 50 years ago suggest the students then studied more thoroughly in preparation for essay examinations than for objective examinations. More recent evidence is scanty and inconclusive.

With respect to the influence of examinations on study, the really important question is not how students say they study for examinations of different kinds—or even how they actually do study—but how these differences affect their achievement. In the absence of adequate research, we venture to make the following inferences:

1. The kind of study and achievement that a test stimulates is probably more a function of the kind of questions asked than of the mode of student response.
2. To the degree that tests in different forms measure the same kinds or aspects of achievement, they should stimulate the same kind of study and have the same effect on achievement.

Many potent factors other than examinations affect how and with what success students study. These factors interact in complex ways to facilitate or to inhibit learning. The chances are small, therefore, that research will ever demonstrate clearly which form of examination, essay or objective, has the more beneficial influence on study and learning.

Emphasis on Writing Ability

Essay tests are also valued for the emphasis they place on writing. However, this is both an advantage and a disadvantage. Written expression is an important skill that essay tests do encourage. However, the practice that essay tests give in writing may be practice in *bad* writing—hasty, ill considered, and unpolished. Worse, skill in writing, or lack of it, may influence the scorer's judgment regarding the content of the answer. Uniform, legible handwriting and fluent, graceful sentences can compensate for some deficiencies in content. On the other hand, flaws in spelling, grammar, or usage can detract from the scorer's evaluation of the content.

Students occasionally use writing skill to compensate for lack of knowledge. Students who are hard put to answer adequately the question asked can transform it subtly into a related question that is easier for them to answer. If they perform well on the substitute task, the reader may not even notice the substitution. Or the student may concentrate on form rather than on content, on elegant presentation of a few rather simple ideas, in the hope that this may divert the reader's attention from the lack of substantial content.

Not all readers of essay examinations are easy to bluff. Then, too, students likely to be most in need of the kind of assistance that bluffing might give them are usually the least able to use such techniques. For this reason, bluffing on essay tests is hardly more serious a problem than guessing one's way to success on an objective test.

Reliability of Essay-Test Scores

The most serious limitation of essay tests as measures of achievement in classroom settings is the low reliability of the scores they typically yield. Low reliability means that there is a good deal of inconsistency between scores obtained from successive administrations of the same test or equivalent tests, or from independent scorings of the same test. On the whole, three conditions are responsible for this low reliability: (1) the limited sampling of the content covered by the test; (2) the indefiniteness of the tasks set by the essay questions; and (3) the subjectivity of the scoring of essay answers.

In general, the larger the number of independent elements in the sample of tasks chosen for an achievement test, the more accurately performance on those tasks will reflect overall achievement in the field. It is true that the answer to a complex essay-test question often involves many separate elements of achievement. Yet they are dealt with as a more or less integrated whole by both the student and the grader, not as independent elements.

Few, if any, experimental studies of the sampling reliability of essay tests relative to that of objective tests have been made. The difficulty of obtaining sufficiently objective scoring of essay-test answers may be part of the reason. But there have been some theoretical analyses of the problem. Ruch (1929) has shown a direct relation between the extensiveness of the sample of tasks in a test and the precision with which different levels of achievement can be differentiated. Posey (1932) demonstrated that examinees' luck, or lack of it, in being asked what they happen to know is a much greater factor in the grade they receive in a ten-item test than in one of 100 items.

On many essay-test questions, the task and the basis for judging an examinee's success in completing it are not clearly specified. Essay questions *can* be explicit; they can guide students to produce those answers that will signify achievements. Often, however, they do not. Similarly, scoring directions *can* be written in a concise, easy-to-follow manner. Again, they often fall short of the mark. The more detailed and explicit the directions to both student and scorer, the more objective and reliable the measurements obtainable from an essay-test question.

The classic studies of Starch and Elliott (1912, 1913a, 1913b) exposed the appallingly wide variations in the grades that typical teachers assigned to the same student's answers to questions in geometry, literature, and history. Later studies confirmed these findings in other contexts (Finlayson, 1951; Vernon and Mellican, 1954). Thus, although it has been elsewhere shown that essay-test answers can be graded reliably when the job is done under careful supervision, the fact that essay tests typically yield highly subjective and unreliable measures of achievement was established beyond dispute.

The score on any test is a means of communicating and recording a measurement or an evaluation. It is useful only insofar as it is meaningful. It must mean something to the person who determined it, not only at the moment of determination, but days or weeks later. It must mean as nearly as possible the same thing to the student who receives it as it did to the teacher who assigned it. To the degree that other qualified observers would assign different scores, the measurement lacks objectivity and hence utility. Measurements of school achievement, like other reports, must be trustworthy in order to be useful. To be trustworthy means that they are capable of independent verification. If the same teacher were to assign totally different scores to the same essay test answer on different occasions—or if different teachers were to disagree in the same way—our confidence in the scores would be shaken and their usefulness seriously diminished.

COMPARISON OF ESSAY AND OBJECTIVE TESTS

The following statements summarize some of the similarities and differences of essay and objective tests.

1. Either an essay or an objective test can be used to measure almost any important educational achievement that any written test can measure.
2. Either an essay or an objective test can be used to encourage students to study for understanding of principles, organization and integration of ideas, and application of knowledge to the solution of problems.
3. The use of either type necessarily involves the exercise of subjective judgment.
4. The value of scores from either type of test is dependent on their objectivity and reliability.
5. An essay-test question requires students to plan their own answers and to express them in their own words. An objective-test item requires examinees to choose among several designated alternatives.
6. An essay test consists of relatively few, more general questions that call for rather extended answers. An objective test ordinarily consists of many rather specific questions requiring only brief answers.
7. Students spend most of their time in thinking and writing when taking an essay test. They spend most of their time reading and thinking when taking an objective test.
8. The quality of an objective test is determined largely by the skill of the test constructer. The quality of an essay test is determined largely by the skill of the test scorer.

9. An essay examination is relatively easy to prepare but rather tedious and difficult to score accurately. A good objective examination is relatively tedious and difficult to prepare but comparatively easy to score.

10. An essay examination affords students much freedom to express their individuality in the answers they give and much freedom for the examiner to be guided by his or her individual preferences in scoring the answer. An objective examination affords much freedom for the test constructer to express personal knowledge and values but allows students only the freedom to show, by the proportion of correct answers they give, how much or how little they know or can do.

11. In objective-test items the student's task and the basis on which the examiner will judge the degree to which it has been accomplished are stated more clearly than they are in essay tests.

12. An objective test permits, and occasionally encourages, guessing. An essay test permits, and occasionally encourages, bluffing.

13. The distribution of numerical scores obtained from an essay test can be controlled to a considerable degree by the grader; that from an objective test is determined almost entirely by the examination itself.

When to Consider Using Essay Tests

Use essay tests in the measurement of educational achievement when:

1. The group to be tested is small, and the test will not be reused.
2. The instructor wishes to encourage to the fullest the development of student skill in written expression.
3. The instructor is more interested in exploring student attitudes than in measuring achievements. (Whether instructors *should* be more interested in attitudes than achievement and whether they should expect an honest expression of attitudes in a test situation seem open to question.)
4. The instructor is more confident of his or her proficiency as a critical reader than as an imaginative writer of good objective-test items.
5. Time available for test preparation is shorter than time available for test grading.

Essay tests have important uses in educational measurement. They also have serious limitations. It would be well for all teachers to be on guard against unsubstantiated claims that essay tests can measure undefined and only vaguely perceived "higher-order mental abilities." They ought also to question the propriety of using essay tests to determine how well students can do what the instructor has not really tried to teach them to do—to analyze, to synthesize, to organize, to develop original ideas and to express them with clarity, grace, wit, and correctness. Above all, they ought to avoid using an essay test when an objective test could do the job better and more easily.

GUIDELINES FOR PREPARING ESSAY ITEMS

Implicit in what has been said in this chapter about the values and limitations of essay tests are a number of suggestions for improving essay-type questions.

1. Ask questions or set tasks that will require the student to demonstrate a command of essential knowledge. Such questions will not simply call for re-production of materials presented in the textbook or classroom. Instead of looking exclusively backward to the past course of instruction, they will also look forward to future applications of the things learned. The questions will be based on novel situations or problems, not on the same ones used for instructional purposes.

2. Ask questions that are determinate, in the sense that experts could agree that one answer is better than another. Indeterminate questions are likely to function in some measure as exercises in exposition, whose relation to effective behavior may be quite remote. Such questions will probably not be especially relevant to the measurement of a student's useful command of essential knowledge. Further, and most importantly, the absence of a good best answer may make it much more difficult for a reader to judge a given student's level of achievement. On controversial questions, which many indeterminate questions are, the reader's opinions and biases may considerably influence any evaluation of the student's answer.

3. Define the examinee's task as completely and specifically as possible without interfering with measurement of the achievement intended. The question should be carefully phrased so that examinees fully understand what they are expected to do. If the task is not clearly evident in the question itself, add an explanation of the basis on which answers will be evaluated. Do not allow students more freedom than is necessary to measure the desired achievement. If the question permits variation in the extent and detail of the answer given but this is not a relevant variable, specify about how long the answer is expected to be.

4. In general, give preference to more specific questions that can be answered more briefly. The larger the number of independently scorable questions, the higher the sampling reliability of the test is likely to be. Narrower questions are likely to be less ambiguous to the examinee and easier for scorers to grade reliably. Occasionally an instructor may find it necessary to base an essay test on only a few very broad questions. These occasions are not frequent, however, and the instructor should be sure that the need for extended answers is sufficient to warrant the probable loss in score reliability.

5. Avoid giving the examinee a choice among optional questions unless special circumstances make such options necessary. If different examinees answer different questions, the basis for comparing their scores is weakened. Clearly, when students choose the questions they can answer best, the range of test scores is likely to be narrower—hence the reliability of the scores would be expected to be somewhat less. Research indicates that this expectation is justified.

When college students in psychology were given the choice of omitting one of five essay questions, Meyer (1939) found surprisingly that only 58 percent of them omitted the question on which they would do least well. He "suggested that unless the various questions are weighted in some suitable fashion the choice form of essay examination be discontinued." Stalnaker (1951) concluded a survey of the problems involved in the use of optional questions with these words:

> No experimental evidence has been published to show that skills and abilities can be adequately sampled by the use of optional questions; on the other hand, several studies have shown that optional questions complicate measurement and introduce factors of judgment which are extraneous to the ability being measured. For sound sampling, it is recommended that optional questions be avoided and that all examinees be asked to run the same race. (p. 170)

Optional questions are sometimes justified on the ground that giving students a choice among the questions they are to answer makes the test "fairer." But if all the questions involve essential aspects of achievement in a course (as they ordinarily might), it is not unfair to any student to require answers to all of them. Furthermore, an opportunity to choose among optional questions may help the poorer student considerably, but may actually distract the well-prepared student.

Optional questions may be justifiable when a test of educational achievement must cover a broad area, and when the students who take it have received unequal training in different areas. Even in such a situation, however, the advantages of using optional questions are highly dubious. Optional tests, separately scored, might be preferable to a common test, yielding a single score, based on different sets of questions.

6. Test the question by writing an ideal answer to it. Writing the ideal answer at the time a question is drafted serves an immediate purpose. It gives the test constructor a check on the reasonableness of the questions and on the adequacy of his/her own understanding. Perhaps some change in the question could make it easier, if that seems desirable, or more discriminating, which is always desirable. Also useful, if it can be arranged, is to have a colleague in the same field try to answer it. Comparison of such ideal answers might shed additional light on the question's suitability and might suggest additional ways of improving it.

The deferred purpose served by drafting an ideal answer to each essay-test question is to provide guidance, and a point of reference, for the later scoring of students' answers. If someone other than the instructor is to grade the questions or to help with the grading, the ideal answer is almost indispensable to uniformity in grading.

GUIDELINES FOR GRADING ESSAY TESTS

As has been mentioned, the efficacy of essay tests as measures of educational achievement depends primarily on the quality of the grading process. The competence of the grader is crucial to the quality of this process, yet even competent graders may inadvertently do things that make the results less reliable than they ought to be. Here are some suggestions for graders of essay-test answers to consider if they are anxious to make their work as precise as possible.

1. Use either analytic scoring or global-quality scaling.   In analytic scoring, crucial elements of the ideal answer are identified and scored more or less separately. The higher the proportion of these crucial elements appearing in the student's answer and the less they are contaminated by inaccuracies or irrelevancies, the higher the student's score. Analytic scoring can pay attention not only to the elements of an ideal answer, but also to relations between these elements, that is, to the organization and integration of the answer. But if these relationships are complex and subtle, analytic scoring may prove to be too cumbersome and tedious to be effective.

An alternative is global-quality scaling. Scorers using this method simply read the answer for a general impression of its adequacy, then transform that impression into a numerical grade, record the grade, and go on to the next answer. A better procedure, which allows the grader to check the consistency of grading standards as applied to different papers, involves the sorting of answers into several piles corresponding to different levels of quality. Sorting before marking permits, even encourages, graders to reconsider their decisions in the light of experience with all the students' answers. It lessens the possibility of giving a higher score to one of two answers which, on rereading, seem to be of equal quality.

As a general rule, global-quality scaling is simpler and faster than analytic scoring. In some situations it may be more reliable. But it does not provide any clear justification of the grade assigned, nor does it give students any indication how their answers fell short of the mark (Mullis, 1984). Analytic scoring can provide such indications. It is well suited to questions that are likely to elicit detailed, uniformly structured answers.

2. Grade the answers question by question rather than student by student.   This means that the grader will read the answers to one question on all students' papers before going on to the next question. Such a procedure is obviously required in the global-quality scaling just described. It is also advantageous in analytic scoring, since concentration of attention on one question at a time helps to develop specialized skill and to foster independent judgment in scoring it (Hales & Tokar, 1975).

3. If possible, conceal from the grader the identity of the student whose answer he or she is grading.   The purpose of this procedure is to reduce the possibility that biases or halo effects will influence the scores assigned. Ideally, the answers to different questions would be written on separate sheets of paper, identified only by a code number. These sheets would be arranged into groups by question for the grading process and then recombined by the student for totaling and recording. By this process one can reduce not only the halo effect associated with the student's name and reputation, but also that which might result from high or low scores on preceding answers.

   4. If possible, arrange for independent grading of the answers, or at least a sample of them.   Independent grading is the only real check on the objectivity, and hence the reliability, of the grading. Since it is troublesome to arrange and time-consuming to carry out, however, it is seldom likely to be utilized by the classroom teacher. But if a school or college were to undertake a serious program for the improvement of essay examinations, such a study of the reliability of essay test grading would be an excellent way to begin.

   To get independent grades, at least two competent readers would have to grade each question, without consulting each other and without knowing what grades the other had assigned. At least 100, preferably 300, answers should be given this double, independent reading. (The answers need not all be to the same question. Reading the answers of 30 students to each of 10 questions would be quite satisfactory.) The correlation between pairs of grades on individual questions would indicate the reliability of the grading procedure. Then the Spearman-Brown formula could be applied to estimate the reliability of grading for the test as a whole (see Chapter 15).

SUMMARY

The main conclusions to be drawn from the ideas presented in this chapter are summarized in the following propositions:

1. The popularity of essay tests is due partly to their convenience in preparation, the security they provide the examiner, and the control they afford of the score distribution.
2. Essay questions are less vulnerable to examinee criticism than are objective questions.
3. The examiner can control the distribution of test scores more easily with essay than with objective tests.
4. An essay test may permit the examiner to assess the examinee's thought processes.
5. Essay tests usually do not provide valid measures of complex mental processes such as critical thinking, originality, or ability to organize and integrate.
6. It is unlikely that students study more effectively in preparation for an essay test than for an objective test.
7. The emphasis essay tests place on the ability to write is both advantageous and disadvantageous.
8. Essay testing is vulnerable to student bluffing, but the actual harm this can do is likely to be small.
9. Essay scores tend to be low in reliability because of limited content sampling, indefinite test tasks, and subjective scoring.
10. Essay scores must possess significant objective meaning to be useful.
11. Essay tests can be efficient when the group to be tested is small.
12. Good essay questions require the examinee to demonstrate command of essential knowledge.
13. Essay-score reliability can be enhanced by making the questions specific enough so that all good answers will be nearly identical.

14. Reliability also can be enhanced by using more questions that call for short answers than by using fewer questions that require long answers.
15. Optional questions should be avoided in essay testing.
16. Advance preparation of an ideal essay-question answer facilitates reliable scoring and permits a test of the quality of the question prior to its use.
17. The reliability of scoring essay responses can be improved by scoring them question by question, by concealing the name of the examinee, and by arranging for several independent scorings.

PROJECTS AND PROBLEMS

Problem: Grading Essay-Test Answers

This activity is based on the essay-test question, the model answer to that question, and five student answers to the question. Your task is to assign a numerical grade to each student answer, using the scale of grades defined below:

9. Much better than the model
8. Slightly better than the model
7. As good as the model
6. Not quite as good as the model
5. A little more than half as good as the model
4. Half as good as the model
3. Not quite half as good as the model
2. Only slightly correct or relevant
1. Totally incorrect or irrelevant

Make an initial grade decision, paying attention only to the completeness and correctness of the statements made and the absence of irrelevant statements. Write a brief statement explaining the grades you give to each answer. Do not confer with any other student in this class in deciding on these grades. Do not change your grade if you discover that others disagree with you.

A committee will collate the grades and report the distribution of grades assigned to each question. Results may be discussed in class.

A. *The Question:*
Identify and comment on the misconceptions (there are at least five) that surround the problem of guessing on objective tests.

B. *Model Answer:*
A number of misconceptions surround the problem of guessing on objective tests. One is that students are likely to do extensive blind guessing on objective tests. The fact is that well-motivated students taking an examination that is appropriate for them do relatively little blind guessing. Another is that students who guess may, if they are lucky, make a high score on an objective test by blind guessing alone. The fact is that the odds against a high score on a reasonably long objective test are astronomical.

A third misconception is that if an objective-test score is corrected for guessing, the effect of luck in guessing is removed or neutralized. The fact is that a correction for guessing hurts the lucky guesser far less than it hurts the unlucky guesser. Another misconception is that students should avoid guessing if the score is to be corrected for guessing. Actually they have the best chance of making a high score by offering an answer to every question, even when the correction is to be applied. Usually an answer will be better than a blind guess. Even if it is not, the penalty is not likely to hurt more than an omission would.

Finally there is the common misconception that guessing involves an element of cheating, with the students trying to get credit for answers they are not sure of. But since the purpose of the test is to measure amount of knowledge, students ought to use all of it they possess to give the best answers they can, even if they are quite uncertain of the correctness of some of them.

C. *Student Answers:*

1. There are many misconceptions that surround the problem of guessing on objective tests. It is some of these misconceptions that will be discussed in this paper.

    One common misconception that surrounds guessing on objective tests is that guessing is not helpful to maintaining a higher grade. We can see that this is truly a misconception because any answer is better than none and the guessed answer could be a right answer.

    Another misconception in this same idea is the view that correction for guessing makes a difference in the score. This is not true because the score is usually the same.

    Another is the psychological advantage.

2. First, the chances of doing well on a test by blindly guessing alone are very slim, contrary to popular belief. Second, very few guesses are really blind guesses. Uncertainty may exist but some basis exists for the choice. Third, it is not undesirable to encourage students to make educated guesses. Life is full of uncertainties we must learn to cope with. We must often make decisions before all the needed information is available. Fourth, tests corrected for guessing yield results almost identical to those not corrected. Why waste valuable time, unless it be for public relations purposes? Fifth, objective tests are no more subject to "guessing" than are essay tests to "bluffing." Sixth, the better students receive the higher grades regardless of whether the test is corrected for guessing or not.

3. Testwiseness is one problem surrounding guessing on objective tests. Students who know "how" to take a test can do well even when they aren't familiar with the material being tested if the questions contain specific determiners which give away the answer.

    Rote learning also promotes guessing on exams when application of knowledge is required.

4. One misconception surrounding the problem of guessing on objective tests is that students really do guess blindly. If a student has any information at all about the subject matter, he is not really guessing blindly; he only does that if he marks answers without any regard to the question.

    A second misconception is that guessing (with some information for background) is harmful. A student will often have to make decisions in life on things of which he is not certain. He will often have to use whatever resources he has available to make choices. This is not a harmful thing.

    A third misconception is that one can get a high score by guessing blindly. The longer the test, the smaller the probability that the student will get a high score by true blind guessing.

    A fourth misconception is that a guessing correction really corrects for guessing. When the formula $R - [W/(k - 1)]$ is used, subtractions are being made for all the questions a student missed, even if he was positive the answer was right; in other words, even though the answer was not a guess.

    A fifth misconception is that guessing is a large problem in objective tests, making luck more important than knowledge. A student with even a moderate command of the material has a better chance on the questions he must guess on because he is not guessing blindly.

    Guessing does not seem to have much of an effect on the reliability of objective-test scores.

5. The first misconception surrounding the problem of guessing on objective tests

deals with a false assumption. Critics suggest that a correction for guessing assumes that incorrectly answered questions are guessed at blindly by the examinee; this not only is incorrect but it also has no relevance in the use of correction for guessing.

The second misconception deals with the correction for guessing. It is assumed (and sometimes so because of false representation) that guessing on a test—or at least its effects—is eliminated by this correction. Again–not true. Corrected and uncorrected tests correlate highly.

The third misconception assumes that if corrected and uncorrected tests correlate highly, then correction for guessing does no good. Perhaps that is so with the correction per se but it has been shown that by telling a class a test will be corrected for guessing (but not necessarily doing this correction) the reliability of the test scores increased. In this sense some good has been done.

The fourth misconception deals with testwiseness. It is assumed that two people knowing absolutely nothing about a subject should both perform at about a chance level. However, a testwise student can pick out specific determiners and irrelevant clues and quite possibly function above the chance level.

The fifth (but not necessarily the last) misconception is that students should never just guess—because it is immoral, or lying, or misrepresentation, etc. Not true! A student might make a good guess based on his basic understanding of the material and justly score better. Actually, not guessing would probably give a less accurate measure of his ability.

9

TRUE-FALSE TEST ITEMS

From one point of view true-false tests seem like a breeze, easier than they ought to be. From another, as many students would testify, they seem unnecessarily difficult, irrelevant, and frustrating. Some would say there are better ways of measuring achievement than by using true-false items. Yet this lack of endorsement is not universally shared among educators. A few, including the authors of this book, regard true-false items much more favorably (Ebel, 1975; Frisbie, 1973).

THE VALUE OF TRUE-FALSE ITEMS

The basic reason for using true-false test items is that they provide a simple and direct means of measuring the essential outcome of formal education. The argument for the value of true-false items as measures of educational achievement can be summarized in four statements:

1. The essence of educational achievement is the command of useful verbal knowledge.
2. All verbal knowledge can be expressed in propositions.
3. A proposition is any sentence that can be said to be true or false.
4. The extent of students' command of a particular area of knowledge is indicated by their success in judging the truth or falsity of propositions related to it.

The rationale supporting the first statement was provided in Chapter 3. The second is almost self-evident. Is it possible to imagine an element of verbal knowledge that could not be expressed as a proposition? The third is a generally accepted definition. The fourth seems to be a logical consequence of the first three. It may, of course, be challenged on the basis of technical weaknesses in true-false items, but it is not likely to be rejected in principle.

To test a person's command of an idea or element of knowledge is to test his or her understanding of it. A student who can recognize an idea only when it is expressed in some particular set of words does not have command of it. Neither does the student who knows the idea only as an isolated fact, without seeing how it is related to other ideas. Knowledge one has command of is not a miscellaneous collection of separate elements, but an integrated structure that one can use to make decisions, draw logical inferences, or solve problems. It is usable knowledge.

Consider how one might test a student's command of Archimedes' principle. Clearly, to offer the student the usual expression of the principle as a true statement, or some slight alteration of it as a false statement, as has been done in items 1 and 2, is to misunderstand the true nature of knowledge.

(1) **A body immersed in a fluid is buoyed up by a force equal to the weight of the fluid displaced. (T)**
(2) **A body immersed in a fluid is buoyed up by a force equal to half the weight of the fluid displaced. (F)**

Instead the student might be asked to recognize the principle in some alternative statement of it, as in items 3 and 4 below.

(3) **If an object having a certain volume is surrounded by a liquid or gas, the upward force on it equals the weight of that volume of the liquid or gas. (T)**
(4) **The upward force on an object surrounded by a liquid or gas is equal to the surface area of the object multiplied by the pressure of the liquid or gas surrounding it. (F)**

Or the student might be required to apply the principle in specific situations such as those described in items 5 and 6 below.

(5) **The buoyant force on a one-centimeter cube of aluminum is exactly the same as that on a one-centimeter cube of iron when both are immersed in water. (T)**
(6) **If an insoluble object is immersed successively in several fluids of different density, the buoyant force upon it in each case will vary inversely with the density of the fluids. (F)**

Sometimes the use of an unconventional example can serve to test understanding of a concept.

(7) **Distilled water is soft water. (T)**

It is a popular misconception that true-false test items are limited to testing for simple factual recall. On the contrary, complex and difficult problems can be presented quite effectively in this form.

(8) **The next term in the series 3, 4, 7, 11, 18 is 29.   (T)**

(9) **If the sides of a quadrilateral having two adjacent right angles are consecutive whole numbers, and if the shortest side is one of the two parallel sides, then the area of the trapezoid is 18 square units.   (T)**

The reason why true-false tests are often held in low esteem is not that there is anything inherently wrong with the item form. It is rather that the form is often used ineptly by unskilled item writers. It has also been alleged that true-false tests are especially susceptible to guessing and that they have harmful effects on student learning, beliefs that have not been checked against experimental data. These alleged weaknesses of true-false items will be dealt with more fully later in the chapter.

The Efficiency of True-False Items

In addition to providing relevant measures of the essence of educational achievement, true-false test items have the advantage of being quite efficient. The number of independently scorable responses per thousand words of test or per hour of testing time tends to be considerably higher than that for multiple-choice items. Research evidence has shown that students can attempt three true-false items in the time required to attempt a pair of multiple-choice items (Frisbie, 1973, 1974). Offsetting this advantage in efficiency is a disadvantage in item discriminating power. Item-for-item true-false tend to discriminate less well between high- and low-achieving students than multiple-choice (Ebel, 1980). In sum, a good one-hour true-false test is likely to be as effective as a good one-hour multiple-choice test.

Compared with other item forms, true-false test items are relatively easy to write. They are simple declarative sentences of the kind that make up most oral and written communications. It is true that the ideas they affirm or deny must be judiciously chosen. It is also true that the ideas chosen must be worded carefully, with a view to maximum precision and clarity, since they stand and must be judged in isolation. For this reason they must be self-contained in meaning, depending wholly on internal content, not on external context. But the basic skill involved in true-false item writing is no different from that required in any written communication situation. Those who have difficulty in writing good true-false test items probably have trouble expressing themselves clearly and accurately in writing.

Comparison of True-False and Multiple-Choice Items

An obvious difference between true-false and multiple-choice items is in the number of alternatives generally offered to the examinee. Another difference is in the definiteness or specificity of the task presented. It may be more difficult to judge whether a statement should be called true or false than to judge which of several alternatives is the best answer to a particular question. For example, students who mark a statement true may not be able to think of a counterexample—a situation or occurrence that would make the proposition false. Their search for a counterexample may be bounded by time limits or by the length to which they can stretch their mind or the depth of their retrieval system to which they can penetrate. The multiple-choice item, however, limits the universe of comparisons that the individual must make. Aside from all these differences, there are substantial similarities between the two item types.

Implicit in most multiple-choice test items are one true statement and several false statements. Like true-false items, multiple-choice items also test knowledge and are based on propositions. When expertly written multiple-choice items are converted to true-false items, and both forms are administered to the same large group of examinees, the scores obtained correlate about as closely as their reliabilities allow (Frisbie, 1973). Figure 9-1 displays items testing essentially the same propositions in both multiple-choice and true-false form.

While most multiple-choice test items are based on propositions, a few, like the example which follows, are not.

Which of the following sentences is stated most emphatically?
a. If my understanding of the question is correct, this principle is one we cannot afford to accept.
b. One principle we cannot afford to accept is this one, if my understanding of the question is correct.
c. This principle, if my understanding of the question is correct, is one we cannot afford to accept.
d. This principle is one we cannot afford to accept, if my understanding of the question is correct.

Items of this kind, which involve some degree of personal judgment, are not derived directly from propositions and cannot easily be converted to true-false form.

There are also questions which are much easier to present as true-false than as multiple-choice items, because only two answers are plausible. For example, when one wishes to ask whether two variables are related, or about the effect of increasing one variable on the size of the other, it is almost impossible to find more than two reasonable alternatives. Here are some examples.

(1) Changing the temperature of a mass of air will change its relative humidity. **(T)**
(2) More amendments were added to the U.S. Constitution during the first ten years after ratification than during the next one hundred years. **(T)**
(3) An eclipse of the sun can occur only when the moon is full. **(F)**
(4) Increasing the length of a test is likely to decrease its standard error of measurement. **(F)**

Commitment to the multiple-choice item form has led some item writers to present what is essentially a collection of true-false statements as a multiple-choice item. Figure 9-2 provides some examples. Though research findings on

Figure 9-1 Corresponding Multiple-Choice and True-False Test Items.

Multiple-Choice Version	*True-False Version*
(1) James wants to put a fence around a garden that is 60 feet long and 45 feet wide. How many feet of fencing will he need? *a.* 90 feet *c.* 120 feet *b.* 105 feet **d.* 210 feet	(1*a*) It will take 105 feet of fencing to put a fence around a garden that is 60 feet long and 45 feet wide. (F) (1*b*) It will take 210 feet of fencing to put a fence around a garden that is 60 feet long and 45 feet wide. (T)
(2) The equation $X^2 + Y^2 = 4$ is represented graphically by **a.* a circle. *b.* an ellipse. *c.* a parabola with its base on the *X*-axis.	(2*a*) The graph of $X^2 + Y^2 = 4$ is a circle. (T) (2*b*) The graph of $X^2 + Y^2 = 9$ is an ellipse. (F) (2*c*) The graph of $X^2 + Y^2 = 1$ is a parabola with its base on the *Y*-axis. (F)
(3) How can one generate enough electric current to light a flashlight bulb? *a.* By rubbing two good conductors of electricity together *b.* By dipping two strips of zinc in dilute sulphuric acid *c.* By connecting the north pole of a magnet to the south pole, using a coil of wire **d.* By rotating a coil of wire rapidly near a strong magnet	(3*a*) One can generate enough electric current to light a flashlight bulb by dipping two strips of zinc in dilute sulphuric acid. (F) (3*b*) One can generate enough electric current to light a flashlight bulb by rotating a coil of wire rapidly near a strong magnet. (T)
(4) What does religious tolerance mean? *a.* Admitting everyone to the same church *b.* Accepting religious teachings on faith *c.* Altering religious belief so that it does not conflict with science **d.* Allowing people to believe what they wish	(4*a*) Religious tolerance means admitting everyone to the same church. (F) (4*b*) Religious tolerance means allowing people to believe what they wish. (T) (4*c*) Religious tolerance means altering religious beliefs so that they do not conflict with science. (F)

this question are mixed (Ebel, 1978a; Hsu, 1979), logic suggests that more reliable measures of achievement can be obtained from independently scored true-false items than from multiple-choice items formed by grouping one true statement with three that are false or by grouping one that is false with three that are true.

COMMON MISCONCEPTIONS ABOUT TRUE-FALSE ITEMS

Attitudes unfavorable to true-false items seem to have arisen mainly from disappointing personal experiences and from hearsay. There have been few

Figure 9-2   Items Better Suited to True-False Than to Multiple-Choice Form.

Multiple-Choice Version	*True-False Version*	
(1) **Which of these is *not* characteristic of a virus?**		
a. It can live only in plant and animal cells.	(1*a*) A virus can live only in plant and animal cells.	**(T)**
b. It can reproduce itself.	(1*b*) A virus can reproduce itself.	**(T)**
c. It is composed of very large living cells.	(1*c*) A virus is composed of very large living cells.	**(F)**
d. It can cause disease.	(1*d*) A virus can cause disease.	**(T)**
(2) **Given $\triangle PQR$ with median *RS*. Which of the following must be true?**		
a. *RS* is perpendicular to *PQ*.	(2*a*) The median of a triangle is perpendicular to the side it intersects.	**(F)**
b. *RS* bisects $\angle QRP$.	(2*b*) The median of a triangle bisects the angle from which it is drawn.	**(F)**
c. $\triangle PQR$ is a right triangle.	(2*c*) A triangle with a median is a right triangle.	**(F)**
d. None of the above.	(2*d*) The median of a triangle divides it into two triangles of equal area.	**(T)**

careful empirical studies of the charges most often brought against them. An analysis of some of the most frequently heard indictments follows.

The Impact of Guessing

A charge against true-false tests that many take quite seriously is that they are subject to gross error introduced by guessing. Several things can be said in response to this charge.

The first is that a distinction needs to be made between blind guessing and informed guessing. Blind guessing adds nothing but error to the test scores. Informed guesses, on the other hand, provide valid indications of achievement. The more a student knows, the more likely that informed guesses will be correct.

The second is that well-motivated students, taking a test of appropriate difficulty with a generous time limit, are likely to do very little blind guessing on true-false tests. They know that thinking is a surer basis than guessing for determining the correct answer. In one study, college students reported an average of only one response in 20 that was equivalent, in their opinion, to a blind guess (Ebel, 1968b). Hills and Gladney (1968) have shown that scores in the chance range are not significantly different from above-chance scores as predictors of college grades. This suggests that scores in the chance range were not in fact the results of pure chance (blind guessing).

The third is that the influence of blind guessing on the scores of a test diminishes as the test increases in length. On a one-item true-false test a student has a 50 percent chance (1 in 2) of getting a perfect score by blind guessing, but on a two-item test it drops to 25 percent, on a five-item test to 3 percent, and on a ten-item test to 0.1 percent. On a 100-item test it becomes less than one chance in a million trillion trillion! The chance of getting even a moderately good score, say 70, on a 100-item true-false test by blind guessing alone is less than one in 1000.

The fourth and most significant response that can be made to this charge is that reliable scores could not be obtained from true-false tests if they were seriously affected by blind guessing. But in fact true-false classroom tests of 100 items have shown reliability coefficients of 0.85 to 0.95. These values are about as high as can be expected for any classroom test, regardless of the form of test item used. They support the conclusion that good true-false tests need not be vitiated by guessing.

Some persons who are somewhat familiar with objective testing believe that the problem of guessing can best be dealt with by "correcting the scores for guessing." This is a misconception. The announcement that test scores will be corrected for guessing may deter *some* students from guessing, but it only magnifies the differences between the scores of lucky and unlucky guessers. In fact, its effect on the validity of the test scores is negligible. If guessing on a true-false test were to be extensive enough to affect the test scores seriously, there is almost nothing that a guessing correction could do to improve the accuracy of the scores.

A Reward for Rote Learning

One of the common criticisms of true-false test items is that they are limited to testing for specific, often trivial, factual details. As a result, the critics say, students are encouraged and rewarded for rote learning of bits of factual information rather than for critical thinking and understanding. In support of this criticism, items like these are cited as typical of true-false tests:

The author of Don Quixote was Cervantes. (T)
The chemical formula for water is H_2O. (T)
The Battle of Hastings was fought in 1066. (T)
Christopher Columbus was born in Spain. (F)
There are six planets in the solar system. (F)

If these were indeed the only kinds of questions that could be asked in true-false form, it would surely be of limited value. However, it is possible to ask questions that not only test students' comprehension of broader principles but also their ability to apply them. For example, one can test understanding of an event or of a process:

King John of England considered the Magna Carta one of his great achievements. (F)
In the laboratory preparation of carbon dioxide one of the essential ingredients is limewater. (F)

One can test knowledge of a functional relationship:

The more widely the items in a test vary in difficulty, the narrower the range of test scores. (T)

If heat is supplied at a constant rate to melt and vaporize a substance, the temperature of the substance will increase at a constant rate also. (F)

One can test the ability to apply principles:

It is easier for a poor student to get a good score (80 percent correct) on a true-false test if the test includes only 50 items than if it includes 100 items. (T)

If an electric refrigerator is operated in a sealed, insulated room with its door open, the temperature of the room will decrease. (F)

The time from moonrise to moonset is usually longer than the time from sunrise to sunset. (T)

The Ambiguity Charge

A third major criticism of true-false test items is that they are frequently ambiguous. Although some do indeed succumb to this charge, ambiguity is not an inherent weakness of the true-false item—especially if the ideas for the items are carefully chosen and if the items themselves are carefully worded. Further, we must make a distinction between intrinsic ambiguity and apparent ambiguity. Students who say, "If I interpret the statement this way, I'd say it is true. But if I interpret it that way, I'd have to say it is false," are complaining about apparent ambiguity. If experts in the field have the same difficulty in interpreting a particular statement, the trouble may be intrinsic ambiguity.

Apparent ambiguity may sometimes be due to inadequacies in the students' knowledge. They have trouble interpreting a statement because the words mean something a little different to them than to the expert, or because the statement fails to evoke the necessary associations that would yield the intended interpretation.

Hence apparent ambiguity is not only unavoidable, it may even be useful. By making the task of responding harder for the poorly prepared than for the well-prepared student, it can help to discriminate between the two. Thus a student's comment that a test question is unclear is not necessarily an indictment of the question. It may be, rather, an unintentional confession of his or her own shortcomings.

Intrinsic ambiguity, on the other hand, the kind of ambiguity that troubles the expert as much as or more than it troubles the novice, is a real concern. It probably can never be totally eliminated, since language is inherently somewhat abstract, general, and imprecise. But in the statements used in true-false test items it should be minimized.

Of course, there is sometimes truth in the charge that true-false test items are ambiguous and lack significance: one reason is that teachers sometimes try to excerpt textbook sentences for use as test items. Even in a well-written text, few of the sentences would actually make good true-false test items. Many statements serve only to keep readers informed of what the author is trying to do or to remind them of the structure and organization of the discussion. Some are so dependent for their meaning on sentences that precede or follow them that they are almost meaningless out of context. Others are intended only to suggest an idea, not to state it positively and precisely. Still others comprise a whole logical argument, involving two or three propositions, in a single sentence. Another category of statements is intended not to describe what is true, but to prescribe what ought to be true. Finally, some are expressed so loosely and so tentatively that there is hardly any possible basis for doubting them. In all the writing we do to preserve the knowledge we have gained and to communicate it to others there seem to be very few naturally occurring nuggets of established knowledge.

For this reason it is seldom possible to find in a text or reference work a sentence that can be copied directly for use as a true statement or transformed by a simple negation for use as a false statement. The writing of good true-false items is more a task of creative writing than of copying. This may be a fortunate circumstance, for it helps test constructors avoid the hazard of writing items that would encourage and reward rote learning.

A special source of ambiguity in true-false test items needs to be guarded against. It is uncertainty on the part of the examinee as to the examiner's standards of truth. If the statement is not perfectly true, if it has the slightest flaw, should it be considered false? Probably not; the item writer's task will be easier, and the test will be better, if she/he directs the examinee to consider as true any statement that has more truth than error in it, or any statement that is more true than its contradiction would be. The test builder's task then is to avoid writing statements that fall in the twilight zone between truth and falsehood.

Of course, even the most competent and careful item writer may unintentionally include a few intrinsically ambiguous items. Such items are usually quite easy to identify after the test has been given. The better students who miss these items will call attention to their ambiguity. If the test is analyzed, the ambiguous items are likely to show low discrimination or high difficulty. Post mortems such as this do nothing to correct past failures, but they can help examiners identify items that need to be revised or discarded and make them more sensitive to avoidable sources of ambiguity.

The Effect on Learning

Critics of true-false tests sometimes charge that their use has harmful effects on learning: that they (1) encourage students to concentrate on remembering isolated factual details and to rely heavily on rote learning; (2) encourage students to accept grossly oversimplified conceptions of truth; and (3) expose students undesirably to error. Let us consider these charges.

True-false items need not emphasize memory for isolated factual details. Good ones present novel problems to be solved and thus emphasize understanding and application. Even those that might require recall of factual details do not necessarily reward rote learning, for facts are hard to remember in isolation. They are retained and can be recalled better if they are part of a structure of knowledge.

There is reason to believe that rote learning is something of an educational bogeyman, often warned against and cited as the cause of educational failure, but seldom practiced or observed. Rote learning is not much fun, and it promises few lasting rewards. Most students and teachers properly shun it. Perhaps its supposed prevalence results from an error in inference. It is surely true that rote learning always results in incomplete learning (that is, lack of understanding), but it does not follow that all incomplete learning is the result of too much rote learning. It may simply be the result of too little learning of any sort.

What of the second charge, that the categorical way in which answers are both offered and scored, is likely to give students a false notion about the simplicity of truth? Evidence in support of this argument is seldom presented, and the argument itself is seldom advanced by those who have used true-false tests extensively. Test writers know students will challenge answers that disagree with their own. Often they will point to the complexity of the entire subject and will insist that a case can be made for the alternative answer. Usually the author concedes that the statement in question is neither perfectly true nor totally false. The discussion that normally follows tends to emphasize, rather than to conceal, the complexity, the impurity, the relativity of truth. On occasion it leads to the conclusion that the item in question was simply a bad item, poorly conceived or carelessly stated.

Now consider the third charge, namely that true-false test items are educationally harmful because they expose the student to error. The argument is that the presentation of false statements as if they were true may have a negative suggestion effect, causing students to believe and remember untruths. However, Ruch (1929) tentatively concluded that the negative suggestion effect in true-false tests is probably much smaller than is sometimes assumed and is fully offset by the net positive teaching effects. Other experimental studies confirm this conclusion, and as Ross (1947) pointed out:

> Whether or not a false statement is dangerous depends largely upon the setting in which it appears. A false statement in the textbook, toward which the characteristic pupil attitude is likely to be one of passive, uncritical acceptance, might easily be serious. But the situation is different with the items in a true-false test. Here the habitual attitude of the modern pupil is one of active, critical challenge. (p. 349)

In light of these findings, we conclude that well-conceived and well-developed true-false test items can contribute substantially to the measurement of educational achievement. The harm some fear they might do is trivial in comparison.

GUIDELINES FOR PREPARING TRUE-FALSE ITEMS

There are five general requirements for a good true-false test item.

1. It should test the examinee's knowledge of an important proposition, one that is likely to be significant and useful in coping with a variety of situations and problems. It should say something worth saying.
2. It should require understanding as well as memory. Simple recall of meaningless words, empty phrases, or sentences learned by rote should not be enough to permit a correct answer.
3. The intended correct answer (true or false) should be easy for the item writer to defend to the satisfaction of competent critics. The true statements should be true enough and the false statements false enough so that an expert would have no difficulty distinguishing between them. Any explanation or qualification needed to justify an unconditional answer should be included in the item.
4. On the other hand, the intended correct answer should be obvious only to those who have good command of the knowledge being tested. It should not be a matter of common knowledge. It should not be given away by an unintended clue. The wrong answer should be made attractive to those who lack the desired command.
5. The item should be expressed as simply, as concisely, and above all as clearly as is consistent with the preceding four requirements. It should be based on a single proposition. Common words should be given preference over technical terms. Sentences should be short and simple in structure. Essentially true statements should not be made false by simply inserting the word *not*.

Here are some pairs of true-false test items that illustrate these requirements. The first of each pair is an acceptable item, while the second is poor.

1. The item tests an important idea.

(1) **President Kennedy attempted to solve the missile crisis by threatening a blockade of Cuba. (T)**
(2) **President Kennedy was 12 years older than his wife. (T)**

The difference in the ages between President Kennedy and his wife might be a subject for comment in a casual conversation, but it has little to do with the important events of the time. The Cuban missile crisis, on the other hand, brought the United States and Russia to the brink of war. How this crisis was handled is a far more important element in world history than a difference in ages between a president and his wife.

(3) **Words like *some, usually, all,* or *never* should be avoided in writing true-false test items. (F)**
(4) **Two pitfalls should be avoided in writing true-false test items. (F)**

Item 4 is the type of textbook sentence that sets the stage for an important pronouncement—but fails to make it. Item 3, on the other hand, tests the examinee's understanding of several important principles. Specific determiners like *some* and *usually* provide irrelevant clues only when used in true statements. If used in false statements they tend to attract wrong answers from the ill-prepared student. Conversely, specific determiners like *all* or *never* should be avoided in false statements, but are useful in attracting wrong answers from the uninformed when used in true statements.

(5) **More salt can be dissolved in a pint of warm water than in a pint of cold water. (T)**
(6) **Some things dissolve in other things. (T)**

A statement like that in item 6 is too general to say anything useful. Item 5, on the other hand, provides a test of the understanding of an important relationship.

2. The item tests understanding. It does not reward recall of a stereotyped phraseology.

(7) **When a hand pushes a door with a certain force, the door pushes back on the hand with the same force. (T)**
(8) **For every action there is an equal and opposite reaction. (T)**
(9) **If the hypotenuse of an isosceles right triangle is seven inches long, each of the two equal legs must be more than five inches long. (F)**
(10) **The square of the hypotenuse of a right triangle equals the sum of the squares of the other two sides. (T)**

Both items 8 and 10 are word-for-word statements of important principles that could be learned by rote. To test a student's understanding it is desirable to present specific applications that avoid the stereotyped phrases, as has been done in items 7 and 9.

3. The correct answer to an item is defensible.

(11) **Moist air is less dense than dry air. (T)**
(12) **Rain clouds are light in weight. (T)**

Since a rain cloud seems to float in the air, it might reasonably be called light in weight. On the other hand, a single rain cloud may weigh more than 100,000 tons. One cubic foot of the cloud probably weighs about the same as a cubic foot of air. Since the cloud contains droplets of water, it could conceivably weigh more per cubic foot than cloudless dry air. On the other hand, moist air alone (item 11) weighs less per cubic foot than does dry air. Should the item also specify "other things being equal," for example, pressure and temperature? It might, but in the absence of mention, a reasonable person is justified in assuming that temperature and pressure should not be taken to be variable factors in this situation.

(13) The proposal that salary schedules for teachers ought to include skill in teaching as one of the determining variables is supported more strongly by teachers' organizations than it is by taxpayers. (F)

(14) Merit is an important factor affecting a teacher's salary. (F)

The first version is much more specific, and much more clearly false than the second. Experts could agree on the answer to the first, but would be troubled by the intrinsic ambiguity of the second. Across the country it is no doubt true that the salaries of good teachers are higher than those of poor teachers. However, it is also true that the salary schedules of many school systems do not include merit as one of the determining factors.

(15) The twinkling of starlight is due to motion in the earth's atmosphere. (T)

(16) Stars send out light that twinkles. (T)

The answer to the second, unacceptable version of this item could be challenged by a reasonable, well-informed person on the following grounds. It is not the light sent out by the star that twinkles—that light is relatively steady. But, owing to disturbances in our atmosphere, the light that reaches our eyes from the star often appears to twinkle. That the second version is unacceptable is due either to the limited knowledge or to the carelessness in expression of the person who wrote it.

4. The answer to a good test item is not obvious to anyone. It tests special knowledge.

A. It is not self-evident.

(17) Frozen foods are usually cheaper than canned foods. (F)

(18) Frozen foods of the highest quality may be ruined in the kitchen. (T)

(19) Most local insurance agencies are owned and controlled by one of the major national insurance companies. (F)

(20) Insurance agencies may be either general or specialized. (T)

Who could doubt the possibility of cooking any kind of food badly? How plausible is the belief that only general or only specialized insurance agencies could be found? The unacceptable versions, items 18 and 20, are too obviously true to discriminate high achievement from low. Both read like introductory sentences lifted from a textbook, sentences that set the stage for an important idea but do not themselves express important ideas.

B. To one who lacks the knowledge being tested, a wrong answer should appear more plausible than the correct one.

(21) **By adding more solute, a saturated solution can be made supersaturated. (F)**
(22) **A supersaturated solution contains more solute per unit than a saturated solution. (T)**

It appears reasonable to believe that adding more solute would turn a saturated solution into a supersaturated solution (item 21). But those who understand solutions know that it doesn't work that way. The added solute won't dissolve in a saturated solution. Only by evaporating some of the solvent, or cooling it, can a saturated solution be made supersaturated. The student who tries to use common sense as a substitute for special knowledge is likely to give a wrong answer (which is all his knowledge entitles him to) to the first item. But the same common sense leads the student of low achievement to answer item 22 correctly. Thus the second version fails to function properly as a test of the student's command of knowledge.

5. The item is expressed clearly.

A. It is based on a single idea.

(23) **The salt dissolved in water can be recovered by evaporation of the solvent. (T)**
(24) **Salt can be dissolved in water and can be recovered by evaporation of the solvent. (T)[1]**
(25) **At conception the sex ratio is approximately 3 boys to 2 girls. (T)**
(26) **Scientists have found that male-producing sperm are stronger and live longer than female-producing sperm, which accounts for the sex ratio at conception of approximately 3 boys to 2 girls. (T)**

An item based on a single idea is usually easier to understand than one based on two or more ideas. It is also more efficient. One can obtain a more accurate measurement of a student's achievement by testing separate ideas separately than by lumping them together and scoring one composite answer right or wrong.

(27) **Individuals who deliberate before making choices seldom find themselves forced to sacrifice one good thing in order to attain another. (F)**
(28) **Life is a continuous process of choice making, sacrificing one human value for another, which goes through the following steps: spontaneous mental selections regarding everything we want, conflicting preferences hold each other in check, hesitation becomes deliberation as we weigh and compare values, finally choice or preference emerges. (T)**

The strong inclination of some teachers to use their tests as opportunities for teaching, or their misguided attempts to use textbook sentences as test items, may account for the appearance of such items as number 28. But if one looks for the central idea in item 28, and asks what misapprehension it might

---

[1] Another unacceptable version that inappropriately combines two ideas might be: Salt dissolves in hot water; sugar dissolves in cold water. (T)

serve to correct, an item like number 27 may emerge. Item 27 is simpler, clearer, and better in almost every way than item 28.

B. It is concise.

(29) **The federal government pays practically the entire cost of constructing and maintaining highways that are part of the interstate highway system. (F)**

(30) **When you see a highway with a marker that reads "Interstate 80," you know that the construction and upkeep of that road is built and maintained by the state and federal governments. (T)**

The wording of item 30 is careless and redundant. It is the *highway* that is built and maintained, not its construction and upkeep. The personal touch ("when you see") may give the appearance of practicality, but does not affect what the item really measures at all. Finally, making item 30 true by including state as well as federal governments as supporters of the interstate highway system probably makes the item easier for the uninformed. Item 29 hits the intended mark more clearly because it is more straightforward and concise.

C. It does not include an artificial, tricky negative.

(31) **Columbus made only four voyages of exploration to the Western Hemisphere. (T)**

(32) **Columbus did not make four voyages of exploration to the Western Hemisphere. (F)**

Some item writers try to turn textbook propositions into false statements for test items simply by inserting the word *not* in the original statement. The result is seldom good. The item usually carries the clear birthmark of its unnatural origin: It reads awkwardly and invites suspicion, which, if the item is indeed false, may give away the answer. Further, these items tend to be tricky. An unobtrusive "not" in an otherwise wholly true statement may be overlooked by even a well-prepared examinee. Such items put students at an unnecessary and undesirable disadvantage.

THE PROCESS OF DEVELOPING TRUE-FALSE ITEMS

The instructor who wishes to write a true-false item for a classroom test should begin by focusing attention on some segment of the knowledge that has been taught. It is assumed that the item writer is in firm command of that segment of knowledge and that it is something any capable student of the subject ought also to understand. This segment of knowledge is, or easily could be, described in a single paragraph such as those found in any good textbook adopted for the class. Accordingly, item writers usually find it easier and more effective to use instructional materials as the source of ideas for test items than to derive those ideas directly from educational objectives.

Suppose now that an item writer singles out a specific paragraph of text intended to help the student develop some segment of knowledge. Take, for example, this paragraph:

> Precise measurement requires careful control or standardization of the conditions surrounding it. Obviously, this control makes the behavior being measured artificial to some degree. Artificiality is a price that usually must be paid to achieve precision. It is a price that scientists and engineers, as well as psychologists and teachers, have usually found worth paying. For tests intended to measure typical behavior, such as personality, attitude, or interest tests, the price may sometimes be too high. That is, the behavior in the artificial test situation may be so poorly related to typical behavior in a natural situation that precise measurement of something hardly worth measuring is so much wasted effort. But for tests of educational aptitude or achievement, the gain in precision resulting from the controlled conditions that formal testing can afford usually far outweighs the slight loss in the relevance of artificial to natural behavior.

The first question the item writer must ask himself or herself is, "What are the most important ideas presented in this paragraph?" There are two possibilities:

1. The controls required for precise measurement make the behavior being measured somewhat artificial.
2. Artificiality is more harmful when personality is being measured than when achievement is being measured.

The next question is how these ideas can be expressed as true-false test items. At this point, a very important suggestion can be offered: *Always think of possible true-false test items in pairs, one true, the other false.* Of course, only one member of the pair is actually used in the test. However, unless a parallel but opposite statement can be made, the proposition is not likely to make a good true-false test item. Here are some item pairs derived from the ideas presented above.

1a. In measurements of behavior, precision and naturalness are directly related. **(F)**
1b. In measurements of behavior, precision and naturalness are inversely related. **(T)**

2a. To obtain precision in the measurement of behavior, naturalness must be preserved. **(F)**
2b. To obtain precision in the measurement of behavior, naturalness must be sacrificed. **(T)**

3a. The purpose of controls in the process of measuring behavior is to make the measurements more precise. **(T)**
3b. The purpose of controls in the process of measuring behavior is to make the behavior being measured more realistic. **(F)**

4a. In measurements of achievement it is desirable to emphasize precision at the expense of naturalness. **(T)**
4b. In measurements of achievement it is undesirable to emphasize precision at the expense of naturalness. **(F)**

4c. In measurements of personality it is desirable to emphasize precision at the expense of

esirable to emphasize precision at the expense

isely than to measure it naturally.   (T)
rally than to measure it precisely.   (F)
sely than to measure it naturally.   (F)
ally than to measure it precisely.   (T)

loped from the two basic ideas specified.
ed the basic ideas, is a reproduction of
ns are designed to test for understanding,
l or heard.
ustrate another trick that sometimes can
is to write statements that compare two
can focus attention on the central pre-
of using arbitrary standards in judging
ility that the examiner's standards might
examinee.
nt always to express an idea as accurately
of saying "a long test," say "a 100-item
moderate difficulty," say "an item that
the examinees answer correctly."

nation

scriminate between those who have and
ent of knowledge, regardless of the type
res. Those who have achieved command
correctly without difficulty. Those who
ractive. To produce items that will dis-
s of item writing. Here are some of the
uced.

tatements in the test. When in doubt,
han to challenge propositions presented
l to discriminate somewhat more sharply
ievement than do true statements. This
escent response set." In the absence of
ly to accept than to question a declarative
nust judge.
-false tests sometimes suggest including
ie statements. But if the false statements
would seem advantageous to include a
s many as 67 percent. Even if students

come to expect a greater number of false items, the technique still seems to work. In one of the author's classes students took a test on which two-thirds of the statements were false. After answering the questions and counting how many they had marked true, they were told the correct number of true statements and were given a chance to change any answers they wished. Most of them changed a number of answers, but they improved their scores very little, on the average. They changed about as many of their answers from right to wrong as from wrong to right.

2. Word the item so that superficial logic suggests a wrong answer.

(1) **A rubber ball weighing 100 grams is floating on the surface of a pool of water exactly half submerged. An additional downward force of 50 grams would be required to submerge it completely. (F)**

The ball is half submerged and weighs 100 grams, which gives one-half of 100 considerable plausibility on a superficial basis. The true case is, of course, that if its weight of 100 grams submerges only half of it, another 100 grams would be required to submerge all of it. Superficial logic also would make the incorrect answers to questions 2, 3, and 4 seem plausible.

(2) **Since students show a wide range of individual differences, the ideal measurement situation would be achieved if each student could take a different test specially designed to test him or her. (F)**

(3) **The output voltage of a transformer is determined in part by the number of turns on the input coil. (T)**

(4) **A transformer that will increase the voltage of an alternating current can also be used to increase the voltage of a direct current. (F)**

3. Make the wrong answer consistent with a popular misconception or a popular belief irrelevant to the question.

(5) **The effectiveness of tests as tools for measuring achievement is lowered by the apprehension students feel for them. (F)**

Many students do experience test anxiety, but for most of them it facilitates rather than impedes maximum performance.

(6) **An achievement test should include enough items to keep every student busy during the entire test period. (F)**

Keeping students busy at worthy educational tasks is usually commendable, but in this case it would make rate of work count too heavily as a determinant of the test score.

4. Use specific determiners in reverse to confound testwiseness. In true-false test items extreme words like *always* or *never* tend to be used mainly in

false statements by unwary item writers, whereas such modifiers as *some, often,* or *generally* tend to be used mainly in true statements. When they are so used they qualify as "specific determiners" that help testwise but uninformed examinees to answer true-false questions correctly. But some *always* or *never* statements are true and some *often* or *generally* statements are false. Thus these specific determiners can be used to attract the student who is merely testwise to a wrong answer.

(7)   **A 50-item test generally will be more reliable than a 75-item test.   (F)**

(8)   **In a positively skewed distribution the mean is always larger than the mode.   (T)**

(9)   **True statements usually are more discriminating than false statements.   (F)**

(10) **A correlation of +.28 is never considered to be higher than a correlation of −.49.   (T)**

5. Use phrases in false statements that give them the "ring of truth."

(11) **The use of better achievement tests will, in itself, contribute little or nothing to better achievement.   (F)**

The phrases "in itself" and "little or nothing" impart a tone of sincerity and rightness to the statement that conceals its falseness from the uninformed.

(12) **To ensure comprehensive measurement of each aspect of achievement, different kinds of items must be specifically written, in due proportions, to test each distinct mental process the course is intended to develop.   (F)**

As in questions 2, 3, and 4, superficial logic is predominant. But this item also displays the elaborate statement and careful qualifications that testwise individuals associate mainly with true statements.

Are teachers playing fair when they set out deliberately to make it easy for some students to give wrong answers to test items? We contend that if they want valid measures of achievement—that is, measures that correctly distinguish between those who have and those who lack command of a particular element of knowledge—it is the only way they can play fair. The only reason a test constructor sets out to make wrong answers attractive to those who lack command of the knowledge is so that correct answers will truly indicate the achievement they purport to measure.

SUMMARY

Some of the main ideas developed in this chapter are expressed in the following 21 statements:

1. True-false items provide a simple and direct means of measuring the essential outcomes of formal education.

2. The low esteem in which true-false tests are sometimes held is due to inept use, not to inherent limitations.

3. True-false items provide information on essential achievement more efficiently than most other item forms.

4. Most important aspects of achievement can be tested equally well with either true-false or multiple-choice items.

5. It is less efficient to group true-false statements to produce a multiple-choice item than to require separate responses to each of the true-false statements.

6. Informed guesses, as opposed to blind guesses, provide useful indications of achievement.

7. Students do very little blind guessing on good true-false tests.

8. The probability of an examinee achieving a high score on a true-false test by guessing blindly is extremely low.

9. True-false items can test students' comprehension of important ideas and their ability to use them in solving problems.

10. True-false items that appear ambiguous only to poorly prepared students are likely to be powerful discriminators.

11. Few textbook sentences are significant enough, and meaningful enough out of context, to be used as true statements in a true-false test.

12. Statements that are essentially (but not perfectly) true or essentially (but not totally) false can make good true-false items.

13. There are no firm empirical data to support the notions that true-false tests encourage rote learning, over-simplified conceptions of the truth, or the learning of false or incorrect ideas.

14. Good true-false items express single, not multiple, ideas.

15. Generally, a good false statement cannot be created by inserting a negative ("not") in a true statement.

16. Generally it is easier to develop test items from instructional materials than from statements of instructional objectives.

17. A useful strategy for developing true-false items is to create pairs of statements, one true and one false, based on a single idea.

18. Ambiguity in items can be minimized by writing statements that contain an internal comparison of alternatives.

19. False statements tend to be more highly discriminating than true statements.

20. Specific determiners can be used in ways that will hinder rather than help the poorly prepared, testwise examinee.

21. False statements can be made to seem plausible by using familiar terms and phrases in seemingly straightforward factual statements.

PROJECTS AND PROBLEMS

Project: Writing True-False Test Items

Using the information in the following paragraphs as directly and simply as possible, write ten pairs of parallel statements, one true and one false. Do not try to test for understanding of the information or for applications of it. For example, if the information given had been:

The highest mountain in the fifty states is Mt. McKinley. It is not Pike's Peak.

An appropriate pair of true-false items would be:

(T) The highest mountain in the fifty states is Mt. McKinley.
(F) The highest mountain in the fifty states is Pike's Peak.

Treat each of the ten paragraphs below in the same way. Place a (T) before the true statement and an (F) before the false statement.

1. Iron is an element. It is not a compound.
2. Ice is less dense than water. It is not more dense.
3. If two angles of a triangle are equal, it is isosceles. It is not equilateral.
4. The Panama Canal is controlled by the United States. It is not controlled by Panama.
5. One third times one third is one ninth. It is not one sixth.
6. The heart pumps blood into the arteries. It does not pump blood into the veins.
7. Words that name objects are nouns. They are not verbs.
8. The first ten amendments to the United States Constitution are known as the Bill of Rights. They are not known as the Articles of Confederation.

9. The best place to look for an account of the French Revolution would be an encyclopedia. It would not be a dictionary.

10. Temperatures change less from season to season on the equator than in the arctic. They do not change more on the equator.

Problem: Tryout of True-False Test Items

This assignment is based on 20 true-false test items that were intended to test for elements of knowledge that most college students are unlikely to have. Decide how you would answer each question and record your answers on a special answer sheet. Then your instructor will read or show you the ten paragraphs on which the questions were based. After you have heard or seen the background information you will be asked to respond again to the 20 questions. This time your answers may be recorded in spaces 21 to 40 on the special answer sheet.

A committee from the class or a test-scoring machine will determine the proportion of correct answers given to each question each time it was taken (that is, before and after "instruction"). The difference between *proportion correct after* and *proportion correct before* will indicate how effective the instruction was in giving information and how effective the item was in measuring it. These differences will be reported to you and will form the basis for a discussion of good and poor true-false test items.

1. Napoleon won most of his military campaigns.
2. Napoleon's downfall was his loss of the battle for Spain.
3. Six of the several known species of penguins are found on the Galapagos Islands near the equator.
4. Adult penguins have no natural enemies on the ice.
5. Sugar is often added to wine during fermentation to make it sweeter.
6. Most wines require fairly long aging periods before they reach the peak of their flavor.
7. Scientists have found that male sperm are stronger and live longer than female sperm; this accounts for the sex ratio of males to females—150 to 100.
8. Human population studies indicate that the general weakness of the male sperm accounts for the relationship of more birth defects, miscarriages, and death among males than females.
9. Infection was the major cause of death for soldiers in the Civil War.
10. Pneumonia was the most common illness suffered by soldiers in the Civil War.
11. After learning something, you forget more in the next few hours than in the next several days.
12. Lessons learned early in the morning are remembered better than those learned just before going to sleep.
13. In cases of severe shock, the victim's feet should be elevated.
14. Small amounts of an alcoholic beverage can be given to shock victims if they are conscious.
15. When selling a home, realtors must be aware of its individual "sex appeal" to the buyer.
16. A man considers price and location as the most important elements when purchasing a home.
17. Due to the many new techniques that have been developed by psychologists, mental illness is not considered to be one of our biggest problems today.
18. Some forms of mental illness can be inherited.
19. A recent survey indicates that many parents give stock to their children.
20. 6.5 percent of the stockholders in the United States are children.

10

MULTIPLE-CHOICE TEST ITEMS

THE STATUS OF MULTIPLE-CHOICE ITEMS

Multiple-choice test items are currently the most highly regarded and widely used form of objective-test item. They are adaptable to the measurement of most important educational outcomes: of knowledge, understanding, and judgment; of ability to solve problems, to recommend appropriate action, to make predictions. Almost any understanding or ability that can be tested by means of any other item form—short-answer, completion, true-false, matching, or essay—can also be tested by means of multiple-choice test items.

The form of the multiple-choice item, with the stem asking or implying a direct question, provides a realistic, naturally appropriate setting for testing student achievement. There tends to be less indirectness and artifice in multiple-choice than in some other item forms. Students often find multiple-choice questions less ambiguous than completion or true-false items. Instructors also find it easier to defend correct answers.

Finally, multiple-choice items seem to both instructors and students to be less susceptible to chance errors resulting from guessing than true-false items. It is easy to exaggerate the harm done by guessing, and to place too much emphasis on the need to limit the amount of guessing students do. Yet no matter how little harm is done by guessing, instructors and students still perceive that it is less detrimental in multiple-choice than in true-false tests.

Finally, two item forms that represent viable alternatives to the traditional multiple choice—alternate choice and multiple true-false—are described near the end of this chapter. Though neither type is regarded as a "more valid" item form than multiple choice, each does possess the potential for yielding more efficient and more reliable measures of achievement.

In spite of their virtues, multiple-choice test items have not escaped the attention of critics. Some of the criticisms reflect a general mistrust of all objective testing techniques. These critics allege that objective-test questions are inevitably superficial, ambiguous, and conducive to guessing. They say or imply that the only good way to test is the old way they prefer to use—namely, essay testing. Other critics find fault with specific test items, alleging that the questions are ambiguous, the correct answers incorrect, or the distracters as good as or better than the intended correct answer. In fact the public disclosure of both test items and their correct answers required by truth-in-testing legislation has facilitated the critics' campaign. The press has been quick to highlight the handful of cases in which ambiguous items have been detected on national scholastic aptitude tests used for making college admission decisions. That the number of such cases is trivial in relation to the number of test items that have been used since the legislation became effective is testimony to the high quality that examiners can achieve with multiple-choice test items.

Few objective tests or test items are so perfect as to be above reproach from a persistent, perceptive critic. But there are at least two weaknesses in the general indictments that have been issued against all multiple-choice tests and items. First, the criticisms are seldom supported by unbiased experimental data, despite the fact that relevant data would be fairly easy to obtain. Most of the flaws pointed out should lower the discriminating power of the items and the reliability of the test scores, yet by and large they fail to do so. In addition, some of the critics, instead of obtaining or even welcoming experimental evidence, tend to discredit statistical methods of testing the quality of items or tests, without suggesting any replacement procedure—other than their own intuitions (and occasionally those of a few friends) and what seems to them to be plain common sense.

In the second place, the critics seldom attempt seriously to make a good case for a better way of measuring educational achievement. Even the most ardent advocates of objective testing do not claim perfection. They acknowledge that multiple-choice test questions can be subject to serious flaws and that, in general, they are not as clearly meaningful and sharply discriminating as they should be. Users of objective tests agree wholly with the observation that the scores are not as reliable as they might be and ought to be for maximum value, but they are not likely to abandon multiple-choice testing until a substitute can be found whose shortcomings are less serious. The implied alternative, essay testing, is clearly much less convenient to use in many situations. In any case, advocates of objective testing are not likely to consider seriously any recommendations accompanied by expressions of disdain for experimental evidence.

The Process of Elimination

Students may sometimes arrive at the correct answer to a multiple-choice test item through a process of elimination. Rejecting responses that seem unsatisfactory, they are finally left with one termed the "right answer," not because they have any basis for choosing it directly, but simply because none of the others will do.

The availability of this process of elimination is sometimes regarded as a weakness of the multiple-choice item form. It is charged that students get credit for knowing something they really don't know. Most specialists in test construction, however, do not disapprove of the process of answering by elimination and do not regard it as a sign of weakness in multiple-choice items in general, or in an item where the process is particularly useful. (It might be noted in passing that an item that uses the response "none of the above" as a correct answer *requires* the student to answer by a process of elimination.) There are two reasons why this process is not generally deplored by test specialists.

In the first place, the function of achievement-test items is primarily to contribute to a measure of general achievement in an area of study. They are not intended primarily to provide an inventory of which particular bits of knowledge or skills a student has. The achievement of a student who answers items 1, 3, and 5 correctly but misses 2 and 4 is regarded as equal to the achievement of another student who answers items 2, 3, and 4 correctly but misses 1 and 5. Identifying exactly which things a student has achieved or failed to achieve is a matter of secondary importance in an achievement test.

In the second place, the knowledge and ability required to properly eliminate incorrect alternatives can be, and usually is, closely related to the knowledge or ability that would be required to select the correct alternative. If education does not consist in the accumulation of unrelated bits of information, if the development of a meaningful network of related facts and concepts is essential, then the fact that a student responds in a reflective, problem-solving manner, choosing the best answer by rational processes (including the process of elimination), should be applauded rather than deplored.

In practice, few multiple-choice test items are likely to be answered correctly merely by eliminating incorrect choices. Far more often the process of choice will involve comparative judgments of this alternative against that. It is unlikely that an examinee who is totally ignorant of the correct answer would have knowledge enough to eliminate with certainty the incorrect alternatives. This is especially likely to be true if the item is well enough constructed so that all the available alternatives, correct and incorrect, have some obvious basic similarity. For these reasons, it seems safe to conclude that the problem of answer choice by a process of distracter elimination need not be regarded as a serious one.

MULTIPLE-CHOICE VERSUS ESSAY ITEMS

It is sometimes suggested that objective tests are inevitably more superficial and less realistic tests of a student's knowledge than are essay tests. The reasoning is that in suggesting possible answers to the student the examiner has done the important part of the task. But most good objective-test items require the examinee to develop, by creative, original thought, the *basis* for choice among the alternatives. Good objective-test items do not permit correct response on the basis of simple recognition, sheer rote memory, or meaningless verbal association. Consider the nature of the thought processes involved in selecting an answer to this question:

A child buys jelly beans which the grocer picks up, without regard for color, from a tray containing a mixture of jelly beans of three different colors. What is the smallest number of jelly beans the child can buy and still be certain of getting at least four jelly beans of the same color?

The answers provided are 4, 7, 10, and 12.

Assume that examinees are seeing this particular problem for the first time, so that they cannot answer it successfully by simply repeating an answer someone else has given them. Assume, too, that problems of this kind are not of sufficient practical importance to have been made the subject of a special unit of study. These assumptions call attention to an important general principle of educational measurement. What a test item measures, that is, what a successful response to it indicates, cannot be determined on the basis of the item alone. Consideration must also be given to the examinee's previous experiences. These may differ significantly for different examinees. But in the case of the foregoing problem, the assumptions mentioned above may be quite reasonable.

How much different would the thought processes be, and how much more difficult would the problem be, if no answers were suggested and the task required production of the answer rather than selection? Producing an answer is not necessarily a more complex or difficult task, or one more indicative of achievement, than choosing the best of the available alternatives (Quellmalz et al., 1980).

Hogan's (1981) thorough review of the research involving comparisons between free-response and objective tests led him to these conclusions: "In most instances, free-response and choice-type measures are found to be equivalent or nearly equivalent, as defined by their intercorrelation, within the limits of their respective reliabilities. Further, the choice-type measure is nearly always more reliable than the free-response measure and is considerably easier to score." Patterson (1926) reached the same conclusion nearly 55 years earlier. But despite the overwhelming empirical support for Hogan's conclusions, many practitioners continue to ignore the research or persist in believing that in their own situation, the two must yield measures of quite different abilities.

An illustration of the use of essay and objective questions to test essentially the same educational achievement is given in Figures 10-1 and 10-2. These tests were devised for use in a dental prosthetics course. The instructor had always used essay questions but was interested in the greater reliability and ease in scoring that objective tests might afford. He was dubious, however, about the prospect of having to write a number of independent objective-test items relating to the same complex process without having one question give away the answer to another.

To explore this possibility, the professor of dentistry supplied an essay-test question and an ideal answer to it. This is displayed in Figure 10-1. Then

Figure 10-1 Essay-Test Question and Answer.

Q. Sometimes a bridge will not go in place properly when being tried in the mouth after being soldered. If the operator should consider it advisable or necessary to unsolder, reassemble, and resolder the bridge, describe how this should be done.

A. The operator should first determine which joint or joints are to be unsoldered. The parts of the bridge should never be separated with a saw or disc, as this leaves a wide space to be filled in with solder. Instead, the bridge should be held in a blow-torch flame in such a way that the flame is directed on the joint to be unsoldered. Only enough heat must be used to melt the solder, and care must be used not to melt or distort an abutment piece. When the parts of the bridge have been separated, they should be pickled in acid to clean them of oxide. It will be necessary to use a disc or stone to smooth and reduce the amount of solder at the joints before the bridge will go into place in the mouth. This must be done till all parts of the bridge can be reassembled in the mouth.
Place some Parr's flux wax on all contact points of the abutment pieces and pontics (this is done with the pieces outside the mouth), then place all pieces back in the mouth. The Parr's flux wax will hold the parts in place, and the wax is soft enough so the pontics can be moved around to a certain extent to get them in the right position. When positioned properly, the joints should be reinforced with sticky wax, which is hard and brittle and will hold the parts firmly together. Then to further reinforce and strengthen the bridge so the parts will not be disarranged while taking the impression, a short piece of wire about 16 gauge should be bent and placed along the buccal or labial surface of the bridge and the approximating teeth and held firmly in place with sticky wax. All this waxing must be done with the field perfectly dry because any moisture will positively prevent the wax from holding.
Then a small, shallow impression tray is selected, filled with a fast-setting impression plaster and a shallow occlusal impression (if for a posterior bridge) or lingual and incisal impression (if for an anterior bridge) is secured. The impression is removed from the mouth, the bridge also removed and reassembled in the impression, the joints filled with Parr's flux wax, the plaster impression given a coat of separating medium, and the exposed parts of the bridge covered with soldering investment. When the investment is set, the plaster impression is cut away and more soldering investment applied in the proper manner to provide for correct soldering. The case is now ready to be heated and soldered in the regular way.

Figure 10-2 Corresponding Multiple-Choice Items.

The following eight items deal with the problem of separating, reassembling, and resoldering a bridge that will not go into place properly after being soldered.

(1) Which joint or joints should be separated?
 a. The joint between pontics and smallest abutment piece
 b. Any single joint (the faulty joint must be located by trial and error)
 c. All that were originally soldered
 *d. Only the one or ones which appear responsible for the failure to fit

Note: Only one of the following two items should be used.

(2) Should the joints be separated using a saw or disc rather than heat?
 a. No, because the saw might damage the original castings
 *b. No, because the saw will leave too large a gap to be filled with solder
 c. Yes, because the use of heat might damage the original castings
 d. Yes, because the saw leaves a clean joint ready for resoldering

(3) Should the flame be concentrated on the joint to be unsoldered? Why?
 a. No, because the bridge may crack if heated unevenly
 b. No, because the abutments must be thoroughly heated before the solder will melt
 *c. Yes, to avoid damage to the other pieces
 d. Yes, to avoid delay in separation

(4) After the bridge has been separated what, if anything, needs to be done before reassembling it in the patient's mouth?
 *a. The pieces should be cleaned in acid, and the joints smoothed with a stone.
 b. The pieces should be cleaned in acid, but the joints should not be smoothed.
 c. The joints should be smoothed, but the pieces need not be cleaned in acid.
 d. Reassembling should begin as soon as the bridge has been separated.

(5) What is used initially to hold the pieces together on reassembly in the patient's mouth?
 a. Sticky wax
 *b. Parr's flux wax
 c. Impression plaster
 d. Soldering investment

(6) Which of the following materials—flux wax, sticky wax, metal wire, and soldering investment—are used to hold the pieces of the reassembled bridge in place prior to taking the impression?
 a. All of them
 b. All but metal wire
 *c. All but soldering investment
 d. Only flux wax and sticky wax

(7) What precaution is necessary in using sticky wax?
 a. It must not be allowed to touch gum tissues.
 b. It must be applied in separate thin layers to avoid cracking.
 c. The surface to which it is applied must be moist.
 *d. The surface to which it is applied must be dry.

(8) What function does the plaster impression have in the process of resoldering the bridge?
 *a. It holds the parts in place while soldering investment is applied.
 b. It holds the parts in place while they are being soldered.
 c. It permits the resoldered bridge to be checked before insertion in the patient's mouth.
 d. It has no function in resoldering the bridge.

a series of multiple-choice items was written on the basis of this essay-type answer. Eight of these are shown in Figure 10-2. Items 2 and 3 are interlocking items; that is, the question asked in item 3 gives some indication as to the best answer to item 2. Hence only one of the two items should be used in any one test.

THE CONTENT BASIS FOR CREATING MULTIPLE-CHOICE ITEMS

Like true-false items, multiple-choice items are developed most conveniently and appropriately on the basis of ideas expressed or implied in instructional materials. The same starting point can be used. In Chapter 9 a paragraph of test material was reproduced and these two ideas were inferred from it:

1. The controls required for precise measurement make the behavior being measured somewhat artificial.
2. Artificiality is more harmful when personality is being measured than when achievement is being measured.

To develop multiple-choice test items on the basis of ideas like these one must:

(a) formulate a question or an incomplete sentence that clearly implies a question (the stem of the item)
(b) provide a good answer to the question in a few well-chosen words
(c) produce several plausible but incorrect answers to the question, termed *distracters*.

Multiple-choice items 1 and 2 that follow were developed on the basis of the first idea from the excerpted paragraph, and items 3 and 4 on the basis of the second.

(1) **What is the relation between the naturalness of a test situation and the precision of the resulting measurement?**
   a. In general, the more natural the situation, the more precise the measurement.
   *b. In general, the more natural the situation, the less precise the measurement.
   c. The nature of the relation depends on the type of trait being measured.
   d. The nature of the relation depends on the type of items used to make the measurement.

(2) **Is it possible to measure natural behavior precisely? Explain.**
   a. No. Natural behavior can be observed, but it cannot be measured.
   *b. No. The controls necessary to achieve precision make the behavior measured somewhat unnatural.
   c. Yes. Precision of measurement does not require artificiality of behavior.
   d. Yes. The degree of precision depends on the process of measurement, not on the thing being measured.

(3) **In achievement testing and in personality testing, is precision (in the resulting measurement) more important than naturalness (in the test situation)?**
   a. Yes, in both achievement testing and personality testing
   *b. No, only in achievement testing
   c. No, only in personality testing
   d. No, naturalness is more important than precision in both kinds of testing.

(4) Is it desirable to emphasize precision at the expense of naturalness in measurements of both achievement and personality?
  a. Yes
  *b. No, only in measurements of achievement
  c. No, only in measurements of personality
  d. No. It is undesirable to emphasize precision at the expense of naturalness in either case.

In the remainder of this chapter, a number of suggestions will be offered for writing good multiple-choice test items. Most of these reflect conclusions that item writers have reached as a result of their own efforts to produce items that will yield dependable indications of achievement, and many are supported by rational inference. Nonetheless, only a few have been tested in rigorous experiments, and the results have not always clearly supported the suggestions (Board & Whitney, 1972; McMorris et al., 1972). Rigorous experiments in this area are difficult to manage, and the effect of violating one or a few suggestions is not likely to be great. On the whole, however, item writers are likely to produce better items if they know and follow the suggestions than if they are ignorant of them or disregard them.

THE MULTIPLE-CHOICE ITEM STEM

The function of the item stem is to acquaint the examinee with the problem that is being posed. Ideally, it should state or imply a specific question. Although one can sometimes save words without loss of clarity by using an incomplete statement as the item stem, a direct question is often better. Not only does a direct question tend to present the examinee with a more specific problem, it also may focus the item writer's purposes more clearly and help him or her to avoid irrelevance or unrelatedness in the distracters.

Attending to Relevance

Irrelevant items fall short in contributing to the purpose for testing for any number of reasons: the stem fails to present a question or specific problem, the wording of the stem is ambiguous, or the question presented is relatively insignificant. A lack of relevance results in frustration for examinees and contributes to unreliable measures. The sample items that follow illustrate poor techniques for beginning the multiple-choice item.

Physiology teaches us that
  *a. the development of vital organs is dependent upon muscular activity.
  b. strength is independent of muscle size.
  c. the mind and body are not influenced by each other.
  d. work is not exercise.

Here the subject of a sentence is used as the item stem and its predicate as the correct response. Obviously, the predicate does not *necessarily* follow: Physiology could teach us a variety of things. Even if the stem were rephrased to read, "What does physiology teach us?" the item would be just as bad.

In comparing the period of heterosexual adjustment of our culture with those of other cultures, it must be concluded that
a. there are tremendous differences that can only be explained on a cultural basis.
 b. there are large differences that must be explained by the interaction of biology and the more influential culture.
 c. although there are some differences, the biological foundation of puberty is fundamental.
 d. in most cultures puberty is the period of heterosexual adjustment.

Here, again, there are any number of conclusions possible on the basis of a study of a particular period of human development. Until the examinee reads all the responses, she or he has no clear idea of what the question is asking. The item as a whole is not focused on any specific problem. This opens the way for confusing multiple interpretations.

Ideally, the intended answer to a multiple-choice question should be a thoroughly correct answer, admitting no difference of opinion among adequately informed experts. This kind of absolute correctness, however, is difficult to achieve except in formal logical systems or in statements that simply reproduce other statements. Few, if any, inductive truths or experimentally based generalizations can be regarded as absolutely true. Test constructors must base many of their items on propositions that are not absolutely true but are strongly probable. They should, however, guard against basing items on statements whose validity would be challenged by competent scholars.

Another guideline to follow is that the stem of a multiple-choice item should ask a question that has a definite answer. Indeterminate questions may provide interesting topics for discussion, but they do not make good items for testing achievement. For example:

Which event in the following list has been of the greatest importance in American history?
a. Braddock's defeat
 b. Burr's conspiracy
 c. The Hayes-Tilden contest
 d. The Webster-Hayne debate

It is unlikely that scholars can agree on which of these events is of the greatest importance in American history. The importance of an event depends on the point of view of the person making the judgment and the context in which that individual is thinking of it.

While each multiple-choice item should have a definite answer, it may not always be an absolutely correct answer. Many good items ask the examinee to choose the best answer, as in this example.

Which statement best characterizes the man appointed by President Eisenhower to be Chief Justice of the United States Supreme Court?
  a. An associate justice of the Supreme Court who had once been a professor of law at Harvard
b. A successful governor who had been an unsuccessful candidate for the Republican presidential nomination
  c. A well-known New York attorney who successfully prosecuted the leaders of the Communist party in the United States
  d. A Democratic senator from a southern state who had supported Eisenhower's campaign for the presidency

For many of the most important questions that need to be asked, it is impossible to state an absolutely correct answer within the reasonable limits of a multiple-choice test item. Even if space limitation were not a factor, two experts would probably not agree on the precise wording of the best possible answer. Items whose "correct" answer is simply the best among the alternatives offered often permit the item writer to ask much more significant questions and free him or her from the responsibility of stating a correct answer so precisely that all authorities would agree that the particular wording used was the best possible wording.

What about items that involve expressions of opinion? If it is an opinion on which most experts agree, then a reasonable multiple-choice item can be based on it.

Which of these statements is most consistent with Jefferson's concept of democracy?
  a. Democracy is part of the divine plan for mankind.
  b. Democracy requires a strong national government.
c. The purpose of government is to promote the welfare of the people.
  d. The purpose of government is to protect the people from radical or subversive minorities.

The responses to this question represent generalizations on the basis of Jefferson's speeches and writings. No authoritative sanction for one particular generalization is likely to be available. Yet scholars familiar with Jefferson's work would probably agree on a best answer to this item. In such cases the use of an item based on expert opinion is entirely justifiable. However, if the item asks the examinee for a personal opinion, it is subject to criticism. For example:

What do you consider the most important objective of staff meetings?
a. To establish good working relations with your staff
  b. To handle routine matters
  c. To help teachers improve instruction
  d. To practice and exemplify democracy in administration

There is one sense in which any answer to this item must be considered a correct answer. On the other hand, what the item writer obviously wanted to do was to test the examinee's judgment against that of recognized authorities in the field of interpersonal relations. It would have been better to ask students directly to "choose the most important objective of staff meetings." Their answers will obviously be what *they* consider the most important objective, but all answers will be open to criticism and possible correction should they differ from the judgment of recognized experts.

But even experts disagree, particularly in areas that experience continual change due to new advancements in the field. An instructor may present one viewpoint or recommend a specific technique, but the textbook adopts a different or opposing position. When it is relevant to examine students on these topics, it may be necessary to specify the authoritative source in the stem. Expressions like "According to your instructor" or "According to Ebel and Frisbie," for example, may be needed to establish a frame of reference from which students should respond. However, such situations probably ought to be quite rare. It seems more relevant for examinees to understand the rationale for a particular point of view than, for example, to remember Smith's viewpoint.

Good multiple-choice items deal with important, significant ideas, not with incidental details, as does the first item following, nor with particular, unique organizations of subject matter, as does the second.

This question is based on the advertising campaign of Naumkeag Mills to retain the market leadership of Pequot bed linen. What was the competitive position of Pequot products in 1927?
  a. Ahead of all competitors among all customers
 *b. Strong with institutional buyers but weak with household consumers
  c. Second only to Wamsutta among all customers
  d. Weak with all groups of consumers

This advertising campaign may indeed provide an excellent illustration of the problems involved and the practices to follow in advertising campaigns. But it seems not entirely appropriate to measure students' ability to handle an advertising campaign by asking them to recall the details of one illustration used in instruction.

The second principle of education is that the individual
  a. gathers knowledge.
  b. makes mistakes.
  c. responds to situations.
 *d. resents domination.

The only person capable of answering this question is one who has studied a particular book or article. Whether a given principle of education is first or second is usually a matter of little importance. Educators have not agreed on any particular list of principles of education or any priority of principles. This item shows an undesirable close tie-up to the organization of subject matter used by a specific instructor or writer.

Informational preambles that serve only as window dressing and do not help the examinee understand the question being asked should ordinarily be avoided. Here are two examples.

While ironing her formal, Jane burned her hand accidentally on the hot iron. This was due to a transfer of heat by
a. conduction.
b. radiation.
c. convection.
d. absorption.

The introductory sentence suggests that the item involves a practical problem. Actually the question asked calls only for knowledge of technical terminology.

In purifying water for a city water supply, one process is to have the impure water seep through layers of sand and fine and coarse gravel. Here many impurities are left behind. Below are four terms, one of which will describe this process better than the others. Select the correct one.
a. Sedimentation
b. Filtration
c. Chlorination
d. Aeration

The primary purpose of a test item is to measure achievement. While much learning may occur during the process of taking a test, deliberate inclusion of instructional materials may reduce its effectiveness as a test more than its instructional value is increased. It might be better to ask the purpose of filtration in purifying city water supplies or the type of filter used.

Novel questions and novel problem situations reward the critical-minded student who has sought to understand what he/she was taught and penalize the superficial learner. Consider this example:

If the radius of the earth were increased by 3 feet, its circumference at the equator would be increased by about how much?
a. 9 feet
b. 12 feet
c. 19 feet
d. 28 feet

Requiring students to predict what would happen under certain unusual, even impossible, circumstances is a good way to measure their understanding of the principle involved. This type of task does a good job of discriminating between the student who can estimate an answer based on a thorough understanding of the principles and the student who must rely on formula and tedious computations.

It is usually desirable to avoid using the same questions or problems in a test that were used during instruction. In general, bona fide questions such as would be asked by a person honestly seeking information are likely to be more important than quiz-type questions, which would only be asked by someone who already knew the answer. Here is an example of a bona fide question:

J. B. Matthews, one-time employee of Senator McCarthy's subcommittee, charged that a large number of supporters of communism in the United States would be found in which of these groups?
a. Wall Street bankers
b. Newspaper editors
c. Professional gamblers
*d. Protestant clergymen

Multiple-choice items sometimes provide unintended clues to the correct answer that offer considerable help to a poorly prepared examinee. In some cases, key words from the stem, or their synonyms, are repeated in the correct answer. In others the correct response is more consistent grammatically or semantically with the stem than is any of the other responses. Finally, sometimes the stem of one item will inadvertently suggest the answer to another item. Here are some examples of items that provide relevant clues in the stem:

When used in conjunction with the T-square, the left vertical edge of a triangle is used to draw
*a. vertical lines.
b. slant lines.
c. horizontal lines.
d. inclined lines.

The use of the word *vertical* in both the stem and the correct response of this item provides an obvious clue.

Minor differences among organisms of the same kind are known as
a. heredity.
*b. variations.
c. adaptation.
d. natural selection.

The plural term *differences* in the stem calls for a plural response, which can only be response *b.*

The major weakness of our government under the Articles of Confederation was that
a. there were no high officials.
*b. it lacked power.
c. it was very difficult to amend.
d. there was only one house in Congress.

There is an obvious relation between lack of power and weakness of government. If a person knew nothing about the Articles of Confederation, common sense would nonetheless dictate the correct response.

Any test item that is either much too easy or much too difficult for a group of examinees cannot provide much useful information about their relative levels of achievement. If on inspection or after tryout an item is found to be inappropriate in difficulty, some corrective action may be needed.

To some extent the difficulty of a multiple-choice test item is inherent in the idea on which it rests. There are, however, techniques that give the writers of multiple-choice test items some control over the difficulty of the items they produce on a given topic. In general, stem questions can be made easier by making them more general or harder by making them more specific. The following pair of items is illustrative.

A tariff is a tax on
 a. gifts of money.
 *b. goods brought into a country.
 c. income of immigrants.
 d. real estate.

Only the most general notions about a tariff are required to respond successfully to this item, which is thus suitable for use at the lowest level of achievement. Much more knowledge of tariffs is required to respond successfully to the following item.

A high protective tariff on Swiss watches in the United States is intended to most directly benefit
 a. Swiss watchmakers.
 b. United States citizens who buy Swiss watches.
 c. United States government officials.
 *d. United States watchmakers.

This pair of items illustrates how the generality or specificity of a question can be used to help control its difficulty.

Striving for Clarity

It is usually desirable to express the stem of the item so that it requests the essential knowledge being tested as directly, accurately, and simply as possible. The following item stem seems needlessly complex:

Considered from an economic viewpoint, which of these proposals to maintain world peace derives the least support from the military potentialities of atomic energy?
 a. An international police force should be established.
 b. Permanent programs of universal military training should be adopted.
 *c. Sizes of standing military forces should be increased.
 d. The remaining democratic nations of the world should enter into a military alliance.

Even after repeated careful readings, the meaning of this item stem is not clear. It involves a negative approach and seems to combine two dissimilar bases for judgment, economics and atomic energy. The wording of this item might seem to reflect lack of clarity in the thinking of the person who wrote it.

It sometimes seems desirable to phrase the stem question to ask not for the correct answer, but for the incorrect answer. For example,

In the definition of a mineral, which of the following is incorrect?
  a. It was produced by geologic processes.
  b. It has distinctive physical properties.
  c. It contains one or more elements.
d. Its chemical composition is variable.

Items that are negatively stated, that is, that require an examinee to pick an answer that is not true or characteristic, tend to be somewhat confusing. They appear unusually attractive to examination writers because so much of the instructional material is organized in terms of parallel subheadings under a main topic. This suggests the easy approach, that of asking for something that is *not* one of those subheadings. However, such questions are rarely encountered outside the classroom and thus lack the practical relevance that is usually desirable. At times negatively worded stems seem to be the best means of stating a problem to achieve both brevity and clarity. This item is an example:

Under which of these circumstances would a speaker at a political rally NOT be protected by the First Amendment?
  a. When asking the audience to join in a protest march
b. When telling the audience to take violent action
  c. When denouncing the president of the United States
  d. When calling for the creation of a new political party

By capitalizing or underlining the negative word, the item writer draws the examinee's attention to it and ensures that the careless reader who knows the answer will not overlook this key word.

The purpose of the words and syntax chosen in writing a multiple-choice test item is to communicate explicit meaning as efficiently as possible. Habits of colorful, picturesque, imaginative, creative writing may serve the item writer badly by impairing the precision and definiteness of a communication. Few written words are read with such careful attention to meaning, expressed and implied, as those in objective-test items. Item writing makes rigorous demands on the vocabulary and writing skill of test constructors as well as on their mastery of the subject matter and their familiarity with the caliber of the students to be tested. Simple carelessness in grammar, usage, punctuation, or spelling may interfere with the effectiveness of an item and will certainly reflect no credit on the item writer. Skill in expository writing and careful exercise of that skill are essential to the production of good objective-test items.

It is well to specify all conditions and qualifications necessary to make the intended response definitely the best of the available alternatives. Consider this example:

What change occurs in the composition of the air in a lighted airtight room in which the only living things are growing green plants?
a. Carbon dioxide increases and oxygen decreases.
*b. Carbon dioxide decreases and oxygen increases.
c. Both carbon dioxide and oxygen increase.
d. Both carbon dioxide and oxygen decrease.

As originally worded this item simply asked, "What change occurs in the composition of the air in a room in which green plants are growing?" Only if one specifies that the room is lighted, so that photosynthesis can take place; that it is airtight, so that changes in air composition will not be neutralized by ventilation; and that there are no other living things that might consume the oxygen faster than it is produced, is it possible to give a firm answer to this question.

Sometimes when item writers seek to limit a question in order to elicit a definitely correct answer, they reduce its dimensions to the point that the question itself becomes inconsequential. For example, it is important to know why the armed forces of the United States were ordered into combat in Korea in 1950, but it is difficult to give a thoroughly correct answer to such a question. On the other hand, it is quite easy to give an unequivocally truthful answer to the question, "What explanation for U.S. military action in Korea was given in an editorial in the *Chicago Tribune* on Friday, June 30, 1950?" But the knowledge this question tests is of dubious value.

Item writers should never settle for a best answer when a correct answer to the same question is available. They should be sure that, in the eyes of competent experts, the best alternative is clearly superior to all the others. At the same time, however, they should not avoid important questions simply because there is no absolutely and completely correct answer. If many descriptive or qualifying ideas are required, the clearest expression may be achieved by placing them in separate introductory sentences.

The term *creeping socialism* appeared frequently in political discussions in the early 1950s. Which of these is most often used to illustrate creeping socialism?
*a. Generation and distribution of electric power by the federal government
b. Communist infiltration of labor unions
c. Gradual increase in sales and excise taxes
d. Participation of the United States in international organizations such as the United Nations

The use of two sentences—one to present background information and the other to ask the question—frequently adds to the clarity of the item stem. Combining these two elements into a single-question sentence probably would make it considerably more complex.

In other situations a separate introductory sentence is necessary to establish the setting or context. Such statements differ from the instructional preambles and window dressing mentioned earlier. Here is an example:

"When we look at the world as a whole, it is clear that the problem of economic progress is really the most important." This statement is best classified as
*a. a value judgment.
b. a scientific conclusion.
c. an established fact.
d. an analogy.

Obviously these statements could be merged to form a single question. But for examinees whose reading skills may not be well developed, greater clarity of task can be achieved by using the format illustrated.

GUIDELINES FOR PREPARING RESPONSES

Once a suitable item stem has been prepared, a correct response should be written, and then the set of distracters (incorrect responses) can be developed. Several different techniques can be employed to prepare plausible distracters, responses that will enhance the clarity and efficiency of the item without providing irrelevant clues that lead the uninformed to the correct response.

Obtaining Distracters

The purpose of a distracter in a multiple-choice item is to discriminate between those students who have command of a specific body of knowledge and those who do not. To do this, the distracter must be a plausible alternative. One way of obtaining plausible distracters is to use true statements that do not correctly answer the question presented in the stem. For example:

What is the principal advantage of a battery of lead storage cells over a battery of dry cells for automobile starting and lighting?
a. The storage cell furnishes direct current.
b. The voltage of the storage cell is higher.
*c. The current from the storage cell is stronger.
d. The initial cost of the storage cell is less.

Lead storage cells do furnish direct current, and at a higher voltage than dry cells, but this is not the reason why the storage cell is preferred. Judgments concerning the relevance of knowledge may be as important as judgments concerning its truth. Multiple-choice items should make frequent use of this device for testing an achievement that is sometimes thought to be testable only by using essay examinations.

Another source of plausible distracters are familiar expressions, phrases that have been used in common parlance and this may seem attractive to students whose knowledge is merely superficial.

Which of these has effected the greatest change in domestic plants and animals?
a. Influence of environment on heredity
b. Organic evolution
*c. Selective breeding
d. Survival of the fittest

Phrases like "organic evolution" or "survival of the fittest," which a student may have heard without understanding, provide excellent distracters at the elementary level of discrimination for which this item is intended.

Here are some specific tactics that item writers can use to generate good distracters for a multiple-choice item.

1. Define the class of things to which all the alternative answers must belong.   For example, if the question asks what cools an electric refrigerator, the class of possible answers is defined as "things that can cause cooling," such as ice, moving air, expansion of gas, and so forth.

2. Think of things that have some association with terms used in the question.   For the electric refrigerator question, these might be such things as "flow of electricity through a compressed gas" or "electromagnetic absorption of heat energy."

3. If the item calls for a quantitative answer, make the responses distinctly different points along the same scale.   For example, in response to the question, "How many questions should the average student answer correctly on a good multiple-choice test?" the alternative answers might be 40 percent, 60 percent, 80 percent, and 90 percent. Such a scale is illustrated in this item.

How did (A) the estimated amount of petroleum discovered in new fields in 1953 compared with (B) the amount extracted from producing fields in the same year?
a. **A was practically zero.**
b. **A was about half of B.**
c. **A just about equaled B.**
*d. **A was greater than B.**

In many situations the precise value of a quantitative answer is less important than knowledge of a general level or relationship. One systematic approach to testing in quantitative situations is to categorize the responses to represent intervals on a scale of quantities. The use of code letters for the two quantities to be compared shortens the response options and probably adds to their clarity.

Sometimes it is possible to establish a qualitative scale of responses, as in this item.

Some cases of lung cancer have been attributed to smoking. What was the status of this idea in 1953?[1]
a. **The theory had been clearly established by medical evidence.**
*b. **It was a controversial matter and some experts considered the evidence to be inconclusive.**
c. **The theory had been clearly disproved by surveys of smokers.**
d. **The theory was such a recent development that no tests of it had been completed.**

[1] This item and others used as illustrations in this chapter were collected from a variety of sources. Some were written originally for use in tests of understanding of contemporary affairs in the early 1950s. Although the item content may be out of date, the principles of item writing are still valid.

The responses to this item represent a scale of values from complete establishment to complete indefiniteness. The use of a qualitative scale of responses helps to systematize the process of test construction and to suggest desirable responses.

4. Phrase the question so that it calls for a "yes" or "no" answer plus an explanation. Here is an example.

Has the average size of farms in the United States tended to increase in recent years? Why?
  a. Yes, because as the soil loses its natural fertility more land must be cultivated to maintain the same output.
*b. Yes, because the use of farm machinery has made large farms more efficient than small farms.
  c. No, because the difficulty in securing farm labor has forced many farmers to limit their operations.
  d. No, because large family farms tend to be subdivided to provide smaller farms for the children.

5. Use various combinations of two elements as the alternatives. Thus four responses might occasionally assume this form:

1. Only A
2. Only B
3. Both A and B
4. Neither A nor B.

An item illustrating this tactic is:

What was the general policy of the Eisenhower administration during 1953 with respect to government expenditures and taxes?
  a. Reduction of both expenditures and taxes
*b. Reduction of expenditures, no change in taxes
  c. Reduction in taxes, no change in expenditures
  d. No change in either expenditures or taxes

If the two elements each have two different values, for example rise-fall, rapidly-slowly, they can be combined in this way to give four alternatives.

1. It rises rapidly.
2. It rises slowly.
3. It falls slowly.
4. It falls rapidly.

6. Finally, if alternatives still remain elusive, consider using a different approach in the item stem. It is also useful sometimes to back off from the writing job and to ask just what the item is supposed to be testing. If the proposition on which it is based is self-evident, or if a plausible false alternative to it does not exist, the idea may just as well be discarded, and a new start made with a better idea.

In developing the distracters it is possible to manipulate the overall difficulty of the item, to make the correct response more or less difficult for examinees to identify. The more homogeneous the responses are, the more fine the content discrimination required, and consequently the more difficult the item will be. Compare the responses of the first item that follows with those of the second.

An embargo is
*a. a law or regulation.
 b. a kind of boat.
 c. an embankment.
 d. a foolish adventure.

Because the responses to this item vary widely, only an elementary knowledge of embargoes is required for successful response.

An embargo is
 a. a tariff.
 b. a customs duty.
*c. the stoppage of goods from entry and departure.
 d. an admission of goods free of duty.

The homogeneity of responses in this second question makes it considerably more difficult.

Another means of making an item easier is to provide more than one basis for choosing the correct answer, as in this item.

Which of the following are outstanding contemporary pianists?
*a. Robert Casadesus and Rudolph Serkin
 b. Patrice Munsel and Marian Anderson
 c. Claude Debussy and Ignace Paderewski
 d. Alan Paton and Alec Guinness

The use of the names of two individuals fitting the specification in the item stem makes it somewhat easier. The examinee need only know one of the contemporary pianists—or know one in each of the three distracters is not a contemporary pianist—to respond successfully.

It has occurred to some item writers that they might use as distracters the wrong answers students give to short-answer or completion items (Loree, 1948). Some useful ideas are quite likely to be obtained in this way, but the gain in quality of items or in ease of item writing seldom seems to justify the labor of obtaining the student responses (Owens et al., 1970; Frisbie, 1973).

Striving for Clarity

Each of the alternative answers offered in a multiple-choice test item should be appropriate to the question asked or implied by the item stem. Careless, hasty item writing can sometimes result in the inclusion of inappropriate answer choices, as in this example:

The chief difference between the surface features of Europe and North America is that
a. the area of Europe is larger.
b. Europe extends more to the south.
c. the Volga River is longer than the Missouri-Mississippi.
*d. the greater highlands and plains of Europe extend in an east-west direction.

Only the correct answer really describes a surface feature of Europe. Either the question should not be limited to "surface features" or the responses given should all conform to that category.

Since multiple-choice responses are all intended to be answers to the same question, they should all be parallel (that is, similar) in grammatical structure, in type of content, in length, and in complexity. Unfortunately this is not always the case.

Slavery was first started
*a. at Jamestown settlement.
b. at Plymouth settlement.
c. at the settlement of Rhode Island.
d. a decade before the Civil War.

The first three responses to this item are places; the fourth is a time. In questions of this type, it is not difficult to visualize an instance in which two responses would be correct. Use of a direct question stem might help to prevent this type of ambiguity.

Since alternative responses are intended to represent a set of distinct options to the stem question, it is helpful to the examinee and to the effectiveness of the test item if they do indeed present clear choices.

Meat can be preserved in brine due to the fact that
a. salt is a bacterial poison.
*b. bacteria cannot withstand the osmotic action of the brine.
c. salt alters the chemical composition of the food.
d. brine protects the meat from contact with air.

Both responses *a* and *b* could be judged correct. Response *b* simply explains why response *a* is correct. In a case like this, it is undesirable to count only one of two almost equally correct responses.

Familiar expressions and phrases provide a useful source of plausible distracters, but obscure distracters are undesirable.

A *chaotic* condition is
 a. asymptotic.
*b. confused.
 c. gauche.
 d. permutabie.

If the words *chaotic* and *confused* represent an appropriate level of difficulty for this vocabulary test, then the remaining terms used as distracters are obviously too difficult. It is unreasonable to expect the examinee to know for sure that one of them might not be a better synonym for "chaotic" than the intended correct answer.

The search for plausible distracters may sometimes induce an item writer to resort to trickery, as in this item.

Horace Greeley is known for his
 a. advice to young men not to go West.
 b. discovery of anesthetics.
*c. editorship of the *New York Tribune.*
 d. humorous anecdotes.

Insertion of the "not" in the first response spoils what would otherwise be the best answer to the question and thus makes the item more a test of students' alertness than of their knowledge of Horace Greeley. Trickery of this kind reflects badly on the ethics of the item writer and is likely to spoil the discriminating power of the item. Such ploys tend to have detrimental effects on well-prepared examinees who are able to detect them. The message to them is "Read *every* word carefully because someone is out to catch you off guard." As a result, students are likely to require more time to make their responses, and their levels of frustration are likely to rise.

Gaining Efficiency

The need for parallel structure between the stem and the responses sometimes requires that all responses begin with the same word. But if the same group of words is repeated in each response, the possibility of including that phrase in the stem should be considered.

Which is the best definition for a vein?
*a. A blood vessel carrying blood going to the heart
 b. A blood vessel carrying blue blood
 c. A blood vessel carrying impure blood
 d. A blood vessel carrying blood away from the heart

This item could probably be improved by using an incomplete statement stem such as, "A vein is a blood vessel carrying . . . ." Occasionally some repetition provides the most convenient way of making the item clear, but in this case, the repetition seems excessive.

Another problem arises when responses are long and complex so that examinees have difficulty perceiving and keeping in mind the essential differences among the alternatives.

Systematic geography differs from regional geography mainly in that
a. systematic geography deals, in the main, with physical geography, whereas regional geography concerns itself essentially with the field of human geography.
b. systematic geography studies a region systematically, while regional geography is concerned only with a descriptive account of a region.
*c. systematic geography studies a single phenomenon in its distribution over the earth in order to supply generalizations for regional geography, which studies the arrangement of phenomena in one given area.
d. systematic geography is the modern scientific way of studying differentiation of the earth's surface, while regional geography is the traditional and descriptive way of studying distribution of phenomena in space.

A better question might ask, "What characteristic of systematic geography distinguishes it essentially from regional geography?"

Brevity in the responses simplifies the task for the examinee by removing an irrelevant source of difficulty. Brief responses also tend to focus attention on the essential differences among the alternatives offered. Other things being equal, the multiple-choice test item having shorter responses will be superior. But a test composed largely of items using one-word responses or very short phrases is likely to place more emphasis on vocabulary than on command of knowledge. The item writer should not sacrifice importance and significance in the questions to gain brevity in the responses. By way of illustration, if the purpose of an item is to test understanding of the word *monogamy*, the first of the following items will probably do the job better than the second.

What is monogamy?
a. Refusal to marry
b. Marriage of one woman to more than one husband
c. Marriage of one man to more than one wife
*d. Marriage of one man to only one wife

A marriage in which one woman marries one man is called
a. unicameral.
b. dualism.
c. monotheism.
*d. monogamy.

It is usually desirable to list the responses to a multiple-choice item rather than to arrange them in tandem, as in this example.

The balance sheet report for the Ajax Canning Company would reveal (a) The company's profit for the previous fiscal year *(b) The amount of money owed to its creditors (c) The amount of income tax paid (d) The amount of sales for the previous fiscal period.

Responses in tandem save some space but are much more difficult to compare than those placed in list form. Another good rule is that whenever the alternatives form a quantitative or qualitative scale, they normally should be arranged in order of magnitude from smallest to largest or largest to smallest. This may avoid some confusion on the part of the examinee and eliminate an irrelevant source of error.

The population of Denmark is about
 a. 2 million.
b. 4 million.
 c. 7 million.
 d. 15 million.

Common practice in writing multiple-choice tests calls for three or four distracters for each item. If good distracters are available, the larger the number of alternatives, the more highly discriminating the item is likely to be. However, as one seeks to write more distracters each additional one is likely to be somewhat weaker. There is some merit in setting one's goal at three good distracters to each multiple-choice item and in struggling temporarily to reach this goal. Not all good distracters are immediately apparent. Some will emerge only after considerable brain racking.

On the other hand, there is no magic in four alternatives and no real reason why all items in a test should have the same number of alternatives. It is quite possible to write a good multiple-choice test item with only two distracters (three responses), and occasionally with only one distracter, as Smith (1958) and Ebel and Williams (1957) have shown. After tryout, one can actually improve some items by dropping those alternatives that don't distract poor students, or that do distract good ones.

Eliminating Unwanted Clues

A common device for adapting multiple-choice items to questions that seem to require several correct answers is to add as a final alternative the response, "all of the above." But use of this response as the correct answer is strictly appropriate only if all preceding alternatives are *entirely correct* answers to the stem question. It is not uncommon on some classroom tests to find "all of the above" as the correct answer for each or most of the items in which it appears. Occasionally just the opposite situation is found. In both cases such a pattern introduces an irrelevant clue to the correct answer or to an incorrect answer. When "all of the above" is used—and it should be used sparingly—it ought to be the correct answer on some occasions, but never on all occasions in which it appears.

The response "none of the above" is also sometimes used, either as the intended answer or as a distracter. It is particularly useful in multiple-choice arithmetic or spelling items where the distinction between correctness and error is unequivocal. But this response, like "all of the above," should *not* be used unless the best answer is a thoroughly correct answer. Here are examples of correct (first) and incorrect (second) usage of these responses.

Which word is misspelled?	**What does the term *growth* mean?**
a. Contrary	*a. Maturation
*b. Tendancy	b. Learning
c. Extreme	c. Development
d. Variable	d. All of these
e. None of these	e. None of these

The overuse of both of these response alternatives probably derives from the misconception that all multiple-choice items should have at least four (or five) response alternatives. These phrases are used as filler when the item writer encounters difficulty in finding a sufficient number of distracters. In such circumstances, the overuse of each becomes a clue to the testwise, underprepared student who recognizes that "all of the above" or "none of the above" is seldom the correct answer when it does appear. As was pointed out in the previous section, there is no compelling reason for all items in a test to have the same number of alternatives.

The use of distracters that are less difficult than the correct answer is sometimes criticized because it permits a student to respond successfully by eliminating incorrect responses. However, students who can respond successfully on this basis usually possess more knowledge than those who cannot. Hence the discriminating power of an item is not impaired by this characteristic. Of course, a distracter which is absurd or highly implausible will contribute little or nothing to the effectiveness of a test item.

Which of the following has helped most to increase the average length of human life?
a. Fast driving
b. Avoidance of overeating
c. Wider use of vitamins
*d. Wider use of inoculations

Some teachers may feel that the abilities of some of their students cannot possibly be underestimated, but they should not let this feeling of frustration lead them to employ such an unreasonable distracter as response *a*.

A lack of parallelism in the alternative choices often leads poorly prepared examinees to the correct answer. There is a tendency for unskilled item writers to express the correct answer more carefully and at greater length than the other alternatives. Sometimes the correct response is more general and inclusive than any distracter. At other times a familiar verbal stereotype is used as the correct answer, allowing some students to respond successfully simply by recalling vaguely that they had encountered those same words before. Here are some examples of items that provide unwanted cues:

How did styles in women's clothing in 1950 differ most from those in 1900?
a. They showed more beauty.
b. They showed more variety.
c. They were easier to clean.
*d. They were easier to live in, to work in, to move in, and were generally less restrictive.

The greater detail used in stating the correct response makes it undesirably obvious.

History tells us that all nations have enjoyed participation in
a. gymnastics.
b. football.
*c. physical training of some sort.
d. baseball.

Response *c* obviously provides a more reasonable completion to the stem than any of the other responses. It represents a consistent style of expression. This is one of the dangers inherent in the use of incomplete statement item stems.

All of these irrelevant clues to the correct answer are undesirable, of course, and should be avoided. It is entirely appropriate to plant such clues deliberately in the distracters to mislead the testwise but poorly prepared student. To give all of the relevant clues—those useful to well-prepared examinees—while avoiding the irrelevant clues is an important skill in writing multiple-choice test items.

ALTERNATE-CHOICE ITEMS

It is possible to write a multiple-choice test item as a simple declarative sentence, one portion of which offers two alternative words or phrases that might be used to complete the sentence. The examinee's task is to choose the version that makes the sentence most nearly true. Here are some examples:

(1) A violin player shortens a string with her finger in order to 1) lower 2) raise the pitch.
(2) Temperatures change 1) less 2) more from season to season on the equator than in the arctic.
(3) If two sides of a triangle are 4 and 6 inches the third side must be 1) greater than 2) less than 10.

These alternate-choice items look suspiciously like true-false items, and in essence they are. Like true-false items, each is based on an important proposition, but unlike true-false items, the basis for establishing truth is built into the item. Whereas the true-false item requires the examinee to search for a counterexample to make a comparison, the alternate-choice item contains the comparison. This fundamental difference is a basis for some of these virtues of alternate-choice items (Ebel, 1983):

1. Because they are based on simple rather than complex relationships, they are easier and more efficient to write than traditional multiple-choice items.
2. Because they present a comparison within the item, they tend to be more easily and clearly stated than true-false items.
3. Because they are stated more briefly than traditional multiple-choice items, students can respond to many more of them in an hour of testing time.
4. Because they permit a longer test than traditional multiple choice, they tend to yield more reliable scores.

The techniques presented in Chapter 9 for writing good true-false items are generally applicable to preparing good alternate-choice items. Instructional materials are used to develop important propositions that serve as the basis for item writing. Pairs of statements, one true and the other false, are written for each proposition. These can be combined into a single statement that provides two choices. However, when propositions lend themselves to using more than two plausible alternatives, the number of choices may be increased, perhaps to as many as five. Here are two examples:

The gas given off in photosynthesis is 1) carbon dioxide, 2) hydrogen, 3) nitrogen, 4) oxygen.
Most of the territorial possessions of the United States were gained as a result of the 1) War of 1812, 2) Civil War, 3) Spanish-American War, 4) First World War.

The attractive features of alternate-choice items are soon lost when the choices become lengthy and increase in number. Then the tandem format makes comparisons more difficult and the unique advantages—ease of preparation and quickness of response—become indistinguishable from those of traditional multiple-choice items.

MULTIPLE TRUE-FALSE ITEMS

Multiple true-false items resemble multiple-choice items in their physical appearance. However, rather than selecting one best answer from several alternatives, examinees respond to each of the several alternatives as a separate true-false statement. These separate statements have a common stem, like a multiple-choice item, but any number of the associated alternatives may be true. The number of alternatives per item or cluster need not remain constant throughout a given test. Here is a sample item:

**An ecologist losing weight by jogging and exercising is
  1. **increasing maintenance metabolism. (T)**
  2. **decreasing net productivity. (T)**
  3. **increasing biomass. (F)**
  4. **decreasing energy lost to decomposition. (F)**
  5. **increasing gross productivity. (F)**

Notice that the alternatives are numbered consecutively throughout the test and each new stem is introduced by two asterisks or some symbol that makes the stem easily identifiable. The next item, for example, might contain choices 6–10, the next, choices 11–14, and so on.

The multiple true-false form has several appealing features relative to the multiple-choice format (Frisbie and Sweeney, 1982). Examinees can make at least three multiple true-false item responses, on the average, in the time required to answer a single multiple-choice item, a decided advantage in an hour of testing time. The longer test permits testing of a greater range or depth of content. In addition, it has been shown that a multiple true-false test prepared by converting items from multiple-choice form yields higher reliability estimates than the original multiple-choice test. Finally, two less critical outcomes can be noted. Students that were examined by both item types expressed an overwhelming preference for multiple true-false items and perceived them to be easier than the multiple choice.

Multiple true-false items can be developed using any of several strategies. Existing multiple-choice items can be converted easily to multiple true-false "clusters," sometimes without significant rewording of the stem. The response choices in some items would need to be modified so that each cluster would not contain a single true statement. The number of items per cluster may vary, and the number of true statements per cluster should vary throughout a given test from "all" to "none." In other words, the test constructor should avoid establishing a pattern for the number of true statements per cluster, just as the position of the keyed response should vary throughout a muliple-choice test.

The shortcomings of "multiple multiple-choice" items, described in Chapter 7, can be overcome by converting them to multiple true-false form. Consider this example from an elementary-level mathematics test:

For which of the quantities below is it more reasonable to estimate the quantity by measuring a sample rather than the whole population?
  I.   **The average life of a new brand of TV tubes**
  II. **The percent of American voters who favor the president's foreign policy**
  III. **The number of teachers in Jefferson School who usually ride the bus to school**
*A. **Both I and II**
 B. **Both II and III**
 C. **I only**
 D. **II only**
 E. **III only**

In multiple true-false form, the item might look like this:

**It would be more reasonable to measure a sample than the whole population to estimate the
  1. **average life of a new brand of TV tubes.   (T)**
  2. **percent of American voters who favor the president's foreign policy.   (T)**
  3. **number of teachers in Jefferson School who usually ride the bus to school.   (F)**

Note that it is possible to add more statements to the multiple true-false cluster quite readily, but to do so to the multiple multiple-choice item would increase its complexity for the item writer and the examinee. Both types of items require the same cognitive tasks, but the second item does the job more efficiently.

Finally, those who prepare multiple true-false items other than by a conversion method can begin the process using the recommendations given earlier for preparing multiple-choice items. The task is simplified somewhat, however, because the item writer is not limited to only one correct answer in the set of responses developed. Any concepts, principles, or applications measured by multiple-choice items can be measured at least as well by multiple true-false items.

SUMMARY

Some of the main ideas developed in this chapter are expressed in the following 26 statements:

1. The most highly regarded and widely used form of objective test is the multiple-choice form.
2. Critics of multiple-choice items tend to exaggerate both the number of faulty items that appear on tests and the seriousness of the consequences of those faults.
3. A student who selects the correct response to a good multiple-choice item by eliminating responses she or he knows are incorrect demonstrates achievement of relevant subject matter.
4. Multiple-choice items should be based on sound, significant ideas that can be expressed as independent and meaningful propositions.
5. The important aspects of educational achievement that can be measured by objective tests are largely identical with those that can be measured by essay tests.
6. The stem of a multiple-choice item should state or clearly imply a specific direct question.
7. A multiple-choice item calling for a best answer can be as effective as one that contains only one absolutely correct answer.
8. Good multiple-choice items can be based on matters of opinion if most experts share that opinion or if the authoritative source is specified.
9. A good multiple-choice item ordinarily should not ask for the examinee's opinion.
10. Items testing recall of incidental details of instruction

or special organizations of subject matter ordinarily are undesirable.
11. The item stem should pose the essence of its question as simply and accurately as possible.
12. Item stems including the word *not*, asking in effect for an incorrect answer, tend to be both confusing to the examinee and somewhat superficial in content.
13. The stem of a multiple-choice item should be expressed as concisely as possible without sacrificing clarity or omitting essential qualifications.
14. Brevity is desirable in multiple-choice responses, but it should not be achieved by reducing significant questions to less important or trivial ones.
15. True statements that do not provide good answers to the stem question often make good distracters.
16. Item writers can make some multiple-choice items easier by making the stem more general and the responses more diverse; they can make items harder by making the stem more specific and the responses more similar to each other.
17. All of the responses to a multiple-choice item should be parallel in type of content, grammatical structure, and general appearance.
18. The responses to a multiple-choice item should be expressed simply enough to make clear the essential differences among them.
19. The responses to a multiple-choice item should be listed rather than written one after another in a compact paragraph.
20. While most multiple-choice items provide at least

four alternative responses, good questions can be written using only two or three alternatives.
21. There is no compelling reason for all multiple-choice items in a test to have exactly the same number of response alternatives.
22. The responses "none of the above" and "all of the above" are appropriate only when the answers given to the question are absolutely correct or incorrect (as in spelling or arithmetic problems).
23. The distracters in a multiple-choice item should be definitely less correct than the answer, but plausibly attractive to the uninformed.
24. The intended answer to a multiple-choice item should be clear, concise, correct, and free of clues.
25. In contrast to multiple-choice items, alternate-choice items offer the advantages of ease of preparation, efficiency in response, and opportunity for broader content coverage.
26. Relative to multiple-choice items, multiple true-false items are more efficient, are easier to prepare, and can yield slightly more reliable scores.

PROJECTS AND PROBLEMS

Project: Writing Multiple-Choice Test Items

Using the information in the following paragraphs as directly and simply as possible, write ten good multiple-choice items. Do not try to test for understanding of the information or for applications of it. For example, if the information given had been:

The national government of Great Britain is located in London. It is not located in Birmingham, Paris, or Berlin.

An appropriate multiple-choice item would be:

Where is the national government of Great Britain located?
a) Berlin
b) Birmingham
*c) London
d) Paris

Treat each of the ten paragraphs below in the same way. Indicate the correct response with an asterisk.

1. A magnet attracts pieces of iron. It does not attract pieces of glass or wood or copper.
2. When heat is applied to a liquid, the molecules of the liquid move faster. The molecules do not expand, or decompose, or combine.
3. A major cause of lung cancer is smoking. Pneumonia, high blood pressure, or excessive use of alcohol are not major causes of lung cancer.
4. If the sides of a rectangle are 5 inches and 12 inches, the diagonal is 13 inches. It is not 17 inches, or 7 inches, or 34 inches.
5. The intelligence quotient involves measures of mental ability. It does not involve measures of physical development, years of schooling, or social maturity.
6. The Elizabethan Age is notable for the amount of great literature produced. It is not notable for improvements in agriculture, for revolutionary uprisings in Europe, or for popular democracy in government.
7. The purpose of the judicial branch of the United States Government is to interpret laws. It is not to make the laws, or to enforce the laws, or to investigate violations of laws.
8. The increasing size of farms in the United States is due mainly to the use of farm machinery. It is not due mainly to the development of farm cooperatives, or high yield varieties, or mortgage foreclosures on small farms.
9. The area of land that was located north of the Ohio River, east of the Mississippi

River, and south of Canada was known as the Northwest Territory. It was not known as the Louisiana Purchase, the Gadsden Purchase, or the Old Dominion.

10. Knowing what force operates through what distance, you can calculate how much work has been done. You cannot calculate how much horsepower was used, or how great was the mechanical advantage, or the velocity of motion.

Problem: Writing Items to Discriminate

Write or copy a short paragraph of from three to seven sentences expressing ideas you think few, if any, of the other members of this class already know. On another sheet, write three different independent items—two true-false and one four-alternative multiple-choice—designed to test the knowledge of these ideas. None of the items should refer directly to the paragraph.

Your items and the paragraph on which they are based will be tried out by your classmates in one of the class meetings. The class will be divided into tryout groups of 6 to 10 members. The items written by members of the group will be circulated within the group to obtain preinformation responses. Each person, except the author of the item, will record his or her responses independently, guarding against being influenced by the responses others may have given. Then the items will be circulated again along with the paragraphs to obtain postinformation responses.

When all this has been done and the responses have been returned to the author of the items, he/she must do these four things:

1. Enter the key (correct response) for each item.
2. Calculate an index of discrimination for each item using this arithmetic:
   a. Number of postinformation correct responses, minus
   b. Number of preinformation correct responses, divided by
   c. Number of total responses, pre or post (that is, one less than the number of members of the group).
3. Add the three indices of discrimination, taking account of signs (that is, subtracting the negative indices).
4. Fasten paragraph, items, responses, and calculations together and turn them in. Be sure your name is on each sheet.

Your instructor may supply you with special forms on which you may write the items. The other side of the form will provide spaces for recording the responses and calculating the discrimination indices.

11

SHORT-ANSWER, MATCHING, AND OTHER OBJECTIVE-TEST ITEMS

SHORT-ANSWER ITEMS[1]

A short-answer test item aims to test knowledge by asking examinees to supply a word, phrase, or number that answers a question or completes a sentence. Completion and fill-in-the-blank are other common labels for short-answer items. Here are several examples:

(1) Who discovered the insulin treatment of diabetes?	Banting
(2) The holy city of Islam is	Mecca
(3) When was the battle of Hastings fought?	A.D. 1066

What is the common name of each of these chemical substances?

(4) $CaCO_3$	limestone
(5) NaCl	salt
(6) $C_{12}H_{22}O_{11}$	sugar
(7) NaOH	lye
(8) NH_3	ammonia

Items 4 through 8 constitute a cluster of similar short-answer items based on the same question.

Short-answer items deal mainly with words and numbers. They ask for

[1] This section owes much to the work of Alexander G. Wesman (1971).

names of persons, places, things, processes, colors, and so forth. They may also ask for English words, foreign equivalents, or symbols that represent words in shorthand, mathematics, chemistry, music, or logic. Common responses also include numbers representing dates, distances, costs, and populations. If they call for a phrase, it is usually something short, specific, and familiar, such as "spontaneous combustion" or "discovery of America." An item that calls for a collection of somewhat longer responses, for example, "Give three reasons why . . ." or "List the traits of . . ." is classified as a short essay question rather than a short-answer item.

This means that short-answer items test mainly for factual information. As the foundation of all reliable knowledge, facts constitute an important substratum. But there is much, much more to knowledge than the facts that can be reported in single words, short phrases, or numbers. What short-answer items can test is much more limited than what true-false or multiple-choice items can test. Thus, while any short-answer item can be converted to a true-false or multiple-choice item, only a few true-false or multiple-choice items can be converted to the short-answer form.

Short-answer items are very much less affected by guessing than are true-false or multiple-choice items. They also are supposed to test recall rather than recognition, which in the eyes of some instructors makes them more demanding and more valid as tests of achievement. However, as we have already seen, not only is blind guessing a rather rare phenomenon, but the harm that it can do to the score on a reasonably good, reasonably long test is actually rather slight. And in response to the contention that recall is a more strenuous mental process than recognition, it may be said that good choice-type items seldom can be answered by simple recognition. In fact, they are more likely than are short-answer items to test understanding and to require reflective thinking.

Despite these limitations, short-answer items have a place in educational measurement. They are reasonably easy to write. They are efficient, providing many separate scorable responses per page or per unit of testing time. And if the group to be tested is reasonably small, the scoring which must be done by the teacher or a competent aide is not unreasonably burdensome.

Short-answer tests are widely and justifiably popular in the primary and intermediate elementary grades, where basic vocabularies are being built in subjects like spelling, geography, and arithmetic, and in those parts of science where names of structures, substances, and symbols must be learned. When used simply, they are the test item of choice when examinees have identifiable reading or writing problems.

Writing Short-Answer Items

1. Word the question or incomplete statement carefully enough to require a single, unique answer. A common problem with short-answer items is that a question which the item writer thought would call for answer A elicits from some of the examinees equally defensible answers B, C, or D. For example, the question, "What is coal?", to which the intended answer was "a fuel," might also elicit such answers as "petrified vegetable matter," "a burning ember," or "impure carbon." To prevent this dual ambiguity—indefiniteness in what is tested and consequent difficulty in scoring—the question should be reworded so as to elicit a more specific answer.

For what purpose is most coal used?
From what substance was coal formed?
What name is applied to a glowing coal in a fire?
Coal consists mainly of what chemical element?

2. Think of the intended answer first. Then write a question to which that answer is the only appropriate response.   The focus of a short-answer question should be on the intended answer. If item writers keep that answer in mind and word their questions accordingly, they will probably succeed in avoiding indefiniteness and multiple correct answers. An alternative, but inferior, method of obtaining short-answer items is to find a textbook sentence from which a word can be deleted to make a short-answer item. For example:

Thunderstorms form when columns of _____ air rise to cooler altitudes.

Possible correct answers to this item include "warmer," "lower," and "moist." This example also serves to illustrate the next three suggestions for writing short-answer items.

3. If the item is an incomplete sentence, try to word it so the blank comes at the end of the sentence.   This will often make the intent of the item clearer and avoid some of the indefiniteness and possibility of multiple answers.

4. Use a direct question, unless the incomplete sentence permits a more concise or clearly defined correct answer.   When an incomplete sentence is arranged so the blank comes at the end, it will often be apparent that a direct question would be just as easy to write and possibly a shade easier to understand. For example:

The holy city of Islam is _____.

versus

What is the holy city of Islam? _____.

However, answers to the question:

Why did the United States declare war on Japan in 1941?

are likely to be more variable and somewhat longer than completions of the sentence:

The immediate cause for the U.S. declaration of war on Japan in 1941 was the bombing of Pearl Harbor.

5. Avoid unintended clues to the correct answer. The word *cooler* in the item on thunderstorms suggests that the air before it rose must have been warmer. Or consider this item:

Steamboats are moved by engines that run on the pressure of _____.

It takes little knowledge or insight to guess that the correct answer to this item must be "steam." For what purpose is a question like this one being asked at all? Focusing on the answer before writing the question is likely to result in more important questions that have more specifically unique answers. It is also important to remember that questions written with a specific answer in mind are likely to be more relevant and more concise than sentences lifted from text material.

Another common but unwanted cue helps the examinee determine the length of the intended responses. Each blank used in a set of short-answer items should be exactly the same length. The short-answer directions should indicate if only a single word or if either a word or phrase may be used as a valid response. Consider this item:

The names of the two rivers that meet at Cairo, Illinois, are the _____ and _____.

The long blank to accommodate "Mississippi" and the short blank intended for "Ohio" make this item easier for all, but particularly for students who are unsure about the names.

6. Word the item as concisely as possible without losing specificity of response. Clear ideas are expressed in concise statements or questions. Excess words waste the examinee's time and may confuse the idea to be expressed.

7. Arrange space for recording answers on the right margin of the question page. This practice not only makes the items easier to score, which is its main justification, but also encourages the use of direct questions or placement of blanks at the end of incomplete sentences.

8. Avoid using the conventional wording of an important idea as the basis for a short-answer item. Use of the usual wording may encourage and reward study to memorize rather than to understand. For example:

Gain or loss divided by the cost equals the gain or loss in _____.

Two lines perpendicular to the same line in the same plane are _____ to each other.

Better versions of these items would be:

To determine the percent of gain on a transaction, by what must the actual gain be divided? _____

If two lines are drawn perpendicular to the same line on a sheet of paper, they are _____.

NUMERICAL PROBLEMS

While numerical problems can be presented as multiple-choice test items, they are most often presented in short-answer form. Numerical problems provide the basis for a wide variety of test items in arithmetic and other branches of mathematics, in the sciences, in bookkeeping, and accounting, and in any fields of study where exact quantitative relationships have been developed.

Numerical problems provide good measures of achievement in learning. They are performance tests that assess application of knowledge. Many novel problems can easily be produced by changing the given quantities and the ways in which they are presented; and these novel problems are an excellent way to test understanding in contrast to mere recall. The answers are usually concise and hence easy to score, even in short-answer form. All these are virtues of numerical problems as short-answer test items. But sometimes there are minor difficulties in using them.

The problem of avoiding a number of correct responses, which plagues other short-answer items, takes a somewhat different form in numerical problems. How precisely correct must the answer be to receive credit? How much partial credit should be given if the process is correct but the answer incorrect because of computational errors? No blanket answer can be given to these questions, but the following suggestions may help to avoid serious difficulties on these points.

1. Use the simplest numbers possible. The purpose of the item is to test understanding of a process, not computational accuracy. If accuracy needs to be tested, test it in separate items, using numbers as complex as may be necessary.

2. If possible, choose the given quantities so that the answer will be a whole number. To do this will help to avoid uncertainty about how far a decimal fraction should be carried out.

3. Specify the degree of precision expected in the answer. If students are uncertain about what they are being asked to do, and if they guess wrongly, the measurement of what they are able to do will be made less accurate.

4. If a fully correct answer must specify the unit of measure in which it is expressed, tell the examinee this as part of the problem. It is easy for a distracted examinee to forget to write the units in which an answer is expressed. If knowing what the units should be is an important part of the problem, ask for them separately, thus:

What number expresses the intensity of illumination on this surface? _____
In what units is this illumination intensity expressed? <u>foot-candles</u>

5. If possible, divide a single complex multiple-step problem into a number of simpler single-step problems. It is a mistake to believe that the more complex the problem, the better it will test the examinees' ability. Just the reverse is usually true. Any complex problem involves a number of procedural choices, as well as a number of quantitative calculations. Each of these can be made the basis of a separate test item. Success in solving the whole problem involves nothing more than success in making the separate choices and calculations. Consider these two items. The first is relatively complex, but the second is more efficient and likely will contribute more to high reliability.

Last year Marcy sold 60 cars at an average price of $2,000. Her goal this year is to sell 50% more cars. If Marcy earns a commission of 10% for each sale, how much more will she earn this year than last year if she reaches her goal?

Last year Marcy sold 60 cars at an average price of $2,000. Her goal this year is to sell 50% more cars. Marcy's commission is 10% for each sale.
1. **How many cars does Marcy hope to sell this year?**
2. **How many dollars did Marcy earn last year from her sales?**
3. **How many dollars does Marcy hope to earn this year?**

Breaking down a complex, multiple-step problem in this way will minimize the problem of partial credit. It will result in more independent indications of achievement or lack of it. That will improve the reliability of the test scores.

6. Express the numerical problem clearly and as concisely as possible. Clarity requires full information and simple direct statements. Conciseness, the elimination of unnecessary words or distracting comments, also aids in achieving clarity. A study was made some years ago to test the hypothesis that inclusion of irrelevant data would improve the measuring characteristics of physics test problems (Ebel, 1937). This hypothesis was based on the assumption that giving the examinee only the numerical information needed was not true to life and might help students who lacked understanding to stumble onto the correct answer. But the inclusion of complicating irrelevant data did not improve the items. Evidently they were quite complicated enough without it.

MATCHING ITEMS

Matching-test items occur in clusters composed of a list of premises, a list of responses, and directions for matching the two. In many clusters the distinction between premises and responses is simply in the names given to them. The two lists can be interchanged without difficulty. In other clusters, such as the following example, it is convenient to use descriptive phrases as the premises and shorter names as responses.

Directions: On the blank before each of the following contributions to educational measurement, place the letter that precedes the name of the person responsible for it.

Premises	*Responses*
__ 16. Developed the Board of Examiners at the University of Chicago	*a.* Alfred Binet
__ 17. Developed high-speed electronic test-processing equipment	*b.* Arthur Otis
__ 18. Published the first textbook on educational measurement	*c.* E. F. Lindquist
	d. E. L. Thorndike
	e. L. L. Thurstone

A wide variety of premise-response combinations can be used as the basis for matching-test items: dates and events; terms and definitions; writers and quotations; quantities and formulas; color samples and names of colors; and so on. Names of an animal's organs or structures can be matched to parts shown on a sketch of the animal.

Closely related to the matching-test item is the classification or key-list item. Responses for this item consist of a list of classes such as the parts of speech, periods of history, classes of plants or animals, types of chemical reactions, cause-effect sequences, branches of government, nations or states, and so on. The premises consist of names, descriptions, or examples that are to be classified among the responses provided. Here is an illustration.

Directions: After each event in the list below, put the number
1. if it happened before the birth of Christ (4 B.C.)
2. if it happened after the birth of Christ but before the Magna Carta was signed (A.D. 1215)
3. if it happened after the Magna Carta was signed but before Columbus arrived in America (1492)
4. if it happened after Columbus arrived in America but before the Declaration of Independence (1775)
5. if it happened after the Declaration of Independence (1775)

36. Battle of Hastings	2
37. Eruption of Mt. Vesuvius	2
38. Gutenberg Bible printed	3
39. Pilgrims landed at Plymouth	4
40. William Shakespeare was born	4

Apart from the use of classes or categories as responses (the key list), classification items differ from typical matching items in that the same response is "matched" to more than one premise, and the number of premises is usually greater than the number of responses. In typical matching items there are more responses than premises.

Matching items have something in common with multiple-choice items in offering explicit alternative answers. They also have something in common with short-answer items. They are usually limited to specific factual information—names, dates, labels, and so on. They are poorly suited for testing understanding. They are also poorly adapted for testing unique ideas, since a cluster of related items is a prerequisite to the writing of such items. Clustering can reduce the breadth of sampling of questions in a test, concentrating attention on particular narrow aspects of achievement.

There are, on the other hand, some attractive features of matching-test items. They are efficient in that they yield many independent scorable responses per test page or per unit of testing time. They may also motivate students to cross-reference and integrate their knowledge and to consider relations among the items in the lists of responses and premises. Yet seldom can a whole test be composed of matching or classification-test items. Some aspects of achievement may, however, be ideally suited to this item form. Here are some suggestions for using it effectively.

1. Choose homogeneous premises and responses for any matching cluster. The premises and responses in the list that follows are not homogeneous.

__ 13. dark, hard wood	a. board foot
__ 14. tool for smoothing	b. drawing
__ 15. 12″ × 12″ × 1″	c. plane
	d. shellac
	e. walnut

Is it necessary to supply a key for the correct answers to the items in this cluster? As this example illustrates, if the lists are not homogeneous, the items are likely to test only the simplest associations and to provide many commonsensical clues to the correct answer.

2. Make the lists of premises and responses relatively short. It is easier to keep short lists homogeneous. The task involves less irrelevant difficulty if examinees do not have to hunt through long lists for a match. Adding responses beyond four or five reduces the chance of successful guessing only a very little. The difference in probability of correct answer by chance between a five- and a six-response item is only about 0.03. Common practice among expert item writers is to use a list of three premises to be matched by one of five responses.

3. Do not attempt "perfect" matching, in which each response is matched once and only once to each of the premises. In perfect matching, the final match may be given away by the other matches. Or if an error is made in one match, there is certain to be an error in another. Thus the items are not wholly independent. Using more responses than premises eliminates these potential dangers of perfect matching.

4. Provide directions that clearly explain the intended basis for matching. While the intended basis may be self-evident in simple matching clusters, in most cases it should be made explicit to avoid any misunderstandings. Classification items usually require fairly detailed directions.

5. Arranging responses or premises or both in alphabetical order, usually prevents give-away clues that can occur in item writing. Item writers are likely to think of a premise and its responses together. If they are written down just as they are thought of, their sequence may make the task of matching easier than it should be. Rearranging one or both lists in alphabetical order will eliminate such clues. However, if any logical order exists among the responses (for example, quantities or dates) preserving that order will remove an irrelevant difficulty from the examinees' task.

6. If the responses are numerical quantities, arrange them in order from low to high.

7. Use the longer phrases as premises, the shorter as responses.
Both of these actions will tend to simplify the examinees' task in finding the correct match, and may eliminate irrelevant difficulty.

TESTING FOR APPLICATION OF KNOWLEDGE

Any good item tests application of knowledge. Good multiple-choice items require more than recall. Yet many of the items discussed in this and the two preceding chapters test for knowledge directly by asking for factual knowledge. There are also items that test for knowledge indirectly by giving the examinee a task that requires knowledge.

Numerical problems, discussed earlier in this chapter, test for application of knowledge. So do dictation or error recognition, spelling tests, tests that require the examinee to add or correct punctuation or capitalization, to edit or proofread copy, or to diagram a sentence. Examinees can be asked to provide all or parts of the proof of a proposition in geometry or to write or to complete the equation for a chemical reaction. They can be asked to interpret the meaning of a table, a graph, a musical score, a cartoon, a poem, or a passage of literary, scientific, or other test material.

Items that require interpretations of these kinds are sometimes referred to as context-dependent items. They are widely used in tests of general educational development, whose purpose is to measure fairly the abilities of students with widely different educational backgrounds. In this they succeed quite well. They are less appropriate, convenient, and efficient in testing for achievement in learning specific subject matter. One should be skeptical of claims that context-dependent items measure *abilities* rather than *knowledge,* for the abilities they measure are almost wholly the results of knowledge.

Many of these indirect tests of knowledge via special applications of that knowledge can be presented in true-false, multiple-choice, alternate-choice, multiple true-false, short-answer, or matching forms. Some are more conveniently presented for response in other ways, such as requiring the examinee to produce a diagram, sketch, or set of corrections. The main point to be made here is that, while achievement in learning usually can be tested most conveniently in one of the common forms of test items, there are occasions when other means may be more convenient and satisfactory. At the same time, there is no virtue in attempting to use several item forms in a test when a single form will do the job well.

SUMMARY

The principal ideas developed in this chapter are summarized in these propositions:

1. Short-answer items are used mainly to test for factual information.
2. A much wider range of achievements can be tested with true-false or multiple-choice items than with short-answer items.
3. The difficulty examinees have in producing the correct answer to a short-answer item is an advantage of limited value.
4. Short-answer items do not provide a more valid measure of real achievement than do choice-type items.
5. Short-answer items are efficient and relatively easy to prepare.
6. Short-answer items need to be conceived and written carefully to avoid the possibility of multiple correct answers.
7. In writing short-answer items, it is advantageous to think first of the answer and then write the question that will elicit it.
8. A direct question generally will result in a less ambiguous short-answer item than will an incomplete sentence.
9. Item writers should avoid "lifting" intact sentences from textual materials as the basis for short-answer items.
10. Numerical problems can provide valid and convenient measurements of achievement.
11. Two difficulties frequently encountered by users of numerical problems center on defining the required accuracy of the answer and deciding how much credit to award for partially correct answers.
12. If a complex, multiple-step problem is broken down into a number of simpler, single-step problems, more reliable measurements of ability ordinarily will be obtained.
13. To test for understanding of a process, it is best to require the simplest possible numerical calculations.
14. Matching items, like short-answer items, usually are limited to testing for factual information.
15. Matching items are efficient and useful in emphasizing relationships between ideas.
16. Short, homogeneous lists should be used in any matching cluster.
17. Perfect matching of the two lists on a one-to-one basis is undesirable.
18. Directions should be explicit about the basis to be used in matching.
19. The list of responses in a matching cluster should be presented in either scrambled or alphabetical order to avoid clues.
20. All good items test for application of knowledge. Some test it directly by asking a question. Others test it indirectly by presenting tasks to be performed.
21. Context-dependent items calling for interpretations are useful mainly in testing for general educational development.

PROJECTS AND PROBLEMS

Project: Writing and Evaluating Short-Answer Items

Use the ten paragraphs from the first project described at the end of Chapter 10 to prepare ten short-answer items. Include a set of instructions for examinees at the top of your paper and list the correct answer(s) to each item on a separate piece of paper.

Your instructor will ask another student to respond to your items with as many "correct answers" as he or she can think of. The quality of your items will be judged, in part, by the number of unintended correct responses the other class member gives to each of your items.

12

THE ADMINISTRATION AND SCORING OF ACHIEVEMENT TESTS

Unless the class is very large, unless the classroom is poorly suited for test administration, or unless other special problems are encountered, test administration usually is the simplest phase of the whole testing process. In the administration of external, standardized tests, the golden rule for the test administrator is: *Follow the directions in the manual precisely.* In classroom testing there is usually no such manual, and the need for rigidly standardized conditions of test administration is much less. Nevertheless, here, as in most other areas, advanced planning usually pays dividends. Also there are some persistent problems associated with test administration, such as the questions of time limits, of guessing on objective tests, and of cheating. These topics, together with the problems of efficient scoring of objective tests, will provide the subject matter of this chapter.

PREPARING THE STUDENTS

Preparing the students for the test goes hand-in-hand with preparing the test for the students. Though each can be accomplished separately, the neglect of either certainly will result in lost effort and less valid measures of achievement. As a start, students should know that a test is coming. Any important test should be announced well in advance. If a test is to have the desirable effects in motivating and directing efforts to learn, students need to know not only when the test is coming but what kinds of achievement the test will require them to demonstrate. This means the teacher should plan tests *before* the course begins, using the instructional objectives and materials prepared in the planning stages of instruction.

Some instructors favor surprise tests in the belief that such tests keep the students studying regularly and discourage cramming. In some situations these tactics may be necessary and effective. However, most instructors see some elements of unfairness in surprise tests. Further, cramming is unlikely to be effective with, or to be encouraged by, a test of students' command of knowledge. This type of learning cannot be achieved in a few short sessions of intensive cramming. Cramming is most essential and effective if the test requires no more than superficial memory of prominent details. Advance announcement and description of test content are likely to do more to encourage productive study than the surprise administration of a test whose nature has been kept secret from the students.

Students tend to seek more information about an upcoming test than most instructors believe they need to know in advance. How many questions will there be? Will there be true-false or only multiple choice? How many points will there be? By answering such questions, the instructor can reduce unnecessarily high levels of anxiety in some students and simultaneously make all students aware that the teacher is striving for the best measure of their performance that is obtainable.

Test-Taking Skills

In addition to knowing that a test is coming, and to having a good general idea of what to expect in it, the students need to know how to give a good account of themselves on the test. The measurement of achievement requires active cooperation from the students. If they lack skill in test taking, their scores may fall short of their true achievements. Test taking is not a highly specialized skill nor is it difficult to master. But almost anyone who has taken more than a few tests can testify from personal experience how easy it is to go astray on an examination, how failure to heed all directions, carelessness, unwarranted assumptions, or ignorance of some crucial rule of the game has marred an otherwise creditable test performance.

What are some of the legitimate and essential test-taking skills that examinees ought to possess?

1. They ought to be aware of the danger of failing to read or listen attentively when directions for taking the test are presented and of the danger of failing to follow those directions exactly.
2. They should find out the basis on which responses will be scored. Will points be subtracted for wrong responses or for errors in spelling, grammar, or punctuation? Will any questions carry more weight than others?
3. They should be aware of the premium that most human scorers, and most

scoring machines, place on legibility and neatness. Accordingly, they should take pains in writing the answers or marking the answer sheet. For students beyond the elementary school level, a general explanation of how a scoring machine reads stray or multiple marks might instill a greater awareness of the need to make clean erasures and to check responses before the answer sheet is turned in.

4. They should put themselves in the best possible physical and mental shape for taking the test. Fatigue induced by an all-night cram session, even when partially offset by stimulants, is a heavy handicap. Examinees should realize that last-minute cramming is a poor substitute for consistent effort throughout the course, particularly if the test they are facing is likely to be a well-constructed measure of their command of knowledge. Some anxiety is useful in motivating examinees to do their best, but jitters are even less helpful than fatigue.

5. Students should pace themselves so as to have time to consider and respond to all the test questions. This means that they must not puzzle too long over a difficult question or problem, or write too extensively on an essay test question, even when a long answer seems easy to write.

6. They should know that ordinary guessing corrections really do not penalize even blind guessing, but simply seek not to reward it. Hence, students should act in their own best interest by attempting to answer all questions, even those that they have only a slight basis for answering.

7. In answering an essay question, students should take time to reflect, to plan, and to organize their answer before starting to write. They should decide how much they can afford to write in the time available. And in all cases they should write something, however flimsy it may seem to be, as an answer.

8. If they are making responses on a separate answer sheet, students should check frequently to be sure their mark actually indicates the response they intended and that it is marked in the spaces provided for that question.

9. If possible, examinees should take time to reread their answers, to detect and correct any careless mistakes. It is a common misconception among teachers and students that the first answer given is more likely to be correct than a changed answer. However, research evidence has shown that answer changing tends to improve test scores when the changes are based on new insights rather than random guessing (Mueller and Wasser, 1977). In addition, Crocker and Benson (1980) found that test quality is not eroded by encouraging students to reconsider their original answers.

Since examinations do count, students and their teachers are well advised to spend some time considering how to cope with them most skillfully. Some good books on the subject, giving more detailed help than we have suggested here, are available (Millman and Pauk, 1969; Divine and Kylen, 1979; Annis, 1983).

Skill in test taking is sometimes called *testwiseness*. Students who are richly endowed with this attribute are supposed to be able to score well on any test, whether they know anything about the subject or not. Further, it is supposed by some that objective tests inevitably are better measures of students' testwiseness than of their real achievements.

There is some basis for this concern. Certain tests, especially some kinds of intelligence tests, include novel, unique, and highly specialized tasks—for example, figure analogies or number series. For test items of this nature the main problem of the examinee is to "get the hang of" solving them. They do not reflect previous learning, nor is the skill developed in solving these test problems likely to be practically useful in other settings. Their use in intelligence testing is justified on the grounds that brighter students will get the hang of solving novel problems sooner, and more fully, than duller students.

Items of this type are seldom used in classroom tests. But there are common faults in item writing that may allow an examinee to substitute testwiseness for knowledge (Sarnacki, 1979). Some of these, involving unintended clues to the correct answer, were discussed in the chapters on true-false and multiple-choice test items. They are outlined and discussed in greater detail in an article by Millman (1965) and his colleagues. In a good test, however, the item writer will avoid dropping very many clues of this or any other kind. Given a test that measures command of knowledge and is free of technical flaws, error in measurement is likely to be due to too little, rather than too much, testwiseness.

Test Anxiety

The problem of test anxiety was mentioned in the preceding section. Anxiety is a frequent side effect of testing, whether that testing occurs in the classroom, on the athletic field, in the art exhibit hall, in the courtroom, in the conference room where a crucial business decision is being discussed, or in the legislative chamber where a bill is being debated. Test anxiety in the classroom is not something unique. It is a part, though hopefully not too large a part, of life itself.

Because human beings are complex and the situations in which they are tested are diverse, it is unlikely that any simple, universal answers will be found to questions concerning the cause and cure of test anxiety. Some research has been done on test anxiety, particularly among young children. However, the measurement of anxiety is no simple problem. It is not surprising that few generalizations of wide applicability can be defended solidly on the basis of research findings. Yet combining what controlled experimentation has reported with common observations of human behavior, we can offer a few generalizations that seem reasonably safe.

1. There is a negative correlation between level of ability and level of test anxiety. Those who are most capable tend to be least anxious when facing a test (Tryon, 1980).
2. There is a positive correlation between level of anxiety and level of aspiration. Those who are most anxious when facing a test tend to be those who have the greatest need or desire to do well on it.
3. Mild degrees of anxiety facilitate and enhance test performance. More extreme degrees are likely to interfere with and depress test performance.
4. The more frequent a student's contact with tests of a specific type given for a specific purpose, the less likely he or she is to be the victim of extreme anxiety.

5. Test anxiety can be educationally useful if it is distributed, at a relatively low level, throughout the course of instruction, instead of being concentrated at a relatively high level just prior to and during an examination. Skillful teaching involves the controlled release of the energy stimulated by test anxiety.

Evidence to support the belief that some students of good or superior achievement characteristically go to pieces and do poorly on every examination is hard to find. Since individuals differ in many respects, it is reasonable to suppose that they may differ also in their tolerance of the kind of stress that tests generate. On the other hand, it is conceivable that apparent instances of underachievement on tests may actually be instances of overrated ability in nontest situations. In other words, a student whose achievement is really quite modest may have cultivated the poise, the ready response, the verbal facility, and the pleasing manners that would ordinarily mark the person as an accomplished and promising scholar. All things considered, a teacher is well advised to take with several grains of salt any claim that a student's test performances never do justice to her/his real achievements.

PRESENTING THE TEST TO STUDENTS

Objective tests generally are presented to students in printed or duplicated booklets. Sometimes the questions for essay or problem tests are written on the chalkboard as the test period begins. This saves duplication costs and helps to maintain test security, but it gives the teacher the double responsibility of copying the questions and of getting the students started to work on them, all at a time when minutes are precious and when everyone is likely to be somewhat anxious to begin working. Then, too, when the chalkboard has been erased, no one has a valid record of exactly what the questions were.

Oral dictation of test questions, especially short-answer or true-false items, can be accomplished with success, but most students prefer to look at each item while they are trying to decide on a response. Some instructors put test items on slides and project them in a semidarkened room. This enables the examiner to pace the students and ensures that each examinee will give at least brief consideration to each item. Studies have indicated that examinees answer about as many items correctly when they are forced to hurry as when they choose their own pace (Curtis & Kropp, 1962; Heckman et al., 1967). With a reasonably rapid rate of item presentation, more items can be used and more reliable scores can be obtained in a given testing period. But there are drawbacks as well. Students generally are unhappy with this type of time pressure. Their attention is not so firmly fixed on their own answer sheet, making test proctoring somewhat more tedious. And make-up tests present a serious and nagging problem.

Probably the best method of test presentation is to duplicate enough copies of the examination for all students. In printed test copy, legibility of print and of format are prime considerations. Some classroom tests are duplicated unskillfully, on inadequate equipment. Questions may be crowded too closely together. Instead of being listed in a column, the response options to multiple-choice questions may be written in tandem to form a continuous, hard-to-read paragraph. Testers can avoid faults like these by taking pains with the layout and duplication of test copy. Examples of good layouts for true-false and multiple-choice test items are shown in Figure 12-1. Some duplication processes permit the use of both sides of the paper. This is economical and, if the papers are stapled only once in the upper lefthand corner, causes the examinees no

Figure 12-1 Sample Layouts of Objective-Test Items.

A. True-False Test Items

(1) The indirect influence of a test on student learning is greater than its direct influence.

(2) Most teachers are quite unaware of the fallibility of their subjective judgments.

(3) For assessing a student's typical behavior, informal observation is more effective than formal testing.

(4) Since pupils differ in ability, the tests used to measure their achievements should, ideally, also differ in difficulty.

(5) It is a good thing for students to study with an eye to doing well on the kind of tests they will have to take.

B. Multiple-Choice Test Items

(1) In what part of the process of preparing, giving, and scoring an objective test in American history would the help of another history teacher be most valuable?
   a. In planning the test
   b. In writing the original item drafts
   c. In reviewing and revising the original item drafts
   d. In scoring the answer sheets

(2) How important is the assignment of marks as a function of educational achievement tests?
   a. It has ceased to be important enough to deserve special attention.
   b. It is definitely less important than the diagnostic values of taking such tests.
   c. It is important enough to justify special efforts to construct valid and reliable tests.
   d. It is the only important function of such tests.

(3) What is the chief weakness of many achievement tests constructed by classroom teachers?
   a. They are speed tests rather than power tests.
   b. They are too difficult.
   c. They are too long.
   d. They test memory of details rather than achievement of objectives.

(4) Is it desirable for classroom teachers themselves to construct most of the tests they use? Why?
   a. Yes, because the process of test construction helps the teacher to diagnose student difficulties.
   b. Yes, because teacher-made tests permit instructors to fit the tests to their own program of instruction.
   c. No, because teachers lack the time to do an acceptable job of test construction.
   d. No, because test construction requires special knowledge and skill that few teachers possess.

problems. The use of a separate cover page on which the directions are printed helps to emphasize those directions and to keep the students from seeing the questions prematurely.

Open-book examinations, in which the examinees are permitted to bring and use textbooks, references, and class notes, have attracted some interest and attention from instructors and educational research workers. Instructors have seen in them a strong incentive for students to study for ability to use knowledge rather than for ability simply to remember it. Such examinations also encourage instructors to eschew recall-type test questions in favor of interpretation and application types. In this light there is much to be said in favor of the open-book examination. On the other hand, students soon learn that the books and notes they bring with them to class are likely to provide more moral than informational support. Looking up facts or formulas may take away from valuable problem-solving time.

An experimental comparison of scores on the same multiple-choice examination, administered as an open-book test in one section and as a closed-book test in another section of the same course in child psychology, was reported by Kalish (1958). He concluded that although "the group average scores are not affected by the examination approach, the two types of examinations measure significantly different abilities." Kalish also suggested some possible disadvantages of the open-book examination:

1. Study efforts may be reduced.
2. Efforts to overlearn sufficiently to achieve full understanding may be discouraged.
3. Note-passing and copying from other students are less obvious.
4. More superficial knowledge is encouraged.

The take-home test has some of the same characteristics as the open-book test, with two important differences. On the pro side is removal of the pressure of time, which often defeats the very purpose of a classroom open-book test. The disadvantage is the loss of assurance that the answers students submit represent their own achievements. For this reason the take-home test often functions better as a learning exercise than as an achievement test. Students may be permitted, even encouraged, to collaborate in seeking answers in which they have confidence. The efforts they sometimes put forth and the learning they sometimes achieve under these conditions can be a pleasant surprise to the instructor. But the take-home test must be scored and the scores must count in order to achieve this result. And, as with any effective testing procedure, the correct answers should be reported to the students, with opportunity for them to question and discuss. One precaution: it is especially hazardous to use a take-home test of low or unknown quality. Student cross-examination can be devastating.

If time limits for the test are generous, as they usually should be for achievement tests, the order of presentation of the items has little effect on student scores, as shown by Sax and Cromack (1966). If time is restricted, the items probably should be arranged in order of increasing difficulty. It is reasonable to suppose that to begin a test with one or two easy questions would help to lessen excessive test anxiety. It also seems reasonable to group together items that deal with the same area of subject matter. However, empirical evidence that these practices improve the validity of the test scores is difficult to obtain.

Finally, for multiple-choice tests, a check of the frequency with which each answer choice is the keyed answer should be made. With four-choice items, for example, response "A" should be the correct answer for about one-fourth of the items. There is a tendency for some item writers to use certain positions, first and last, for the keyed answer. The unintentional use of a pattern in keying items provides an advantage to the testwise, uninformed examinee and serves to lower the quality of the test generally. If the position of the correct answer is determined by a random procedure, each position likely will be used an equal number of times.

TEST-ADMINISTRATION CONSIDERATIONS

As we have stated earlier, the actual administration of most tests involves relatively few and simple problems. Since the time available for the test is usually limited, and seldom as long as some of the students wish, every available minute should be used to good advantage. By giving preliminary instructions the day before the test, by organizing test materials for efficient distribution, and by keeping last-minute oral directions and answers to questions as brief as possible, the teacher can ensure that students have the maximum amount of time to work on it. Corresponding provisions for efficient collection of materials and advance notice to the students that all work must stop when time is called help to conclude the test on time and in an orderly fashion.

To aid the students in pacing themselves, it is helpful for the teacher to write a statement like this on the chalkboard near the beginning of the test.

No more than _____ minutes remain for you to work on this test.
If you have not reached item _____ you are working too slowly.

By changing the numbers entered in these statements every 10 or 15 minutes, the teacher can help the students find time to consider all questions.

During almost any test administration, some students are likely to feel the need of asking an occasional question. Questions such as those growing out of errors in the test copy or ambiguities in the directions or test questions require answers if the students are to respond properly. Teachers should help students understand the tasks but should stop short of giving clues to the answer. Sometimes the dividing line is hard to determine.

Such questions as those stimulated by obvious but noncritical typographical errors should not even be asked. Since the process of asking and answering a question during the course of an examination is always disturbing to others, even if it is done as quietly and discreetly as possible, and since the answer to one student's question might possibly give that individual an advantage over the others, students should be urged to avoid all but the most necessary questions. Discussion of this point can well be undertaken prior to the day of the examination.

Special consideration may need to be given in settings where some examinees use English as a second or foreign language. In classroom testing situations, these students should be encouraged to ask questions related to general vocabulary or cultural situations presented in test items, information with which they may not be familiar. In some cases special test administrations may be appropriate to permit additional testing time for slower readers. The general goal of good test administration is to present and maintain the conditions that will permit all examinees to demonstrate their true level of achievement without giving advantage to any examinee.

The Problem of Cheating

In addition to giving directions, answering questions, and helping students keep track of time, the instructor has at least one other major responsibility during the course of administering a test. That is to prevent cheating. This problem, which students, teachers, and educational administrators tend to agree is serious, seems to receive more attention in the popular press than in technical books and articles on testing. Cheating on examinations is commonly viewed as a sign of declining ethical standards or as an inevitable consequence of increased emphasis on test scores and grades.

Any activity of a student or group of students whose purpose is to give any of them higher grades than they would be likely to receive on the basis of their own achievements is cheating. Thus the term covers a wide variety of activities, such as:

1. The sidelong glance at another student's answers
2. The preparation and use of a crib sheet
3. Collusion between two or more students to exchange information on answers during the test
4. Unauthorized copying of questions or stealing of test booklets in anticipation that they may be used again later on
5. Arranging for a substitute to take an examination
6. Stealing or buying copies of an examination before the test is given, or sharing such illicit advance copies with others.

Although these various forms of cheating differ in seriousness, none can be viewed with indifference. The typical student has many opportunities to cheat. Some circumstances may even encourage examinees to cheat, but none justifies their doing so. Students may conclude, not without some justification, that the ethical standards of many of their peers are not very high, at least where cheating on examinations is concerned. They may go on to infer that this fact requires them to lower their own standards or justifies them in doing so. Whatever other conditions may contribute to it, cheating would not occur if all students were to recognize that it is always dishonest and usually unfair.

Some acts of cheating are no doubt motivated by desperation. The more extreme the desperation, the more ambitious and serious the attempt to cheat is likely to be. A major factor contributing to cheating is carelessness on the instructor's part in safeguarding the examination copy before it is administered and in supervising the students during the examination.

Emphasis on grades is sometimes blamed as a primary cause of cheating. But since grades are, or should be, symbols of educational achievement, we cannot indict grading as a cause of cheating without also indicting the goal of achievement in learning. Does anyone really want to do that? No doubt most students would find it easier to resist the temptation to cheat if no advantage of any consequence were likely to result from the cheating. But refusal to recognize and reward achievement may be as effective in reducing achievement as in reducing cheating. Such a price seems too heavy to pay.

Increased use of objective tests has also been cited as a cause of cheating. The mode of response to objective tests makes some kinds of cheating easier, but the multiplicity of questions makes other kinds of cheating more difficult. No form of test is immune to all forms of cheating. The quality of a test, however, may have a direct bearing on the temptation it offers to students to cheat. Demand for detailed, superficial knowledge encourages the preparation of crib sheets. If the examination seems to the students unlikely to yield valid measures of their real achievements, if it seems unfair to them in terms of the instruction they have received, if their scores seem likely to be determined by irrelevant factors anyway, the "crime" of cheating may seem less serious.

What cures are there for cheating? The basic cure is related to the basic cause. Students and their teachers must recognize that cheating is dishonest and unfair and that it deserves consistent application of appropriate penalties— failure in the course, loss of credit, suspension, or dismissal. Reports on the prevalence of cheating, no doubt sometimes exaggerated, should not be allowed to establish cheating as an acceptable norm for student behavior or to persuade instructors that cheating is inevitable and must be accommodated as gracefully as possible.

It is the responsibility of the instructor to avoid any conditions that make cheating easy—before, during, or after an examination. The security of the examination must be safeguarded while it is being written and duplicated and when it is stored. If the class is large and if students must sit in close proximity, alternate forms of the examination should be distributed to those sitting in adjacent seats. Alternate forms can easily be prepared by arranging the same questions in different order. Finally, instructors should take seriously the task of proctoring their examinations as part of their responsibility to the majority of students who will not cheat and who should not be penalized for their honesty.

Teachers have considerable authority in their own classroom. They should not overuse it under stress or underuse it when the situation demands it. If a teacher is satisfied beyond any reasonable doubt that a student is cheating, she or he needs no other justification for:

1. Collecting the examination materials and quietly dismissing the student from the room
2. Voiding the results of the examination, requiring an alternative make-up examination, or giving the student a failing grade on the examination
3. Bringing the incident to the attention of the school authorities if further action seems necessary

One frequently mentioned proposal for dealing with the cheating problem is the establishment of an honor system. Such systems seem to work best in educational institutions of moderate size with rich traditions that encourage strong group identification and loyalties. The spirit of honor on which the system depends seldom arises or maintains itself spontaneously. It must be cultivated carefully and continuously. The things that must be done, or avoided, to maintain personal honor and the honor of the group usually are defined clearly in a code or by well-rehearsed tradition. The degree to which student experience with an honor system in such an environment cultivates a general and lasting spirit of personal honor in a world where no such system is in effect is open to question. That such systems have worked to limit, or eliminate, cheating in certain institutions seems beyond doubt. That they sometimes break down, disastrously, is also beyond doubt. The adoption of the honor system as a feasible answer to the problem of cheating on examinations is a highly questionable practice in any school.

Loss of Test Security

Instructors and administrators, especially at the college level, are occasionally beset by rumors that copies of this or that examination are "out" in advance of the scheduled administration of the examination. Sometimes the rumors are founded on fact. More often they result from misinformation that anxious students are only too eager to pass along. Finally the rumor (not so identified, of course) reaches the ears of the instructor, often via one or a number of anonymous telephone calls. What is the instructor to do?

Clearly, the instructor must determine whether or not the rumor is founded on fact, a task that must be pursued with the most vigorous effort. If the instructor is ready to enlist the aid of the informants and if they are willing to help, even anonymously, the task may be possible. If the informants are unable or unwilling to supply any leads, then they should be told courteously but plainly that their information is worthless and their transmission of it harmful.

If verifiable evidence is obtained that some students have, or have seen, advance copies of the examination, the only reasonable course of action is to prepare a new examination, even if it means changing the form of the examination and possibly losing a night of sleep. But if such evidence cannot be obtained even by a thorough search, the rumor had probably best be allowed to die as quietly as it will.

Problems of this kind are most likely to arise and to cause most serious difficulties on college campuses, which is not to say that they are totally absent from high schools. Care in safeguarding examinations before they are given is the best preventative. But it is also helpful to be ready to respond wisely, and vigorously if the situation warrants, when the rumors that a test is out *do* begin to circulate, as they almost surely will sooner or later.

TEST-SCORING PROCEDURES

Student answers to objective-test items may be recorded either on the test copy itself or on a separate answer sheet. Tests given in the elementary grades are almost always arranged so that the answers can be recorded in the test booklet. This avoids complicating the task of responding for the beginner. Cashen and Ramseyer (1969) found that the test scores of first-grade students were lowered substantially when they were required to record their answers on a separate answer sheet. Scores of second-grade students were lowered somewhat, but those of third-grade students were affected very little. Recording answers in the test booklet lessens the danger of purely clerical errors and makes the corrected test copy easier to use for instructional purposes. The use of a separate answer sheet, on the other hand, makes the scorer's task much easier. It also makes possible the reuse of the test booklet. If a scoring machine is to be used, the answers must be recorded on an answer sheet that the machine is designed to handle.

If the answers are to be recorded on the test booklet, space for the answers should be provided near one margin of the test pages. To speed scoring and minimize the possibility of errors, the scorer may record correct answers on the columns of a separate answer key card, using one column for each page of answers and positioning the answers in the column so that they will match the answer spaces on the test copy.

In scoring the answers recorded in test booklets, the scorer may find it helpful to mark the answers, using a colored pencil. A short horizontal line through the student's response can be used to indicate a correct response. Sometimes it is advantageous to mark all responses using, in addition to the horizontal line for correct responses, an "X" to indicate an incorrect response and a circle around the answer space to indicate an omitted response.

Responses are indicated on most separate answer sheets by marking one of the several response positions provided opposite the number of each item. Such answer sheets may be scored by hand, using a stencil key with holes punched to correspond to the correct responses. Transparent keys, which can be prepared on the film used to make transparencies for an overhead projector, have some advantages, as Gerlach (1966) has noted. When a separate answer sheet and a punched key are used, it is possible to indicate incorrect or omitted items by using a colored pencil to encircle the answer spaces that the student marked wrongly or did not mark at all. This kind of marking is useful when the answer sheets are returned with copies of the test for class discussion.

Most classroom tests of educational achievement are scored by the instructor. If the test is in essay form, the skill and judgment of the instructor or of someone equally competent are essential. The task of scoring an objective test is essentially clerical and can often be handled by someone whose time is less expensive than an instructor's time and whose skill and energy are less in demand for other educational tasks.

Some school systems and colleges maintain central scoring services. Usually these services make use of small scoring machines, several of which are now available. But even if all the scoring is done by hand, a central service has the value of fostering the development of special skills that make for rapid, accurate scoring. Institutional test-scoring services often provide statistical and test analysis services as well, and sometimes they even offer test duplication services that provide expert assistance in the special problems of test production and in the maintenance of test security.

Instructors sometimes use the class meeting following the test for test scoring. Asking each student to check the answers of a classmate may on occasion be a reasonable and rewarding use of class time, but often the process tends to be slow and inaccurate. A difficulty encountered by one student on one test paper may interrupt and delay the whole operation. Most important, if the student scorers are concentrating on mechanical accuracy of scoring, as they probably should be, the circumstances will not favor much learning as a by-product of the scoring process.

But students can and usually should have the chance to learn from the mistakes they make on a test. Ordinarily the best occasion for this learning is *after* the tests have been scored and the answer sheets returned to the students. The correct answer to each item can be recorded on the chalkboard, on a duplicated handout, or best of all, directly on the student's answer sheet. With this information students can satisfy themselves of the accuracy with which their answers have been scored. Distributing copies of the test booklet will allow students to discover the nature of their mistakes and to clarify any misunderstandings. The teacher can prevent protracted arguments over the correctness of any particular answer by asking the protesting student to state his/her case in writing, with a promise of credit if the case seems to merit it. Discussions of this kind contribute to the feeling that students are being treated openly and fairly. Test reviews can also contribute enough to an increase in students' command of knowledge to be well worth the time required.

Scoring Machines

Recent advances in computing technology have contributed to the development of an array of electronic scoring machines that are practically useful and economically accessible to school districts and colleges of all sizes. These optical scanners can be operated independently by relatively unskilled workers or they can be integrated into a variety of complex computer equipment configurations. They may be attached to a large computer directly or they may send information to such a computer over transmission lines. They can be attached to a microcomputer or minicomputer. As a self-contained system, some scanners can read the answer sheets, compute the score for each, and print the score on the answer sheet. Smaller machines do so at the rate of 300 sheets per hour, but larger ones process as many as 6000 or more per hour. Most machines require that specially printed answer sheets be used, forms produced with a type of paper and ink that are compatible with the optical sensing system of the machine. These special forms are available in a variety of sizes and can accommodate more than 200 five-choice multiple-choice items per form.

Freestanding complex optical scanners provide flexibility and efficiency for a variety of situations (Frisbie, 1978a). The large, high-capacity machines are relatively expensive and tend to be used by universities and national testing agencies that deal with large volumes of test scoring. In addition to the quick and accurate scoring that optical scanners provide, they make it possible to use computers efficiently to create frequency distributions, test statistics, reliability estimates, and class score rosters. They provide information that allows the test constructor to evaluate the test and revise the items for future use. It is difficult to exaggerate the contribution that optical scanners and computers can make to the efficient use of objective tests and to the progressive improvement of tests through test analysis.

Correction for Guessing

Scores on objective tests are sometimes corrected for guessing. The purpose of such a correction is to reduce to zero the gain in score expected to result from blind guessing. In other words, a guessing correction is intended to give the student who guesses blindly on certain questions no reasonable expectation of advantage in the long run over the student who omits the same questions.

Suppose a student were to guess blindly on 100 true-false test items. Since there are only two possible answers, one of which is certain to be correct, the student has reason to expect a score somewhere around 50. Another student, knowing no less than the first but reluctant to guess blindly, might attempt no answers and thus receive a zero. Without correction for guessing, the score of the first student would be higher than that of the second when, in fact, the two scores should be the same.

To correct the first student's score for guessing, it is necessary to subtract from that score an amount equal to the expected gain from blind guessing. Since on a true-false test the student can expect to answer one question wrongly for every question he/she answers correctly, the number of wrong answers is simply subtracted from the number of right answers. If the questions provided three equally likely answers instead of two, the student would expect to give two wrong answers to every right answer. In this case one would subtract one-half of the number of wrong responses from the number of right responses to correct for guessing. If multiple-choice items list five alternative possible answers to each question, only one of which is correct, the expected ratio of wrong to right answers is 4 to 1 and the guessing correction would call for subtracting one-fourth of the number of wrong answers from the number of right answers.

Logic of this kind leads to a general formula for correction for guessing

$$S = R - \frac{W}{N - 1} \qquad\qquad 12.1$$

where

S stands for the score corrected for guessing
R for the number of questions answered rightly
W for the number of questions answered wrongly, and
N for the number of possible alternative answers equally likely to be chosen in blind guessing.

It is easy to see that this formula becomes

$$S = R - W \qquad\qquad 12.2$$

in the case of two-alternative (true-false) items, or

$$S = R - \frac{W}{4} \qquad\qquad 12.3$$

in the case of five-alternative multiple-choice test items.

Instead of penalizing the student who guesses, one could correct for guessing by rewarding the student who refrains from guessing. That is, instead of subtracting 50 units from the score of the guesser, we could add 50 units to the score of the nonguesser. This too would eliminate the expected advantage from blind guessing. The assumption in this case is that if the nonguesser had guessed, she/he would have given the right answer to one-half of the true-false items. On three-alternative items the nonguesser would have given correct answers to one-third of the items.

Logic of this kind leads to a second general formula for guessing correction

$$S' = R + \frac{O}{N} \qquad\qquad 12.4$$

where

S' is the score corrected for guessing on the basis of items omitted

R is the number of items answered correctly

O is the number of items omitted, and

N is the number of alternative answers whose choice is equally likely on the basis of blind guessing.

Again, it is easy to see that this general formula becomes

$$S' = R + \frac{O}{2} \qquad\qquad 12.5$$

in the case of true-false items, or

$$S' = R + \frac{O}{5} \qquad\qquad 12.6$$

in the case of five-alternative multiple-choice test items.

If the same set of test scores is corrected for guessing in two different ways, by subtracting a fraction of the wrong answers and by adding a fraction of the omitted answers, two different sets of corrected scores will be obtained. But although the two sets of scores will differ in their average value (with the omit-corrected scores being higher in all cases) and in their variability (with the omit-corrected scores being more variable almost always), the two sets of scores will be perfectly correlated. If student A makes a higher score than student B when the appropriate fractions of their wrong responses are subtracted from the total of their right responses, A will also make a higher score than B when the appropriate fraction of their items omitted is added to the total of their correct responses.

Correction for guessing by subtracting a fraction of the wrong responses is sometimes criticized on the ground that it is based on a false assumption—the assumption that every wrong response is the result of blind guessing. But the falseness of that assumption (and usually it is completely false) does not invalidate the correction formula that rests on it: No such assumption is made in the formula for guessing correction on the basis of items omitted and yet the two formulas yield scores that agree perfectly in their relative ranking of students. Scores corrected by subtraction may be regarded logically as too low in absolute value, just as those corrected by addition may be regarded logically as too high in absolute value. But they are equally sound in relative value. With scores on tests of educational achievement, the absolute value is usually far less significant than the relative value.

It is also worth noting here that if no items are omitted, scores corrected for guessing by subtracting a fraction of the wrong responses correlate perfectly with the uncorrected scores, that is, with the numbers of right responses. This indicates that the magnitude of the effect of a guessing correction depends on the proportion of items omitted. Only if considerable numbers of items are omitted by at least some of the students will the application of either formula for correction for guessing have an appreciable effect.

Here are some considerations that should influence the test maker's decision regarding the use of a correction for guessing on objective achievement tests:

1. Scores corrected for guessing will usually rank students in about the same relative positions as do uncorrected scores.
2. The probability of obtaining a respectable score on a good objective test by blind guessing alone is extremely small.
3. Well-motivated examinees who have time to attempt all items guess blindly on few, if any, of them.
4. Seldom is any moral or educational evil involved in the encouragement of students to make the best rational guesses they can.
5. Students' rational guesses can provide useful information about their general level of achievement.
6. If a test is timed, a guessing correction removes the incentive for slower students to guess blindly.
7. Scores corrected for guessing may include irrelevant measures of the examinee's testwiseness or willingness to gamble.

Contrary to what students sometimes seem to believe, the typical correction for guessing applies no special penalty to the one who guesses. It simply tends to eliminate the advantage to the student who guesses blindly in preference to omitting items. Testwise students know they have nothing to lose, and perhaps something to gain, by making use of every hunch and scrap of information in attempting to answer every item. The test-naive student, or the one who tends to avoid taking chances, may be influenced by a guessing correction to omit many items on which his or her likelihood of correct response is well above the chance level (Rowley and Traub, 1977; Wood, 1976). To the degree that scores corrected for guessing give a special advantage to the bold or testwise student, their validity as measures of achievement suffer.

DIFFERENTIAL ITEM WEIGHTING

All objective-test scores are obtained by adding weighted response scores. The simplest system of scoring weights, and the one most often used, is +1 for the correct response to each test item and 0 for any response not correct. Correction for guessing involves a slightly more complex set of scoring weights, such as +1 for each correct response, -1 or $-\frac{1}{2}$ or $-\frac{1}{3}$, and so on, for each wrong response, and 0 for each omitted response.

Some test constructors believe that certain items in their test should carry more weight than others because they are more important items—items of better technical quality, items of greater complexity or difficulty, or items that are more time-consuming. For example in a test composed of 50 true-false and 25 multiple-choice items, the test constructor may decide that each multiple-choice item should be worth two points and each true-false item should be worth only one point.

Reasonable as such differential weights seem to be on the surface, they seldom make the test to which they are applied a more reliable or valid measure. Nor do they ordinarily make the test a much worse measure. Like guessing corrections, to which they are closely related, they tend to have relatively small effects. The data shown in Table 12-1 support this generalization (Evaluation and Examination Service, 1982.) Each of four instructors requested a slightly different weighting scheme when presenting their examination for test scoring. The value in the last column shows the correlation between uncorrected scores (weights of +1 and 0) and corrected scores using the requested weights. The rank order of students was essentially the same in both test-score distributions and the Kuder-Richardson reliabilities were nearly identical. There is no obvious advantage to using the differential weights in any of these cases. Sabers and White (1969) reached the same conclusion:

> . . . from the point of view of test construction, weighted scoring is probably not worth the effort. The same advantages can be gained by adding more items or by selecting only the best items from a larger pool. From the administrative

Table 12-1 The Effect of Differential Item Weighting Applied to Four Tests

Test Number	No. of Students	No. of Items	Type of Weighting	Correlation
1	83	41	Rights = +4 Wrongs = −1	.945
2	50	160	Rights = +1 (1–140) Rights = +3 (141–160)	.923
3	34	105	Rights = +1 (1–70) Rights = +2 (71–105)	.983
4	21	90	Rights = +1 (1–45) Rights = +3 (46–90)	.976

point of view, unweighted scoring saves time and offers fewer possibilities for errors in calculating the scores; in addition, the resulting raw scores are probably easier to interpret.

If an achievement test covers two areas, one of which is judged to be twice as important as the other, then twice as many items should be written over the more important area. This generally will result in more reliable and valid measures than if an equal number of items is written for each area and those for the more important area are double-weighted.

Complex or time-consuming items should be made to yield more than one response, each of which can be independently scored as right or wrong. The advantages of multiple true-false items for such situations were described in Chapter 10. Very difficult items are likely to contribute less than moderately difficult items to test reliability. Giving the more difficult items extra weight lowers the average effectiveness of the items and thus lowers the effectiveness of the test as a whole.

It has occurred to some test constructors that differential weighting of responses to test items might be useful in improving test reliability or validity. For example, in a question like the following:

A child complains of severe pain and tenderness in the lower abdomen, with nausea. What should the child's mother do?
a. Give the child a laxative.
b. Put the child to bed.
c. Call the doctor.

Choice of the first response might result in a score of -1, of the second in a score of 0, and of the third in a score of $+1$. In this case the scoring weights were determined a priori. It has also been suggested that they might be determined experimentally, so as to maximize test reliability or validity.

But in this case also the experimental results have been disappointing (Downey, 1979). Seldom have any appreciable, consistent gains in reliability or validity been found. It seems clear that to gain any real advantage by this means one would need to write items with this purpose specifically in mind. Most item writers, even skilled professionals, have enough difficulty writing items good enough for simple right-or-wrong scoring. To make them good enough for more finely graded differential weighting seems a formidable task. Test improvement via additional, good, simply scored items looks more promising to most item writers.

Exceptions will be found, of course, to the generalization that differential weighting of items, or of item responses, is not worthwhile in the scoring of classroom tests of educational achievement. But it is a good general guide to the constructor of an educational achievement test to settle for simple right-or-wrong scoring of individual items, with each item carrying the same weight as every other item, regardless of its importance, complexity, difficulty, or quality. Increasing the number of scorable units and making each unit as good as possible seem generally more effective than differential weighting of items or responses as a means of test improvement.

COMPUTER-ASSISTED TEST ADMINISTRATION

Computerized testing has long been a part of the computer-assisted instruction programs that have developed to greater levels of complexity as computer technology has improved and become more accessible. Today computers are used for test-administration purposes primarily in programs of individualized instruction, for both formative and summative evaluation. Though it is possible to administer any kind of objective or essay test with a computer, the practicalities associated with doing so have not made it a popular mode for testing a large group of examinees with the same test items.

The computer offers speed and accuracy in computing and storing that make it a logical candidate for taking on test administration chores. It can be programmed to select items for each examinee according to content specifications and item difficulty. It can use the examinee's score on a given item to decide which item should be presented next. It can score an item immediately and store the result in any of several locations in its memory. It can use its internal clock to monitor the amount of time each examinee takes to respond to each item. It can store information about test-item performance as well as examinee performance. It can provide examinees with their test score as soon as they respond to the last test item. It seems that the potential of the computer for streamlining test administrations is bounded only by our imaginations in telling the computer what it can do for us.

There are problems to be resolved, however, before mass testing by computer becomes commonplace. There must be a large pool of test items in the computer's bank, so that, for test security purposes, every examinee does not receive exactly the same items that those previously tested received. The items different examinees receive must be relatively equivalent in content and difficulty, otherwise their test scores will not be comparable. There is no assurance that a bank of test items can be maintained without permitting unauthorized access to those items. One computer whiz seems able to "outfox" the other to break security codes designed to limit access and preserve confidentiality. The old-fashioned lock and key still appears to be the safest way to store test items or booklets in preparation for test administration. Further discussion of the role of computers in testing and of the future trends of computerized testing appears in Chapter 19.

SUMMARY

Some of the main ideas presented in this chapter are summarized in these statements:

1. Students should be told in advance when an important test is to be given and what the nature of the content is to be.
2. Students at all educational levels should be taught essential test-taking skills.

3. The test developer should avoid clues in the test items that enable an examinee to substitute test-wiseness for command of knowledge.
4. Test anxiety is seldom a major factor in determining a student's score on a test.
5. Objective classroom tests usually are, and should be, presented in duplicated test booklets.
6. Both open-book and take-home tests offer advantages that are outweighed by their disadvantages relative to in-class, closed-book tests.
7. There is no conclusive research evidence that supports the ordering of items in a test according to difficulty level or on the basis of subject-matter areas.
8. The position of the correct answer in multiple-choice items should be distributed somewhat evenly so that overuse or underuse of a position does not provide a clue to examinees.
9. The test administrator should help students to adjust their rate of work on a test to the time available.
10. Special test-administration procedures for classroom tests may be needed to accommodate students with language handicaps.
11. The instructor should be responsible for both the prevention and the punishment of cheating on classroom examinations.
12. The development of an honor system is not a promising solution to the problem of cheating during examinations.
13. The instructor should be responsible for preserving the security of a test prior to its administration.
14. The use of separate answer sheets facilitates rapid clerical or machine scoring of objective tests.
15. Recent advances in computer technology have made test-scoring machines more readily available for use by schools in scoring classroom tests.
16. The purpose of using a guessing correction is to reduce to zero the expected score gain from blind guessing.
17. One may correct scores for guessing by subtracting a fraction of the wrong responses from, or by adding a fraction of the omitted responses to, the number-right score.
18. Scores corrected for guessing usually will rank the examinees in about the same order as uncorrected scores.
19. The probability of getting a respectable score on a good objective test by blind guessing alone is small.
20. Students should be encouraged to make rational guesses on the answers to objective-test items.
21. Giving different weights to different items in a test, or to different correct or incorrect responses within an item, seldom improves score reliability or valid score use appreciably.
22. Despite the apparent advantages of computer-administered testing, important practical problems must be resolved before mass testing by computer becomes commonplace.

PROJECTS AND PROBLEMS

Project: Test Administration and Scoring

Each of the statements below is a hypothesis that could be tested—supported or refuted—with evidence from a research study. Choose one of the statements and describe a study you could conduct in a single classroom to gather evidence to "test" the hypothesis. Limit your description to no more than about 250 words.

1. Students do very little blind guessing on good classroom objective tests.
2. The use of a separate test answer sheet by young students will not adversely affect their test scores.
3. The use of differential scoring weights for items judged more or less important than others will not affect the rank order of students' scores appreciably.
4. Students' rate of work on a test is directly related to their levels of test performance.
5. Directions to "not make any marks on your test booklet" (except to record the intended answer when answer sheets are not used) adversely affect both student rate of work and overall test performance.
6. Students score higher on multiple-choice and true-false tests presented in written form than on those presented orally.

Your description of a study will be evaluated on the basis of its feasibility for providing evidence about the hypothesis you chose. Its completeness will be judged by the adequacy with which subjects, measures, and data-gathering procedures are described.

13

USING TEST AND ITEM ANALYSIS TO EVALUATE AND IMPROVE TEST QUALITY

What makes an achievement test a good test? This question concerns both students and teachers whenever a test is given. The answer has direct implications for instruction and for further test development work. With respect to instruction, the feedback loop that leaves and then returns to the performance-assessment component of the Basic Teaching Model (described in Chapter 2) is significant. It indicates that the teacher should assess the quality of the tools of assessment. If students' performances are below expectation, perhaps the explanation lies in the methods of evaluation rather than in inadequate learning on the students' part. Tests should be evaluated, then, to determine if the scores they yield have value for the purpose for which they were originally intended.

There is another practical reason for instructors to evaluate and analyze the test scores and the test from which they were derived. When tests have been scored and returned to students for discussion, considerable learning can occur. However, unless the test review session has been planned well by the teacher in advance, the opportunities for learning can be preempted by lengthy debates about correct answers and item semantics. A teacher who is prepared with information about poorly performing test items and possible explanations for them stands a better chance of maintaining control of the class session and clearing up misconceptions or misunderstandings revealed by the test-item data.

A third reason for analyzing and evaluating a test after its administration relates to the teacher's professional development. Test and item data can reveal technical flaws and errors of judgment made by the item writer. By making use of these data, teachers can improve their item-writing skills and, at the same time, revise their test items for future use. Eventually a large pool of high-quality test items will accumulate, and the ability to develop high-quality items will be enhanced in the process.

TEST CHARACTERISTICS TO EVALUATE

The characteristics to consider in judging the quality of an achievement test are the same ones that the test developer considers in trying to build a good test. Some of these important factors are relevance, balance, efficiency, specificity, difficulty, discrimination, variability, and reliability. Though some of these characteristics are evaluated with different criteria for content-referenced or group-referenced measures, each is important to consider, regardless of the type of score interpretation the test is intended to provide.

Relevance and Balance

Relevance indicates the extent to which the test items reflect the test specifications and contribute to achieving the stated purpose for testing. Assessing the relevance of test items requires judgments rather than quantitative criteria. Are the test specifications and purpose sufficiently explicit to allow the test reviewer to decide which items are relevant and which are not? In view of the test purpose, does an item like this belong in this test? Items that are judged to be relevant are not necessarily of high quality, but they are items that appear to measure the abilities that the test constructor set out to measure.

Most test constructors seek *balance* in their tests. They hope that the items they select for inclusion in the test will sample representatively all of the important tasks—knowledge, skills, and understandings—outlined in the test plan. The table of specifications developed in the test-planning stage is intended to be a guide to choosing items for the test. An assessment of test balance is simply a judgment about the extent to which the ideal specifications were achieved in terms of content representativeness.

Efficiency and Specificity

A test that yields a large number of independently scorable responses per unit of testing time is an efficient test. *Efficiency* is a relative characteristic that must be judged by comparing a test with other hypothetical tests that could have been used to serve the same purpose. In general a multiple-choice test will be more efficient than an essay test, and a true-false test more efficient than a multiple-choice test. A multiple true-false test may be the most efficient of the four types. But items of any given type may be more or less efficient as well. For example, multiple-choice items that contain implausible distracters are less efficient than those that do not. Unnecessarily lengthy true-false items are less efficient than shorter but relevant statements. Relevance need not and should not be sacrificed to achieve greater efficiency.

A test shows high *specificity* if a testwise novice in the subject matter achieves a near chance score on it. Under such circumstances there is good assurance that the test measures content specific to the objectives of instruction rather than general information. To the degree that any achievement test is a test of reading or writing ability or general intelligence, it suffers in specificity. The most useful evidence for assessing specificity is obtained from the responses of proficient test takers who do not have competence in the field covered by the test.

Difficulty and Discrimination

Tests that are too easy or too difficult for the group tested yield score distributions that make it hard to identify reliable differences in achievement levels between members of the group. Useful norm-referenced score interpretations are less likely to be obtained under such circumstances. The goal with respect to test *difficulty* is to obtain a mean score that is about halfway between a perfect score and the expected chance score. The difficulty of a test is determined by the difficulty of each of the items that comprise it. The ideal difficulty of a 100-item, four-choice multiple-choice test is 62.5, and ideally each item should be answered correctly by about 62.5 percent of the group.

The ability of a test to discriminate between high- and low-achieving students is a function of the ability of each of the items to do just that. If a large proportion of the "good" students get an item right and a small proportion of the "poor" students get it right, that item is discriminating properly and is contributing to the test purpose. *Discrimination* is closely related to difficulty in that items that are too hard or too easy are not as capable of discriminating between high- and low-achieving students as items of moderate difficulty.

Variability and Reliability

As long as differences in student learning exist, and as long as the purpose for testing is to identify such differences, the distribution of test scores should exhibit high *variability*. The larger the standard deviation of the scores, the more successful the test constructor has been in capturing the individual differences in achievement. The role of difficulty and discrimination in obtaining variability should be apparent. Extremely easy or hard tests yield skewed distributions with relatively small standard deviations. Tests composed of items of moderate difficulty stand the best chance of discriminating between levels of achievement and producing high score variability.

The *reliability* of the scores for a group of examinees is the most important *statistical* measure of the quality of the scores. Of course, no matter how high the reliability estimate is for a set of scores, unless relevance is present, the test user may have succeeded in measuring some irrelevant abilities quite accurately. The goals of high score variability, high discrimination, and moderate difficulty all contribute to the major aim of achieving high test-score reliability.

All of these test characteristics are important to consider in evaluating the quality of an achievement test, and the evaluation of each can provide clues regarding the ways in which the test items might be revised and improved for future use. Further discussion of each characteristic can be found in the remaining sections of this chapter and in Ebel (1972).

THE PROCESS OF ITEM ANALYSIS

The analysis of student responses to objective-test items is a powerful tool for test improvement. Item analysis indicates which items may be too easy or too difficult and which may fail, for other reasons, to discriminate between the better and poorer examinees. Item analysis sometimes suggests why an item has not functioned effectively and how it might be improved. A test composed of items revised and selected on the basis of item-analysis data is almost certain to be much more reliable than one composed of an equal number of untested items.

Item analysis begins after the test has been administered and scored. Many different processes of item analysis and many different indices of item quality have been developed (Davis, 1952; Turnbull, 1956; Sato, 1980). A procedure simple enough to be used regularly by classroom teachers, but complete and precise enough to contribute substantially to test improvement, has been chosen for detailed discussion in this chapter. It requires six steps:

1. Arrange the scored test papers or answer sheets in score order from highest to lowest.
2. Identify an upper group and a lower group separately. The upper group is the highest-scoring 27 percent of the group and the lower group is the lowest-scoring 27 percent.
3. For each item, count the number of examinees in the upper group that chose each response alternative. Do a separate, similar tally for the lower group.
4. Record these counts on a copy of the test at the end of the corresponding response alternatives.
5. Add the two counts for the keyed response and divide this sum by the total number of students in the upper *and* lower groups. Multiply this decimal value by 100 to form a percentage. The result is an estimate of the index of item difficulty.
6. Subtract the lower-group count from the upper-group count for the keyed response. Divide this difference by the number of examinees in one of the groups (either group, since both are the same size). The result, expressed as a decimal, is the index of discrimination.

An Example

An illustration of the data obtained by this process for one item is presented in Figure 13-1. Answer sheets from a contemporary affairs test were available for 178 students, so the upper and lower groups consisted of the 48 students having the highest and the 48 having the lowest scores. The keyed response is marked with an asterisk. The figures in parentheses following each response alternative indicate how many of the upper group (first figure) and how many of the lower group (second figure) chose each response. Of the 48 in the upper group, 47 students chose the first response (the keyed answer) and 1 chose the fourth response. Of the 48 students in the lower group, 24 chose the first response, 10 the second, 5 the third, and 7 the fourth. Two of the lower-group students failed to respond to the item at all.

The moderate degree of difficulty of the item is indicated by the 74 percent of correct response in the two groups combined, calculated as follows:

a. Add the two counts for the keyed response:

47 + 24 = 71

b. Divide this sum by the total number of students:

71 ÷ 96 = 0.74

c. Convert the decimal value to a percentage:

0.74 × 100 = 74%

This difficulty value is actually an estimate of the difficulty index that would be obtained if we determined the percentage of the entire group, all 178 students, that answered the item correctly. The estimate will be quite satisfactory for large classes but it may be fairly inaccurate for smaller classes. For small classes, of course, tallying the responses of all students to compute the difficulty index would not be terribly time-consuming.

Figure 13-1 Illustration of Item-Analysis Data.

74% What change in life expectancy (number of years a person is likely to live) has been
0.48 occurring?

    *a. It has been increasing. (47–24)
    b. It has been declining due to rising rates of cancer and heart disease. (0–10)
    c. It has increased for young people but decreased for older people. (0–5)
    d. It has remained quite stable. (1–7)
       Omits (0–2)

The reasonably good level of discrimination of the item is indicated by the difference in proportions of correct response between the upper and lower groups [(47 − 24) ÷ 48 = 0.48]. And each of the distracters functioned well, since each attracted some responses, and these were largely from students in the lower group.

SELECTION OF THE CRITERION GROUPS

The type of item analysis we describe in this chapter, like most such procedures, makes use of an internal criterion for the selection of groups of high and low achievement. That is, the total score on the test to be analyzed is used as the criterion rather than some other independent (external) measure of achievement. In order to conclude that an item showing high discrimination is a good item, one must assume that the entire test, of which that item is a part, is a good test.

Such an assumption is ordinarily quite reasonable. Most test constructors come close enough to the mark on their first attempt to make the total score a fairly dependable basis for distinguishing between students of high and low achievement. However, it must be conceded that item analysis using an internal criterion can only make a test a better measure of *whatever it does measure*. To make the test a better measure of what it *ought* to measure, one would need to use some better criterion than the total score on the test itself. Obviously this would be an external criterion. Yet an external criterion has no real advantage over an internal criterion unless it is truly a better measure than the test of whatever the test is supposed to measure.

The use of total test score as a basis for selecting upper and lower groups for item analysis has two important advantages. The first is relevance. Within limits set by the wisdom and skill of the test constructor, the score on a teacher-made test does come closer than any other measure is likely to come to measuring what that person wished to measure. The second is convenience. The total score on the test whose items are being analyzed is always readily available.

The selection of highly discriminating items, using total test score as the criterion, results in a test whose items are valid measures of what the whole test measures. In this sense, item analysis is a technique of item validation. But the kind of analysis and selection we have been considering does not demonstrate, and might not even improve, the validity of the test as a whole. What it can do to the test as a whole, and this is no small thing, is to make the test more reliable, and thus probably more valid too.

Step 3 in the process of item analysis called for the counting of responses in upper and lower 27 percent groups. Why 27 percent? Why not upper and lower fourths (25 percent), thirds (33 percent), or even halves (50 percent)? The answer is that 27 percent provides the best compromise between two desirable but inconsistent aims: (1) to make the extreme groups as large as possible and (2) to make the extreme groups as different as possible. Truman Kelley (1939) demonstrated that when extreme groups, each consisting of approximately 27 percent of the total group, are used, one can say with the greatest confidence that those in the upper group are superior in the ability measured by the test to those in the lower group.

Although upper and lower groups of 27 percent are best, they are not significantly better than groups of 25 or 33 percent. Test analysts who prefer to work with simple fractions like one-fourth or one-third should feel free to use upper and lower fourths or thirds. However, those who do should guard against the intuitive feeling that 33 percent is better than 27 percent because it involves groups of larger size or that 25 percent is better than 27 percent because the difference between the groups is greater. In each case the supposed advantage is slightly more than offset by the opposing disadvantage. The optimum value is 27 percent.

Counting the Responses

The counting of responses to the items is likely to be the most tedious and time-consuming part of the analysis. However, for many classroom tests the number of papers in each extreme group may be less than ten, which makes the task seem less formidable. A chart can be developed that has items numbered down the left side and response alternatives labeled across the top as column headings. The chart helps to organize the work and, if many copies of it are duplicated at one time, a supply can be kept on hand for future tests or to share with colleagues. Often clerical staff or volunteer aides can perform the tallying work and computation with minimal guidance.

Some teachers obtain response counts by a show of hands in class, as suggested by Diedrich (1960), or by using student volunteers. But neither of these approaches is recommended here, because each fails to maintain the confidentiality of the test scores that students and their parents should expect to be respected. Optical scanners and computers are the most efficient tools available for obtaining the item-analysis counts and indices. Many school districts and colleges with data-processing and computing facilities make such analysis available to teachers. Some institutions share computer programs and equipment to make these services readily accessible.

THE INDEX OF DISCRIMINATION

The index of discrimination that results from step 6 was first described by Johnson (1951). Since then it has attracted considerable attention and approval (Engelhart, 1965). It is simpler to compute and to explain to others than such other indices of discrimination as the point-biserial correlation, biserial correlation,

Flanagan's coefficient (Flanagan, 1939), and Davis's coefficient (Davis, 1946). It has the very useful property, which most of the other correlation indices lack, of being biased in favor of items of middle difficulty. As we have already seen, it is precisely these items that provide the largest amounts of information about differences in levels of achievement and that thus contribute most to test reliability. If the primary goal of item selection is to maximize test reliability, as it probably should be for most classroom tests, the items having highest discrimination in terms of this index should be chosen. Item difficulty need not be considered directly in item selection, since no item that is much too difficult or much too easy can possibly show good discrimination when the upper-lower difference index is used.

Item discrimination indices of all types are subject to considerable sampling error (Pyrczak, 1973). The smaller the sample of answer sheets used in the analysis, the larger the sampling errors. An item that appears highly discriminating in one small sample may appear weak or even negative in discrimination in another sample. The values obtained for achievement test items are also sensitive to the kind of instruction the students received relative to the item. Hence the use of refined statistics to measure item discrimination seldom seems to be warranted.

But even though one cannot determine the discrimination indices of individual items reliably without using large samples of student responses, item analysis based on small samples is still worthwhile as a means of overall test improvement. How much better a revised test composed of the most discriminating items can be expected to be will depend on how large the samples and how small the sampling errors are.

Biserial and Point-Biserial Indices

The biserial and point-biserial correlation coefficients are presented as discrimination indices in some item-analysis reports generated by a computer. Their computation is too complex and time-consuming to warrant our attention, but because they are popular indices of discrimination, it is worth comparing each with the upper-lower difference index discussed above.

The *biserial correlation coefficient* describes the relationship between two variables: score on a test item and score on the total test for each examinee. High positive correlations are obtained for items that high-scoring students on the test tend to get right (item score = +1) and low-scoring students on the test tend to get wrong (item score = 0). Such items are interpreted to be high in discrimination. Negatively discriminating items show the opposite relationship: Most students with high test scores have scores of zero on the test item and many with low test scores have scores of +1 on the item. The *point-biserial correlation coefficient* differs from the biserial coefficient computationally and theoretically, but for item-analysis purposes the two can be interpreted in essentially the same manner.

When both are computed with data from the same test item, the biserial coefficient will yield a value that is always at least a fourth larger than the point-biserial (Guilford, 1965, p. 324). Neither coefficient is as biased in favor of items of moderate difficulty as is the case with the upper-lower index. Thus, it is possible to obtain relatively high point-biserial or biserial discrimination indices for very hard or very easy items. This point is worth remembering when selecting items on the basis of their discrimination indices to build a test or to determine which items may be in need of revision.

THE INDEX OF DIFFICULTY

Historically, two measures of item difficulty have been used. One, which is slightly harder to calculate but slightly less confusing to interpret, defines the index of difficulty of a test item as the percentage of a defined group of examinees who did *not* answer it correctly. Under this definition the larger the numerical value of the index of difficulty is, the more difficult the item. The second measure defines the difficulty index as the percentage of the group who answered the item correctly. The larger the value of the index is, the *easier* the item. Despite the minor confusion associated with it, the second definition is used in this book because it has been so consistently adopted by measurement specialists in the literature related to achievement testing.[1]

The value of the index of difficulty of a test item is not determined solely by the content of the item. It reflects also the ability of the group responding to the item. Hence, it is more appropriate to say, "When this item was administered to that particular group, its index of difficulty was 63 percent," than to say, "The index of difficulty for this item is 63 percent."

The Distribution of Item-Difficulty Indices

It is quite natural to assume, and many test constructors do assume, that a good test intended to discriminate well over a fairly wide range of levels of achievement must include some easy items to test the poorer students and some difficult items to test the better students. But the facts of educational achievement testing seldom warrant such an assumption. The items in most achievement tests are not like a set of hurdles of different heights, all of which present essentially the same task and differ only in level of difficulty. Achievement test items do differ in difficulty, but they differ also in the kind of task they present.

Suppose a class of 20 students takes a test on which 12 of the students answer item 6 correctly but only 8 answer item 7 correctly. A reasonable assumption

---

[1] The definition of item difficulty used in previous editions of this book was the percent of the group that either responded *incorrectly* or omitted the item.

is that any student who answered the harder question (item 7) correctly should also answer correctly the easier question (item 6). Anyone who missed the easier question would also be expected to miss the harder. But such assumptions and expectations are often mistaken when applied to educational achievement tests.

Table 13-1 presents data on the responses of 11 students to six test items. A plus (+) in the table represents a correct response, a zero (0) an incorrect response. In this exhibit the students have been arranged in order of ability, and the items in order of difficulty. Note that the item missed by good student B was not one of the most difficult items. Poor student J missed all of the easier items but managed correct answers to two of the more difficult items.

It is possible to imagine a test which would give highly consistent results across items and across students when adminstered to a particular group. Results would be called consistent if success by a particular student on a particular item practically guaranteed success on all other items in the test that were easier for the group than that item. Correspondingly, failure on a particular item would almost guarantee failure on all harder items if student responses were highly consistent. But a test showing such a degree of consistency among the responses would also be characterized by much higher reliability than ordinarily obtained with the same number of items. Such tests can be imagined but are seldom met with in practice. This is another reason why specifications requiring that the test include items ranging widely in difficulty are seldom warranted.

Most item writers produce some items that are ineffective (nondiscriminating) because they are too difficult or too easy. Efforts to improve the accuracy with which a test measures, that is, to improve its reliability, usually have the effect of reducing the range of item difficulty rather than increasing it. The differences in difficulty that remain among items highest in discrimination are usually more than adequate to make the test effective in discriminating different levels of achievement over the whole range of abilities for which the test is expected to be used.

Some data from a simple experimental study of the relation between spread of item-difficulty values, on the one hand, and spread of test scores and level of reliability coefficients, on the other, are presented in Figure 13-2.

Three synthetic tests of 16 items each were "constructed" by the selection of items from a 61-item trial form of a social science test. This trial form had

Table 13-1 Responses of 11 Students to Six Test Items

Student	A	B	C	D	E	F	G	H	I	J	K
Item 1	+	+	+	+	+	+	+	+	+	0	0
Item 2	+	+	+	+	+	+	0	+	0	0	+
Item 3	+	0	+	0	0	+	+	+	+	0	0
Item 4	+	+	0	+	0	0	+	0	0	+	0
Item 5	+	+	+	+	+	0	0	0	0	0	0
Item 6	+	+	0	0	+	0	0	0	0	+	0

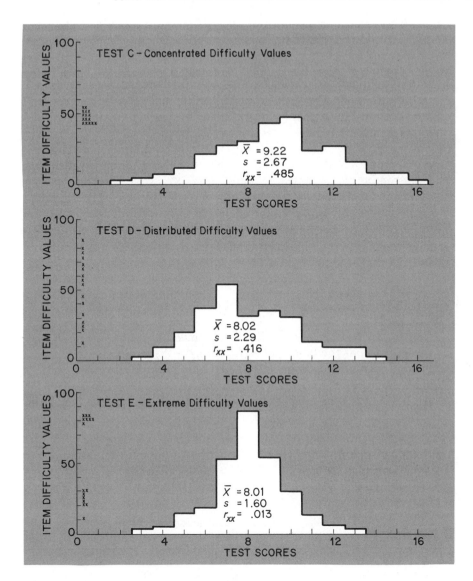

Figure 13-2 Relation of Distribution of Test Scores to Distribution of Item Difficulty Values.

been administered to over 300 college freshmen and an item analysis performed to yield indices of difficulty and discrimination for each item. The items constituting the three 16-item tests were selected so as to yield tests differing widely in difficulty distributions.

> In Test C, the items selected were *concentrated* in difficulty values as near the middle of the entire distribution of difficulty values as possible.
>
> In Test D, the items selected were *distributed* in difficulty values as uniformly as possible over the entire range of available difficulty values.

In Test E, the items were selected for *extreme* difficulty values, including the eight easiest and the eight most difficult items.

When these three 16-item tests were scored on a set of 253 answer sheets for the 61-item tryout form, the distributions of scores displayed in the histograms of Figure 13-2 were obtained. The distributions of item difficulties are indicated by the tally marks along the vertical scales to the left of each histogram.

Note the inverse relation between the spread of item difficulties and the spread of test scores. The wider the dispersion of difficulty values, the more concentrated the distribution of test scores. Note, too, the very low reliability of scores on the test composed only of very easy and very difficult items and the somewhat higher reliability of the scores from those tests composed of items more nearly in the mid-range of difficulty. In short, the findings of this study support the recommendation that items of middle difficulty be favored in the construction of achievement tests.

ITEM SELECTION

One of the two direct uses that can be made of indices of discrimination is in the selection of the best (that is, most highly discriminating) items for inclusion in an improved version of the test. How high should the index of discrimination be?

Experience with a wide variety of classroom tests suggests that the indices of item discrimination for most of them can be evaluated in these terms:

Index of Discrimination	Item Evaluation
0.40 and up	Very good items
0.30 to 0.39	Reasonably good but possibly subject to improvement
0.20 to 0.29	Marginal items, usually needing and being subject to improvement
Below 0.19	Poor items, to be rejected or improved by revision

It probably goes without saying that no special effort should be made to secure a spread of item-discrimination indices—the higher each item-discrimination index, the better. Of two tests otherwise alike, the one in which the average index of item discrimination is the higher will always be the better, that is, the more reliable.

A simple relation can be shown to exist between the sum of the indices of discrimination for the items of a test and the variance of the scores on the test (Ebel, 1967). It is expressed in the formula:

$$s_x^2 = \frac{(\Sigma\, D)^2}{6}$$

This formula indicates that the score variance, s_x^2, is directly proportional to the square of the sum of the discrimination indices, $(\Sigma\ D)^2$. Since it is true in general that the larger the score variance for a given number of items, the higher the reliability of the scores, the formula also indicates that the greater the average value of the discrimination indices, the higher the test reliability is likely to be.

ITEM REVISION

The second use that can be made of indices of item discrimination is in the revision of the test items. Five items illustrating the revision process on the basis of item-analysis data are presented and discussed here. These items were written to test the background knowledge of high school students in the natural and social sciences areas. They were administered to a large cross section of students in a preliminary item tryout. Then item-analysis data were used to select the most satisfactory items for the final form of the test. Among the items that were rejected there appeared to be some that could be salvaged by revision. After making revisions, the items were tried out with another representative group of students and reanalyzed. Results of the tryouts before and after revision are indicated in the following paragraphs.

The first item deals with the distinction between the terms *climate* and *weather*.

37%   **What, if any, is the distinction between climate and weather?**
0.13

    a. **There is no important distinction. (1–6)**
    b. **Climate is primarily a matter of temperature and rainfall, while weather includes many other natural phenomena. (33–51)**
  c. **Climate pertains to longer periods of time than weather. (43–30)**
    d. **Weather pertains to natural phenomena on a *local* rather than a *national* scale. (23–13)**

This item is somewhat too difficult for the group tested (only 73 correct responses among 200 students) and does not discriminate well (only 13 more good than poor students answered it correctly). Examination of the response counts indicates that response *b* was attractive to a considerable number of good students and that response *d* was more attractive to good students than to poor. Since the stem of the question seemed basically clear and since the intended correct response seemed reasonable, efforts in revision were concentrated on changing distracters *b* and *d*. It appeared that response *b* could be made less attractive by making it simpler and somewhat more specific. Since response *d* seemed much too plausible to the better students in the group being tested, it was "spoiled" by substituting a more obviously incorrect response. The revised item (revisions in uppercase letters) reads:

62% **What, if any, is the distinction between climate and weather?**
0.58

    a. **There is no important distinction. (2–22)**
    b. **CLIMATE IS PRIMARILY A MATTER OF RAINFALL, WHILE WEATHER IS PRIMARILY A MATTER OF TEMPERATURE. (3–25)**
    *c. **Climate pertains to longer periods of time than weather. (91–33)**
    d. **WEATHER IS DETERMINED BY CLOUDS, WHILE CLIMATE IS DETERMINED BY WINDS. (4–20)**

Analysis data of the revised item reveal that the revisions were effective. The changed item is much easier and much more highly discriminating than the original. Only nine of the good students chose distracters. Equally important is the fact that these revisions did not appreciably increase the number of poor students choosing the correct response. It is interesting to note that on the second tryout the number of poor students who chose response *a* increased markedly, even though this response had not been altered.

The next item deals with the common misconception that meteors are "falling stars."

36% **Do stars ever fall to the earth?**
0.35

    a. **Yes. They may be seen often, particularly during certain months. (12–28)**
    b. **Yes. There are craters caused by falling stars in certain regions of the earth. (30–43)**
    c. **No. The earth moves too rapidly for its gravitational force to act on the stars. (5–11)**
    *d. **No. The falling of a single average star would destroy the earth. (53–18).**

This item again is somewhat too difficult, though its discriminating power is fairly good. The item might be made somewhat easier by revising the response *b*. This response can be legitimately criticized as "tricky" because there are *meteor* craters. Hence in the revision, this response alone was changed.

42% **Do stars ever fall to the earth?**
0.56

    a. **Yes. They may be seen often, particularly during certain months. (20–68)**
    b. **NO. PLANETS LIKE THE EARTH HAVE NO ATTRACTION FOR STARS. (1–4)**
    c. **No. The earth moves too rapidly for its gravitational force to act on the stars. (9–14)**
    *d. **No. The falling of a single average star would destroy the earth. (70–14)**

Note that the difficulty of the item improved only slightly, but the change obviously spoiled the attractiveness of the second response. However, the change did not increase the proportion of poor students choosing the correct answer. Apparently most of their choices shifted to response *a*, which had not been modified in the revision.

The next item attempted to deal with the relationship between the number of time zones spanning a geographic area and the size of that area.

23% **There are eleven time zones in the U.S.S.R. This fact indicates that**
0.09
   a. **much of the area of the U.S.S.R. is above the Arctic Circle. (12–26)**
   b. **the U.S.S.R. is wider (east-west) than it is long (north-south). (56–40)**
   *c. **the U.S.S.R. occupies a large geographic area. (27–18)**
   d. **some areas of the U.S.S.R. are above the equator and some are below the equator. (5–16)**

This item is much too difficult and is very low in discrimination. The major problem appears to be with choice *b*. It was a very attractive choice overall, but more attractive to good students than to poor ones. A new second response was written that was expected to be less closely related to the idea expressed by the keyed response.

49% **There are eleven time zones in the U.S.S.R. This fact indicates that**
0.58
   a. **much of the area of the U.S.S.R. is above the Arctic Circle. (4–32)**
   b. **MOST OF THE AREA OF THE U.S.S.R. IS IN THE EASTERN HEMISPHERE. (11–25)**
   *c. **the U.S.S.R. occupies a large geographic area. (78–20)**
   d. **some areas of the U.S.S.R. are above the equator and some are below the equator. (7–23)**

This revision improved both the difficulty level and discrimination of the item markedly. Most good students were able to decide on the correct response, but it appears that poor students distributed themselves nearly evenly across all four responses, much as would be expected if the examinees were blindly guessing.

The next item deals with cause of shortage in the ground water supply.

48% **Water shortages in many localities have been caused by which, if any, of these factors?**
0.17
   a. **Removal of natural plant cover allowing faster run-off into streams (17–13)**
   b. **Increased demands for water in homes, businesses, and industry (15–26)**
   c. **Neither *a* or *b* (12–22)**
   *d. **Both *a* and *b* (56–39)**

This item is of appropriate difficulty but is not highly discriminating. In this case it appeared that the fault might lie with the design of the item itself. The question was framed in such a way that there were two important, correct answers, and hence it was necessary to include each of these as a single, supposedly incorrect response and to make "both" the correct response. This approach is apparently somewhat confusing. Furthermore, no opportunities are provided for the use of bona fide distracters. In the revision one of the correct responses was placed in the stem of the item and three bona fide distracters were provided as follows:

53% **WHAT FACTOR, OTHER THAN INCREASED WATER USE, HAS BEEN RESPONSIBLE**
0.62 **FOR WATER SHORTAGES IN MANY LOCALITIES?**

    a. **RESTRICTION OF STREAM FLOW BY HYDROELECTRIC DAMS (3–22)**
    b. **DISTURBANCE OF NORMAL RAINFALL BY ARTIFICIAL RAINMAKING (3–18)**
    c. **INTENSIVE FARM CULTIVATION, WHICH PERMITS MOST RAINFALL TO SOAK INTO THE GROUND (10–38)**
  *d. **REMOVAL OF NATURAL PLANT COVER ALLOWING FASTER RUN-OFF INTO STREAMS (84–22)**

The item was made somewhat easier and much more discriminating. In this case, the revision process worked in a way that gladdened the heart of the item writer.

The final item to be illustrated deals with knowledge of the type of information found on a physical map of a region.

12% **A physical map of a state would show**
0.21

    a. the state's railway network. (20–25)
    b. average rainfall by month for the state. (20–34)
    c. the location of the largest cities in the state. (38–40)
  *d. the state's highest elevation. (22–1)

The item writer decided that this item called for too fine a discrimination. All responses were attractive to good students because no single response seemed best. Some physical maps do show major transportation systems and some maps show rainfall patterns, though not usually monthly averages. Finally, major cities are occasionally used as points of reference on physical maps. Each distracter was modified to reduce its attractiveness to good students while maintaining a certain level of plausibility for poor students.

43% **A PHYSICAL MAP OF A STATE WOULD SHOW THE STATE'S**
0.40

    a. **AVERAGE SUMMER RAINFALL. (2–11)**
    b. **POPULATION DENSITY. (20–25)**
    c. **MOST IMPORTANT CITIES. (15–40)**
  *d. **HIGHEST ELEVATION. (63–23)**

The revised item turned out to be reasonably discriminating and easier, but it is still a bit more difficult than most item writers would prefer. Either students are not clear about the unique features of a physical map or the second and third distracters still represent legitimate correct answers relative to keyed response *d*.

These five items do not illustrate all the possible ways in which item-analysis data may be interpreted to aid in item revision. What they do indicate is the general nature of the process and the fact that it *may* be highly successful.

ITEM ANALYSIS WITH CONTENT-REFERENCED MEASURES

The procedures for item analysis described in this chapter are equally useful for judging the quality of items from group-referenced and content-referenced measures. However, the standards used to differentiate good and poor items in the two types of measures vary, and, consequently, an item earmarked for revision for one type of measure may be selected without change for use in the other type.

In the preparation of items for content-referenced measures such as mastery tests, minimum-competency tests, and some professional certification tests, item writers need not make a conscious decision to write items that will be about moderate in difficulty. The rigid content specifications of the test should indicate with some precision what the test items should measure. If the pool of examinees is expected to be well prepared, the item writer should expect difficulty indices in the range 70–100 percent. By these standards no well-written test item likely will be judged to be too easy, but items can be identified that are too difficult. However, items that, say, 95 percent of a group answers correctly are not automatically good items for a content-referenced measure. For example, those that contain several implausible distracters or that give internal clues suggesting the correct response are still bad items. The analysis of content-referenced items for appropriate difficulty should include a review of the items for technical adequacy. The reviewer should be convinced that a high proportion of the students actually knew the content measured by items showing high difficulty indices.

The upper-lower difference index can be used to assess the quality of content-referenced items as well, but generally it is much less useful in this situation. No test item, regardless of its intended purpose, is useful if it yields a negative discrimination index. But many good items used in content-referenced measures may have discrimination indices of zero or near zero. The explanation for this phenomenon relates to the fact that score distributions from content-referenced measures tend to be quite negatively skewed and low in variability. The upper and lower criterion groups tend to be very similar in terms of total test score. In some cases, in fact, the average true scores for the two groups may be barely distinguishable.

Alternative indices to the upper-lower index or point-biserial correlation have been proposed for use with items from content-referenced measures. Cox and Vargas (1966) suggested a pre-post difference index to judge the ability of items to discriminate. The proportion of students who answer an item correctly prior to instruction (pre) is subtracted from the proportion of the same group who respond correctly after instruction (post). The larger the value of the index, the more highly discriminating the item is judged to be. Another index, used primarily for items from mastery tests, is based on the phi correlation coefficient. An item index is computed by correlating item score (0 or +1) with the mastery decision (Master or Nonmaster) using a two-by-two table like that shown below. If "masters" tend to answer correctly (A is large) and "nonmasters" tend to answer incorrectly (D is large also), the item discriminates well between the two levels of achievement. When the values B and C are large, the item shows negative discrimination. The phi coefficient has greater practical utility than the pre-post difference index because it requires no pretest administration. But unless the number of nonmasters is sufficiently large, the phi index will provide a misleading indication of the quality of discrimination of the items.

MASTERY DECISION

		Master	Nonmaster
ITEM SCORE	+1	A	B
	0	C	D

The index of discrimination can be used to select the best items for inclusion in a content-referenced measure, also. To do so, items first must be grouped according to the content categories outlined in the table of specifications. Then the number of items required from each category can be selected on the basis of their discrimination indices. This procedure will ensure that the content balance required to make valid score interpretations will be achieved.

SUMMARY

Some of the principal ideas developed in this chapter are summarized in these 18 statements:

1. Item analysis is a useful tool in the progressive improvement of achievement tests.
2. Specific criteria of relevance ought to be written as a basis for determining what kinds of items are appropriate for inclusion in a test.
3. The degree of match between a table of specifications and the test-item content is an indication of the degree of balance achieved in the test.
4. An efficient test includes as many independently scorable responses per unit of testing time as is possible without sacrificing relevance.
5. Persons who lack special competence in the subject covered by the test will obtain scores near the chance level if the test is properly specific.
6. A group-referenced test is appropriate in difficulty if its mean is midway between a perfect score and the expected chance score.
7. The more variable the scores from a test, the more

likely it is that the test has succeeded in differentiating between examinees who possess different amounts of the abilities measured by the test.
8. The most significant statistical measure of the quality of an achievement test is the reliability of its scores.
9. Item analysis begins with the counting of responses made by good and poor students to each of the items in the test.
10. While logical objections can be made to the use of the total score on a test as a criterion for analyzing the items in the test, the practical effect of these shortcomings is small and the practical convenience of disregarding them is great.
11. It is convenient and statistically defensible to consider as "good" students those whose scores place them in the upper 27 percent of the total group, and to consider as "poor" students those whose scores place them in the lower 27 percent of the total group.
12. A convenient and highly satisfactory index of dis-

crimination is simply the difference in the proportions of correct response between the upper and lower 27 percent groups.

13. The proportion of correct responses to an item in the upper and lower 27 percent groups combined provides a satisfactory estimate of the difficulty index of the item.

14. For most classroom tests it is desirable that all of the items be of middle difficulty, with none of them extremely easy or extremely difficult.

15. In general, the wider the distribution of item-difficulty values in a test, the more restricted the range of scores will be and the lower the reliability of those

scores will be.

16. Good norm-referenced achievement-test items should have indices of discrimination of 0.30 or more.

17. The higher the average discrimination index for items in a test, the more variable the scores are likely to be and the more reliable the scores are expected to be.

18. The same item-analysis procedures are appropriate for items from both content-referenced and group-referenced measures, but the standards for differentiating between good and poor items are likely to vary for the two situations.

PROJECTS AND PROBLEMS

Project: Interpreting Item-Analysis Data

The responses of 30 students to four test items are summarized in the four tables below. Assume that these four items were among many others on the same norm-referenced test, but not necessarily ordered as shown below. The keyed answer is indicated by an asterisk; the upper, middle, and lower groups (U, M, and L) contain 8, 14, and 8 students, respectively.

Calculate the difficulty index and the Upper-Lower Difference discrimination index for each item. Prepare an evaluation of each item, including possible explanations for why the item performed as it did. In each case make recommendations for modifying the item to improve its performance on future tests.

		1	2*	3	4	5	Omit
1. Diff =	U	0	4	3	0	1	0
Disc =	M	0	6	3	2	3	0
	L	0	5	2	1	0	0
	T	0	15	8	3	4	0

		1	2	3	4	5*	Omit
2. Diff =	U	0	0	0	0	6	2
Disc =	M	1	0	0	1	8	4
	L	1	1	1	0	1	4
	T	2	1	1	1	15	10

		*1	2	3	4	5	Omit
3. Diff =	U	1	0	7	0	0	0
Disc =	M	6	1	4	2	1	0
	L	5	0	1	1	1	0
	T	12	1	12	3	2	0

		1	2	*3	4	5	Omit
4. Diff =	U	2	2	2	1	1	0
Disc =	M	2	3	3	3	3	0
	L	2	1	1	2	2	0
	T	6	6	6	6	6	0

14

GRADING AND REPORTING STUDENT ACHIEVEMENT

THE NEED FOR GRADES

The uses made of grades are numerous and often crucial. They are used as self-evaluative measures and also to report students' educational status to parents, future teachers, and prospective employers. They provide a basis for important decisions about educational plans and career options. Education is expensive. To make the best possible use of educational facilities and student talent, it is essential that each student's educational progress be watched carefully and reported as accurately as possible. Reports of course grades serve somewhat the same function in education that financial statements serve in business. In either case, if the reports are inaccurate or unavailable, the venture may become inefficient.

Grades also provide an important means for stimulating, directing, and rewarding the educational efforts of students. This use of grades has been attacked on the ground it provides extrinsic, artificial, and hence undesirable stimuli and rewards. Indeed, grades are extrinsic, but so are most other tangible rewards for effort and achievement. Most workers, including those in the professions, are grateful for the intrinsic rewards that sometimes accompany their efforts. But most of them are even more grateful that these are not the only rewards. Few organized, efficient human enterprises can be conducted successfully on the basis of intrinsic rewards alone.

To serve effectively the purpose of stimulating, directing, and rewarding student efforts to learn, grades must be valid. The highest grades must go to those students who have achieved to the highest degree the objectives of instruction in a course. Grades must be based on sufficient evidence. They must report the degree of achievement as precisely as possible under the circumstances. If grades are assigned carelessly, their long-run effects on the educational efforts of students cannot be good.

Some students and teachers minimize the importance of grades, suggesting that *what* students learn is more important than the *grade* they get. Their conception rests on the assumption that there generally is not a close relationship between the amount of useful learning a student can demonstrate and the grade he or she receives. Others have made the same point by noting that grades should not be regarded as ends in themselves and by questioning the use of examinations "merely" for the purpose of assigning grades.

It is true that the grade a student receives is not in itself an important educational outcome—by the same token, neither is the degree or diploma toward which the student is working, nor the academic rank or professional reputation of those who teach that individual. But all these symbols can be and should be valid indications of important educational attainments. It is desirable, and not impossibly difficult, to make the goal of maximum educational achievement compatible with the goal of highest possible grades. If these two goals are not closely related, the fault would seem to rest with those who teach the classes and assign the grades. From the point of view of students, parents, teachers, and employers there is nothing "mere" about the grading process and the grades it yields. Stroud (1946) underscored this point.

> If the marks earned in a course of study are made to represent progress toward getting an education, working for marks is *ipso facto* a furtherance of the purposes of education. If the marks are so bad that the student who works for and attains them misses an education, then working for marks is a practice to be eschewed. When marks are given, we are not likely to dissuade pupils from working for them: and there is no sensible reason why we should. It simply does not make sense to grade pupils, to maintain institutional machinery for assembling and recording the gradings, while at the same time telling pupils marks do not amount to much. As a matter of fact they do amount to something and the pupil knows this. If we are dissatisfied with the results of working for marks we might try to improve the marks. (p. 632)

Grades are necessary. If they are inaccurate, invalid, or meaningless, the remedy lies less in deemphasizing grades than in assigning them more carefully so that they more truly report the extent of important achievements. Instead of seeking to minimize their importance or seeking to find some less painful substitute, perhaps instructors should devote more attention to improving the validity and precision of the grades they assign, and to minimizing misinterpretations of grades by students, faculty, and others who use them.

Grades and Success

Those who question the value of grades often cite as evidence the low correlations that have been reported between grades and subsequent success in life (Hoyt, 1965). High grades do not infallibly predict success. Low grades do not invariably foretell failure. But if these observations should lead us to conclude that learning has nothing to contribute to living or that grades cannot report amount of learning, we would be foolish indeed. Evidence that might seem to support such unreasonable propositions ought to be examined very closely.

There are at least three reasons why low correlations have been reported. One is that learning is not the only requirement for success in living. It is a necessary but not a sufficient condition. Other ingredients like ambition, opportunity, personality, and luck have much to do with success.

A second reason is the imperfection of our measures of achievement in learning. Some teachers do not have skill enough or take pains enough to measure and report student learning accurately. A third reason is the difficulty of defining success in living and of measuring it reliably. To the extent that our measures of learning and of living are unreliable, the correlation between those measures is bound to be low.

Surely education is intended to contribute to success in life. Instructional programs are designed to help students learn what they must know in order to succeed. Grades should report how much students have learned of what we have been trying to teach them. If those grades are only weakly related to later success, something must be wrong with the instructional program or with our assessments of what students learned from it or both. For grades to be unrelated to success is neither rational nor tolerable.

THE PROBLEMS OF GRADING

The problems of using grades to describe student achievement have been persistently troublesome at all levels of education (Cureton, 1971). An important and fundamental reason why problems of grading are difficult to solve permanently is because grading systems tend to become issues in educational controversies. Odell (1950) noted that research on grading systems did not become significant until after the turn of the century. At about that same time, the development of objective tests was ushering in the somewhat controversial "scientific movement" in education. The rise of progressive education in the third and fourth decades of this century, with its emphasis on the uniqueness of the individual, the wholeness of mental life, freedom and democracy in the classroom, and the child's need for loving reassurance, led to criticisms of academic narrowness, the competitive pressures, and the common standards of achievement for all students implicit in many grading systems. The recent renewed emphasis on "back to basics" and on pursuit of academic excellence has been accompanied by pleas for more formal evaluations of achievement and more rigorous standards of attainment (The National Commission on Excellence in Education, 1983).

These unsteady shifts in educational doctrine influence some educational leaders to espouse one philosophy, some another. Some teachers find it easy to accept one position, some another, even when they teach in the same educational institution. Since somewhat different grading systems are implied by each of these different philosophical positions, it is not surprising that differences of opinion, dissatisfaction, and proposals for change tend to characterize teacher reactions to grading systems.

Another reason why grading systems present perennial problems is that they require teachers, whose natural instincts incline them to be helpful counselors and advocates, to stand in judgment over the deeds of others. "Forbear to judge, for we are sinners all," said Shakespeare, echoing the sentiments of the Sermon on the Mount: "Judge not, that ye be not judged." It is never difficult to assign a student a good grade, particularly if it is higher than he or she really expected. But since the reach of many students exceeds their grasp, there are likely to be more occasions for disappointment than pleasure for both students and teachers.

No system of grading is likely to be found that will make the process of grading easy, painless, and generally satisfactory. This is not to say that present grading practices are beyond improvement. It is only to say that no new grading system, no matter how cleverly devised and conscientiously followed, is likely to solve the basic problems of grading. The real need is not for some new system. Good systems already exist. Even the articles about grading written over a half a century ago seem pertinent today. The same problems that were troublesome then remain with us, and some of the remedies proposed then are still being proposed.

The issues that contribute to making grading a controversial topic are primarily philosophical in nature. There are no research studies that can answer questions like: What should an "A" grade mean? What percent of the students in a class should receive a "C"? Should spelling and grammar be judged in assigning a grade to a paper? What should a course grade represent? These "should" questions require value judgments rather than an interpretation of research data; the answer to each may vary from teacher to teacher. But all teachers must ask similar questions and find acceptable answers to them in establishing their grading policies. With careful thought and periodic review, most teachers can develop satisfactory, defensible grading practices that will yield accurate measures of the achievements of their students. And by attending to the principles that enhance the reliability and validity of other achievement measures, policies and procedures can be developed to produce relevant, mean-ingful grades at all educational levels.

The Shortcomings of Grades

Two major deficiencies of grades, as they are assigned in many educational institutions, are: (1) the lack of clearly defined and generally accepted definitions of what the various grades should mean and (2) the lack of sufficient, relevant, and objective evidence to use as a basis for assigning grades. One consequence of the first shortcoming is that grading standards and the meanings of grades tend to vary from instructor to instructor, from course to course, from department to department, and from school to school within districts (Terwillinger, 1971). Another consequence is that teacher biases and idiosyncrasies tend to reduce the validity of grades. One outcome of this second shortcoming is that the grades tend to be unreliable. Another is that grades become inflated—their face value is higher than their actual value (Hendrickson, 1976).

The absence of explicit definitions for each grade permits teachers to either consciously or unknowingly be influenced by extraneous factors in assigning grades. Research on this point from two and three decades ago probably is characteristic of present practice (Carter, 1952; Hadley, 1954; Palmer, 1962). Some instructors deliberately use high grades as rewards and low grades as punishments for behavior unrelated to the attainment of instructional objectives.

The studies of Starch and Elliott (1912, 1913a, 1913b) on the unreliability of teachers' grades on examination papers are classic demonstrations of the instability of judgments based on presumably absolute standards. Identical copies of an English test paper were given to 142 English teachers, with instructions to score it on the basis of 100 percent for a perfect paper. Since each teacher looked at only one paper, no *relative* basis for judgment was available. The scores assigned to the same paper ranged all the way from 98 to 50 percent. Similar results were obtained with test papers in geometry and in history.

Typically grades such as those Starch and Elliott collected for single examination papers are not highly reliable. For semester grades, however, reliabilities in the range of 0.70 to 0.80 are not uncommon. Semester grades are based on much more extensive and comprehensive observations of student attainments, perhaps as many as 80 hours of observation. Even so, one hour of intensive "observation" under the controlled conditions of a well-standardized achievement test can yield measures with reliability estimates in excess of 0.90. If the tools of performance assessment are not well designed, their collective worth over a semester may be exceeded by a reliable and valid commercially prepared instrument that takes no time for the teacher to prepare and a small fraction of class time to administer. Our purpose here is not to argue for replacing teacher-made evaluation tools with standardized measures, but to dramatize the unfortunate state of affairs in which some teachers find themselves at grade-assignment time. We are not facing utter chaos, but considerable room for improvement exists.

WHAT MEANING SHOULD GRADES CONVEY?

A grading system is primarily a method of communicating measurements of achievement. It involves the use of a set of specialized symbols whose meanings ought to be clearly defined and uniformly understood by all concerned. Only to the degree that the grading symbols have the same meaning for all who use them is it possible for grades to serve the purposes of communication meaningfully and precisely.

The meaning of a grade should depend as little as possible on the instructor who issued it or the course to which it pertains. This means that the grading practices of an instructor, of a department, or indeed of an entire educational institution are matters of legitimate concern to other instructors, other departments, and other institutions. It means that a general system of grading ought to be adopted by the faculty and administration of a school or college. It requires that the meaning of each grading symbol be clearly defined. General adherence to this system and to these meanings ought to be expected of all who issue grades. Such a requirement would in no way infringe the right of each instructor to determine which grade to give a particular student. But it would limit the right of instructors to set their own standards or to invent their own meanings for each of the grades issued.

A particular grade obtains its meaning from three distinct sources. First, a grade represents the comparison of a student's performance with either some absolute standard or a relative standard defined by the performance of a specified group. Second, a grade represents quality of performance with respect to either amount of effort expended or amount of achievement demonstrated. Finally, a grade represents either the amount of knowledge possessed at the end of instruction or the amount of learning attributable to the instructional program. The remainder of this section is a discussion of the issues associated with choosing between the alternative meanings that each of the three sources can contribute to the overall meaning of a grade.

Absolute versus Relative Grading

A grade represents a teacher's summary evaluation of how well a student has performed a set of tasks in one instructional unit or over a series of several units. These judgments of goodness cannot be made in the absence of a standard of comparison. Performance that is described as good, inferior, adequate, excellent, or superior obtains its qualitative label when the evaluator compares the performance in question with a performance standard. The standard is either absolute or relative.

Each of the two major grading systems used in the United States since the turn of the century is based on either absolute or relative grading standards. In the early years almost all grading was in percents. A student who learned all that anyone could learn in a course, whose achievement could be regarded as flawless, could expect a grade of 100 (percent). A student who essentially knew nothing about the course content would, theoretically, be given a grade of zero. A definite percent of "perfection," usually between 60 and 75 percent, ordinarily was regarded as the minimum passing grade. The absolute standard to which all students' performances were referenced was the domain of content— the knowledge, skills, and understanding—that defined the course. Because a student's grade presumably is assigned independently of the grades of other students in the course, percent grading usually is characterized as "absolute grading."

The other major type of grading system is based on the use of a small number of letter grades, often five, to express various levels of achievement. In the five-letter A-B-C-D-F system, truly outstanding performance is assigned a grade of A. The B indicates above-average achievement; C is the average grade; D indicates below-average achievement; and F is used to report failure— achievement insufficient to warrant credit for completing a course. The relative standard to which each student's performance is referenced is the distribution of performance of other students in the class. Thus, letter grading is sometimes characterized as "relative grading."

Of course each letter in the grading system can be defined in absolute terms instead of relative terms. A grade of D may indicate achievement of the minimally essential knowledge and understandings; C may represent adequate rather than average achievement; B may indicate a level of advanced achievement with respect to course content; and A may be used to represent exceptional or meritorious achievement. Such general definitions would require substantial refinement to communicate the absolute levels of achievement in any particular course or grade-specific subject matter. The point is, it is not the use of letter symbols that distinguishes absolute and relative grading, it is the nature of the standard against which performance is compared that differentiates the two.

The decision to use either an absolute or a relative grading standard is the most fundamental decision a teacher must make with regard to performance assessment. When the absolute standard is chosen, all methods and tools of evaluation must be designed to yield content-referenced interpretations. Absolute standards for grading must be established for each component that is to contribute to the course grade—tests, papers, quizzes, presentations, projects, and other assignments. If the decision is to use a relative standard, all measures must be geared to providing norm-referenced interpretations. Of course in both cases criterion-referenced decisions need to be made as long as several grading symbols are available. The basis for determining the criterion points will be content-referenced in one case and group-referenced in the other.

Though a clear majority of institutions now use letter grading with relative standards, percent grading is by no means dead. Some institutions still use percent grades exclusively; others convert to letter grades from percent grades. Many professional examining boards still prefer to define passing scores in terms of percent scores, even though, in some cases, the raw scores are transformed to a percent scale using relative-grading methodology. Some instructors voice a preference for absolute grading over relative grading for philosophical reasons but find the task of establishing standards overbearing or, in some cases, too arbitrary.

Achievement versus Effort

After the decision has been made about the use of absolute or relative standards, the instructor must decide which aspects of performance or which forms of achievement will be included in the grade. Undoubtedly some teachers base some of the grades they issue on factors other than the degree of achievement of instructional objectives. They likely will continue to do so, because grades can be used as instruments of social control in the class, and because some degree of such control is essential to effective teaching. But the use of grades for these purposes ought to be rare, for it leads to distorted meanings of the grades issued. Indirectly it conveys to students that social behavior rather than school learning is the most significant purpose of their school program.

One of the important requirements of a good grading system is that the grades indicate as accurately as possible the extent to which students have achieved the instructional objectives in their course of study. If developing students' attitudes toward something or developing their willingness to put forth effort is one of the specific objectives of instruction, and if the instructor has planned instructional procedures to help students develop these behaviors, then it is quite appropriate to consider such behavior in assigning grades. But often this is not the case. Accordingly, attitude and effort probably should be excluded from consideration in determining the grade to be assigned.

We have argued that grades can and should serve to stimulate, direct, and reward student learning. Certainly students who exert greater effort and demonstrate greater desire to learn than others ought to be rewarded for their labors. But the *major function* of grading should not be reserved for this purpose. A significant challenge facing each teacher is to identify the forms of reward, other than grades, that appear to stimulate students to perform near their optimum levels of cognitive capability. This is no easy task, since students respond differently to words of praise, written notes, smiley faces, and special privileges. The point is that effort and attitude need to be enhanced and sustained through some form of recognition and reward, but grades should not carry this extra burden.

Status versus Growth

Some instructors believe that grading is fairer if the grades are based on the amount of improvement students have shown rather than on the level of achievement they demonstrate at the end of instruction. Scores on a pretest, and on other preliminary observations, are used to provide a basis for estimating initial status. The differences between these and subsequent test scores or other indications of achievement are used to estimate the amount of change or growth. Hence, high grades are assigned to students who show large gains and low grades to those who display small amounts of change or no growth.

Unfortunately, growth measures are characteristically quite unreliable. Since each test score or observation includes its own errors of measurement, subtracting these scores from other measurements results in an accumulation of errors rather than a cancellation. A difference score is more error-laden than either of the scores from which it was derived and, thus, may consist mainly of errors of measurement. Harris (1963) and others have pointed out the difficulty of using this approach. If their tests are appropriate and reliable, instructors may safely use the difference between pretest and posttest mean scores as a measure of their own instructional effectiveness. But few classroom achievement tests are good enough to provide reliable measures of short-term gains in achievement of individual students.

In addition to the unreliability concern, there are other problems with growth measures. One is that for most educational purposes, knowledge that a student is good, average, or poor compared with his or her peers is more useful than knowledge that the student changed more or less rapidly than others during a certain period of time. Another is that students who get low scores on the pretest have a considerably greater likelihood of showing subsequent large gains in achievement than their peers who earned higher scores initially. Students are quick to learn that, under circumstances of grading on the basis of growth, their pretest scores should be as low as possible to permit the greatest possible observable gain.

It is true that status grading seems to condemn some students to low grades in most subjects, semester after semester. Low grades discourage effort, which in turn increases the probability of more low grades. So the vicious cycle continues, bringing dislike of learning and, possibly, early withdrawal from school. If students are taught to dislike school by constant reminders of their low achievement, the remedy probably is not to try to persuade them that their rate of growth toward achievement is more important than status achieved, for that is a transparent falsehood. The remedy is probably to provide varied opportunities to excel in several kinds of worthwhile activities. The planning and implementation of such efforts certainly would require an alert, versatile, and dedicated teacher. When it is accomplished, though, grading on the basis of status achieved will no longer mean that some students must always win while others must always lose. Instead some students will be able to enjoy some of the rewards of excellence in their own specialties. Cohen (1983), for example, has described alternative procedures for grading the achievement of exceptional students who have been "mainstreamed."

CONSIDERATIONS IN ESTABLISHING A GRADING SYSTEM

The Grade Scale

In general, letter grades and percent grades represent two extremes in terms of precision in grading. Those who advocated letter grades when they were first introduced suggested that the bases on which grades usually are determined are not reliable enough to justify the apparent precision of percent grading. They claimed that the best most instructors could do is to distinguish about five different levels of achievement. Many instructors seemed to agree with this view. Nonetheless, from time to time there has been increased or renewed interest in refining the grading scale by adding plus and minus signs to the basic letters, or decimal fractions to the basic numbers.

The notion that grading problems can be simplified and grading errors reduced by using fewer categories is an attractive one. Its weakness can be exposed by carrying it to the limit. If only one category is used, if everyone is issued the same grade, all grading problems vanish, but so does the value of grading. A major shortcoming of two-category grading, and to a lesser extent of five-category grading, is this same kind of loss of information. To trade more precisely meaningful grades for grades easier to assign is probably a bad bargain for education.

The use of fewer, broader categories in grading does indeed reduce the frequency of errors in grading. That is, with a few broad categories more of the students receive the grade they deserve because fewer wrong grades are available to give them. But each error becomes more crucial. The apparent difference between satisfactory and unsatisfactory, or between B and C, is greater than the difference between 87 percent and 88 percent. If a fallible instructor (and all of them, being human, are fallible) gives a student a grade of 86 percent when omniscient wisdom would have assigned a grade of 89 percent, the error has less consequence than if the instructor assigns a C when a B should have been given, or an "unsatisfactory" grade when it should have been "satisfactory." Hence the use of fewer categories is no royal road to more reliable grading. And, as noted previously, reducing the number of categories reduces the information conveyed by the grade.

Pass-Fail Grading

Some proposals for improving grading have gone even further than the five-letter system in reducing grading categories. The use of only two grades, such as S for satisfactory and U for unsatisfactory, P for pass and F for fail, or credit versus no credit, has been adopted by some institutions, at least for some course work. Pass-fail grading enjoyed considerable popularity at the postsecondary level during the late 1960s as a response to several pressures from faculty to lessen grading problems, from students to eliminate the threat of low grades, and from the academic community to try something new. The pros and cons of pass-fail grading have been outlined and discussed in some detail by Ebel (1979).

Almost every school or college offers some courses in which the aim is to provide certain experiences rather than to develop specific competencies. For such courses neither grades nor pass-fail decisions seem appropriate. Instead, students who attend enough course meetings to get a large proportion of the desired experience should simply be given credit for attendance. Courses in the appreciation of art, music, or literature, in recreational pursuits, in social problems, or in great issues may belong in this category of ungraded courses. But most other courses do not. Most courses do aim to develop competencies. Such courses call for assessments of achievement, and for them pass-fail grading is a poor substitute for more detailed and precise reporting of achievements.

Most of us want to be valued as persons. Most of us don't particularly want to be evaluated. But we can't enjoy the first without enduring the second. The weakness of pass-fail grading is that by doing a poor job of evaluating it keeps us from doing a good one of valuing.

Letters versus Numbers

The successful revolt against percent grading was aided by the substitution of letter grades for numbers. Letters helped to emphasize the contrast between clearly relative grading and supposedly absolute percent grading. But the use of letters creates at least two problems. One is that the letters must always be transformed to numbers before they can be added or averaged. The other is that letters imply *evaluations* of achievement rather than measurements.

For both these reasons the return to numerical symbols in grading would be advantageous. This advantage must be weighted against the confusion likely to result from introduction of a new set of symbols, with new and unfamiliar meanings. If an educational institution sets out with vigor to improve its grading system, a change in the set of symbols used may help to dramatize and reinforce other, more subtle changes.

Single or Multiple Grades

Achievement in most courses of study is a conglomerate of many factors. There is knowledge to be imparted and understanding to be cultivated; there are abilities and skills to be developed, attitudes to be fostered, interests to be encouraged, and ideals to be exemplified. Correspondingly, the bases used for determining grades include many aspects or indications of achievement: home-work, class participation, test scores, apparent attitude, interest, and motivation, and even regularity of attendance and helpfulness to the teacher. How can a single symbol do justice to these various aspects of achievement?

The answer of many educators is that it cannot. A grade, some say, is a hodgepodge of uncertain and variable composition. They suggest that grades can be improved by making them more analytical and descriptive. For example, multiple grades or written reports and progress charts have been proposed as improvements over the traditional single letter or number, especially at the elementary school level. Expanded reporting forms, for example, are essentially lists of instructional objectives for a subject area that show when formal instruction was presented for each objective and when the student presented evidence of attainment of each (Frisbie, 1976). Such reports are more explicit in communicating what students can do than are letter grades alone. Some school districts use a dual grading system to separate academic progress and the extent of effort exerted. The intent of the dual system is twofold: (1) to provide more information than can be conveyed by a single symbol and (2) to make the academic grade a purer indicator of the level of subject-matter competence attained by students.

The dual system is no panacea for the ills of grading; however, under some conditions it can improve grading considerably. Multiple grades require that clear distinctions be made between the aspects of achievement each represents and that sufficient evidence unique to each aspect be obtained as a basis for determining each grade. Finally, the larger the number of separate grades reported at one time, the more likely it is that the multiple grades will be influenced by considerable halo effect. That is, the teacher's overall impression of the student may influence each of the grades more than any unique evidence related to each of the separate aspects of achievement. Certainly any advantages multiple grading may have to offer an educational institution cannot be realized until the shortcomings of the single-symbol system have been addressed adequately.

There is an eclectic grading system that may appear to be complex, but that has promise for satisfying the needs of proponents of either content-referencing or norm-referencing. This system depends on content-referenced measures to make passing decisions and uses group-referenced measures to make relative distinctions among those who have passed. Only a single grade is assigned to each student, but a failing grade and a passing grade (A, B, C, and D) are referenced to knowledge, skills, and understandings that have been identified as minimally essential. Passing grades in this system reflect the relative standings of students in a class in learning things that the teacher regards as "beyond basics," or important to success in studying more advanced aspects of the subject matter. The eclectic system offers these advantages:

1. Teachers are less likely to assign a barely passing grade (D) to students who have not mastered basic skills than they might be under a relative grading system.

2. Students who fail at first can be retested to improve their grade when they improve their skills. They are not relegated to failure simply because on one occasion they demonstrated less learning than others.

3. Students who excel are rewarded according to their level of achievement. There are incentives to go beyond the minimum essentials defined for passing.

4. The system represents a reasonable compromise for faculties that are split by advocates of an either-or system, absolute versus relative standards.

THREATS TO THE VALIDITY OF GRADES

A distinction should be made between the aspects of performance that a teacher *evaluates* and the *subset* of those that are appropriate to use for assigning course grades. Components that contribute to determining course grades should reflect students' competence with respect to the instructional objectives. The components of a grade should be academically oriented; they should not be tools of discipline or rewards for pleasant personalities or good attitudes. A student who is assigned an A grade should have a firm grasp of the skills and knowledge taught. If the student is merely marginal academically but very industrious and congenial, an A grade would be misleading and would render a blow to the motivation of the excellent students in class. Instructors can, and probably should, give feedback to students with respect to a variety of traits and characteristics, but only behaviors that reflect academic achievement should be used to determine grades. In their recommendations regarding standards and expectations, the National Commission on Excellence in Education (1983) stated that "grades should be indicators of academic achievement so they can be relied on as evidence of a student's readiness for further study." Grades contaminated by other factors give students a false sense of readiness and provide misinformation to those who seek to guide students in their future educational endeavors.

Several aspects of student performance have been labeled as potentially invalid grading components because they represent behaviors that do not reflect directly the attainment of the important objectives of instruction (Frisbie, 1977). Though some exceptions could be noted, these variables generally should not be used in determining course grades.

Students at all levels should be encouraged to attend classes because the lectures, demonstrations, and discussions presumably have been designed to facilitate their learning. If students miss several classes, then their performance on examinations, papers, and projects likely will suffer. If the instructor reduces their grade because of absence, such students are submitted to a form of double jeopardy. For example, a college instructor may say that class attendance counts 10 percent of the course grade, but for students who miss several classes this may effectively amount to 20 percent. Teachers who experience high rates of "cutting" in their classes probably need to examine their classroom environment and instructional procedures to determine if changes are needed. There ought to be more productive means of encouraging students to attend classes than to threaten to lower their grade.

Most small classes and college seminars depend to some degree on student participation for their success. When participation is an important ingredient in learning, participation grades may be appropriate. In such cases the instructor should ensure that all students have sufficient opportunity to participate and should maintain systematic notes regarding frequency and quality of participation. Waiting until the end of the grading period and relying strictly on memory makes a relatively subjective task even more subjective and unreliable. Participation probably should not be graded in most classes, however. Dominating and extroverted students tend to win, and introverted or shy students tend to lose. Instructors may want to provide evaluative information to students about various aspects of the students' personalities, but grading should not be the means of doing so.

Neatness in written work, correctness in spelling and grammatical usage, and organizational ability all are worthy traits and are assets in most vocational endeavors. To this extent it seems appropriate that teachers evaluate these aspects of performance and provide students with constructive comments about them. However, unless the course objectives include instruction in these skills, students should not be graded on them in the course. For example, students' essay examination scores should not be influenced directly by their spelling ability, and neither should their course grades. Students whose skills in written expression are weak can and do learn the important knowledge of science, social studies, literature, and other academic subjects. Their writing skills can and should be evaluated in such courses, but their course grades should not suffer directly because of their writing deficiencies. To the extent that they do, these grades are misleading to both students and parents and serve to moderate rather than stimulate future performance in the subject area.

Most instructors are attracted to students who are agreeable, friendly, industrious, and kind. They try to ignore or may even reject those who display opposite characteristics. To the extent that certain personalities may interfere with class work or have limited chances for employment in their field of interest, constructive feedback from the instructor may be necessary. An argumentative student who receives a C grade should have only a moderate amount of knowledge about the course content. The C should not reflect the student's disposition directly.

Some instructors are more generous in their grading than they ought to be because they fear that lower grades might bruise their students' self-images. However, as Sadler (1983) has argued, this philosophy is not defensible:

> The desire to label everything as good rests on two false assumptions, namely (1) that any negative reaction is bound to stifle personal development and creativity, and (2) that evaluating a performance as a performance is equivalent to judging a person as a person. Not everything produced by human beings, even honest and diligent ones, is good, and students are not so naive. (p. 75)

Judgments about writing and speaking skills, personality traits, effort, and motivation are made by teachers constantly as they interact with their students. To exclude most of these factors from the judgments made about academic progress and promise is no easy task. But accurate and meaningful grades depend on it.

GRADING COURSE ASSIGNMENTS

The assignments discussed in this section are the activities prescribed by the teacher primarily to allow students to demonstrate their level of competence. In this sense, each is a form of summative evaluation and a planned part of performance assessment. Assignments used for formative evaluation purposes, usually labeled homework, are used to provide practice for the learner.

Homework assignments that are intended to provide instruction or formative feedback probably should not be graded and included among the components that enter into course grading. Consider Freddy, for example, who is learning to identify prepositions as they occur in a sentence. On each of the first five daily assignments Freddy missed four to eight sentences out of ten. On the sixth and seventh days he missed none. He missed only one out of 20 on the test given the eighth day. What grade best represents Freddy's level of achievement? Though he may not have caught on as rapidly as some of his peers, Freddy appears to be able to identify prepositions. Some form of grading might be used to motivate and direct Freddy and his classmates, but all such grades need not enter into determining the final course or term grade.

Perhaps the most frequent shortcoming associated with grading assignments such as papers, reports, presentations, and projects is the failure of the teacher to specify in advance what the important aspects of the final product should be. As a result of the lack of "feedforward," as Sadler (1983) has labeled it, some students present incomplete assignments because they misunderstood the teacher's intent, and grading becomes a chore for the teacher because the criteria that distinguish better assignments from poorer ones have not been explicated. The grading guide that seems so logical to prepare for scoring essay items is equally beneficial to the teacher for grading assignments. It can help to accomplish these things:

1. When presented to the students at the time the assignment is made, potential misunderstandings about what to do can be overcome. The nature of the final product can be described completely, and the relative importance of various aspects of it can be presented. Often an example of an A assignment from a previous class is helpful.
2. Opportunities for extraneous factors to influence grading are reduced because the relevant elements have been defined. Grading variables and evaluation variables can be separated, so that a conscious effort can be made by the teacher to make comments about the nongraded aspects of the work.

3. Grading is done efficiently because little time is needed to decide which parts of the assignment to weight most heavily. Less time is needed to judge completeness as well.

4. Feedback to students can be somewhat diagnostic because missing work and student misconceptions are more readily identified.

We discussed in a previous chapter the importance of preparing students for important examinations so that they know what to expect and can prepare themselves further. A grading guide can serve this same useful function for assignments, and, if used wisely by the grader, it also can contribute to more valid and reliable measures of achievement.

COMBINING GRADING COMPONENTS

When instructors determine a course grade by combining grades or scores from tests, papers, demonstrations, and projects, each component carries more or less weight in determining the final grade. To obtain grades of maximum validity, instructors must give each component the proper weight, not too much and not too little. How can they determine what those weights actually are and what they ought to be? And if these two sets of figures are disparate, what can instructors do? It is not easy to give a firm, precise answer to the question of how much influence each component ought to have in determining the composite grade. But several guiding principles can be offered.

In general, the use of several different kinds of indicators of achievement is better than use of only one, provided that each indicator is relevant to the instructional objectives and provided also that it can be observed or measured with reasonable reliability. Other considerations equal, the most reliable components should be assigned the greatest weight.

If component measures of achievement are highly correlated, the problem of weighting them is far less critical than if they are fairly unrelated. For most courses the various measurable aspects of achievement are related closely enough that proper weighting is not a critical problem. Ideally the component measures used to determine the final grade will collectively measure all of the important objectives in the course. However, two components that cover unique objectives should have greater combined weight than two components that measure many of the same instructional objectives. Note that the emphasis here is on the uniqueness of the objectives and not on the importance of each. More important objectives should have been measured with more components (more test items, more writing samples, more demonstrations) to ensure greater influence in the course grade.

The actual weight that a component of a final grade *does* carry depends on the variability of its measures and the correlations of those measures with measures of the other components. This makes the precise influence of any given component quite difficult to assess. As a first approximation to the weight of a component, the standard deviation of its scores serves quite well. If one set of scores is twice as variable as another, the first set is likely to carry about twice the weight of the second in their total.

Table 14-1 shows that the influence (weight) of one component (for example, scores on one test) on a composite (the sum of scores on three tests, in this example) depends on the variability of the test scores. The top section of the table displays the scores of three students, Tom, Dick, and Harry, on three texts, X, Y, and Z, along with their total scores on the three tests. Dick has the highest total and Tom the lowest. The next section shows how the students ranked on the three tests. Each of them made the highest score on one test, middle score on a second, and lowest score on the third. But note, for future reference, that the ranks of their total scores on the three tests are the same as their ranks on Test Z.

The third section of the table gives the maximum possible scores (total points), the mean scores, and the standard deviations of the scores on the three tests. Text X has the highest number of total points. Test Y has the highest mean score. Test Z has scores with the greatest variability.

On which test was it most important to do well? On which was the payoff for ranking first the highest, and the penalty for ranking last the heaviest? Clearly on Test Z, the test with the greatest variability of scores. Which test ranked the students in the same order as their final ranking, based on total scores? Again the answer is Test Z. Thus the influence of one component on a composite depends not on total points or mean score but on score variability.

Table 14-1 Weighted Test Scores

Tests	X	Y	Z	Total
Student scores:				
Tom	53	65	18	136
Dick	50	59	42	151
Harry	47	71	30	148
Student ranks:				
Tom	1	2	3	3
Dick	2	3	1	1
Harry	3	1	2	2
Test characteristics:				
Total points	100.0	75	50	225.0
Mean score	50.0	65	30	145.0
Standard deviation	2.5	5	10	6.5
Weighted scores:	×4	×2	×1	
Tom	212	130	18	360
Dick	200	118	42	360
Harry	188	142	30	360

Now if the three tests should have carried equal weight, they can be made to do so by weighting their scores to make the standard deviations equal. This is illustrated in the last section of the table. Scores on Text X are multiplied by 4, to change their standard deviation from 2.5 to 10, the same as on Test Z. Scores on Test Y are multiplied by 2, to change their standard deviation to 10 also. With equal standard deviations the tests carry equal weight, and give students having the same average rank on the tests the same total scores.

When the whole possible range of scores is used, score variability is closely related to the extent of the available score scale. This means that scores on a 40-item objective test are likely to carry about four times the weight of scores on a 10-point essay-test question, provided that scores extend across the whole range in both cases. But if only a small part of the possible scale of scores is actually used, the length of that scale can be a very misleading guide to the variability of the scores.

The most efficient means of ensuring proper weighting involves the computation of standard scores, perhaps T-scores, for each grading component. Then each component will be represented on a score scale that yields the same standard deviation, 10 for T-scores, for each measure. If an instructor has promised a class, for example, that the final grade will be based on five components, weighted as follows:

Unit Test I	20%
Unit Test II	20%
Term Paper	10%
Final Exam	30%
Term Project	20%

the T-scores of each component can be multiplied by 2, 2, 1, 3, and 2, respectively, to achieve the desired weighting.

One final admonition regarding relative grading and combining scores: It is a mistake to convert test scores to letter grades, record these in a grade book, and then reconvert the letter grades to numbers (A = 4, B = 3, and so on) for purposes of computing final averages. A better procedure is to record the test scores and other numerical measures directly. These can be added, with whatever weighting has been adopted, to obtain a composite score that can be converted to a final grade.

Recording of scores rather than letters saves time in the long run, but more importantly, it contributes to higher grading accuracy. Whenever a range of scores, some higher and some lower, is converted to the same letter grade, information is lost. Each B, whether a high B or low B in terms of the score on which it was based, is given the same value in the reconversion process. Some of the reliability the teacher struggled to achieve in developing each measure is lost in the process. For this reason it is desirable to record raw scores rather than scores obtained after conversion to letter grades.

METHODS OF ASSIGNING GRADES

The procedures an instructor follows for assigning course grades are dictated largely by the meaning the instructor has chosen to attribute to the symbols. The multitude of methods used in practice generally can be categorized in terms of their dependence on either absolute or relative standards (Frisbie, 1978b). The popular variations of these two types and their corresponding strengths and weaknesses are described in this section.

Relative-Grading Methods

One popular variety of relative grading is called "grading on the curve." The "curve" referred to usually is the normal distribution curve or some symmetric variant of it. The norm-referenced basis for this type of grading is complicated by the need to establish arbitrary quotas for each grading category. What proportion of the grades should be As? Bs? Ds? Once these quotas are fixed, grades are assigned without regard to actual level of achievement. Thus the highest 10 percent may receive an A even though the top 20 percent may have achieved at about the same level. Those who "set the curve" or "blow the top off the curve" are merely among the top group, including those who may have scored 20 points lower. The bottom 5 percent may each be assigned an F, even though the bottom 15 percent may be indistinguishable in achievement. Alternative procedures used with grading on the curve are described in some detail by Terwillinger (1971). Regardless of the quota-setting strategy used, this relative-grading method seldom carries a defensible rationale for most courses.

The "distribution-gap" method, another relative-grading variation, is based on the relative ranking of students in the form of a frequency distribution of the composite scores. The frequency distribution is examined carefully for gaps—several consecutive scores that no students obtained. A horizontal line is drawn at the top of the first gap ("Here are the As!") and a second gap is sought. The process continues until all possible grade ranges (A–F) have been identified.

The major fallacy with this technique is the dependence on chance to form the gaps. The size and location of gaps may depend as much on random measurement error as on actual achievement differences between students. If the scores from an equivalent set of measures could be obtained from the group, the smaller gaps might appear in different locations or the larger gaps might turn out to be somewhat smaller. Errors of measurement from different measures do not necessarily cancel each other out as they are expected to do on repeated measurement with the same instrument.

The major attraction of the distribution-gap method is that when grades are assigned, few students appear to be right on the borderline of receiving a higher grade. Consequently, instructors receive fewer student complaints and fewer requests to reexamine test papers to search for "that extra point" that would, for example, change a C grade to a B. In situations where the distribution of scores is highly variable, this grading method is likely to yield grades that are similar to those assigned by some other relative-grading methods. However, when scores are relatively homogeneous, the distribution-gap method actually may be as inequitable to some students as it appears to be.

One other widely used and generally sound relative-grading procedure might be labeled the *standard-deviation method,* owing to the dependence on the standard deviation for determining the grade cutoff points that form equal intervals on the score scale. The first step in this method is to build a frequency distribution for the total or composite scores. Then the median and the standard deviation of the composite scores are computed. Cutoff points for the range of C grades (average performance) are determined by adding one-half of the standard deviation to the median and subtracting one-half of the standard deviation from the median. Add one standard deviation to the upper cutoff of the Cs to find the A-B cutoff score. Subtract the same amount from the lower cutoff of the Cs to find the D-F cutoff. Review borderline cases by using number of assignments completed, quality of assignments, or some other relevant achievement data to decide if any borderline grades should be raised or lowered. Measurement error exists in composite scores, also. A variation of this method that describes the use of relative grading on an institutional basis has been iilustrated in considerable detail by Ebel (1972).

Absolute-Grading Methods

Various methods that depend on percent scores as their basis have a long-standing history, but their popularity has diminished greatly since the early part of this century. Percent scores from tests, papers, and other projects are interpreted as the percent of content, skills, or knowledge over which students have command, a domain-referenced interpretation. For example, a test score of 83 percent means that the student knows 83 percent of the content represented by the instructional objectives from which test items were prepared and sampled. Percent scores are converted to grades by comparing the scores with performance standards established by the instructor for each grading category.

Many instructors assign grades to percent scores using arbitrary standards similar to those set for grading on the curve. That is, students with scores in the 93–100 range are assigned an A, 85–92 is a B, 78–84 is a C, and so on. The restriction here is on the score ranges rather than on the number of students eligible to receive each of the possible grades. But what rationale should be used to determine each grade-category cutoff score? Why should the cutoff for an A be 93 rather than 94 or 90? A major limitation of percent grading as used by some teachers is the use of fixed cutoff points that are applied to every grading component in the course. It seems indefensible to set grade cutoffs that remain constant throughout the course and over several consecutive offerings of the course. What does seem defensible is for the instructor to establish cutoffs for each grading component, independent of the others. For example, the range for an A might be 93–100 for the first test, 88–100 for a term paper, 87–100 for the second test, and 90–100 for the final exam.

Those who use percent grading find themselves in a bind when the highest score obtained on a test was only 68 percent, for example. Was the test much too difficult or did students prepare too little? Was instruction relatively ineffective? Some instructors proceed to adjust the scores by replacing the perfect score, 100 percent, with the highest score, 68 percent in this case. For example, if the highest score was 34 out of 50 points, each student's percent score would be recomputed using 34 as the maximum rather than 50. Though such an adjustment may cause all concerned to breathe easier, the new score can no longer be interpreted as originally intended—the amount of content sampled by the test the student knows. A new domain has been established. What useful interpretation can be made of the new scores?

A final shortcoming of percent grading should be noted. The range of percent scores usually is limited to 70–100 because the passing score generally is 70 percent. The test constructor must exhibit great skill to prepare items that will yield scores distributed in this narrow range and that, at the same time, will measure relevant learning as reflected by the instructional objectives. Methods that allow for a lower passing score would permit a greater potential range of scores, likely would yield more reliable scores, and likely would result in more reliable grade assignments, assuming that the full range of grades (A–F) is to be used.

A second method of absolute grading, called here the *content-based method*, depends heavily on the judgments of the instructor in deciding the type and amount of knowledge students must display to earn each grade on the A–F scale. It is the method most compatible with mastery or quasi-mastery teaching and learning strategies, but it need not be limited to pass-fail or satisfactory-unsatisfactory grading scales. The procedural steps for establishing performance standards and cutoff scores are outlined below for a 50-item test built to measure achievement in two units of instruction.

1. First, the grade to be assigned to those who demonstrate minimum passing achievement must be established. We will use D for illustration purposes, but it could be C, as is common in graduate-level courses. The instructor must develop a description, preferably in writing, of the type of knowledge and understanding a student who barely passes should possess. Similar descriptions must be developed to describe C, B, and A performances.
2. With the descriptions in hand, the instructor reads the first test item and decides if a student with minimum achievement should be able to answer it correctly. If so, a D is recorded next to the item number and the same procedure is applied to item number two. If not, the question is posed in terms of C-level achievement. This process continues until the first item has been classified. If the instructor decides that even A students should not necessarily be able to answer the item correctly, another symbol, say N, is used to classify the item.

(Few such items should exist on a test built by the instructor.) For items that are worth more than a single point, like some essay or problem items, the instructor must decide the minimum number of points to be earned by students in each grade category.

3. This process continues, item by item, until each item has been classified. The estimated cutoff score for a D is determined by adding the number of "D" symbols preceding the items. Assume that number is 17 for this example. Then the number of C symbols is tallied and added to 17 to obtain the cutoff score for C performance. This process continues until a tentative cutoff score for each grade has been determined. The result might look like this:

$$
\begin{aligned}
A &= 48\text{--}50 \\
B &= 40\text{--}47 \\
C &= 29\text{--}39 \\
D &= 17\text{--}28 \\
F &= 0\text{--}16
\end{aligned}
$$

4. The final cutoff scores can be obtained by adjusting the estimated cutoff score down by 2–4 points, depending on test length. The adjustment accounts for negative measurement error, the fact that our measures are less than perfectly reliable. Obviously positive measurement error will affect some students' scores, but most instructors prefer to give the benefit of doubt to students when it comes to matters of chance. With a 2-point adjustment, the cutoff scores for earning the grades D through A in our example are 15, 27, 38, and 46, respectively.

The content-based method is not without limitations. The instructor must exercise subjectivity in describing the performance that A students, for example, must display. Instructors in the same field or those teaching the same course may not agree on the knowledge students should be able to demonstrate at each point on the grading scale. They are likely to disagree to some extent about the classification of test items as well. Yet this method is unlikely to be labeled as arbitrary if instructors are willing and able to define performance standards in writing and are able to supply a defensible rationale for their classification judgments. Other methods of determining cutoff scores—passing scores, in particular—are described in the next chapter.

A final word relates to the use of grading contracts, agreements between teacher and student specifying the achievements toward which the student will strive and the grade the teacher will assign as a result. Taylor (1980) reviewed over 100 reports describing contract grading and concluded that ". . . contract grading appears to have a permanent place among the most appropriate current methods of assigning grades to students." However, studies of the effects of contracting generally showed that students liked it, teachers assigned more high grades than when conventional methods were used, and student achievement was no higher than with conventional grading. Contract grading appears to be best suited to very small classes or independent studies, courses in which students are given the flexibility to pursue individual interests. In such cases a written agreement should be mandatory so that no misunderstanding will exist regarding what will be accomplished, by whom, and by what deadline.

SUMMARY

Some of the main ideas developed in this chapter are summarized in these statements:

1. Measurements and reports of student achievement are essential in education, and no better means than grades seem likely to appear.
2. Grades must be reliable and valid to serve their purposes of stimulating, directing, and rewarding student efforts to learn.
3. There is nothing wrong with encouraging students to work for high grades if the grades are valid measures of achievement.
4. Though they cannot possibly predict success in life, school grades can reflect accurately a student's success in learning the knowledge that is essential to success.
5. Grading is frequently the subject of educational controversy because the grading process is difficult, different philosophies call for different grading systems, and the task of grading is sometimes unpleasant.
6. The major shortcomings of grades relate to a lack of clearly defined and scrupulously observed meanings for the grades and also to the lack of sufficient good evidence to use as a basis for assigning them.
7. Grading standards often vary from instructor to instructor and from institution to institution.
8. Grades will tend to lose their meaning if the institution lacks a clearly defined grading system or does not require instructors to grade in conformity with the system.
9. The selection of either absolute or relative standards as a basis for grading will be influenced more by philosophical considerations than by empirical ones.
10. Grades should be based primarily on achievement, as reflected by instructional objectives, rather than on attitude or effort.
11. Grades that indicate achievement status tend to be more reliable, meaningful, and constructive than grades that indicate growth.
12. The more grading symbols available in the system,

the more reliable the grades will be, but the less convenient the system may be to use.
13. Pass-fail grades cannot serve the major purposes of grading as well as more finely scaled grades.
14. A return to numerical grades would emphasize their use as measurements and would simplify the calculation of grade-point average.
15. The use of multiple grades on various aspects of achievement can improve grading but requires extra effort relative to using a single grade.
16. Aspects of student behavior that do not indicate achievement directly and that are usually inappropriate as components of a course grade include: attendance, class participation, neatness and skill in written expression, and student deportment.
17. Measures used primarily as tools of formative evaluation generally should not be components of a grade intended to represent summative achievement or status.
18. A grading guide for an assignment can be used effectively to communicate the nature of the work to students and to attain valid grading of the assignment.
19. The weight carried by each component measure in a composite score is determined mainly by the variability of the scores from each component.
20. Highly precise weighting of the components on a numerical basis is not crucial to the quality of the grades assigned, especially when the number of components is not small.
21. Relative grading methods that divide the score scale into equal intervals are preferable alternatives to strict grading on the curve or to the use of score "gaps."
22. It is illogical and impractical to expect that a fixed set of cutoff scores, such as 90–100 = A, can be used for all graded work in a course.
23. A defensible absolute grading method requires that the instructor prepare written definitions of the performance standards to be used for assigning grades.

PROJECTS AND PROBLEMS

Problem: Weighting Test Scores in a Composite

A group of five students received the scores shown in Table A on each of three tests. Compute a composite score for each student so that the weight of each test in the composite is the same for each test.

Table A

Student	Test 1	Test 2	Test 3
Barbara	38	25	15
Donald	35	19	39
Michael	32	31	27
Rodney	30	23	22
Amanda	40	27	29

Problem: Assigning Grades

Assume that the 15 scores in Table A were obtained by different students on a single test. Use the standard-deviation grading method to assign grades to the 15 students. Use the median score as the middle of the C grades and use one-half of a standard deviation as the distance between consecutive grade cutoff scores. List the minimum score required to obtain each grade (A–F) and show the number of each grade assigned by this method.

15

USING STANDARDIZED TESTS

CHARACTERISTICS OF STANDARDIZED TESTS

The term *standardized test,* when used precisely, refers to a test that:

1. has been methodically and expertly constructed, usually with tryout, analysis, and revision;
2. includes explicit instructions for uniform (standard) administration and scoring; and
3. provides tables of norms for score-interpretation purposes, derived from administering the test in uniform fashion to a defined sample of students.

Used loosely, the term can refer to almost any published test or inventory, whether standardized in the manner just described or not. Tests or measures that have been well standardized provide the means for making score comparisons among examinees who attempted the same tasks under the same testing conditions and time constraints, and whose responses were scored with the same procedures. Of course not all standardized tests, as the term is commonly used, are intended to yield norm-referenced comparisons. Criterion-referenced and domain-referenced achievement tests and some personality measures, all of which may be commercially prepared and uniformly administered, provide no tables of norms.

Standardized tests serve the same function in education and psychology that are served by standard weights and measures in commerce and science.

If every meat market had its own type of scale and concept of how much a pound is, we could not be sure that a pound of ground beef purchased at one market would be more or less than a pound obtained at another. The same problem would face the consumer at the gas station, the fabric shop, and the candy counter. Without standardized tests, the achievements and abilities of students from different classrooms and schools could not be assessed readily with a common yardstick. If each elementary teacher in a district were to develop a geography test to measure student achievement, we would likely find tests that varied markedly in the breadth and depth of tasks required, the number of items, the amount of testing time allowed, the quality of test items, and the reliability of the scores obtained. Certainly it would be illogical and inappropriate to make score comparisons among students from different classrooms and schools under such circumstances.

TYPES OF STANDARDIZED TESTS

In Chapter 2 we distinguished the term *test* from the broader term *measure*. We will retain that distinction here and simply indicate that various types of standardized personality measures will be discussed in Chapter 18. Our concern here, then, is with standardized tests of achievement, aptitude, and intelligence.

Test Batteries

Some standardized tests are developed, published, and administered in coordinated sets known as *test batteries*. The number of tests or subtests in the set may vary from four or less to ten or more, the number of items per test may vary from 35 or fewer to 100 or more, and the time per test may range from ten minutes to more than an hour. The administration of batteries such as the *Iowa Tests of Educational Development* or the *Differential Aptitude Tests* may require two to four half-day test sessions.

A primary advantage of using a battery over a collection of separate tests, whether for achievement or aptitude measurement, is that the battery provides comparable scores from the same norm group for all of its subtests. This is important if a student's achievement in mathematics computation, for example, is to be compared with his or her achievement in mathematics concepts or mathematics applications. If uncoordinated tests are used, a student might seem to do better on Test A than on Test B simply because students of lower achievement were more prominent in the norm group of Test A. It is for this reason that aptitude batteries are used most frequently in employment and vocational counseling to help the client understand his or her areas of strength and weakness.

An achievement-test battery can provide comprehensive coverage of most of the important aspects of achievement at the elementary school level, many at the secondary level, and some at the college level. The more uniform the educational programs of the students, the more suitable is a uniform test battery for all of them. Such a battery can be selected to avoid duplication in the content covered by the several subtests and to minimize the number of serious omissions.

Use of a battery of tests that was developed as an integrated whole thus offers substantial advantages. The only significant disadvantage is the lack of flexibility. A battery may include some subtests that are of little interest to particular users and may omit others they would have preferred. But this is part of the price that must be paid for the advantages of convenience in use, comprehensiveness of coverage, and comparability of scores.

Single-Subject Tests

Tests that measure achievement in one content area, or that measure a single type of aptitude, differ in several respects from their counterparts that might be found, at least by name, in a battery. The content coverage tends to be broader and more detailed in a single-subject test. Such tests usually contain more items and require more testing time than the corresponding battery subtest.

Single-subject tests tend to be used for specific purposes, to make some kind of instructional decision, rather than to simply describe students' relative achievement or aptitude levels. For example, readiness tests used at the primary level help the teacher group students of similar reading or arithmetic achievement levels for instructional purposes. A mathematics test might be used to decide which eighth-graders are most likely candidates for studying algebra in the ninth grade. Reading tests are used to help select reading materials most appropriate for developing the reading skills of each student. Special aptitude tests for musical, artistic, and mechanical ability are used to help students make vocational and educational decisions about future actions.

Some single-subject tests resemble a battery in that they contain subtests or they provide subtest scores. A reading test, for example, may yield a vocabulary score, a comprehension score, and a total score. Some English language tests provide scores on vocabulary, spelling, punctuation, grammar, word usage, and capitalization. Generally such subtest scores are so highly correlated with one another that their separate diagnostic value is quite limited. However, the total score is probably a comprehensive indicator of overall achievement in the content domain defined by the test specifications.

The standardized tests of intelligence to be described more fully in Chapter 17 are most appropriately classified as single-subject tests. That is, the trait that such tests attempt to measure generally is a single unitary characteristic. Despite the differences among intelligence tests in what they purport to measure and in the theory on which they are based, and despite the fact that some yield subtest scores, intelligence tests are less like batteries and more like single-subject tests.

INTERPRETATION OF STANDARDIZED TEST SCORES

Seldom are the raw scores obtained by students on standardized tests interpreted directly. Instead, raw scores are converted to some other score scale to facilitate interpretation. These new score scales are designed to enhance norm-referenced interpretations by referring to a single reference group or to several reference groups that have been linked to the same score scale.

Status Scores

Status scores indicate how a student's test performance compares with those of others in a single reference group—a class, school, school district, or national group. Status or standing in the group generally is expressed as a percentile rank, but standard scores like those described in Chapter 4 frequently are used as well. In most cases the stanines, T-scores, or normal-curve equivalents are normalized standard scores derived from percentile ranks. Status scores are needed primarily to determine intraindividual differences in achievement across subtests in a test battery. Note that status scores mask growth or change when students are tested with a significant time lapse between administrations unless (a) the single reference group is broadly defined to include several consecutive age-grade groups or (b) the status scores are based on the same reference group on the various occasions.

Developmental Scores

Developmental scores indicate how a student's test performance compares with those of others in a series of reference groups (Hoover, 1983). These groups differ systematically and developmentally in average achievement and are defined in terms of chronological age or school grade. Score scales most frequently used to express developmental level include grade equivalents, age equivalents, and expanded standard scores.

Grade- and age-equivalent scores are most appropriately used with elementary school subjects that are studied continuously at increasing levels of skill and complexity over many years. To obtain a table of equivalents, the test must be given to a large number of students in each of the several grades for which it is intended. Then the median raw score of students in each grade, or of each age, is determined. The numerical designation of the grade (or the age in years) is considered to be the grade equivalent (or age equivalent) of that particular raw score. Both grade and age equivalents usually are indicated to the nearest tenth, each tenth corresponding roughly to one month of schooling in a school year of approximately ten months. A grade-equivalent of 7.4, for example, represents the median performance of seventh-graders in their fourth month.

Usually the actual equivalents reported in a table are obtained by graphically plotting the median test scores against their corresponding grade or age values, drawing a smooth curve through the points, and reading the score equivalents for each grade or age value from the curve. Suppose, for example, that a reading test is given to a large representative sample of students in grades 3 through 8 at the beginning of December and to another similar sample about five months later at the end of April. The median scores for each grade might look like those shown in Table 15-1.

These data have been plotted in Figure 15-1. Note that the median score for the third grade in the December testing is plotted as Grade 3.3 (third grade, plus three months). The other December medians are plotted in a similar fashion and the April medians are plotted as 3.8, 4.8, and so on. Table 15-2 presents the grade equivalents of some of the raw test scores. These were obtained from Figure 15-1 by reading straight across from the test-score value to the curve and then straight down to the corresponding grade level (to the nearest tenth of a unit).

Age equivalents are obtained similarly, though since the age data are less uniform than the grade data, more points are plotted for age equivalents. Often only four age levels per year are used, indicated, for example, by the numbers 11.0, 11.3 (three months past the eleventh birthday), 11.6, and 11.9.

Grade- and age-equivalent scores are easy to interpret because they are tied to a score scale that is understood by individuals with little test or statistical sophistication. They are subject to misinterpretation just as are status scores, but there is no convincing evidence that developmental scores are more grossly misused or misinterpreted than are status scores (Hoover, 1983). Common sense and knowledge about developmental scales are the key ingredients to responsible interpretation of grade- and age-equivalent scores.

If a bright fifth-grade girl gets a grade-equivalent score of 8.4 on an arithmetic test designed for grades 5 and 6, how should this score be interpreted? Chances are this test was not administered to eighth-graders, so the value 8.4 is the estimated grade equivalent (by the process of extrapolation). The typical student in the eighth grade, fourth month, would score about the same as our

Table 15-1   Median Reading-Test Scores in Grades 3–8

	MEDIAN RAW SCORE	
Grade	December	April
3	33	42
4	45	57
5	59	64
6	72	74
7	77	81
8	82	85

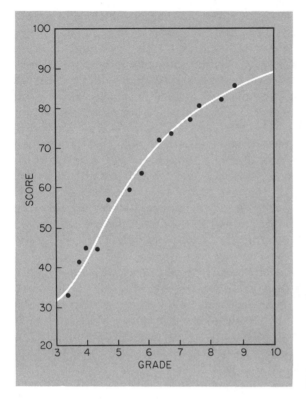

Figure 15-1
Plot of Median Raw Scores Against Grade Levels.

fifth-grader did on this test. However, this does not mean our fifth-grader can do the same arithmetic as the typical eighth-grader. She would need to take a test designed for eighth-graders for us to know how she would perform on arithmetic content studied by eighth-graders. Students who obtain grade-equivalent scores significantly above or below their own grade level should be retested with a higher- or lower-level test form if the user wishes to obtain more precise indications of the developmental levels of such students. Often the percentile rank, a status indicator, is helpful in making judgments about the value of out-of-level testing for a particular student.

Table 15-2 Grade Equivalents of Reading-
Test Scores

Score	Grade	Score	Grade
85	8.8	55	4.8
80	7.6	50	4.5
75	6.8	45	4.1
70	6.2	40	3.8
65	5.6	35	3.4
60	5.2	30	2.8

Score Profiles

Only if scores on the several tests used are comparable is a profile of student scores meaningful. Scores will be comparable if they are expressed on the same status score scale (all percentile ranks or all the same type of standard score) and if the same reference group is used for each one. An example of one student's score profile is shown in Figure 15-2. The horizontal lines on the chart represent various percentile ranks, spaced as they would be if scores on the vertical scale were normally distributed. There is a vertical line on the chart for each test in the battery. The percentile rank values shown across the top of the chart for each test are marked as dots on the vertical scales and connected by lines to form the profile. Larry Hill's performance is about average, overall. (His percentile rank for the total test is 52.) His best achievement levels are in

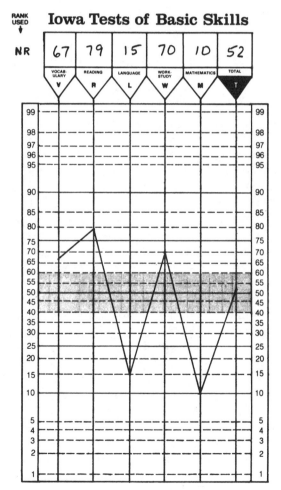

Figure 15-2
Example of Student Profile Chart. (© 1978 by The University of Iowa)

reading, vocabulary, and work-study skills. His poorest are in language and mathematics.

Profiles are most useful for identifying individual needs of students and for vocational and educational planning. A profile also might be used to identify students who should be tested more extensively or to determine if impressions formed from classroom testing and observation are confirmed. Profiles represent a very compact form of visual communication, making them convenient for reporting and explaining test results to both students and parents.

Percentile Bands

Some test publishers stress the fact that test scores are subject to error by choosing not to report an exact percentile rank equivalent for each raw score. Instead they provide a range of values within which the "true" percentile rank probably lies. This range is called a *percentile band*. For example, the test manual may show that the percentile rank for a test score of 37 is between the values 28 and 57; it may go on to stress that the exact percentile rank equivalent is unknown, since it depends on the unknown size and sign (positive or negative) of the error of measurement in the score.

The principle employed in computing percentile bands is the same one involved in using the standard error of measurement (Chapter 5) to find the raw-score range in which the true score probably lies. The width of the percentile band depends on two factors—the reliability of the scores and the degree of certainty that the band includes the true value. Unreliable tests or high degrees of certainty lead to broad percentile bands. Unfortunately, the broader these percentile bands, the less useful information the test provides.

One use of percentile bands in a battery of tests is in deciding whether or not a difference between any two scores is large enough to be meaningful. Most manuals suggest that if two percentile bands overlap, there is probably insufficient evidence to conclude that achievements in the two areas differ. If they do not overlap, it is safe to regard the scores as truly different. The purpose of these recommendations is to guard against attaching too much importance to score differences that might be due solely to errors of measurement.

There is a possibility of underinterpreting test scores using percentile bands just as one might overinterpret scores without the use of bands. In cases where a test yields highly reliable scores, relatively wide bands may result from selecting high levels of confidence for interpretation. In such cases the user might be better off relying on the percentile rank if additional information is available for decision making. Generally the larger a score difference, the more confident the user can be that a corresponding achievement difference actually exists. But such interpretations usually are made in a decision-making context using other corroborative test data or auxiliary information pertinent to the decision. When only a test score is available as the basis for making an important decision about an examinee—and this should be an extremely rare occasion— percentile bands are more likely to help than to hinder the process.

Subtest Scores

Just as tests that constitute a test battery provide separate measures of different aspects of achievement, so it is possible to subdivide a single test into separately scored parts to obtain measures of several different aspects. The desire to obtain as much information as possible from a test sometimes leads the test developer to offer a large number of part scores, each of which is based on only a few test items. There are three cautions to note with regard to interpreting subtest scores. First, as the number of part scores increases, the reliability of each probably diminishes. On many tests, a part score based on as few as 10 or 15 items may measure sampling error more than it does true achievement.

A second caution relates to the validity of each subtest score. Some test publishers give unique names to each of several subtests to indicate the separate aspects of achievement they expect each to be measuring. When subtest scores are provided, the developer should provide subtest correlations in the test manual as evidence that the subtests are sufficiently unique measures to warrant giving them separate titles. If the correlations are too high, and regardless of the reliability of each, the subtest scores are likely to be measures of a single unitary trait or skill. The responsible test user should focus interpretations on total test scores in such cases and ignore the availability of the subtest scores.

Finally, increasing the number of scores a test yields complicates the process of using it without producing a corresponding gain in value. Often all the test users really want and need, and all they have time to use effectively, is a single, overall measure of achievement in an area. On a single-subject standardized achievement test, therefore, the provision of a number of part scores should be viewed more with skepticism than with acclaim.

NORMS

Norms, which report how students actually do perform, should not be confused with *standards,* which reflect estimates of how well they should perform. The standard of correctness in arithmetic problems is 100 percent. The norm of student achievement on any given arithmetic test may be only 85 percent. Yet this latter percentage functions as a kind of standard on which to base comparisons of an individual with his or her peers. Few students are regarded as failures in an area of study if their performance is above the norm or average. Few are regarded as successes if their performance is below it. It is in this context that highly differentiated norms lose much of their significance. For example, norms for ninth-grade girls of Hispanic descent attending parochial schools in the rural Midwest are more highly differentiated than those for just ninth-grade girls. If the differentiation were carried far enough, the only reason why individual students would not score exactly at the norm appropriate for them would be that their scores include some measurement error.

In addition, norms should not be confused with the various types of scores that are used to report them. Percentile ranks, stanines, grade-equivalents, and standard scores are all types of scores, derived from raw scores, to report normative performance; they are not norms themselves. Norms are differentiated by certain characteristics of the reference group that comprise them. There are age norms and grade norms, local norms and national norms, group norms and individual norms, to name only a few. It is possible to combine the characteristics of a norm group in a variety of ways in an attempt to build highly differentiated norm groups. As indicated earlier, however, there is little practical value accrued in providing such fine classifications.

Characteristics of Useful Norms

To be accurate, test norms must be based on the test scores of large and representative samples of examinees who have been tested under standard conditions, and who take the test as seriously, but no more so, as will other students for whom the norms are needed. That complex sentence outlines a very complex and difficult process.

Norms obviously must be obtained from students in schools that are willing to take time out from their other responsibilities to help with the norming administration. That very willingness may make them somewhat atypical of the population of schools and students generally. To get enough cooperation to provide a reasonably large norm group is hard enough. To make it a representative sample is even harder. First the developer must decide which population the norm sample is supposed to represent. Then the ideal sample that will represent that population must be identified. Finally, the cooperation of school administrators must be secured and the students in the sample must actually be tested. It is no wonder that Baglin (1981) questioned whether "nationally" normed really means nationally. In his review of three recent norming studies conducted by publishers, the percentage of school districts originally invited to participate that actually took part was as low as 13 percent in one study and only as high as 32 percent in another.

In the early days of standardized testing, publishers sometimes prided themselves on the large samples on which their norms were based. However, these large numbers often had been obtained by testing all students in a few very large school systems. But since there are great differences between school systems in the general level of abilities of their students and in the quality of education provided, scores from only a few school districts cannot provide dependable norms for a broader population of districts. The relevance and representativeness of a set of test norms cannot be assessed adequately without considering such factors as community type and size, school curricular emphasis and diversity, and students' levels of motivation, aspiration, and general ability.

The administration of tests to obtain normative data can take significant amounts of time away from the schools' other important activities. The reluctance of schools to cooperate is somewhat understandable, but it would be quite wrong for administrators and teachers to believe that test administration has no direct educational value for the participating students. A school that "doesn't have time" to cooperate in the tryout or norming of a standardized test suitable to its students' abilities must have a phenomenal program and must be making amazingly good use of teacher and student time doing things that are more important. Unfortunately some of these same schools complain of the irrelevance of norms provided by the publishers from whom they must select tests for their standardized testing program.

Individual versus Group Norms

A serious error that some test users make is to use norms composed of individual student scores to interpret average scores from schools, school districts, or some other aggregate. Although the mean of the school averages must be the same as the mean for the individual student scores, the school averages are likely to be far less variable than the student scores. The standard deviation of the school means is smaller than that for the student scores. The *average* score in a truly excellent school may be lower than the scores obtained by one-third of the students in all schools, and the average score in a very poor school may be better than the scores of one-third of all students. In other words, when such inappropriate interpretations are made, the percentile ranks of the school averages are not likely ever to be lower than 33 or higher than 66. Degrees of excellence or of deficiency are likely to be underestimated drastically. The only proper basis for evaluation of school averages, a type of treatment-referenced interpretation, is a separate table of norms for school averages. And the quality of school norms should be judged by the same criteria of relevance and representativeness as were recommended for individual student norms.

Alternatives to National Norms

Because accurate national norms are difficult to obtain and are of limited relevance in many local situations, some test specialists have suggested that they should be abandoned in favor of purely local norms. Though local norms are adequate for student evaluation, they provide no basis for judging whether the school's performance is better or worse than that of other schools. After all, average performance within a group is always represented by the fiftieth percentile, a stanine of 5, or a *T*-score of 50.

There is another alternative, however, that schools and test publishers could pursue cooperatively. Schools in similar situations, with similar interests and similar problems, could band together to form a kind of "common market" for educational testing. If they use the same tests under the same standard conditions, they can pool the scores obtained, student scores and school averages separately, and thus gain the benefits of external standards of achievement. Such an association may even be developed along the same lines as are used to establish athletic conferences for interscholastic competition. Some state education departments now provide such normative data through the statewide competency-testing programs they administer.

CERTIFICATION OF OCCUPATIONAL COMPETENCE

Most of the tests used for certification and licensure purposes are regarded as standardized, but because the procedures used in test development, scoring, and determining of the passing score are seldom publicized, it is difficult to determine if these tests are standardized by our definition. Nonetheless, the use of tests for credentialing is unmistakably on the upswing, despite the charge by some that written tests are unable to yield valid measures of the important aspects of professional or technical competence.

Let it be granted without argument that no written test can assess *all* aspects of skill or competence in the practice of a profession or trade. The best it can do is to indicate whether examinees know enough about the work they hope to do to be intellectually qualified. It cannot reveal how skillfully, or with what wisdom, they will use the knowledge at their command. But the aspects of competence that written tests can assess *are* important, and written tests can do an efficient, valid job of assessing them. That scores from such tests are sometimes used inappropriately or unwisely by credentialing bodies is not an indictment of the tests, however, as some may claim.

Those who are responsible for the development of tests to be used in certifying competence should themselves be highly competent test developers. In some cases they are; unfortunately in many they are not. Usually, and quite understandably, they are first and foremost experts in the profession or trade in which competence is to be examined and certified. They may work under the supervision of a specialist in testing, and they may gradually acquire through experience some sophistication in methods of testing. However, lacking special training for the job they are asked to do, they may sometimes show less than the desired competence in doing it. All around the world there are many untrained or poorly trained test constructors doing their very limited best to handle some very important responsibilities. Universities that offer training in educational measurement probably could do much more than they have done to provide good preservice and in-service training for these workers.

Tests used to certify competence ought to be highly valid tests. They ought to measure with high precision the important abilities the profession has concluded are necessary for safe and competent practice. To some this suggests that the tests should be validated against "appropriate" criterion measures. Unfortunately, as pointed out in Chapter 6, the problem of obtaining valid criterion measures is no easier than building a comprehensive test of the relevant abilities. Whether the test is validated directly, or indirectly via some criterion, there is no escape from the exercise of expert judgment in determining what ought to be measured and how it ought to be measured. The absence of this kind of judgment in test development is a frequent and serious weakness of many tests of professional or technical competence.

THE PASSING SCORE

There is a popular belief that any person who takes a test either passes or fails it. For tests used to measure amount of achievement, this is patently false. However, it is substantially true of the criterion-referenced measures used to certify competence to practice in the trades and professions.

A second widespread belief is that when a test is used to pass or fail examinees, the distinction between the two outcomes is clear-cut and unequivocal. This is almost never true. Determination of a minimum acceptable performance level always involves some rather arbitrary and not wholly satisfactory decisions.

Of the several approaches to the problem of setting a passing score, one could be considered ideal. The first step is to decide on the minimum essentials of competence, what every practitioner must know or be able to do in order to practice safely and effectively. A written description of these abilities establishes the *standard* for minimum competence. Tasks designed to test whether the applicant possesses this knowledge and ability are developed to constitute the test. Theoretically, the passing score on such a test should be a perfect score. In practice, of course, to insist on a perfect score as the minimum passing score would be almost to guarantee that no one would pass. First, minimum essentials are not matters of consensus; second, the item writer's ability to test them unequivocally also is not perfect; and finally, the examinee's performance is not flawless enough to make a perfect score a reasonable minimum score. There needs to be some margin for errors on all counts. Alternatives to the ideal approach that have greater practical utility are described below.

Five Alternative Approaches

The first approach is to broaden the scope of ability to be tested somewhat, replacing the "minimum essentials" concept with the concept of "important fundamentals." Test construction is handled in the same manner, but the passing score is set somewhat below 100 percent correct. Conventionally, passing scores on such tests have been 75, 70, or even 65 percent correct. This approach is more practical than the ideal, but it has two weaknesses. The first is that the "conventional" passing score is an arbitrary percentage with no clearly rational justification. This weakness can be overcome to some degree by using this line of reasoning:

1. On a well-constructed objective test, no examinee, however weak, should actually get a score less than the expected chance score on that test, but one or two should get close to that expected chance score.
2. On a well-constructed objective test the very best examinees should get scores at or near the maximum possible score.
3. Hence, the ideal mean score on such a test falls at a point midway between the maximum possible score and the expected chance score.
4. The passing score might then be defined as a point midway between the ideal mean score and the expected chance score.

How this reasoning applies to two hypothetical tests is shown in Table 15-3.

If the test does not meet the criteria of goodness expressed by points 1 or 2—that is, it is too easy or too difficult to give a mean score near the ideal mean and is insufficiently discriminating to give a low score near the expected chance score—a better estimate of the passing score might be obtained by employing these modifications:

1. Average the lowest score and the expected chance score.
2. Average the actual mean and the ideal mean.
3. Define the passing score as a point midway between the two averages.

If the divergence between actual and ideal values is extreme, it might be advisable to forget the ideal values and define the passing score as the point midway between the mean score and the lowest score.

The other weakness of this first approach is that this definition still leaves substantial elements of chance in determination of the passing score. The items may be more difficult, or less difficult or less discriminating, than the test constructor intended. Whether an examinee passes or fails a specific test may be determined by the questions in the test rather than by his or her actual level of professional competence. This weakness can be overcome by using a second approach.

The second approach, commonly referred to as the "Ebel method," involves determining the passing percentage from a subjective analysis of the relevance and difficulty of each item in the test. Table 15-4 illustrates four categories of relevance and three categories of difficulty and gives the expected percentages of passing for items in each category. These expected percentages are not fixed but, as determined by the judges, may vary on each occasion in which the

Table 15-3 Passing Scores on Two Hypothetical Tests

	True-false	*Four-alternative*
Number of items	100.0	100.00
Expected chance score	50.0	25.00
Ideal mean score	75.0	62.50
Minimum passing score	62.5	43.75

Table 15-4 Relevance, Difficulty, and Expected Success on Test Items

Relevance Categories	DIFFICULTY LEVELS		
	Easy	Medium	Hard
Essential	100%	—	—
Important	90	70%	—
Acceptable	80	60	40%
Questionable	70	50	30

method is used. Each number in the table expresses the percentage of items in that category that a minimally qualified (barely passing) applicant would likely answer correctly.

Suppose, for example, that the number of items in a 100-item test falling in each category when the ratings of five judges were pooled were as shown in the second column of Table 15-5. Multiplying each of these numbers by the expected proportion of correct answers gives the products shown in the fourth column of Table 15-5. The sum of these products divided by 500 gives an estimate of the appropriate passing score.

The third approach assumes that competence is essentially a relative term, and that the task of a certification test is simply to select the most competent and to reject those who are least competent. The test is still based on important

Table 15-5 Passing Score Estimated from Item Characteristics

Item Category	Number of Items*	Expected Success	Number × Success
Essential	94	100	9,400
Important:			
Easy	106	90	9,540
Medium	153	70	10,710
Acceptable:			
Easy	24	80	1,920
Medium	49	60	2,940
Hard	52	40	2,080
Questionable:			
Easy	4	70	280
Medium	11	50	50
Hard	7	30	210
	500		37,130

$$\frac{37,130}{500} = 74.26 \text{ or } 74\% = \text{passing score}$$

* Actually the number of placements of items in the category by all five of the judges.

fundamentals, but the passing score is not defined as some proportion of correct answers. Instead, it is defined as that score above which 50 percent, or 66 percent, or 90 percent of all scores fall. This means that the poorest one-half, one-third, or one-tenth of the applicants must fail, regardless of the absolute level of their performance.

The obvious drawback of this approach is that it allows the passing score to vary according to the general level of competence of the examinees at a specific testing. If the general level is high, some fairly well-qualified applicants may fail. If it is low, some poorly qualified candidates may pass.

Whether the passing score should be defined as a percent of the total score or as a percent of applicants to be passed probably should depend on the expected stability of the examinations in level of difficulty compared to the expected stability of the group of examinees in levels of ability in future test administrations. If an examiner is more confident of the stability of the examination difficulty than of examinee-group ability, he or she may choose the percent-of-total-score approach. But if one's confidence leans in the other direction, then the passing score should probably be determined by a percentage of applicants.

A fourth approach combines the second and third, retaining some of the advantages of both. The decision rule for the passing score might be: 75 percent correct responses is passing as long as at least 60 percent of the examinees but no more than 80 percent of the examinees exceed this score. An adjustment can be made if too many or too few examinees pass. If less than 60 percent of the examinees exceed the 75 percent score, the new passing score is the point midway between the 75 percent score and the score that 60 percent of the examinees do exceed. If more than 80 percent of them exceed the 75 percent score, the new passing score is the point midway between the 75 percent score and the score that 80 percent of the examinees do exceed. The figures used in this example—75 percent of the items, and 60 percent and 80 percent of the examinees—are simply illustrative. An examining body might want to raise or lower any of them, depending on its circumstances. The object in setting these values is to keep the amount of content knowledge, and the proportion of passes and failures, within what seem to be reasonable bounds while making reasonable allowance for the unavoidable errors of measurement. This fourth alternative has not been widely used but would seem to have considerable merit as a rational solution to a difficult problem.

The fifth approach uses the performance of certified practitioners as a basis for setting the passing score. It requires the certification test to be given to a large and representative sample of professionals who are actually practicing. A decision is made by the certifying body that any applicant who scores above the lowest quarter, lowest fifth, or lowest tenth of those actually practicing the profession deserves to be certified to practice it also. If the supply of applicants is good, and if the profession is seeking to upgrade itself rapidly, it may set the passing score fairly high on the scale of actual practitioner performances.

One problem with the fifth approach, of course, is getting the scores of a sufficient sample of practitioners, and getting them to take the test conscientiously. A solution to this problem might be to break the test into representative sets of 15 to 25 items, asking each respondent to answer only those in one set. From their performance on these sets, synthetic score distributions of the entire test could be constructed. This procedure, by limiting the proportion of the test exposed to any one person, would help to safeguard test security also.

It is clear that a variety of approaches can be used to solve the problem of how to determine the passing score. Because the procedures associated with different approaches vary, we should not be surprised to find that these approaches do not converge to the same result. Some have a content-referenced basis and some have a group-referenced basis. Anyone who expects to find the "real" passing score by any one of these approaches, or by any other approach, will certainly be disappointed. A "real" passing score simply does not exist. All that any examining authority can hope for, and all that any of their examinees should expect, is that the basis for defining the passing score be stated clearly, and that the definition be as rational as possible. Additional approaches to defining the passing score and related considerations have been described by Livingston and Zieky (1982).

SELECTION OF STANDARDIZED TESTS

Sources of Information

For those who wish to identify published and unpublished tests that measure a particular trait, or those who seek descriptive information or critical reviews of existing measures, a wide variety of sources is available. Most information will be found in print, but much of it is accessible through computer retrieval systems as well.

The *Mental Measurements Yearbook* (*MMY*) generally is regarded as the most comprehensive source of information about published tests. The eighth edition (Buros, 1978), the most current at the time of this writing, includes such descriptive information about each test as author, publication date, number of forms and levels, number of scores reported, administration time required, and prices for tests and scoring services. In addition, critical reviews by testing specialists and a bibliography of sources in which the measure was used are provided. *Tests in Print* (Mitchell, 1983) is a summary reference to information detailed in all the *MMY*s published previously. All the information in the *MMY*, including that in the forthcoming edition, has been encoded in computer-retrievable form so that it is accessible through a computer literature search. This is a significant development for test users. It means that the severe publication lag that has plagued *MMY* users in the past will be cut drastically, permitting access to current information even before the publication date of the next printed revision.

Tests and Measurements in Child Development: Handbook II (Johnson, 1976) contains descriptive information about over 1200 unpublished measures of child behavior. The validity and reliability evidence provided for the various measures should be examined carefully by potential users, because unpublished measures generally have been subjected to less critical review than their published counterparts.

A series of handbooks organized by grade levels has been developed by the Center for the Study of Evaluation (CSE) to provide judgments of the quality of tests available for use in educational settings. Characteristics evaluated are measurement validity, examinee appropriateness, administrative usability, and normed technical excellence. Methods used to arrive at summary judgments about the tests reviewed are described in each publication: *CSE-ECRC Preschool/ Kindergarten Test Evaluations* (1971), *CSE Elementary School Test Evaluations* (1976), and the three volumes of *CSE Secondary School Test Evaluations* (1974). A sixth volume, *CSE-RBS Test Evaluations: Tests of Higher Order Cognitive, Affective, and Interpersonal Skills* (1972), covers measures not ordinarily classified as achievement, aptitude, or intelligence tests.

The most current information about standardized tests is in publisher catalogs and the tests themselves. Those who are charged with selecting tests for a school testing program should review a specimen set for each test under consideration. For a nominal fee, the publisher will provide a copy of one form of the test and the accompanying test manuals to individuals who are authorized to use standardized tests. Publisher representatives can answer questions about their tests and processing services through either telephone inquiries or school visits requested by the test-selection committee.

Some tests have been reviewed by measurement specialists in professional publications such as the *Journal of Educational Measurement* or *Measurement and Evaluation in Guidance*. These reviews, as well as validity studies published in *Educational and Psychological Measurement,* can be identified readily through a computerized literature search for a very modest price.

Finally, college and university faculty members in education and psychology departments often are available to consult with school personnel regarding test selection and use. Some universities are willing to provide consultation and test-scoring services to school districts through their campus measurement and test-scoring centers. The same services are supplied by some state education departments through area or regional centers established throughout the state to serve school districts.

Selection Criteria

Sources of information available to committees or individuals responsible for selecting standardized tests were described in the previous section. But what information should be sought from these sources, and how should the information be weighed in arriving at a selection decision? The answers to these questions are developed in the remainder of this section.

Validity. Without question, test content—what the items or test tasks require the examinee to know—is the most important factor to assess. How well the tests or subtests match the curriculum in terms of content coverage and emphasis must be determined in selecting achievement tests. For tests of aptitude and intelligence, a review of the item content is still the primary source of validity evidence. The item types used should be familiar to students, the format of the tests should make them easy for students to use, and the diagrams and figures employed should be legible.

Technical adequacy. A test that has been judged to be sufficiently valid to allow the district to accomplish its purpose for testing should be scrutinized further for technical adequacy. The reliability of test and subtest scores should be assessed from data supplied in the technical manual and comments made by reviewers of the test. Data should be provided in the manual about the equivalency of alternate test forms that may be available. When developmental scores are provided, the user should search for evidence that sufficient data were gathered in the norming process so that reliance on interpolation and extrapolation was not too great in building the norms tables. Sufficient information should be supplied in the manual to permit users to decide that the norm group is a relevant one with which to compare the scores of students in their school district.

Practical considerations. Tests that survive a validity and technical screening should be evaluated in terms of certain other important considerations. Schools do not have unlimited funds, but cost should not carry more weight in the decision than validity or technical adequacy. If necessary, trade-offs in scoring and reporting services should be made so that the district can use the most valid measures available. In addition, test administration time required should be weighed in relation to direct instructional time lost. The adequacy of the manuals and other publisher aids for users should be assessed. Finally, tests under consideration should be viewed in terms of the entire district testing program. Is there an appropriate achievement battery available that was normed on the same group that was used to norm the intelligence test that is under consideration? Is the elementary school battery that is under review linked to a battery that could be used at the middle school or secondary school level? Of course this question is relevant only to the extent that the upper-level batteries themselves have been judged to be appropriate in validity and technical quality.

The test-selection committee must work systematically to gather, organize, and summarize the data about each test under consideration. One useful method of organization involves developing a two-dimensional grid with specific test-selection criteria listed vertically down the page and test titles listed horizontally across the top. Each cell of the table might contain summary information and a symbol representing the committee's overall evaluation of the corresponding criterion for the test to which it pertains.

SUMMARY

The main ideas developed in this chapter can be summarized in the following 20 statements:

1. A standardized test is one that has been expertly and carefully constructed, is administered under standard (uniform) conditions, and provides tables of norms for score interpretation.
2. Achievement-test batteries provide for comprehensive coverage of achievements and for comparable scores in different areas of achievement.
3. Single-subject tests provide greater breadth and depth of coverage than their counterparts included in a battery.
4. Status scores permit norm-referenced interpretations and are needed to make intraindividual comparisons from the results of a test battery.
5. Developmental scores depend on the use of multiple reference groups and are most useful for elementary school subjects that are studied continuously over a long period of time.
6. A grade-equivalent score in arithmetic of 7.4 for a fifth-grade girl ordinarily does not mean that she is ready for seventh-grade mathematics.
7. Profiles of test scores indicate both the student's general level of achievement and his or her specific strengths and weaknesses.
8. Percentile bands call attention to the lack of precision in educational measurements but may complicate or distort the interpretation of the results somewhat.
9. Part scores from a single test must be sufficiently reliable to be useful.
10. Norms report what is, and standards report what ought to be, but national norms inevitably function as a kind of local standard.
11. To be accurate, test norms must be based on large and representative samples of examinees, tested under standard conditions.
12. The adequacy of test norms depends on both the number of students and the number of schools of a specified nature represented in them.
13. Individual student norms are not appropriate to use for the interpretation of school or district average scores.
14. Similar schools that cooperate in administering the same tests can secure highly relevant and useful norms by pooling their test data.
15. The essential functions served by tests of technical or professional competence would be served better if those who develop such tests (a) were trained better and (b) were more attentive to the problems associated with test validity.
16. The passing score may be defined as (a) some fraction of the total test score, (b) some fraction of applicants to be passed, or (c) a score higher than that obtained by some fraction of certified practitioners.
17. The passing score may be defined on the basis of the pooled judgments of experts about the relevance and difficulty of each item in the test.
18. Passing scores cannot be discovered; they must be defined, but the definition should be as clear and as rational as possible.
19. Both descriptive and evaluative information about particular standardized tests can be found in print or accessed by computer retrieval.
20. Systematic procedures for selecting a standardized measure should give high priority to test validity, technical adequacy, and a number of practical considerations.

PROJECTS AND PROBLEMS

Project: Interpretation of Standardized Test Scores

The accompanying table gives the scores of Roland Elkins, a fifth-grade student in your school, on a series of tests of basic skills taken at midyear. Complete the table by determining the stanine equivalents for the local percentile ranks.

Mrs. Elkins has made an appointment to talk with you about the test scores, which she has not seen. Write out the main ideas that you would try to explain to her. You probably should touch on:

1. What raw scores, grade equivalents, percentile ranks, and stanines mean. (These tests were not corrected for guessing. The standard error of measurement of these grade-equivalent scores is about 0.4.)
2. Why local percentile ranks differ from the publisher's percentile ranks, and what the difference indicates in this case.
3. What the scores indicate about the achievements of Roland, in general and more specifically.

Basic Skills Test Scores for Roland Elkins

Test	Raw Score	Grade Equivalent	Publisher's Percentile	Local Percentile	Local Stanine
Vocabulary	21	5.3	46	46	
Reading	37	5.3	46	37	
Language	78	5.7	55	49	
Study skills	57	5.3	48	42	
Arithmetic	27	4.2	16	9	
Composite	—	5.2	45	37	

16

USING STANDARDIZED ACHIEVEMENT TESTS

THE STATUS OF STANDARDIZED ACHIEVEMENT TESTING

The standardized achievement test has become an institution inseparable from the school programs and activities it has been designed to serve. In fact, Levine (1976) has argued that the achievement test has become so uncritically accepted among educators and the general public that its validity "as a measure of eductional accomplishment is virtually unquestioned." To some extent he may be correct. We do seem to question most of the measures we encounter in other aspects of our lives, particularly whenever they yield results inconsistent with our hopes or expectations. When the bathroom scale gives a higher reading than we expect, how many of us first wonder if the scale is functioning properly? When stopped for a speeding violation, how many drivers first question the accuracy of the radar? But when achievement-test results turn out to be lower than we expect, the critical finger rarely is pointed first at the tests themselves. Levine's point is that we may too frequently try to explain substandard achievement-test results in terms of teacher quality, funding, and physical resources and simply assume the appropriateness of the measures that provided those results.

Levine's premise appears to be consistent with current practice; there is no evidence that the use of standardized achievement tests is on the downswing. In fact, their continued use is recommended explicitly by the celebrated National Commission on Excellence in Education (1983):

Standardized tests of achievement (not to be confused with aptitude tests) should be administered at major transition points from one level of schooling to another and particularly from high school to college or work. The purposes of these tests would be to: (a) certify the student's credentials; (b) identify the need for remedial intervention; and (c) identify the opportunity for advanced or accelerated work. The tests should be administered as part of a nationwide (but not Federal) system of State and local standardized tests. (p. 28)

In outlining the evidence for concluding that we are a nation at risk, the Commission reported 14 "indicators of risk," 11 of which depended on the use of standardized test scores as criteria. Reactions to the Commission report by educators and the public already have included a reassessment of our educational standards and the establishment of procedures for monitoring the accomplishment of them. Teacher-made achievement tests undoubtedly must play a major role in this process, but standardized achievement tests will have continued significance as well.

The efforts of those who develop and market standardized achievement tests show no signs of waning. Several test publishers have broadened their achievement-test offerings by providing standardized criterion-referenced tests. Two basic types of services are available, but both actually involve objectives-referenced tests. One service includes a bank of instructional objectives from which teachers may choose those that are most consistent with their own classroom objectives. The publisher then will select several items from a test-item pool to match each of the chosen objectives and develop test booklets to be used by the teacher. Results may be reported as the percent of items answered correctly for each objective, or, if a criterion score for mastery is selected, a mastery decision is reported for each objective measured.

The other service is based on individualized instruction, sets of instructional objectives, and tests to be used for placement, formative evaluation, and post-testing. Some of these testing programs are geared primarily to diagnosing learner difficulties for the purpose of planning remedial instruction. Suggestions for appropriate instructional strategies to be used by the teacher are included with some programs. Most of the tailor-made criterion-referenced tests included in such instructional packages are untried measures that probably are convenient for teachers to ' ε but likely are no better than those that teachers might develop on their own. There is no basis for providing norms for such tests, because each is a unique creation based on the specifications supplied by the user. In sum, these so-called criterion-referenced tests are more accurately labeled objectives-referenced tests, and though they are commercially prepared, they more closely resemble teacher-made tests than standardized achievement tests.

Whether or not the standardized achievement test has become an institution is debatable. What seems certain, however, is that good standardized achievement tests will continue to be needed to help educators monitor the effectiveness of their efforts and to report the outcomes of those efforts to those to whom educators are accountable. Careful test selection and wise test-score interpretation and use can make positive contributions to fulfilling these needs.

THE NATURE OF CURRENT ACHIEVEMENT TESTS

The economic necessity, or advantage, of limiting the content of a particular test to the topics most frequently taught has restricted the subject areas for which standardized tests are available primarily to fields that enroll large numbers of students. This effect has been particularly apparent in recent years. More and more the offerings of test publishers have tended to concentrate on tests of general knowledge rather than on those of specific course content. There are numerous tests of intelligence, numerous batteries of tests of general educational development, and numerous tests of reading and of arithmetic. But the more specialized the subject and the more advanced the level, the more limited the potential sales market, and thus the fewer the offerings.

Some test developers and publishers argue that this trend is educationally desirable. They contend that it is general educational development that is important, not a student's knowledge of the subject matter of specific courses. No doubt they are honestly persuaded that this is so, despite the obvious fact that their belief serves well to support large-volume sales of general tests. But they must be mistaken.

In most walks of life where knowledge is used, general knowledge is not adequate. What the doctor or the lawyer or the editor or the artisan needs is specific knowledge. The English teacher may claim that her students studying *King Lear* or *Silas Marner* are learning to understand and interpret and appreciate literature in general. But what one learns mostly in studying *King Lear* is that particular play. Under a competent teacher, one learns what Shakespeare perceived and expressed about particular aspects of human frailty or nobility evoked by a specific situation. The quotations one remembers are specific quotations. The general ability we speak of probably consists entirely of an organized and integrated body of particulars.

Another factor that has caused a reduction in the variety of tests offered by publishers is persistent criticism from test specialists of the inadequacies of some of the "standardized" tests that were published in such abundance, and so hurriedly, during the early days of the testing movement. The critics succeeded in improving the general level of test quality, but at the cost of restricting those tests more and more to fields where large-volume sales could be anticipated.

In these circumstances it is legitimate to wonder if the critics have served education well. Is there not a place, is there not a need, for tests that cover smaller units of instruction; tests that can be supported with smaller-volume sales because they are less ambitiously conceived and less elaborately developed;

tests that may even lack alternate forms, or norms, or validity studies? Test publishers could perform an educational service by selecting, cataloging, and editing the best of the many good tests that are produced around the country by expert teachers who also are skilled in test construction. Published tests of achievement need not be limited to those that have been painstakingly standardized, and they ought not to be limited to subjects where the volume of sales is certain to be large.

USES OF STANDARDIZED ACHIEVEMENT-TEST SCORES

The primary and essential use of standardized achievement-test scores is to provide a special kind of information on the extent of student learning. It is special because it is based on a consensus of expert teachers with respect to what ought to be learned in the study of a specific subject, a consensus external to and independent of the local teacher. It thus provides a basis for comparing local achievements with external norms of achievement in comparable classes. It is useful information because it helps to inform students, teachers, administrators, and the public at large of the effectiveness of the educational efforts in their schools. In differentiating between the functions of teacher-made classroom tests and standardized achievement tests, Linn (1983) aptly summarized the role of the latter:

> For the school or district as a whole, the traditional standardized test provides a general summary of the achievement of its students. By themselves, the scores do *not* reveal anything about the causes of performance, but they do provide a general reading of the current status in comparison to the nation at large. By comparison of scores from one year to another, the school or district can also get an indication of improvement or decline in performance. (p. 180)

Schools sometimes have been criticized for setting up testing programs, giving and scoring the tests, and then doing nothing with the test scores except to file them in the principal's office. If the school faculty and the individual teachers do not study the test results to identify levels and ranges of achievement in the school as a whole and within specific classes; if they do not single out students of high and low achievement; and if the scores are not reported and interpreted to students, parents, and the public, these criticisms are justifiable. But if they mean that no coherent program of action triggered specifically by the test results and designed to "do something" about them emerged from the testing program, then the criticisms probably are not justified.

What a good school faculty "does" about standardized test scores is something like what good citizens do with information they glean from a newspaper. Having finished the evening paper, they do not lay it aside and ask themselves, "Now what am I going to do about all this, about the weather, the accidents, the crimes, the legislative decisions, the clothing sales, the stock market reports, the baseball games won and lost, and all the rest?" They may, of course, plan specific actions in response to one or two items. But most of what is memorable they simply add to their store of latent knowledge. In hundreds of unplanned ways it will affect the opinions they express later, the votes they cast, and the other decisions they make. Information can be very useful ultimately, even when it triggers no immediate response.

Educators who properly deplore judging teacher competence solely on the basis of student test scores sometimes fail to see that it is equally unwise to take action on school or student problems solely on the basis of those same test scores. Seldom do standardized test scores by themselves provide sufficient guidance for wise and effective educational actions. It follows that these test scores should be regarded primarily as sources of useful information, not as stimuli and guides to immediate action.

The ultimate, and occasionally immediate, actions that are taken on the basis of standardized achievement-test scores fall into two general classes, instructional and evaluative. If the tests are given at the start of or during a specific course, they can serve as learning exercises or problems, or as guides to

1. placement in differentiated instructional "tracks,"
2. individualized instruction,
3. remedial instruction.

The fall testing programs that have become more popular recently are intended to serve primarily these purposes.

If the tests are given at the end of a course or unit of instruction, their primary function is summative evaluation of students' success, teachers' effectiveness, and the curriculum's adequacy. To argue that terminal evaluations come too late to do any good is to ignore the fact that students are likely to continue to study in other courses or units, that teachers are apt to continue to teach, and that the curriculum, or some revision of it, will be used in the future. Sometimes summative evaluation data for one purpose can be viewed as formative evaluations for another. Past successes and failures are useful guides to future improvements. In life there is no such thing as an absolutely final examination.

A school faculty or teacher who sees the need and has the opportunity should not hesitate to develop a program for action based partly on the scores provided by standardized tests of achievement. But neither should feel that the testing was a waste of time unless such a program is developed. The immediate purpose to be served by standardized test scores is the provision of information, information that can contribute to the wisdom of a host of specific actions stimulated by other educational needs and developments.

Diagnostic Testing

Like several other concepts in education, diagnostic testing is more cherished as an ideal than effectively demonstrated in practice. Taking their cue from medicine, and noting that some students seem to be ailing educationally, the advocates of diagnostic testing propose to identify the causes of the educational ailments and to correct them. In the early days of objective testing, diagnostic tests in a number of school subjects proliferated. Now, outside the fields of elementary reading and arithmetic, few standardized diagnostic tests are available. Even in those two fields, it is being recognized that diagnostic tests are no clear indicators of the sources of a student's difficulties in learning. They are simply tools that a skilled diagnostician can use to help identify the problems.

One of the reasons for the lack of success in educational diagnosis in most fields other than elementary reading and arithmetic is that the medical model is inappropriate. Learning difficulties are not attributable in most cases to specific or easily correctable disorders. Instead they usually result from accumulations of ignorance and of distaste for learning. Neither of these causes is hard to recognize; neither is easy to cure. Diagnosis is not the real problem, and diagnostic testing can do little to solve that problem.

Another reason for this lack of success in educational diagnosis is that effective diagnosis and remediation take a great deal more time than most teachers have, or most students would be willing to devote. The diagnosis of reading difficulties is a well-developed skill, and remedial treatments can be very effective. Because reading is so basic to other learning, the time required for diagnosis and remediation is often spent ungrudgingly. But where the subject of study is more advanced and more specialized, the best solution to learning difficulties in one area, say algebra, physics, economics, or German, is to put off study in that area and cultivate learning in other areas that present fewer problems.

Few standardized achievement tests are useful diagnostic aids for work with individual students, despite the claims made in some publishers' manuals. However, most can provide considerable group diagnostic information, particularly those that provide special reports showing mean test-item scores or mean sub-category scores within tests. Instructional planning for a class can be enhanced by taking such data into account; instructional materials can be selected or developed to improve learning in deficient areas; and time can be reallocated from topics on which students have demonstrated high levels of accomplishment.

Any achievement test can provide "diagnostic" information of value to individual students if they are told which items they missed. With the teacher's help, these students can then correct the mistakes or misconceptions that led them astray. Highly specific "diagnosis" and "remediation" of this sort can be effective and ought to be encouraged. Good diagnosis and remediation also take place informally in the give-and-take of recitation and discussion. This, too, ought to be encouraged. But more general, formal, and elaborate efforts at diagnosis through testing have seldom been effective.

COMMUNICATING TEST RESULTS

The most basic use to be made of test scores is to report them to all who need to know, along with a simple interpretation of what they mean (Ebel, 1961b). They should be reported to students, and usually to their parents as well. Some test publishers provide a narrative report, like that shown in Figure 16-1, along with a profile or score listing to facilitate interpretation for students and their parents. Narratives are convenient prose summaries that deemphasize technical jargon and numbers and provide a permanent record to which parents can refer outside the context of a parent-teacher-student conference.

Teachers should receive test scores for initial review and should keep them at hand for ready reference on future occasions. Summaries of the score

Figure 16-1 Sample Narrative Report of Test Results. (© 1978 by The University of Iowa)

| PUPIL RECORD FOR ▼ | Iowa Tests of Basic Skills | PROFILE NARRATIVE REPORT | 9-68150 |

KIM ALTON

Grade: 6   Sex: F
Birth Date: AUG, 1967   Age 11/03
I.D. Number:

SUBTESTS	SCORE			PROFILE
	GE	S	PR	NATIONAL PERCENTILE RANK
VOCABULARY	55	4	36	
READING	63	5	52	
SPELLING	80	7	80	
CAPITALIZATION	87	7	86	
PUNCTUATION	86	7	87	
LANGUAGE USAGE	86	7	83	
LANGUAGE, TOTAL	85	7	88	
VISUAL	70	6	66	
REFERENCES	69	6	64	
WORK STUDY, TOTAL	70	6	69	
MATH CONCEPTS	55	4	33	
MATH PROBLEMS	61	5	48	
MATH COMPUTATION	65	6	61	
MATHEMATICS, TOTAL	60	5	46	
COMPOSITE	67	6	62	

APPROXIMATE READING LEVEL
THE FIRST HALF OF THE SIXTH GRADE

Teacher: MR. MORTON   School: ARMSTRONG
Date Tested: NOV, 1978   System: SUNNYVALE
Test Form: 7   Level: 12
Process Number: 000-0666-000

LEGEND FOR SCORES: GE=Grade Equivalents, S=Stanines, and PR=Percentile Ranks

HOW WELL IS KIM LEARNING THE BASIC SKILLS?

TO OBTAIN INFORMATION TO ANSWER THIS QUESTION, KIM WROTE THE IOWA TESTS OF BASIC SKILLS, (FORM 07, LEVEL 12) IN NOV, 1978. KIM ATTENDS ARMSTRONG SCHOOL IN SUNNYVALE, AND IS IN SIXTH GRADE. MR. MORTON IS KIM'S TEACHER.

KIM'S OVERALL ACHIEVEMENT IN THE BASIC SKILLS IS BEST SHOWN IN HER COMPOSITE SCORE. KIM'S COMPOSITE GRADE EQUIVALENT SCORE OF 67 SHOWS THAT HER TEST PERFORMANCE WAS APPROXIMATELY THE SAME AS THAT MADE BY THE TYPICAL STUDENT IN THE SIXTH GRADE AT THE END OF THE SEVENTH MONTH. KIM'S STANDING IN OVERALL ACHIEVEMENT AMONG SIXTH GRADERS NATIONALLY IS SHOWN BY HER COMPOSITE PERCENTILE RANK OF 62. THIS MEANS THAT OVERALL KIM SCORED BETTER THAN 62 PERCENT OF SIXTH GRADERS NATIONALLY AND THAT 38 PERCENT SCORED AS WELL OR BETTER. KIM'S OVERALL ACHIEVEMENT APPEARS TO BE SOMEWHAT ABOVE AVERAGE FOR HER GRADE.

HOW WELL A STUDENT IS DOING IN READING IS A BIG FACTOR FOR SUCCESS IN SCHOOL WORK GENERALLY. KIM'S APPROXIMATE READING LEVEL IS THAT OF THE FIRST HALF OF THE SIXTH GRADE. KIM'S LEVEL OF READING DEVELOPMENT IS ABOUT AVERAGE FOR HER GRADE. SHE SHOULD HAVE LITTLE OR NO DIFFICULTY WITH HER SCHOOL READING ASSIGNMENTS.

THE IOWA TESTS OF BASIC SKILLS COVER MANY IMPORTANT SKILL AREAS. LET US EXAMINE THESE TO SEE KIM'S AREAS OF STRENGTH AND WEAKNESS. KIM IS HIGHEST IN SPELLING, CAPITALIZATION, PUNCTUATION, AND LANGUAGE USAGE. THESE ARE RELATIVE STRENGTHS ON WHICH KIM CAN BUILD DURING THE COMING YEAR. AREAS OF GREATEST NEED APPEAR TO BE VOCABULARY, AND MATHEMATICS CONCEPTS. IT IS HERE THAT KIM NEEDS MOST WORK.

TEACHER'S COPY

©1978, The University of Iowa. All rights reserved. Printed in the U.S.A.

distributions should be reported to administrators, the school board, and the community. If these communications are made, many other important uses of the test scores will be made spontaneously. It is no more necessary to develop a comprehensive, formal program for using the scores than for using a dictionary or a typewriter. If the scores are at hand, along with a guide to their interpretation, they will be used whenever the occasion arises.

School officials have sometimes been negligent about reporting the results of their testing programs. Sometimes they have been unnecessarily cautious. Most test scores are not especially difficult to understand. When understood, they are rarely dangerous. A school should seldom, if ever, require all students to take a test whose results are not to be reported to them or to their parents. Students and parents are partners with teachers and administrators in the educational process. The process works best if they are admitted to full partnership. In many states educational authorities have ruled that parents have a right to know their children's test scores and any other information on file about them. In addition, the Family Educational Rights and Privacy Act of 1974, also commonly known as the Buckley Amendment, gives students and parents specific rights related to access to records, the accuracy of the recorded information, and the release of personal records.

JUDGING TEACHER COMPETENCE

Should the results of standardized tests of student achievement given in a school program be used to evaluate the competence of teachers? The popular answer from teachers and many other professional educators is an emphatic No! Surely test results can never tell the whole story of a teacher's effectiveness. A superintendent who notes low achievement-test scores for a particular class and who concludes solely on the basis of this evidence that the teacher is incompetent would be no wiser than a physician who notes a patient's complaint of pains in the lower abdomen and summarily concludes that the patient's appendix must be removed. Fortunately not many superintendents and not many physicians are foolish enough to jump to conclusions like these.

But would it not be equally foolish to deny, a priori and in all cases, that poor student achievement *might* be the result of poor teaching—just as we cannot preclude the possibility of pain in the lower abdomen being caused by appendicitis? If we agree that quality of teaching influences the quality of educational achievement, then we must agree also that good measures of achievement have something to contribute to the complex process of evaluating teacher competence. If we do not agree that good learning requires good teaching, why try to hire good teachers or even to train them in the first place?

It is quite proper to call attention to the limitations of standardized tests as measures of student achievement and to their additional limitations as bases for inferring teacher competence. Figure 16-2 lists some of the limitations

A. *As measures of student achievement*
  (1) Lack of complete relevance to the objectives of a given course
  (2) Lack of perfect score reliability owing to a limited number of items or poor item quality
  (3) Susceptibility to coaching
  (4) Tendency to lose validity with repeated use
  (5) Possibility of improper administration or scoring
  (6) Possibility of inappropriate or unreliable norms

B. *As bases for inferring teacher competence*
  (1) Sensitivity to conditions other than teacher competence that affect learning
      a. Pupil ability levels
      b. School, family, and community support for learning
      c. Quality of educational curricula and instructional materials
  (2) Insensitivity to the teacher's contributions that do not directly foster learnings
      a. Motivation
      b. Guidance
      c. School morale
      d. Direction of co-curricular activities
  (3) Imperfection as measures of student achievement

Figure 16-2 Limitations of Standardized Test Scores.

of both uses. But these limitations are by no means so serious, so inherent, and so unavoidable as to completely deny any relationship with student achievement or teacher competence. However, those who object most strongly to the use of standardized tests for these purposes would probably object with equal vigor to any other definite bases for measuring achievement or competence. It is more the fact that judgments are being made than the basis on which they are made that causes the concern.

Yet despite the difficulty of the task and the uncertain quality of the result, judgments of teacher competence do have to be made. Almost every school and college has, and uses, procedures for differentiating the better from the poorer teachers. Teachers do differ in effectiveness. The students of good teachers learn more important things, and learn them better, than do the students of poor teachers. Hence standardized test scores do provide one kind of evidence of teacher effectiveness. They never tell the whole story, but they do reveal one important facet. They should never be used exclusively or blindly, but neither should any other evidence of a teacher's competence or lack of it. The indications they can give should not be denied or disregarded.

SCHOOL TESTING PROGRAMS

Local schools and school systems frequently supplement teacher-made achievement tests with schoolwide testing in order to

1. provide information needed for instruction and guidance,
2. evaluate local school achievement against external standards, and
3. stimulate and direct continuing efforts to improve curriculum and instruction locally.

Sometimes these school testing programs are well planned and competently handled, sometimes the results are put to good use, and sometimes the testing program is supported strongly by the faculty and community. Unfortunately, these desirable conditions do not always exist. In some cases a school's testing program is imposed by an administration that believes all good schools have such programs, without knowing very clearly what range of educational purposes they serve. In that situation the school's testing program is not likely to be very good or very popular.

Most educators agree that a school testing program should not be imposed by administrative fiat on an unprepared and, hence, possibly unwilling school staff. But to democratize the approach by appointing a committee of teachers and administrators to plan the testing program may develop into the classic "the blind leading the blind." The first requirement of a good program is not that it be democratically planned, but that it be *competently* planned. Of course the teachers who must administer the testing program and use its results should understand what is to be done, and why. Their support for the program should be sought. However, program support will be easier to secure if the planning is done competently rather than haphazardly.

A school that is planning to adopt or to modify its testing program has two main options. One is to tailor a program to fit its own needs and purposes. This is an attractive alternative if the school has teachers, counselors, and administrators who know enough about tests and testing programs to plan a good one. The other is to participate in a cooperative interscholastic testing program such as the Iowa Testing Programs, the Michigan School Testing Service, or the Educational Records Bureau.

The main advantage of the local program lies in its specific fit to local conditions. Its main disadvantages are (1) that it needs more expertness and time to plan and operate than the cooperative program requires and (2) that it may lack relevant external standards of comparison. The external cooperative testing program may not ideally meet all of the local school's needs, but it is likely to bring expert planning, efficient and economical operation, relevant norms, and professionally competent resources for score interpretation and use. Unless a school feels sure of the competence of its staff for development of its own testing program, it should probably give careful consideration to a cooperative program.

A good testing program is likely to cost as much as several dollars per student per year. These costs cannot be disregarded. On the other hand, if viewed in the perspective of other educational costs and of the educational value received, they are by no means high. A school that absolutely cannot afford a good testing program can hardly afford to operate at all.

Testing Problems Cited by Teachers

Teachers in some school systems occasionally have questioned the value of their testing program or have complained about the apparent waste of time and money in referring to standardized testing. Here are some of the most common expressions of dissatisfaction.

1. "The tests are not appropriate for my class because our curriculum does not deal with some of the test content. Teachers should be involved in the selection of tests so that such mismatches can be avoided."
2. "The tests are just another burden piled on top of other responsibilities for which too little time exists. Preparation for test administration and hand scoring booklets or test answer sheets takes time outside of the instructional day. Tests seem to be another source of the erosion of valuable instructional time."
3. "Students do not always know in advance that the tests will be given and/or how the results will be useful to the school or to them. Some do not work at their best because they don't think the scores will count."
4. "Several students don't take the test seriously and, consequently, are disruptive of others during the test administration. The tests are so easy that most finish early and then disturb others who have not finished. The validity of scores of the entire group is lowered under these circumstances."
5. "So much time passes from when the tests are given to when the results are distributed that the scores just are not useful for instructional planning."
6. "The results simply show up in the mail box and nothing is said or done to assist teachers in using the scores to evelute or improve teaching."

The first comment, related to the mismatch between test content and what is taught, is perhaps the most common and seemingly the most simple to resolve. However, it presents a dilemma in test selection, because, as Linn (1983) has pointed out, "allowing the match between instructional materials and test items to be too close risks losing the capability to measure understanding." He went on to explain that the greatest loss is in the ability to generalize about what students *might* be able to do:

> Literal match of instruction and testing in the sense of practice on the items that appear on the test destroys the measurement value of the test. Inferences about skills and knowledge that are made on the basis of test results become suspect when the match becomes too close. To test whether a student can apply skills and knowledge to solve a new problem, the problem must be new. Practice on the problem as part of instruction insures match and may improve scores, but eliminates any conclusions regarding problem solving. (p. 187)

The mismatch dilemma illustrates the need for both nationally prepared tests, available from test publishers, and locally developed tests specified to the school curriculum. Neither test can accomplish the purposes of the other entirely.

Each comment enumerated above represents a source of concern or frustration for teachers in that school setting. The solutions are not simple in any one case, although recommendations have been made earlier in this chapter about how to deal with some of them. Together these problems point out the need for a responsible test coordinator who is trained to anticipate testing problems and is able to organize the test administrations so that (a) teachers will understand the school's purpose for testing and (b) students will be motivated to perform at their best. If qualified, such a person could consult with teachers who need assistance with test-score use or those who experience student problems during test administrations.

SUMMARY

The following 11 statements summarize the principal ideas developed in this chapter:

1. The standardized criterion-referenced tests offered by publishers are essentially objectives-referenced tests that have few advantages over good teacher-made achievement tests.
2. Economic considerations tend to restrict the content of standardized achievement tests to subjects that almost all students study, or to areas of general education rather than to specific subjects.
3. The primary and essential use of standardized achievement-test scores is to provide information to all who are concerned with the educational process.
4. Standardized achievement-test scores are useful primarily in facilitating instruction and in evaluating its results.
5. Except in the fields of elementary reading and arithmetic, diagnostic testing has proved to be of little educational value.
6. If scores obtained from a school testing program

are reported and interpreted to teachers, students, and parents, no other formal or elaborate program for using them is necessary.
7. The chief justification for a local school testing program is the use the school makes of the test scores obtained.
8. Standardized achievement-test scores provide information that can *contribute* to evaluations of teacher competence, but such scores should never be used as the sole basis for evaluating teachers.
9. It is more important for a school testing program to be *competently* planned than to be democratically planned.
10. In general, tests from locally designed testing programs are likely to be somewhat more relevant to local needs, but somewhat less expertly designed, than those from external testing programs.
11. The degree of match between test content and instructional content determines the extent to which test results can be explained in terms of either remembering or understanding.

PROJECTS AND PROBLEMS

Project: Notes on a Published Test

Choose from your instructor's files a published test that seems likely to be useful to you in your work. Prepare a concise summary of the principal features of the test, following the outline given below.

A. Identifying information
1. Name of the test
2. Publisher (and address)
3. Date of publication
4. Authors (and their positions)

B. Descriptive information
  1. Types and numbers of items
  2. Fields of knowledge sampled
  3. Means for recording and scoring answers
  4. Scores provided
  5. Time required
  6. Cost per pupil tested
C. Interpretive information
  1. Type and adequacy of norms
  2. Score reliability and measurement errors
  3. Data on item difficulty
  4. Evidence for test validity
D. Evaluative information
  1. Readability and attractiveness of test and answer sheets
  2. Readability and completeness of directions for administering, scoring, and interpreting
  3. Favorable and critical comments from other reviewers (Buros or periodicals)
  4. Summary of your own evaluation

17

STANDARDIZED INTELLIGENCE AND APTITUDE TESTS

THE CONCEPT OF INTELLIGENCE

Despite widespread acceptance of the idea that intelligence exists, there seems to be no consensus as to just what it is. It presumably has a biological basis in neuroanatomy or brain physiology. Various levels of mental deficiency have been associated with metabolic defects and certain types of prenatal environmental stress (e.g., oxygen deficiency, viral infection, and injurious drugs). But thus far no biological basis for differences in intelligence among normal humans has been determined clinically.

In its common and informal usage intelligence is often characterized as brightness or sharpness. These words suggest responsiveness, perceptiveness, cleverness, and ability to cut through appearances and confusions to reach understanding. Lack of intelligence is associated with dullness, which suggests a lack of responsiveness, perceptiveness, or understanding. But these metaphors help very little in understanding the nature of the construct.

Psychologists who study cognitive processes and mental development and functioning differ in their conceptions of intelligence (Wagner and Sternberg, 1984). Some call it ability to learn, that is, to do work in school, the same ability that Alfred Binet (1911) was interested in detecting with his early tests. Others characterize it as ability to reason, to solve problems, and use the "higher mental processes." Still others emphasize original thinking and the ability to adapt to novel situations. In some discussions "creativity" is posited as a component of intelligence, as some see it, or as a separate, related psychological construct, as others see it.

Operational and Analytical Definitions

One possible solution to the problem of defining intelligence is to use an operational definition, as is done with a variety of other personality measures. The test used to measure the trait defines what is being measured. That is, intelligence *is* whatever the test measures. But different tests measure different kinds of intelligence, depending on the nature of the tasks of which they are composed. Obviously this approach, whatever its virtues in helping us to think more concretely about what we mean by intelligence, is not going to yield a single, generally acceptable definition.

Another possible solution is to use the methods of factor analysis on the responses of a wide variety of persons to a wide variety of tasks designed to measure intelligence. Factor analysis is a statistical technique that involves examining the correlations between a large number of item responses to determine if certain homogeneous subsets of items, called factors, can be identified. This approach has shed much light on the extent to which proficiency on certain tasks tends to be related to, or independent of, proficiency on other tasks. But it has provided no compelling definition of intelligence. Different researchers have not used the same kinds of test tasks, and, even when they have, they have interpreted their findings somewhat differently. Spearman (1927), for example, found a common, general intellectual factor, but Thurstone (1938) found seven primary mental abilities. The multidimensional "structure of intellect" model proposed by Guilford (1966) is quite elaborate but of mostly theoretical interest. The tasks he used to conceptualize the measurement of intelligence were subdivided finely into 120 aspects of intellectual functioning based on the process, product, and content characteristic of each aspect. Finally, Vernon (1971) is one of several factor analysts to propose a hierarchical theory of intelligence that helps to explain much of the correlational data accumulated on the structure of intelligence.

Because the multitude of definitions proposed by psychologists provides no convergence or consensus, the measures of intelligence available for use in our schools do not have a common basis. The implication for those who must select intelligence tests for their school testing program is clear. The operational definition and theoretical bases of each test under consideration must be reviewed and the test tasks must be examined in terms of the school's purpose for testing. In most cases the nature of the test items will provide a clearer indication of what is being measured than will whatever criterion-related or construct evidence the publisher supplies to support its intended use.

THE NATURE OF INTELLIGENCE TESTS

The different conceptions of the nature of intelligence have contributed to the development of a wide diversity of tasks for testing it. Examples of some of the most widely used types are presented in this section. As you read each of these items, try to describe the characteristics of individuals who likely would answer the items correctly and those who likely would not. When you have read all the items, try to synthesize your descriptions to arrive at a verbal description of intelligence.

I. Verbal

1. *Synonyms (or antonyms)*
   Identify the pair of words in each set that are either synonyms or antonyms.
     a. accident   *b.* bad   *c.* evil   *d.* worry
     a. accept   *b.* make   *c.* object   *d.* order

2. *Verbal analogies*
   snow: flake: *a.* cloud: fleecy   *b.* hail: storm
                   c. icicle: eaves   *d.* rain: drop

3. *Commands*
   The task is to obey simple commands.
   "Give me the pencil."
   "Put the book on the shelf."

4. *Sentence completion*
   While most teachers agree that educational tests are useful, one occasionally hears the suggestion that education could go on perfectly well, perhaps much better than in the past, if tests and testing were _____.
     a. abolished   *c.* criticized   *e.* praised
     b. continued   *d.* investigated

5. *Sentence interpretation*
   Given sentence: The date must be advanced one day when one crosses the International Date Line in a westerly direction.
   Interpretive question: If a ship approaches the International Date Line from the east on Tuesday, what day is it on board the ship after the line has been crossed?

II. Quantitative

6. *Digit span*
   The examiner says a series of numbers and asks the subjects to repeat them, forward or backward. The maximum number the student can repeat is his digit span.

7. Number series
     1   3   5   7   9   ?
     1   2   3   5   8   ?

8. *Arithmetic computation*
   Add 23 to 66.
   Divide 96 by 16.

9. *Arithmetic reasoning*
   How many 5¢ candy bars can be bought with 30¢?
   If concrete is to be made with 4 parts of sand to 1 part of cement, how many shovels of cement should be put with 16 shovels of sand?

10. *Relative magnitudes*
    How much larger than ⅓ is ½?
    A dollar is how many times as much as a dime?

11. *Water jar problems*
If you have a 7-quart jar and a 3-quart jar how can you get exactly 8 quarts of water?

III. Information

12. *General*
How many legs does a dog have?
What is the special name for a doctor who takes care of teeth?

13. *Common sense*
Why are street lights turned off in the morning?
Why do houses have windows?

14. *Absurdities*
What is foolish about these statements?
"The fish I tried to catch got away, but it made a delicious meal."
"If I get to the clubhouse first I'll put an X on the door. If you get there first, rub it out."

IV. Object or Figure

15. *Object naming*
Examiner points to a cup, a book, a glove, or what have you, and asks the subject to name the objects.

16. *Object assembly*
The task is to assemble pieces of a puzzle to form a common object in limited time.

17. *Picture vocabulary*
Given several pictures in a set, the examinee is asked to indicate which best illustrates the meaning of a particular word.

18. *Picture completion*
Tell me what part of this picture is missing.

19. *Figure analogies*
A: B:: C:?

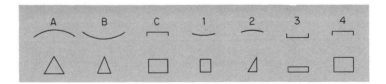

20. *Matrix progression*
    What figure belongs in the blank space?

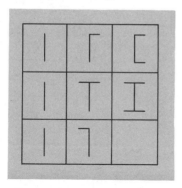

21. *Maze tracing*
    The task is to find a clear path through a maze of lines.

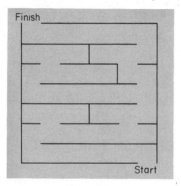

22. *Figure drawing*
    Draw a picture of a man.

V. Abstract Process

23. *Similarity (and difference)*
    Which of these is most like a calf?
    (a) a colt   (b) a cat   (c) a pony
    In what way is a tennis ball different from a baseball?

24. *Classification*
    The examinee is directed to sort a set of words, objects, or symbols into a given
    set of categories.

25. *Sequence*
    Arrange the following words in the proper order:

afternoon	morning
daybreak	noon
evening	sunrise
midnight	twilight

26. *Coding*
Given a simple code, the task is to translate a set of symbols into the code.

Code	———	+	X	– – – –	=
	1	2	3	4	5

Task	X	X	+	=	———	+

School-Related Tasks

Some of the exercises used to test intelligence—giving synonyms, interpreting sentences, computing, and solving problems—are objects of specific instruction in school. Hence, almost identical tasks likely are to be found in general achievement-test batteries. Abilities to handle other tasks such as analogy problems, recognition of absurdities, and problems of classification and sequence usually are learned incidentally in school, at play, at home, or elsewhere.

It is sometimes assumed that what a student succeeds in learning incidentally is a better indication of intelligence than the person's success in intentional learning in school. The assumption may be justified, but the evidence and logic needed to justify it are not obvious. Teaching does indeed assist learning, but it does not make learning automatic nor does it eliminate the need for effort and ability on the part of students. Intelligence contributes to learning in school as well as out of it.

Obviously, if we wish to compare the intelligence of children who have been to school with those who have not, we should not use tasks that the school tries to teach. As a general principle, if we seek to infer basic ability to learn from measurements of success in learning, we must first try to equalize opportunities to learn and then select as test items only problems to which all children probably have been exposed. Yet, as Coleman and Cureton (1954) have pointed out, even if opportunities for in-school learning were equalized, there would still remain great differences in the availability of incidental learning. These differences in environments and life styles among different families, different neighborhoods, and different regions of the country cannot, and probably should not, be eliminated.

Nonverbal and Culture-Fair Tests

Some developers of intelligence tests have attempted to minimize, or to eliminate entirely, the influence of verbal ability on test scores. The tasks they use are based on objects, drawings, or figures that require assembly, classification, arrangement, selection, or some other form of manipulation. Sometimes even the instructions involve no words, but are given in pantomime.

These tests are useful if students who do not all speak the same language must be tested with the same test, or if a student with a severe language handicap must be tested. They may be appealing to those who seek measures of basic intelligence, uncontaminated by learning, particularly language learning. But there is no good reason to believe that these nonverbal tests get any closer to basic native intelligence than do the verbal tests. Ability to do well on them can be learned also. And since verbal facility is so important an element in school learning, and in most other areas of human achievement, the major application for nonverbal tests seems to be with individuals who have significant language problems or with those whose native language is not English.

Most intelligence tests not only require some degree of adeptness with a particular language, but also assume familiarity with a particular culture. This quality limits their usefulness in other cultures. However, attempts to build culture-free tests have failed because testing requires communication, and communication is impossible in the absence of culture and the symbols, concepts, and meanings it embodies.

Attempts to build "culture-free" tests by eliminating items that discriminate between different cultures have been no more successful. If carried far enough, they result in eliminating all the items. There is no difference between individuals in their response to any test item that cannot be attributed to differences in culture, if culture is defined inclusively enough. Each of us lives in a somewhat different culture. Not only Eskimos and Africans, but also Vermonters and Virginians, farmers and city dwellers, boys and girls, even first-born and next-born in the same family live in somewhat different "cultures." The differences are not equally great in all these instances, but they exist as differences in all cases, and they can be used to support the contention that any item that discriminates is unfair. It is logically impossible for a culture-free test to discriminate among individuals, and there is no reason to use a test that does not discriminate between those who have more or less of an ability that is of interest to the user.

Tests of Abstract Intelligence

Those who conceive of intelligence as an abstract ability to think tend to favor test tasks that present novel problems, such as number series, water-jar problems, figure analogies, matrix progressions, or maze tracings. So long as the task is a problem requiring thought, so long as it is novel, its exact nature seems relatively unimportant to those who adhere to the abstract viewpoint. Since the ability being tested is presumably a unitary, generally applicable trait, any of a variety of novel problems may be used. The assumption is that the examinee's success with any such task will depend not on the problem but only on the examinee's ability to reason.

But problem-solving ability tends to be specific. That is, the ability to think is a product of knowledge, of knowing what to think and how to think. Thinking is always based on content, and the best way to learn how to think is to acquire the requisite knowledge (Ebel, 1982). What examinees have or have not learned does make a difference in their ability to handle the tasks that supposedly involve only abstract reasoning. A little judicious coaching in such cases often can prove effective in improving examinee performance. In addition, however, the influence of relevant incidental learning is a factor that cannot be discounted. Thus the claim that these tasks measure abstract intelligence is open to question.

Individual and Group Measures

The earliest tests of intelligence were administered individually, but group-administered tests became necessary in World War I to deal with the mass of army recruits that needed to be screened for assignment to various duties. Army Alpha, the test developed by psychologists in 1917 to classify military personnel, is regarded as the first group intelligence test (Yerkes, 1921). Descendants of both individual and group tests are still in use, because each type has special advantages and unique limitations.

Because of their special properties, individual intelligence tests usually are administered to young children, students with reading disabilities or deficits, and other special cases. Group tests, because they are more economical of time and money, are generally used for routine testing of older children and young adults. Individual tests usually are presented orally and allow oral, free responses that can be scored semiobjectively. The less flexible group test usually is given in objectively scored multiple-choice format. Some researchers have hypothesized that certain characteristics of the examiner (e.g., age, race, sex) can affect examinee performance on individual tests and thereby lower test validity. But the evidence to date fails to give full support to these notions. Graziano et al. (1982), for example, concluded from their review of related studies that examiner race, per se, does not affect performance on intelligence tests. In general, there is no important difference between individual and group tests in the reliability or validity of the scores they yield.

INTELLIGENCE-TEST SCORES

A concept that has contributed greatly to the popularity, and to the misunderstanding, of intelligence tests is the IQ score itself. One reason for this popularity and corresponding misunderstanding is that IQ seems to be a common denominator for all measurements of mental ability. Regardless of the content of the test, whether verbal or nonverbal, whether based on school learning or on novel problems, if its scores come out as IQs, the public seems to regard these numbers as sacrosanct indicators of "intelligence." The fact that different tests are based on quite different tasks is glossed over by the use of the same kind of unit to express the measurements obtained. Were it not for this apparent generality of mental ability, and for the apparent simplicity of its measurement, the concept of abstract intelligence probably would not have gained such a strong following in many educational circles. To compound the problem, two different types of IQ scores have been used, each with a significantly different basis and, consequently, a unique interpretation.

Intelligence Quotient

The German psychologist Stern (1914) suggested the use of intelligence quotients as meaningful interpretations of mental-test scores. Later, when he discovered that they were being represented as indices of permanent, general mental ability, he suggested that steps be taken to "kill the IQ." Stern's wish to end the use of the quotient has been fulfilled, for all practical purposes, but the IQ symbol lives on.

The apparent simplicity of the IQ concept is another reason for its popularity and for the misunderstandings associated with it. The *ratio IQ* is computed from the formula:

$$IQ = 100 \times \frac{\text{mental age}}{\text{chronological age}} \qquad 17.1$$

Since the pioneer work of Alfred Binet, most mental-test scores have been expressed as years and months of mental age. If a student taking an intelligence test answers correctly as many of the items as does the average student who is 11 years and 3 months of age, then the examinee's mental age is reported as 11 years and 3 months, or 135 months. But if the student's chronological age is only 10 years and 6 months (126 months) his IQ is:

$$100 \times \frac{135}{126} = 107$$

The ratio IQ is easy to understand in terms of its calculation and meaning, but like many other generalizations, it fits the facts none too well (Ebel, 1979).

Deviation IQ

To make IQ scores generally applicable to all groups in society, most test developers have shifted from ratio IQs to deviation IQs. *Deviation IQs* are not really quotients at all; they are standard scores. At each age, a score one standard deviation above the mean for the age group is represented by an IQ of 116 in that group. An IQ of 84 represents performance one standard deviation below the mean. All other IQs are similarly located with reference to a mean of 100 and a standard deviation of 16. An exception to this, for example, is the Wechsler scales, which use a standard-deviation value of 15.

Some test publishers do not use the term *deviation IQ* but do use the same score scale with a different label. For example, the *Cognitive Abilities Test* uses "standard age scores," essentially age-equivalent scores on a scale having a mean of 100 and a standard deviation of 16. The "cognitive skills quotient" provided by the *Kuhlmann-Anderson Test* also is a standard score scale with a mean of 100 but a standard deviation of 15. In these and some other cases, publishers have sought to rid themselves and their test of the association with the old ratio IQ by adopting a new name for what is essentially the deviation-IQ score scale.

Other Quotients

The success and popularity of the ratio IQ encouraged the development and use of other quotients in the early days of standardized testing. The *Educational Quotient (EQ)*, for example, was the ratio of educational age to chronological age, times 100. Educational age was represented by an age-equivalent score from an achievement test. The *Achievement Quotient (AQ)* was educational age divided by mental age, times 100. From this ratio the notions of "under-achievement" and "overachievement" evolved.

Both of these ratios depend on assumptions that are even more questionable than those involved in the IQ ratio. And they are subject to even greater errors and ambiguities. Fortunately these ratios have fallen into disuse. Unfortunately, however, the notions of underachievement and overachievement, which involve the same questionable assumptions and operational difficulties, are still popular. Thorndike's (1963) discussion of the limitations of these concepts is still relevant today.

THE INHERITANCE OF INTELLIGENCE

Several issues related to intelligence testing should be examined by teachers and others who use IQ scores. These are not actually philosophical issues that require a value judgment, but they are hard questions addressed by researchers that have resulted in incomplete findings of controversial interpretation. It is important for educators to realize that these issues are still open and unresolved, so that IQ scores will not be misused or misinterpreted on the basis of mis-understood research findings.

Heredity versus Environment

One particular aspect of the nature of intelligence has been the focus of controversy for more than a century. To what extent is it a native, inborn characteristic? To what extent is it acquired and affected by environmental circumstances? It was Galton's (1883) interest in intelligence as an inheritable trait that opened up the modern era of the scientific study of intelligence. Since his time, hundreds of scholars have both theorized and accumulated research data in an effort to resolve the controversy.

Studies of descendants of the same parents have seemed to show mental ability or the lack of it to run in families. Further, comparisons of the intelligence of identical twins, fraternal twins, and siblings have pointed toward a correlation between degree of genetic similarity and degree of similarity in measured intelligence. On the other hand, studies of children reared in foster homes have revealed an increase in intelligence in favorable environments and a decrease in unfavorable ones. Some researchers, notably Jensen (1969), have tried to quantify the impact of heredity and environment on intelligence by partitioning the observed test-score variance into fractional parts attributable to the two factors.

The difficulties that have prevented a clear-cut, generally accepted answer to the heritability question are mainly these two:

1. The lack of any clearly identifiable biological structure or function that determines intelligence and that could be subject to the laws of heredity.
2. The impossibility of isolating the influences of heredity and environment and of controlling and manipulating them sufficiently to obtain unequivocal results.

Few are inclined to challenge the statement that a particular individual's intelligence has an inherited biological base, or that individuals differ in the quality of that base. Extreme cases of mental deficiency often are either inherited or caused by adverse prenatal conditions. In other instances, disease or accident may act to damage some part of the brain or nervous system. However, among normal individuals it is difficult to find cause-effect evidence to link specific qualities of the biological base with corresponding differences in developed intelligence.

In this respect mental intelligence may be analogous to physical health. Just as one person may be born with physical deformities or physiological deficiencies that impair health throughout life, so another may be born with anatomical or physiological deficiencies of the brain and nervous system that impair intelligence throughout life. For the vast majority of human beings, however, both physical health and mental intelligence depend heavily on what happens to us, and more importantly, on what we ourselves do with the capabilities we inherit.

Testing Young Children

If intelligence were a biological "given," the sooner after birth it could be measured the less contaminating the influence of environment, and the more accurate the measurement should be. Unfortunately, no one has discovered a satisfactory way of testing the ability to learn before a person has actually learned anything measurable. One can assume that intelligence is there all right, but just inaccessible. An alternate assumption is that it does not exist in any real sense until it has been developed.

The intelligence of infants has been measured and studied extensively (Bayley, 1933, 1949, 1955). One salient finding is that early measurements correlate poorly with later measurements. Bloom (1964) concluded from his review of the research that the correlation is about 0.45 between scores obtained at ages 1 and 17. Some attribute this apparent instability to inadequate measurements, particularly the low reliabilities obtained in measuring the intelligence of infants and preschoolers. Others claim that the instruments used at different age levels actually measure different traits or different aspects of intelligence. Scores on tests of psychomotor development do not predict well scores on verbal and quantitative cognitive-abilities tests. A third explanation is that the low relationship is due to actual changes in the developing intelligence. Whatever the explanation, the measurements taken at an early age are not good predictors of subsequent educational development or measurements of intelligence.

Implications for Teaching

It is obvious that individuals display different degrees of ability to learn. Since these differences are self-evident, why they exist may seem to be a matter of purely academic interest that should hardly concern the classroom teacher. Yet a teacher's hypotheses about the source and nature of the differences can have important consequences in his or her teaching. If a teacher believes such differences reflect inherited capabilities that set limits to what a person can learn, she or he may "waste" little time trying to teach those whose capacities are perceived to be limited. And if inherited capacity rather than acquired background knowledge is viewed as the main determinant of future learning, the classroom may become a sort of educational quarry where the stones of hidden talent are sorted for polishing. By contrast, if teachers believe that there are no effective biological limits to learning, they will not despair of making reasonable effort to help students learn more, and they will concentrate on developing ability rather than on prospecting for it.

Teachers who see intelligence as an inherent characteristic that limits the learning of some students have tended to use IQ scores more to explain why some students do not learn than to help all students to learn more. Some have tended to explain away intelligence as just another characteristic in which races differ. Instead of using intelligence-test scores to ensure equality of educational opportunity, they have used them to deny it. No doubt this helps to explain why some school systems have either dropped or considered dropping intelligence tests from their testing programs.

If there were clear evidence that important biological differences in learning ability existed among schoolchildren, that these differences accounted to a significant degree for variations in school achievement, and that intelligence tests could measure these biological differences, then we ought to accept the evidence and take it into account in our teaching practices. But the evidence is far from clear or conclusive.

For whatever reasons, students do exhibit differences in learning ability, and they do achieve at varying rates and levels. Certainly such differences cannot be ignored and the sources of such differences should not be overlooked entirely. But teachers are more likely to identify successful instructional interventions by examining carefully the full range of conditions for learning—knowledge prerequisites, desire and interest in learning, and other entering behaviors. We do well not to imagine barriers to learning where none exist, or to assume that brightness gives easy access to knowledge.

USING INTELLIGENCE TESTS IN SCHOOLS

The uses of scores from tests that claim to measure intelligence, mental ability, cognitive skills, mental maturity, cognitive abilities, or mental development—as indicated by their title or their stated purpose—fall into two broad categories: clinical diagnosis and guidance. In the first case the tests are likely to be administered individually and interpreted by a specialist—school psychologist, special educator, counselor, or diagnostic specialist. The purpose is to identify or verify suspected disabilities or deficiencies so that students who are so diagnosed can be placed in appropriate programs and classrooms for remediation or special assistance. In the second case the tests are administered by teachers to groups of students, usually classrooms. The purpose is to obtain information that will guide teachers, the student, parents, and counselors in making decisions about current instructional plans or future educational programs.

For clinical diagnostic purposes the intelligence test ordinarily is one of several tools used by the diagnostician to complete a psychological assessment. Hennessy (1981) has indicated that the diagnosis of learning problems or learning disabilities accounts for the most frequent use of mental-ability measures in the schools. The important roles of the teacher in this process are to recognize the signs of abnormal behavior or deficient progress, to refer the student to a staff member who has the requisite training to perform an assessment, and to work as a team member with the specialist, parents, and the student in implementing the most appropriate instructional program.

IQ scores derived from general intelligence tests have extremely limited value for the classroom teacher, even when separate verbal and quantitative percentile ranks or stanines are provided. The uses that might be made of the scores can, in most cases, be accomplished with the scores from a valid achievement-test battery. It is a generally accepted and well-documented principle that the best predictor of future academic achievement is current achievement status. Thus, teachers who seek information to guide their decisions to group students for instruction, to identify instructional materials consonant with the abilities of their students, and to determine the most effective pace for their teaching might be as far ahead to use achievement-test scores as scores from measures of mental ability.

Beyond the elementary school level, intelligence-test scores and/or scores from aptitude tests or batteries are useful in counseling students about course and educational program selection decisions and for vocational guidance. Here, too, the longitudinal record of school grades and achievement-test scores are equally useful sources of information. Some publishers recommend that scores from their intelligence test be used to identify highly talented and gifted students who might benefit from special programs or promotion to a grade level above their agemates. For many such tests this may, indeed, be an appropriate use. But none of these decisions is so inconsequential that it should be made on the basis of a single test score or without considering the potential concomitant social and academic effects.

Intelligence tests have a place in the school testing program. Their broad function is to help identify students who, on the basis of their extreme scores, should be tested further prior to placing them in the instructional program. Their specific function is to aid in the diagnosis of learning problems. In neither case is it appropriate to make decisions about a student without considering achievement and anecdotal data about him or her as well.

TESTS OF SPECIAL APTITUDE

Somewhat related to tests of general intelligence, but often sounder conceptually and more useful practically, are tests of special aptitude. They are sounder conceptually because what is to be measured is more restricted and defined more clearly. Fewer assumptions about the origin of the aptitude or its stability are made in interpreting the scores. They are more useful practically because their purposes are more specific and more readily attainable.

Some tests of special aptitude, such as scholastic aptitude, are quite comprehensive. Others, such as those of engine lathe aptitude, are rather specific. Often aptitude tests are grouped into batteries to provide for measurement of diverse aptitudes or to permit differential predictions of aptitudes for diverse activities. Texts by Cronbach (1984), Anastasi (1982), and Mehrens and Lehmann (1984) describe the content and intended uses of particular aptitude tests and test batteries.

Aptitude tests are sometimes criticized for seeking to predict success in training programs rather than on the job. A medical aptitude test, for example, is judged to be valid if it assigns the highest scores to those who do best in medical schools, but success in medical school does not always forecast success in medical practice. Yet we must not forget that criteria of success in training programs are easier to define and to measure than criteria of on-the-job success, and also that short-range predictions can be made with greater accuracy than can long-range predictions. Both of these arguments would seem to support aptitude tests as they are presently constituted.

SUMMARY

The following conclusions are based on the ideas presented in this chapter regarding the use of intelligence measures:

1. Because of the variety of definitions proposed for intelligence, and the lack of consensus regarding how to measure it, schools should not use the results from different tests as though they were measures of the same thing.
2. Educators should prefer verbal to nonverbal intelligence tests, particularly for group testing, and tests that emphasize abilities developed in school rather than those that result from incidental learning.
3. Instead of choosing tests that purport to be "culture-free" or "culture-fair," schools should choose tests whose content is relevant to the learning tasks of the school.
4. Schools should avoid using tests that try to measure abstract intelligence, abstract mental abilities, or "the higher mental powers."
5. Except in special cases, schools should not spend time and money on individually administered intelligence tests, even with very young students.
6. Educators should abandon the concept of IQ in favor of percentile ranks or standard scores for use with specific tests of aptitude for learning.
7. Underachievers or overachievers should not be identified on the basis of intelligence-test scores.
8. Teachers should examine thoroughly the full realm of learning conditions in planning instruction rather than focus attention only on differences in abilities to learn.
9. Test users should not be surprised to get somewhat different IQ scores from somewhat different tests, or to find that the same student's IQ score shifts upward or downward from time to time.
10. Teachers should regard intelligence tests as useful measures of general ability in school learning, an ability that is based on prior learning.
11. Group intelligence tests should not be regarded as *essential* to a good school testing program.

18

MEASURES OF OTHER ASPECTS OF PERSONALITY

PERSONALITY MEASURES

Published measures of personality range from rather comprehensive personality inventories and temperament surveys to rather specific instruments designed to assess, for example, hypnotic susceptibility in children or the dimensions of alcohol addiction in adults. That they are relatively abundant is reflected by the fact that nearly a fifth of the 1184 entries in the *Eighth Mental Measurements Yearbook* (Buros, 1978) were categorized as personality measures. They are measures, as distinguished from tests in Chapter 2, because the questions or statements in them require responses that cannot be, and are not intended to be, judged as correct or incorrect.

Despite the variety and number of personality measures, their usefulness in the process of education is open to question. Not only are some personality measures of uncertain or poor technical quality; even more serious is the fact that in many cases test constructors have not carefully specified what precisely is being measured. As a result, convincing evidence for valid use of these measures often is impossible to obtain.

What Is Personality?

As used in ordinary speech, the term *personality* is broad and all-encompassing. Much like the term intelligence, it has been defined and used in a variety of ways by scholars and researchers. Perhaps the most common conception is the one that views personality as a set of cognitive and noncognitive traits that interact to explain how an individual behaves. Included are such elements as intellect, achievement, stature, values, attitudes, sexual orientation, health, voice quality, appearance, and so on. Those who refer to an individual as having "no personality" clearly have some other conception in mind. Obviously we are not likely to obtain a single, meaningful measure of "how much a person has" of such a complex mixture of characteristics. Instead, we must attempt to measure aspects of the total personality.

But this trait approach does not solve the problem, even if we limit ourselves to the behavioral or observable aspects of personality. Traits we have semantically differentiated—friendliness, tolerance, integrity, loyalty, ambition, and optimism, and so on ad infinitum—overlap and interact so that it is difficult to define any of them clearly. Traits that cannot be defined clearly can never be measured precisely. Even when researchers do present clear definitions, as long as those definitions vary substantially from one another, our collective understanding of the trait is not advanced.

For ages human beings have sought to discover the underlying elements of behavior. The ancients thought they had it in their theory of the four humors—blood, phlegm, yellow bile, and black bile—which they envisioned as contributing warmth, inertia, anger, and melancholy, respectively, to a person's temperament. Jung (1959), Kretschmer (1936), and others have tried to identify and distinguish a limited number of personality types. Currently, factor analysts are engaged in a search for some simple structure of basic determiners of behavior, so far without apparent success.

It is not even clear that personality traits can be properly regarded as causes of observed behavior. Perhaps they are only names for the behavior, which itself is the consequence of previous experience(s) interacting with a present situation. Do some high school students refuse to study *because* of a lack of motivation? Or is lack of motivation simply the term we use to describe their behavior, which is in fact the result of many previous experiences and current competing interests? We call generous a woman who drops a $50 bill in the collection plate at church. Does she do this *because* she is generous or does the word *generosity* simply name a class of similar behaviors? If personality traits are not causes of behavior, perhaps educators should not waste too much time trying to measure them. If in fact trait names only *describe* behavior, then why measure traits at all, except to name a behavior or set of behaviors that the individual has already exhibited?

Using Personality Measures in Schools

If schools had systematic, rational programs for personality development, it would be essential to include personality measures in the school's total program of evaluation. But few schools have such programs, and the limited versions that some schools have tried, designed to develop such traits as ambition, honesty, patriotism, and piety, have not been notably successful. Nor are there any clear guides as to the directions personality development should take. Surely the world would be a poorer place to live if all of us had the same "good" personality. Some of us have "difficult" personalities—difficult for our families and friends and even for ourselves. But if one were to eliminate from the list of the world's great men and women those who had serious personality defects or abnormalities of one kind or another, at most only a handful would remain.

This does not mean that our schools can ignore the serious personality problems some of our students face. For the student's sake, as well as for the order, effectiveness, and harmony of the school, these problems need to be solved as well as possible. But personality development probably cannot and should not replace cognitive development as the central mission of the school.

The needs, wishes, preferences, desires, and interests of students—all aspects of personality—are important for teachers to know about, particularly so when individualized instructional programs are being used. The Basic Teaching Model described in Chapter 2 indicates that assessing the entering behaviors of students is an essential ingredient in the instructional process. Entering behavior means more than achievement status or scholastic ability. Knowledge of the likes, dislikes, interests, hobbies, and aspirations of students is useful for developing and selecting instructional materials, for formulating examples and illustrations, and for providing application contexts for assignments and instructional activities. For example, supplemental reading material can be chosen to help increase the desire to read in some students—a sporting goods catalog for those who like athletics or outdoor activities, cookbooks for those who express an interest in baking and cooking, and brochures and magazines on new cars for those who dream about their first automobile purchase. These types of information, aspects of personality, can be obtained by the teacher without employing any of the published personality measures, and the information requires no special assistance for interpretation.

A significant problem associated with most personality measurement is that paper-and-pencil instruments are not well suited to it. Much of personality has to do with typical behavior in actual situations. But the behavior exhibited on a paper-and-pencil test is a limited, artificial kind. Even if students know with reasonable accuracy how they would behave in the situation described (and often they do not), they may find it advantageous to report something else. It is possible for examinees to "fake good" on most personality measures if they choose to do so. Sometimes the purpose of the measure is disguised, but the more this is done the less confidence one can have that the responses are really related to the behavior that needs to be measured. Finally, no matter how disguised, a paper-and-pencil measure remains essentially a cognitive task for the examinee. The emotion that plays so large a part in responses that truly reflect personality is all but absent from responses made on paper with a pencil.

A final problem with personality measures involves the matter of invasion of privacy. Personality measures cause more trouble on this score than either aptitude or achievement tests. The questions on personality measures often ask about intimate personal or family affairs, questions that may embarrass respondents (Do you ever wet the bed?) or irk their parents (Do your parents quarrel?). Such questions invite faking and are almost universally resented.

In sum, personality measures have limited value for use in the schools because (a) the traits are difficult to define and may not even exist, (b) they are susceptible to faking and essentially present cognitive tasks, and (c) many are likely to probe sensitive areas, and thus are likely to be resented. In view of these problems, and because most schools ordinarily are not equipped to carry out systematic programs of personality development, personality measures probably have no place in the school testing program. This does not, of course, rule out selective, clinical use of adjustment inventories or problem checklists to aid counselors helping troubled students. But no one concerned in this process—counselor, student, teachers, or parents—should expect a personality measure to reveal much of a person's basic structure of personality or to contribute very much to the solution of the problem.

Motivation

One of the personality traits that teachers most often would like to measure is motivation. They see some of their students studying hard and others avoiding study as much as possible. They explain the difference by saying that some students are well motivated and others are not. But is motivation a cause or is it simply a description of the observed result? Is motivation a mysterious spiritual essence or is it the result of a complex interaction of beliefs, values, and choices? Can it be measured apart from its manifestation in how hard the student actually works at learning?

The idea that motivation may be more a consequence than a cause, and that it probably never can be "measured" effectively by a paper-and-pencil instrument, does not mean that teachers or students can ignore it. Hard work is essential to learning, and getting students to work hard is an essential part of teaching. The techniques of motivation are varied and their results are not highly predictable. Often the essential motivational factors are out of the teacher's reach, even out of the school's. Sometimes, however, they are not. Some teachers are generally successful in motivating students, in some cases outstandingly so. But it is safe to bet that their special techniques and procedures do not include a paper-and-pencil measure of motivation.

Interest Measures

Interests typically are measured by asking subjects directly what they like or would like to do. Two different approaches are used most commonly.

The *Strong Vocational Interest Blank* (Strong, 1943) uses brief designations of such things as occupations, amusements, and activities and asks the respondent to indicate whether he or she likes, dislikes, or is indifferent to them. The *Kuder Preference Record* (Kuder, 1939) presents triads of activities and asks the respondent to choose which she or he likes most and least of each triad.

Another significant difference between these two approaches has to do with the standards against which subjects' interests are measured. Scoring weights for alternative responses to the Strong were derived from the responses of successful individuals in each occupational group represented by the items. By contrast, the Kuder development was based on assigning items to various interest scales on the basis of student responses that led to a clustering of interest categories. Some of these clusters included activities that were mainly musical, clerical, scientific, and so on. Thus, the scores reported indicate interests in types of activities rather than in particular occupations. The 1974 revision of the Strong, named the *Strong-Campbell Interest Inventory,* was designed to eliminate the sex bias involved in the former separate forms for men and women and to limit the items to activities with which adolescents would be familiar. Additional descriptive information about these and other measures used in the schools for measuring interests and career awareness is provided by Mehrens and Lehmann (1984), Nitko (1983), and Dawis (1980).

Both the Strong-Campbell and the Kuder have been widely used and thoroughly researched. The interests measured by both show considerable stability over time, and both are valuable as predictors of later occupational choice. But it is important to remember that interest inventories are just that: A high interest score does not mean that the person will succeed in a particular occupation. What it does mean is that *if* that person succeeds, he or she probably will be happy in that career.

ATTITUDE MEASURES

What Are Attitudes?

Attitudes constitute one aspect of an individual's personality. The concept of an attitude, like that of personality, is not easy to define precisely. It may be defined very generally as "the sum total of a [person's] inclinations and feelings, prejudice or bias, preconceived notions, ideas, fears, threats, and convictions about any specific topic" (Thurstone and Chave, 1929). Or it may be defined more narrowly as "a relatively enduring organization of beliefs around an object or situation predisposing one to respond in some preferential manner" (Rokeach, 1968).

Attitudes result from our tendency to reach general conclusions on the basis of specific experiences. This ability to generalize is very useful. It is largely responsible for our intellectual development. Without it, all that we learn and know would be specific and, hence, limited in use. It gives us laws of science, of ethics, and of government. It also gives us attitudes, biases, and misconceptions.

To have an attitude toward something is to be biased, favorably or unfavorably. Bias is commonly deplored and its opposites—open-mindedness, tolerance, fairness—tend to be cherished. But to remain open-minded, a person must leave questions undecided. It is good to stay open-minded, to give a fair hearing to all sides of a question, if no immediate action is required. However, it is not good to use open-mindedness as an excuse for evasion of responsibility when hard choices must be made. Remaining open-minded is not always possible or good. We like others to be open-minded to our ideas, but not to be easily persuaded when contrary ideas are presented.

One conceptual framework for describing what an attitude is, and how it might be measured, views an attitude as having three components: an internal or visceral part that is felt, a cognitive part that can be expressed orally or in writing, and an action component that is expressed by overt behavior. Thus it is possible for an individual to feel one way about an object, to say another thing about it, and to behave in either way toward the object. Because some attitudes are held so privately, we can never be sure that the cognitive or behavioral expression of it is a valid indicator of the attitude. Therein lies a key obstacle to those who wish to measure attitudes.

Attitudes develop and change in a number of different ways. Some that involve mainly feelings are often the result of conditioning. A child may be conditioned to fear thunderstorms or mice or snakes by the anxious behavior of a fearful parent or sibling. Another may be conditioned to fear small dogs by the aggressive playfulness of a particular puppy. A third may be conditioned to love books or reading by the pleasant experience of being read to at bedtime.

Other attitudes develop as cognitive generalizations. A politician's words or actions, or what we know about that person's friends or supporters, may cause us to like and to trust him or her. If we do, we probably are generalizing on the basis of a limited number of observations or even from hearsay testimony. In this same way some of us probably develop attitudes toward the people of other countries, not based on the collective actions of those people, but on the basis of statements or actions of one or more natives of those countries.

Cognitive attitudes closely resemble knowledge. The chief difference between them is in how universally they are accepted, or how easily they can be shown to be true. What we believe is made up of our knowledge and our attitudes. Those propositions that most informed people regard as true constitute knowledge. Those on which significant differences of opinion exist we term attitudes. In other words, attitudes are personal beliefs.

Why Different People Have Different Attitudes

There are several reasons why the beliefs we call attitudes differ from person to person. One is that so many of them involve broad generalizations, with much relevant and occasionally contradictory evidence. Another is that they deal less with things as they are than with things as they ought to be. Personal goals and values affect them. Consider these examples:

> Earl Warren was an outstanding Chief Justice.
> Communism is evil.
> Pollution of our air and water must be stopped.
> Minimum-competency testing is good for our schools.

These propositions all are more or less debatable. They are too general and too loaded with value judgments to be *proved* true or false. But individuals and governments, after reflection and deliberation, will decide to act as though they were either true or false. Despite their somewhat limited justifiability, attitudes are powerful determiners of action.

Attitudes have a noteworthy self-sustaining and reinforcing property. Once people develop an attitude toward something or someone, once they arrive at an emotional feeling or a cognitive generalization about it, further experience is more likely to support than weaken it. This is because human beings tend to observe and to remember selectively. They notice and believe incidents that support the correctness of their attitudes and ignore or discredit incidents that seem to call the attitudes into question. The vulnerability of a person's attitudes, the fact that they are not universally believed or easily shown to be true, makes one who holds them use every opportunity to strengthen and defend them.

A well-established attitude is very difficult to dislodge. Seldom can one person induce another to change an attitude, however ill-founded it may seem. If a change comes—and attitudes do change—it is likely to be as a result of a voluntary, internal decision. If evidence against an attitude accumulates, or if clinging to it entails penalties, the holder may gradually soften and ultimately reverse it.

The Measurement of Attitudes

Attitudes affect behavior and are sometimes expressed overtly, allowing them to be measured by observers using rating scales. However, the difficulties of finding qualified observers and of finding sufficient relevant incidents to observe usually make measurement based on direct observation unattractive. The easier and generally better way is to ask subjects directly what they believe or what they like to do. Thus measurements of attitudes are usually based on self-reports that reflect the cognitive aspect of subjects' attitudes.

Instruments used to measure attitudes usually are referred to as *attitude scales*. Although many elaborate techniques of scale construction have been developed (Edwards, 1957), including Guttman's (1950) scalogram analysis, Coomb's (1964) unfolding, and Lazarsfeld's (1959) latent structure analysis, only two have come into wide use. These methods involve either scaled statements (Thurstone and Chave, 1929) or scaled responses (Likert, 1932).

In the Thurstone technique, a large set of statements describing varying levels of attitude toward something like an institution (for example, school) or a development (for example, nuclear disarmament) is assembled or written. Judges are asked to sort these statements into groups that fall in equally spaced intervals along a continuum from highly favorable to highly unfavorable. Statements on which judges display high disagreement in their sorting are eliminated. From those that remain, a smaller set that samples statements from each interval along the entire continuum is selected. These statements constitute the attitude scale.

Each selected statement carries a scale value determined by the average of its placements by the several judges along the original continuum. Ordinarily the continuum ranges from 11 (most favorable) to 1 (most unfavorable). The subject whose attitude is to be measured is given the scaled statements in random order, without knowledge of their scale values, and is asked to indicate which statements she or he endorses or accepts. The individual's score is the average of the scale values of these statements.

Statements like these might appear, along with others, in a scale of attitudes toward permissiveness in child rearing:

	Scale Value
Children should be free to do as they please with their own playthings.	9.5
Decisions on matters of conduct should be made by parent and child jointly.	6.3
In modern times children are being allowed too much freedom.	3.5

The Likert technique also starts with a set of statements, though usually not so many are required. Further, instead of expressing various levels of the attitude, the statements are intended to be clearly favorable or unfavorable. Neutral statements intentionally are avoided. Subjects respond to each item using a five-point scale of agreement:

	NUMERICAL SCORES	
	Favorable	Unfavorable
Strongly agree	5	1
Agree	4	2
Uncertain	3	3
Disagree	2	4
Strongly disagree	1	5

Their score on the item depends, as indicated above, on the extent to which they agree with a statement favoring the attitude or disagree with a statement opposing it.

Here are three statements that might appear on a scale of political liberalism:

Unemployment insurance tends to encourage idleness.
Government serves the businessman better than it serves the laborer.
A family can live quite comfortably on welfare.

Items that discriminate best between those receiving the highest and those receiving the lowest scores on the total scale are retained for the final form of the scale.

The Likert technique is easier to use in developing an attitude scale than is the Thurstone technique, and it gives almost equally good results. It is currently the most widely used technique. More advanced treatments of these and other forms of scale construction are provided by Edwards (1957), Torgerson (1958), and Fishbein and Ajzen (1975). Shaw and Wright (1967) have collected and published a number of sample scales and have cited references regarding the reliability and validity of each.

The Role of the Schools in Developing Attitudes

The cultivation of various presumably desirable attitudes is frequently mentioned as an educational objective. Yet teachers and schools seldom have a systematic program for the attainment of such objectives, and almost never is a serious attempt made to measure the extent to which such objectives have been achieved.

Beyond question, schooling does lead to attitude changes. Many of these changes are results of the acquisition of new knowledge that calls old attitudes into question. Many are the results of conditioning. For example, a teacher who radiates enthusiasm for his/her subject and also demonstrates a genuine interest in students as individuals will probably foster an enduringly favorable attitude toward that field of study. On the other hand, a poorly managed school may condition students to dislike the whole process of education.

Regardless of how attitudes are changed, it seems very doubtful that a teacher or a school should set out deliberately to inculcate certain systems of belief. It seems even more doubtful that an institution designed for the education of a free people should use techniques of conditioning to inculcate the attitudes it approves. Clearly, attitudes accepted as a result of conditioning have not been freely chosen on their merits, as those of a member of a free society ought to be.

What this means is that a teacher or a school should not make the cultivation of a particular set of attitudes one of its explicitly stated and publicly announced primary objectives. Inevitably good teachers will have personal attitudes that they believe to be both good and true. Inevitably these attitudes will affect the knowledge they choose to teach and perhaps even their manner of teaching. Inevitably these and other attitudes will get talked about in good class discussions. The teacher's attitudes will not remain hidden from the students. But under no circumstances should students be required to accept the teacher's attitudes as a condition of satisfactory achievement. What they should be expected to do is to gain command of knowledge and upon this basis form their own attitudes.

Such a procedure is not only the educationally ethical one, it is also likely to be the most effective pedagogically. A frontal attack on other people's attitudes is likely only to strengthen their commitment to them. But if attitudes are recognized as theirs to hold or to change, if they are challenged to examine their attitudes critically—that is, in the light of relevant knowledge, if resources relevant to them are increased, they may find personal satisfaction in adopting new attitudes. Attitude modification by indirection is probably the best strategy.

Neither this strategy nor any other will guarantee adoption by students of a single "ideal" set of attitudes, but this lack of certainty is more to be applauded than deplored. If the propositions that constitute our attitudes are uncertain knowledge, it is good to have different ones held and defended. Efforts to defend them, plus the test of time, are quite likely to lead ultimately to knowledge, which can then properly replace the uncertainty of attitudes. And if we must live with some degree of error in our beliefs, as we inevitably must, it is best that such error not be universally accepted as truth.

Thus, the fact that attitudes are almost impossible to measure as educational achievements is no serious loss. We shouldn't include them among our explicit objectives, and we shouldn't try to teach them in any case. The fact that they are very difficult to measure as outcomes of instruction, however, has probably helped to keep the feet of idealistic teachers in paths of virtue.

SUMMARY

The main ideas presented in this chapter can be summarized in the following propositions:

1. The concept of personality is broad and the factors that influence its development are complex.
2. Personality trait names tend to be satisfactory for describing behavior but not for explaining it.
3. The central mission of the schools should be cognitive development rather than personality development.
4. Information on certain aspects of students' personalities should be obtained by teachers in the process of assessing entering behavior.
5. Personality tests are resented more often and more deeply as unwarranted invasions of privacy than are tests of cognitive development or abilities.
6. Teachers tend to be more successful in influencing

the motivation of their students than in measuring it.
7. Strong's technique for interest measurement calls for expressions of liking, indifference, or dislike for particular activities; Kuder's technique calls for choice among alternative activities.
8. Attitudes are personally held generalizations that are open to questions.
9. A person's attitudes tend to be self-reinforcing and difficult to change.
10. The two principal techniques of attitude measurement are those developed by Thurstone, which uses scaled statements, and by Likert, which uses scaled responses.
11. Schools probably should not set out to develop directly certain "desired" attitudes in their students.

19

RECENT DEVELOPMENTS IN EDUCATIONAL MEASUREMENT

The major topics addressed in this chapter relate to issues and practices that are contributing to major changes in educational measurement. The purpose of each section is to stimulate the awareness of readers, to describe briefly the nature of the ideas or activities, and to provide references for further detailed reading. In each case these advances will impact all of us directly, regardless of our role as educator, student, parent, taxpayer, or measurement specialist.

THE IMPACT OF COMPUTERS ON TESTING

A textbook description of the current developments in the use of computers for testing purposes is likely to be out of date before it reaches its intended audience. The technology changes so rapidly that no document describing "current" equipment and computer programs is likely to live up to its billing for very long. Nonetheless, these continuous updates of both hardware and software are implemented in the classroom at a snail's pace by comparison. In fact, the use of computers for classroom testing activities is much less popular than is their use for other instructional purposes.

The most prominent use of computers in the classroom is to provide individual instruction to students. Such instruction often takes the form of drill and practice exercises, particularly for remediation purposes, and program writing. There are programs to improve computer literacy and there are games, for either learning or recreational purposes. Though we expect that nearly every elementary and secondary school has at least one computer, most generally a microcomputer, we should not expect that students are spending significant portions of instructional time using it. A recent survey of over a thousand schools that have microcomputers showed that the typical elementary school student accessed the computer for less than a half hour each week, but high school students got nearly an hour per week (Center for Social Organization of Schools, 1983). Another noteworthy finding of the study was that in about half of the schools, only one or two teachers at most were regular computer users.

Computers are efficient and accurate but are no wiser than the programmer who instructs them on how to perform specific tasks. They can store large amounts of information and retrieve any portion of it on command, but they have access only to information that the user has directed them to store. The proliferation of computer programs has made computers accessible to so many because the need to learn the computer's language and to write programs to direct its work has been eliminated. The need to speak "computerese" has nearly vanished because the commercially prepared programs are so "user friendly." Thus teachers actually can save valuable planning and instructional time or accomplish tasks that were once considered too time-consuming if they have access to the appropriate software. With respect to classroom testing, available software can be used to store test items in the computer, retrieve stored items to assemble a test, administer different but comparable tests to students, score tests, provide information about the quality of the test items, record scores and compute grades, and assist with test-score interpretation.

Test Development

Test-item banking is not a new concept, but until the recent emergence of the microcomputer, its use was restricted primarily to large mainframe computers such as those found in corporations and at colleges and universities. A *bank* is a set of test items stored in computer memory and retrieved on demand when a test is to be prepared. Each item is stored with a unique number code that classifies it on any of several dimensions: item type, content measured, difficulty level, and date of last use. Some programs provide the capability of storing test-item statistics obtained from previous uses of the item, and some will automatically transfer the statistics to the bank as part of the test-scoring process. Some will store textual material, test directions, or reading passages, and some can handle diagrams and figures as well.

Test assembly from a bank simply requires that the user supply the number code for each stored item desired in the test. A separate printer can then print the items in final format for ready duplication. Since the keyed response usually is stored with each item, an answer key can be printed along with the test copy. Or, the scoring key can be stored temporarily in preparation for computer scoring of the test.

Test Administration

Large-scale test administration using the computer is still quite uncommon, owing to the need for a large number of computer terminals at one time, but individual testing by computer is much less rare. For example, some states now administer their driver's license written test by computer terminal. A key advantage of this procedure in conjunction with item banking is that tests need never be printed. The computer can be directed to select items from the bank in a prescribed fashion so that, if the bank is large enough, no two examinees would be administered the same set of items.

A new and promising test-administration approach, *adaptive testing*, uses the advantages of the computer and requires a relatively new theory of testing called *item response theory*. (Item response theory is described briefly in a subsequent section of this chapter.) Adaptive testing is based on the assumptions that the trait being measured can be described by a single continuum and that the responses of examinees to test items can be used to place the individuals on the continuum. The computer selects from the bank a test item that an average examinee would be expected to answer correctly. If the test taker answers correctly, a more difficult item is chosen for the next try. If the first answer was incorrect, an easier item is chosen for the second try. Since each item in the pool has been calibrated in advance to a particular location on the continuum, the examinee's position on the continuum can be located through successive selections of easier and harder items. A chief advantage of adaptive testing over conventional testing is that only about half the number of items are needed to obtain "equivalent" results (Green, 1983). There are problems yet unresolved with adaptive testing, but its anticipated advantages—shorter testing time, adaptability to more valid item types, and greater test security—make it one of the most promising developments for educational and psychological testing in the last decade of the century.

Finally, computer test administrations have promise for providing more valid test scores from handicapped examinees than can be obtained from paper-and-pencil tests. No writing is required and, with the availability of voice synthesizers, no reading may be needed. For those who lack the fine motor coordination required to use the keyboard of a standard computer terminal, a touch-sensitive screen on the monitor provides an alternative. There is no way to predict the magnitude of the impact of these devices in providing opportunities in education and employment for those who heretofore have seen mostly barriers. But there is every reason to be optimistic!

Scoring and Analysis

Until recently most electronic scoring of test answer sheets was done by optical scanners that were too large, too expensive, and too complex to be considered for direct use by teachers. Fortunately the combination of engineering advances and plummeting prices have made small scanners available at affordable costs. Those that can be connected directly to a microcomputer allow the user to feed the answer sheet into the scanner and have the responses and test score stored in the computer in a matter of minutes and seconds. Once the information is stored in the computer, score rosters, test statistics, item statistics, and interpretive reports can be printed with the aid of software that has been written to perform any or all of these separate tasks.

Computer scoring of objective tests allows for more efficient use of the teacher's time. Computer test analysis and reporting provides useful information that many teachers have not found the time to calculate and summarize on their own. Obviously not every classroom should have an optical scanner, even where there may be a microcomputer in each. But if every school building had its own scanner, much time would be saved, more useful information would be at hand, and improved instruction should result.

Recordkeeping

The chores associated with recording test scores in grade books or on student records and with combining scores to arrive at final grades are handled readily by a computer. Several software packages exist to perform this function, and a number of others include this function as part of a broader test-scoring package. In many cases a master class list can be developed by the computer from the names students code on their test answer sheet. Scores from subsequent tests, assignments, papers, and other projects can be entered using the keyboard of a terminal, or they can be coded on test answer sheets and transferred to the computer record by an optical scanner. Of course the computer is unable to make all the decisions a teacher needs to make. How should the grading components be weighted? How many B grades should there be in the class? These and other philosophical questions that were discussed in Chapter 14 still require the teacher's judgment. But the computer will do the clerical and arithmetic tasks in less time and with greater accuracy than a teacher could hope to do.

Software Packages

Most schools and school districts do not have the resources at hand to develop their own computer programs or even to modify existing programs. They must rely on the software available through computer stores and software firms. With the wide variety of packages available, it seems unfortunate that the user cannot count on the computer to select the most appropriate package for specified use, yet. Hsu and Nitko (1983) have provided an excellent summary of testing software available for microcomputers. In addition, they have developed a review form that organizes the relevant questions a prospective user should ask in evaluating a software package.

Some software packages can be used with more than one brand of computer, but most are intended for only a single brand or model. Most small computers are designed to understand only one programming language, such as BASIC or FORTRAN. As a result, programs written in another language will be as foreign to it as Greek may be to some of us. Computers have the same problem we have when spoken to in an unfamiliar tongue. The wise shopper will be sure that a software package is compatible with the computer with which it is to be used and will attempt to view a demonstration or seek a free trial period before purchasing a package.

MANDATED ASSESSMENT

Mandated assessment is the term that describes the collective testing programs organized at both the state and local level in response to legislation enacted by state governments. The nature of the mandate varies from state to state regarding the flexibility accorded local school districts to implement an assessment program and to use the results. In some states school districts have the option of conducting an assessment, but in others the legislation requires an assessment at specified grade levels, in specified subject areas, and for specified purposes in every district. Virtually every state has enacted some kind of statewide assessment law.

The Need for the Mandate

Large-scale testing at the state level is not a new phenomenon, but the nature of the current activity, particularly with regard to minimum-competency testing, is relatively recent. The forces that had the most significant bearing on this development have been outlined by Womer (1981) as these:

1. The control of school matters has shifted from the local level to the state and federal governments because of the increased dependence of schools on state funding directly or federal funding indirectly.
2. The offer of federal monies in the 1970s brought with it a mandate for assessing the impact of funded programs. Since the dollars were channeled through the states for distribution to local districts, state education agencies bolstered their staffs to perform the program evaluation.
3. The test-score decline of the 1970s and the public observations of high school graduates with deficient preparation in the basic skills alarmed government officials at all levels. The outcry from parents, school boards, and legislators for accountability was translated into a demand for assessment and, in cases where deficiencies were detected, remediation.
4. A greater awareness of the need to establish educational equity created a demand for programs that would enhance opportunities for minority and disadvantaged students. States were faced with the task of evaluating the programs that were designed to attain equity.

The emphasis on measuring school effects or school program differences has caused some measurement specialists to look beyond the traditional standardized achievement tests that have been an integral component of school testing programs for years. They claim that the norm-referenced measures that have been used to sort students according to their achievement are not appropriate for measuring either what students have learned or whether students are learning what they are expected to learn (Tyler, 1981). Airasian and Madaus (1983) have drawn the same conclusion. Standardized tests are designed to measure individual differences rather than group (school) differences, and their content is based on the national "lowest common denominator" curriculum. That is, test content is an adequate sample of what most schools consider important, but it does not reflect well the curriculum of specific schools. Furthermore, test items are selected based on their statistical properties rather than on content appropriateness. Items that measure knowledge or skill that nearly all students have learned are not included on norm-referenced standardized tests because such items do not discriminate well between high and low achievers; they do not contribute effectively to sorting students on the achievement continuum.

The perceived inappropriateness of traditional standardized tests for measuring program effectiveness created a need for new measures, geared to the curricula of particular schools. The expertise for test planning, development, scoring, and reporting has been furnished in most cases by state education departments. Where assessment is optional, local school districts have relied on educational consultants and guidelines supplied by state departments to develop their assessment programs. The need for assessment has been expressed in a national movement, but it has been addressed independently by state governments. Consequently, the nature of assessment programs varies within and between states, depending on the nature of the mandate legislated.

The Nature of Assessment Programs

The extreme diversity of the dimensions of state testing programs makes it impossible to describe the typical one. For example, in some programs every student in certain grades is tested, but other programs test only a sample of students in those grades. The most comprehensive programs use both procedures, testing all students in reading and mathematics, for example, and testing a sample of students in science, citizenship, or social studies. According to survey results reported by Pipho (1980) and Roeber (1980), statewide testing programs vary on these dimensions as well:

1. *Grade level.* The *least* popular levels for testing are K, 1, 2, and 7, but at least one state tests at each of these grade levels.
2. *Test content.* Reading, mathematics, and writing appear in more programs than any other areas, but at least 17 other content areas are tested by one or more states.

3. *Test development.* Some state agencies build their own instruments, others purchase them from publishers, and still others contract with some testing agency to build tests to meet written specifications.

4. *Performance standards.* Minimum standards are mandated by some state legislation. In some states the state education department establishes performance standards while in others local districts have that responsibility. Some programs require no standard or establish no performance standard.

Using Assessment Results

It should be evident from the diverse nature of the state testing programs that assessments are conducted for a variety of purposes and the results are used in diverse ways. Among the major users of assessment results are local schools and school districts. Scores are used by administrators to examine trends over time and within or between grades in the subject areas tested. Graduation and grade-promotion decisions are made by some districts on the basis of assessment scores. Assessment data are used to evaluate instructional programs locally or are provided to funding agencies as evidence of program accomplishment. In addition, once areas of strength and weakness are determined, staff and other resource-allocation decisions are made with the help of assessment results.

Legislative bodies and state education department personnel use assessment scores for a range of purposes. The results permit trend analysis and the identification of districts that consistently show excellence or demonstrate a need for intervention. Exemplary schools are identified and studied to determine how their successful programs or practices might be implemented in other schools. Special programs supported by state or federal funds are evaluated with assessment data, in both the formative and the summative senses. Often decisions about future funding, either temporary or permanent, are made with the help of scores from assessment measures. Other potential uses have been identified by Powell (1981).

Despite the apparent value of assessment data and its potential uses, not enough is known about how assessment data actually are used. Assessments that are planned with specific purposes in mind and are implemented with technical care can yield valuable information. But such information derives its value primarily from its utilization—whether it is used and whether it is used appropriately. Assessment scores should be subjected to the same kinds of validity and reliability scrutiny that is attached to using standardized test results in school testing programs. For example, districts that look for performance changes must be concerned with the reliability of the difference scores, the comparability of tests on the different occasions, and the practical significance to be attached to differences of varying magnitudes.

Minimum-Competency Testing

The frequent expressions of public dissatisfaction with student achievement have caused some legislative bodies to mandate assessments in the form of competency testing. The purpose of the assessment is to determine if students have learned the minimum knowledge and skills expected of students who, for example, should be promoted to the ninth grade or awarded a high school graduation diploma. The purpose of the law is to redirect the efforts of students and teachers toward learning and to end the issuance of diplomas of questionable meaning.

Both reason and past experience suggest that these purposes can be achieved. The presence of minimum-competency tests encourages teachers and students to work hard to achieve satisfactory results. It is an elementary principle of the management of any enterprise that to obtain good results one must pay attention to those results. Where competency tests are used, achievement in learning is likely to matter more than it would in their absence.

Testing for minimum competence is hardly an ideal way of holding schools accountable: It focuses too much on the lower end of the achievement scale, limiting the scope to only the most absolutely essential competencies; it requires the application of a somewhat arbitrary and hard-to-defend categorical distinction between competence and incompetence along a continuous scale of achievement. However arbitrary and fraught with error they may be, and however inadequate they may be for assessing the overall effectiveness of a school's educational program, competency tests are a step in the right direction. When developed soundly, they are much better than nothing at all in the way of systematic public review of student attainments in learning.

What kind of test should be used to determine minimum competence? A domain-referenced test, one that represents a sample of the behaviors defined by the domain of important competencies, seems most appropriate (Ebel, 1978b). Some assessments are based on objectives-referenced measures that examine a limited number of discrete competencies and yield scores that are not generalizable beyond the tasks included in the test. Such tests may be useful as formative evaluations during instruction, but they are less accurate and efficient than domain-referenced measures for summative evaluation of competence after instruction has been completed. Competence is like a fabric composed of a multitude of fibers of knowledge, an integrated network of concepts and understandings. To assess competence, one must probe the fabric to determine its extent and its strength. To mark out on the fabric separate, arbitrarily defined portions and to treat them as distinct parts of total competency is unrealistic, unnecessary, and unprofitable.

Minimum-competency testing is not likely to cure all the ills of contemporary education, but it will do much to correct one of the most serious of the ailments. It will help to restore concern for the cognitive development of students to highest priority in the mission of the school. It should motivate teachers to teach purposefully and students to work harder to learn. In the process, the practice of issuing meaningless diplomas to undereducated graduates could be virtually ended.

NATIONAL ASSESSMENT OF EDUCATIONAL PROGRESS

The quest for school accountability that emerged in the post-Sputnik era made both educators and legislators realize that no useful mechanism existed to provide information about how much young people nationwide have learned in school. No dependable guides existed for steering public policy regarding priorities for educational spending or needed curriculum reform. With the assistance of Carnegie Corporation and Ford Foundation funding, plans were laid in the mid-1960s for a project that would survey the knowledge, skills, and attitudes of young Americans in several subject areas. The National Assessment of Educational Progress (NAEP) was designed to monitor the attainment of educational objectives and to report this information to educational decision makers, practitioners, and the public. Details regarding the development of NAEP and activities associated with the initial assessments have been described by Merwin and Womer (1969) and in publications distributed by the Education Commission of the States.

Initial assessments in each of ten learning areas—science, writing, citizenship, reading, literature, music, social studies, mathematics, career and occupational development, and art—have been updated periodically to gauge progress. More limited assessments, called "probes," have been conducted in such areas as basic life skills, health, and energy. The reports of each assessment include selected exercises (test items) and the proportion of the sample tested that chose each multiple-choice alternative. Because these items are in the public domain, teachers and school districts can use them to compare the performance of their student groups with relevant subgroups for which NAEP has reported results. In fact, some states use NAEP items in some of their assessment measures so that national normative comparisons can be made. All reports from NAEP are available from the Superintendent of Documents, U.S. Government Printing Office, Washington, D.C. 20402.

Many of the factors that shaped the initial structure and goals of NAEP in the 1960s have changed over time. There is less public confidence in the ability of the school to do its job, and there are greater demands for some form of accountability. The once modest role of the federal government in education has changed to a prominent one. Beginning in the late 1970s, charges were made that NAEP was failing to serve the audience that needed serving and that its results needed to be more useful (Comptroller General, 1976;

Wiley, 1981). Subsequently, the funding for NAEP to the Education Commission of the States was not renewed and the contract was awarded to Educational Testing Service, based on a redesign of the purposes and technical procedures proposed for future assessments (Messick et al., 1983). Included in the new plans for NAEP are assessment of functionally handicapped students, assessment of limited-English speaking students, and computer-assisted assessment procedures.

National Assessment has been, and likely will continue to be, a positive influence on educational policy and practice. The flurry of high-quality state assessment programs is due in part to the model provided by NAEP and to the cooperative support of the NAEP consultants to state education departments. The new design for NAEP promises to provide a barometer of the educational progress of the nation and modes of information dissemination that will be palatable to policymakers and practitioners alike.

ITEM RESPONSE THEORY

The science of a field is built on a theoretical foundation that attempts to describe how the important concepts, objects, or traits of that field are related. The area of mental measurement is no exception. Classical test theory developed early in this century to help explain what happens when one "measures" a psychological characteristic of an individual. Such concepts as item difficulty, item discrimination, standard error of measurement, and reliability, as we have used them in this text, are based on certain assumptions associated with classical test theory. This theory has served us well in the past and undoubtedly will continue to do so. However, the limitations imposed by the assumptions of classical theory have caused psychometricians to explore alternative explanations for the mental-measurement process. The most prominent result of this search was the invention of *item response theory,* alternately labeled *latent trait theory* or *item characteristic curve theory.* The complex mathematical foundation of item response theory precludes a detailed treatment of it in this text. However, a general overview of the theory is presented here for those who wish to develop an understanding of the differences between classical and item response theories.

The Need for Another Theory

The major thrust of classical test theory is to provide a framework for explaining how a group of individuals can be measured so that those individuals can be rank-ordered according to how much of the measured trait each has. The result of such measurement is a relative ranking of persons; the highest score is assigned to the person who possesses the most and the lowest score to the person who possesses the least. When the goal of measurement is to establish such rankings, norm-referenced score interpretations are made, but content-referenced interpretations generally are not appropriate. Ability or achievement levels cannot be determined in an absolute sense (How much does she know?), only in a relative sense (How much does he know in relation to what his classmates know?). Why is this so?

Scores obtained from classical measures depend on a group mean and the amount of score variability in that group (standard deviation) for interpretation purposes. Standard scores, for example, indicate an examinee's position in the group relative to the mean. The magnitude of one's score reflects the distance from the mean. Thus a student with a *T*-score of 72 on an English usage test ranks high relative to his or her peers, but unless we know something about the achievement level of the peer group, we do not know much about the absolute amount of knowledge the student possesses. In sum, an individual's score on such a test depends on the difficulty level of the items, which in turn is a function of the overall ability level of the group with which she or he is tested. Item response theory is intended to overcome some of these limitations.

Classical versus Item Response Theory

An illustration may help to distinguish between the two theories. Suppose we wish to measure the weight of four individuals by using a set of ten rocks and a fulcrum and beam much like a see-saw or teeter-totter. To illustrate measurement under classical theory, we will further assume that each of the rocks weighs a different amount but we do not know how much any one rock weighs. To begin, we place one of the rocks on one end of the see-saw and have the first individual, Tom, sit on the other end. If Tom's weight causes his end of the beam to go to the ground, he is given a score of one, otherwise his score is zero. The weights of Jane, Greg, and Diane are measured similarly with the same rock, and the process is repeated with each of the ten rocks. The scores from each weighing are shown in Table 19-1 along with the total raw score for each person and their corresponding *T*-score. Since the rocks did not have preset weights and no common standard such as pounds was used, the raw score is simply "number of rocks exceeded in weight." We do

Table 19-1   Weight Scores from a Classical-Theory Measure

	1	2	3	4	5	6	7	8	9	10	Total	T
Tom	1	0	0	1	0	1	0	0	1	0	4	41
Jane	1	1	1	1	1	1	1	0	1	1	9	64
Greg	1	0	0	1	1	1	0	0	1	0	5	45
Diane	1	0	0	1	1	1	1	0	1	0	6	50

ROCK NUMBER spans columns 1–10.

Note: The *T*-score is based on a raw-score mean of 6.0 and a standard deviation of 2.13.

not know how much any one individual weighs, but the *T*-score tells us who weighs the least and the most. In addition, it tells us the relative distance between individuals in terms of amount of weight possessed.

Now we will use the basis of item response theory to measure the weights of the same individuals using the same rocks. A necessary first step is to use these ten rocks to measure the weights of a large group of individuals, say 500. These data are used to arrive at the weight of each rock in some unit of measurement (but not the familiar "pound"). With the aid of some "heavy" mathematics, a weight value can be assigned to each rock, so that, no matter which other rocks might be used to measure any other group of individuals, the weight values will remain the same. This process is called *calibration*. Once a rock has been assigned a value, we know that anyone who causes that rock to rise when we measure his or her weight will have a weight score at least as high as the value assigned to that rock.

Now that we know the weight of each rock, we can select them in order from lightest to heaviest to successively measure the weight of each of the four individuals. Using the same process we used above, we obtain the scores from weighing as shown in Table 19-2. The weight value of each rock is shown in the row across the top of the table. The last column shows the weight range of each individual. The true weights of these individuals, chosen for illustration, were 37, 63, 46, and 51. If our sample of rocks had included these exact weights, the weight scores would have reflected these true weights more precisely. Note that we could add the separate scores of each individual and arrive at the same raw and *T*-scores shown in Table 19-1. It is possible to make both absolute and relative interpretations of the data from the item response theory measure.

If we translate the rocks to test items, the data in these two tables can be viewed as responses to achievement-test items. In terms of test items, the rock-weight value is analogous to an item-score value that is closely associated with the difficulty level of the item. The more knowledgeable an examinee is, the higher the probability is that she or he will correctly answer a given test item. The item-calibration process makes use of this probability relationship in arriving at an item-score value. An item-score value, say 15, is assigned so that individuals who have an ability score of 15 have a 50-50 chance of answering

Table 19-2 Weight Scores from an Item-Response-Theory Measure

| | ROCK WEIGHT | | | | | | | | | | |
	12	23	31	35	44	47	53	56	62	71	Weight
Tom	1	1	1	1	0	0	0	0	0	0	35–44
Jane	1	1	1	1	1	1	1	1	1	0	62–71
Greg	1	1	1	1	1	0	0	0	0	0	44–47
Diane	1	1	1	1	1	1	0	0	0	0	47–53

the item correctly. Hard items have large item-score values and easy items small values. Individuals whose actual ability score is 15 are likely to answer correctly most items whose score values are below 15 and to answer incorrectly most items whose score values exceed 15. This will happen to the extent that the test items are adequate discriminators, regardless of their difficulty levels.

Note the items in Table 19-1 that did not help to discriminate between individuals of different achievement levels: 1, 4, 6, 8, and 9. These same items did not discriminate between individuals on the item response theory measure either, but two of those, items 4 and 10, were required to establish the upper or lower weight ranges for Tom and Jane, respectively. For example, if item 10 had not been used, we would not have an achievement estimate for Jane, except to say that her score exceeds 62.

The process of calibrating items is obviously an important part of developing measures with item response theory. Hambleton (1979), Wright (1977), and Lord and Novick (1968) have presented more complete descriptions of the statistical models, assumptions, and procedures for calibrating items and selecting those that will maximize the precision of the ability estimates.

Item response theory is being used increasingly by test publishers for test development, equating scores on alternate test forms, and developing test norms. Others use it for adaptive testing, developing minimum-competency tests, and evaluating school programs with content-referenced measures. There exist many theoretical, statistical, and practical problems to resolve before item response theory begins to exert the impact that many psychometricians anticipate. No doubt its grounding in complex statistical theory and methodology and its dependence on the computer for computational facility will continue to limit its direct accessibility to general practitioners. Nonetheless, the indirect influence of item response theory is likely to be felt by all who use tests, whether for measuring school achievement, professional competence, or skills required for employment.

SUMMARY

The main ideas presented in this chapter are summarized in the following statements:

1. Computers can be as useful to teachers in assisting with the management function as with the teaching function.
2. Test assembly and administration can be made more efficient with the use of computers without sacrificing test quality.
3. Teachers wishing to use computer-assisted testing more often are faced with the problem of how to select appropriate software than with the problem of how to design and create the software they need.
4. State and district assessment programs required by law are intended to evaluate the general quality of education students are receiving, or to identify specific competencies they possess on graduation from high school.
5. The widespread increase of mandated assessments has been influenced by a shift from local control to state and federal control of education funds and by public demands for greater accountability of the schools.
6. State assessment data has a variety of potential uses for local schools and state legislatures, but there is no clear evidence that the potentials are being realized in many programs.

7. Tests of minimum competence serve to focus attention on cognitive learning and to contribute to the audit of diploma granting. Because they focus on only one end of the achievement scale, they are of limited value as indicators of the overall progress of the school.

8. A major contribution made by the National Assessment of Educational Progress was to provide an assessment model that could be adapted for mandated state assessment programs.

9. Classical test theory has served educational testing well as a foundation for test development and test use, and it will continue to do so in the future.

10. Item response theory shows promise for solving some of the most perplexing problems encountered by test specialists.

11. Item response theory is no replacement for classical test theory but is a useful expansion of psychometric theory.

PROJECTS AND PROBLEMS

Project: Statewide Assessment

Obtain current information about the status of statewide assessment in your state or in another of interest to you. If there is no state-mandated assessment, summarize the major chronological steps of the proposed assessment legislation in the state you chose. If there is mandated testing, describe the nature of the program and its effects. Include the following in your description:

1. Grade levels at which testing occurs and the frequency of the assessment in each.
2. The nature of the content in the measures used and how the tests are developed.
3. Whether there are performance standards mandated or, if not, the procedures recommended for setting standards.
4. The intended use of the results by state government agencies and local school districts.
5. The findings from the most recent assessment, including trends that incorporate scores from previous years.

Conclude your paper with your personal evaluation of the quality of the program and the impact it has had in the state. Make recommendations that you believe would improve the program or the use of the results.

REFERENCES

AARON, R. I. 1971. *Knowing and the function of reason.* Oxford: Oxford University Press.

AIRASIAN, P. W. & MADAUS, G. F. 1983. Linking testing and instruction: Policy issues. *Journal of Educational Measurement,* 20, 103–118.

ANASTASI, A. 1982. *Psychological testing* (5th ed.). New York: Macmillan.

ANDERSON, J.R. 1983. *The architecture of cognition.* Cambridge, MA: Harvard University Press.

ANDERSON, R. C. 1972. How to construct achievement tests to address comprehension. *Review of Educational Research,* 42, 145–70.

ANNIS, L. F. 1983. *Study techniques.* Dubuque, IA: William C. Brown.

AYRES, L. P. 1912. *A scale for measuring the quality of handwriting of school children.* New York: Russell Sage Foundation, Bulletin 113.

BAGLIN, R. F. 1981. Does "nationally" normed really mean nationally? *Journal of Educational Measurement,* 18, 97–107.

Bakke v. *California.* 1978. 438 U.S. 265.

BAYLEY, N. 1933. Mental growth during the first three years. *Genetic Psychology Monographs,* 14, 1–92.

————. 1949. Consistency and variability in the growth of intelligence from birth to eighteen years. *Journal of Genetic Psychology,* 75, 165–96.

————. 1955. On the growth of intelligence. *American Psychologist,* 10, 805–18.

BINET, A. 1911. Nouvelles recherches sur la mesure du niveau intellectuel chez les enfants d'ecole. *Année Psychologique,* 17, 145–201.

BLOOM, B. S. 1964. *Stablility and change in human characteristics.* New York: Wiley.

————. 1968. Learning for mastery. *Evaluation Comment,* 1, UCLA Center for the Study of Evaluation.

————, ENGELHART, M. D., FURST, E. J., HILL, W. H., & KRATHWOHL, D. R. 1956. *Taxonomy of educational objectives. Handbook I: The cognitive domain.* New York: David McKay Co.

BOARD, C. & WHITNEY, D. R. 1972. The effect of selected poor item-writing practices on test difficulty. *Journal of Educational Measurement,* 9, 225–34.

BOULDING, K. E. 1967. The uncertain future of knowledge and technology. *Education Digest,* 33, 7–11.

BRODY, W. & POWELL, N. J. 1947. A new approach to oral testing. *Educational and Psychological Measurement,* 7, 289–98.

Brown v. *Board of Education.* 1954. 347 U.S. 483.

BUROS, O. K. (Ed.). 1978. *The eighth mental measurements yearbook.* Highland Park, NJ: The Gryphon Press.

CARTER, R. S. 1952. How invalid are marks assigned by teachers? *Journal of Educational Psychology,* 43, 218–28.

CASHEN, V. M. & RAMSEYER, G. C. 1969. The use of separate answer sheets by primary age children. *Journal of Educational Measurement,* 6, 155–58.

CENTER FOR SOCIAL ORGANIZATION OF SCHOOLS. 1983. *National survey of school users of microcomputers.* Baltimore: Johns Hopkins University.

CENTER FOR THE STUDY OF EVALUATION. 1971. *CSE-ECRC preschool/kindergarten test evaluations.* Los Angeles: University of California at Los Angeles, Graduate School of Education.

————. 1972. *CSE-RBS test evaluations: Tests of higher order cognitive, affective, and interpersonal skills.* Los Angeles: University of California at Los Angeles, Graduate School of Education.

————. 1974. *CSE secondary school test evaluations.* Los Angeles: University of California at Los Angeles, Graduate School of Education.

————. 1976. *CSE elementary school test evaluations.* Los Angeles: University of California at Los Angeles, Graduate School of Education.

COFFMAN, W. E. 1966. On the validity of essay tests of achievement. *Journal of Educational Measurement,* 3, 151–56.

————. 1971. Essay examinations. In R. L. THORNDIKE (Ed.), *Educational measurement* (2nd ed.). Washington, D.C.: American Council on Education.

COHEN, M. R. & NAGLE, E. 1934. *An introduction to logic and the scientific method.* New York: Harcourt Brace and Co.

COHEN, S. B. 1983. Assigning report card grades to the mainstreamed child. *Teaching Exceptional Children,* 15, 86–89.

COLEMAN, W. & CURETON, E. E. 1954. Intelligence and achievement: The "jangle fallacy" again. *Educational and Psychological Measurement,* 14, 347–51.

COMPTROLLER GENERAL. 1976. *The national assessment of educational progress: Its results need to be made more useful* (Report to Congress, HRD-76-113). Washington, D.C.: Author.

COOK, D. L. 1955. An investigation of three aspects of free-response and choice-type tests at the college level. *Dissertation Abstracts,* 15, 1351.

COOMBS, C. H. 1964. *A theory of data.* New York: Wiley.

COUNTS, G. S. 1932. *Dare the school build a new social order?* New York: The John Day Co.

COX, R. C. & VARGAS, J. 1966. *A comparison of item selection techniques for norm-referenced and criterion-referenced tests.* Paper presented at a meeting of the National Council on Measurement in Education, Chicago.

CROCKER, L. M. & BENSON, I. J. 1980. Does answer-changing affect test quality? *Measurement and Evaluation in Guidance,* 12, 233–39.

CRONBACH, L. J. 1951. Coefficient alpha and the internal structure of tests. *Psychometrika,* 16, 297–334.

————. 1983. What price simplicity? *Educational Measurement: Issues and Practice,* 2, 11–12.

————. 1984. *Essentials of psychological testing* (4th ed.). New York: Harper & Row.

———— & MEEHL, P. E. 1955. Construct validity in psychological tests. *Psychological Bulletin,* 52, 281–302.

CURETON, L. W. 1971. The history of grading practice. *Measurement in Education,* 2(4).

CURTIS, H. A. & KROPP, R. P. 1962. *Experimental analyses of the effects of various modes of item presentation on the scores and factorial content of tests administered by visual and audio-visual means.* Tallahassee, FL: Florida State University, Department of Educational Research and Testing.

DAVIS, F. B. 1946. *Item analysis data* (Harvard Education Papers No. 2). Cambridge, MA: Harvard University, Graduate School of Education.

————. 1952. Item analysis in relation to educational and psychological testing. *Psychological Bulletin,* 49, 97–121.

DAWIS, R. V. 1980. Measuring interests. In D. A. PAYNE (Ed.), *New directions for testing and measurement: Recent developments in affective measurement* (77–92). San Francisco: Jossey-Bass.

Debra P. v. Turlington. 1979. 747 F. Supp. 244 (M. D. Fla.).

DECECCO, J. P. & CRAWFORD, W. R. 1974. *The psychology of learning and instruction* (2nd ed.). Englewood Cliffs, NJ: Prentice-Hall.

DIEDRICH, P. 1960. *Short-cut statistics for teacher-made tests* (Evaluation and Advisory Service Series No. 5). Princeton, NJ: Educational Testing Service.

DIVINE, J. H. & KYLEN, D. W. 1979. *How to beat test anxiety and score higher on your exams.* Woodbury, NY: Barron's Educational Series.

DORR-BREMME, D. W. 1983. Assessing students: Teacher's routine practices and reasoning. *Evaluation Comment,* 6, UCLA Center for the Study of Evaluation.

DRESSEL, P. L. 1978. Advanced placement examinations. Review in O.K. BUROS (Ed.). *The eighth mental measurements yearbook.* Highland Park, NJ: The Gryphon Press, 627–29.

DYER, H. S. 1958. What point of view should teachers have concerning the role of measurement in education? *The fifteenth yearbook of the National Council on Measurements Used in Education.* East Lansing, MI: Michigan State University.

EBEL, R. L. 1937. Some effects of irrelevant data in physics test problems. *School Science and Mathematics,* 37, 327–30.

————. 1951. Estimation of the reliability of ratings. *Psychometrika,* 16, 407–24.

————. 1953. Maximizing test validity in fixed time limits. *Educational and Psychological Measurement,* 13, 347–57.

————. 1961a. Must all tests be valid? *American Psychologist*, 16, 640–47.

————. 1961b. How to explain standardized test scores to your parents. *School Management*, 5, 61–64.

————. 1967. The relation of item discrimination to test reliability. *Journal of Educational Measurement*, 4, 125–28.

————. 1968a. The value of internal consistency in classroom examinations. *Journal of Educational Measurement*, 5, 71–73.

————. 1968b. Blind guessing on objective achievement tests. *Journal of Educational Measurement*, 5, 321–25.

————. 1972. *Essentials of educational measurement* (2nd ed.). Englewood Cliffs, NJ: Prentice-Hall.

————. 1975. Can teachers write good true-false test items? *Journal of Educational Measurement*, 12, 31–36.

————. 1978a. The ineffectiveness of multiple true-false items. *Educational and Psychological Measurement*, 38, 37–44.

————. 1978b. The case for minimum competency testing. *Phi Delta Kappan*, 59, 546–49.

————. 1979. *Essentials of educational measurement* (3rd ed.). Englewood Cliffs, NJ: Prentice-Hall.

————. 1980. Are true-false items useful? In R. L. EBEL (Ed.), *Practical problems in educational measurement*. Lexington, MA: D. C. Heath.

————. 1982. Proposed solutions to two problems of test construction. *Journal of Educational Measurement*, 19, 267–78.

————. 1983. The practical validation of tests of ability. *Educational Measurement: Issues and Practice*, 2, 7–10.

EDUCATIONAL TESTING SERVICE. 1963. *Multiple-choice questions: A close look*. Princeton, NJ: Author.

————. 1980a. *Test use and validity*. Princeton, NJ: Author.

————. 1980b. *Test scores and family income*. Princeton, NJ: Author.

EDWARDS, A. 1957. *Techniques of attitude scale construction*. New York: Appleton-Century-Crofts, Inc.

ENGLEHART, M. D. 1965. A comparison of several item discrimination indices. *Journal of Educational Measurement*, 2, 69–76.

EURICH, A. C. 1931. Four types of examinations compared and evaluated. *Journal of Educational Psychology*, 22, 268–78.

EVALUATION AND EXAMINATION SERVICE. 1982. *Evidence for not weighting objective test items* (EES Memo No. 51). Iowa City, IA: University of Iowa.

FINLAYSON, D. S. 1951. The reliability of the marking of essays. *British Journal of Educational Psychology*, 21, 126–34.

FISHBEIN, M. & AJZEN, I. 1975. *Belief, attitude, intention, and behavior: An introduction to theory and research*. Reading, MA: Addison-Wesley.

FLANAGAN, J. C. 1939. General considerations in the selection of test items and a short method of estimating the product-moment coefficient from the tails of the distributions. *Journal of Educational Psychology*, 30, 674–80.

FRISBIE, D. A. 1973. Multiple choice vs. true-false: A comparison of reliabilities and concurrent validities. *Journal of Educational Measurement*, 10, 297–304.

————. 1974. The effect of item format on reliability and validity: A study of multiple choice and true-false achievement tests. *Educational and Psychological Measurement*, 34, 885–92.

————. 1976. Expanded reporting forms—points to ponder. *The Clearing House*, 49, 371–72.

————. 1977. Issues in formulating course grading policies. *National Association of Colleges and Teachers of Agriculture Journal*, 21, 15–18.

————. 1978a. *Freestanding complex optical scanners*. Paper presented at the meeting of the National Council on Measurement in Education, Toronto.

————. 1978b. Methodological considerations in grading. *National Association of Colleges and Teachers of Agriculture Journal*, 22, 30–34.

———— & SWEENEY, D. C. 1982. The relative merits of multiple true-false achievement tests. *Journal of Educational Measurement*, 19, 29–35.

GALTON, F. 1883. *Inquiries into human faculty and its development*. London: Macmillan.

GERLACH, V. S. 1966. Preparing transparent keys for inspecting answer sheets. *Journal of Educational Measurement*, 3, 62.

GLASER, R. L. 1962. Psychology and instructional technology. In R. L. GLASER (Ed.), *Training research and education* (559–78). Pittsburgh: University of Pittsburgh Press.

————. 1963. Instructional technology and the measurement of learning outcomes. *American Psychologist*, 18, 519–21.

————. 1968. Adapting the elementary school curriculum to individual performance. *Proceedings of the 1967 Invitational Conference on Testing Problems*. Princeton, NJ: Educational Testing Service.

———— & NITKO, A. J. 1971. Measurement in learning and instruction. In R. L. THORNDIKE (Ed.), *Educational measurement* (2nd ed.). Washington, D.C.: American Council on Education.

GRAZIANO, W. G., VARCA, P. E., & LEVY, J. C. 1982. Race of examiner effects and the validity of intelligence tests. *Review of Educational Research*, 52, 469–97.

GREEN, B. F. 1983. Adaptive testing by computer. In R. B. EKSTROM (Ed.), *New directions for testing and measurement: Measurement, technology, and individuality in education*. San Francisco: Jossey-Bass.

Griggs v. *Duke Power Co.* 1971. 401 U.S. 424.

GRONLUND, N. E. 1981. *Measurement and evaluation in teaching* (4th ed.). New York: Macmillan Publishing Co.

GUILFORD, J. P. 1965. *Fundamental statistics in psychology and education.* New York: McGraw-Hill.

————. 1966. Intelligence: 1965 model. *American Psychologist,* 21, 20–25.

GUTTMAN, L. 1950. The basis for scaleogram analysis. In S. STOUFFER (Ed.), *Measurement and prediction.* Princeton, NJ: Princeton University Press.

HADLEY, S. T. 1954. A school mark—fact or fancy? *Educational Administration and Supervision,* 40, 305–12.

HALES, L. & TOKAR, E. 1975. The effect of the quality of preceding responses on the grades assigned to subsequent responses to an essay question. *Journal of Educational Measurement,* 12, 115–18.

HAMBLETON, R. K. 1979. Latent trait models and their applications. In R. E. TRAUB (Ed.), *New directions for testing and measurement: Methodological developments* (13–32). San Francisco: Jossey-Bass.

HARRIS, C. W. (Ed.). 1963. *Problems in measuring change.* Madison, WI: University of Wisconsin Press.

HARROW, A. J. 1972. *A taxonomy of the psychomotor domain: A guide for developing behavioral objectives.* New York: David McKay Co.

HECKMAN, R. W., TIFFIN, J., & SNOW, R. E. 1967. Effects of controlling item exposure in achievement testing. *Educational and Psychological Measurement,* 27, 113–25.

HENDRICKSON, H. R. 1976. Grade inflation. *College and University,* 52, 111–16.

HENNESSY, J. T. 1981. Clinical and diagnostic assessment of children's abilities: Traditional and innovative models. In P. MERRIFIELD (Ed.), *New directions for testing and measurement: Measuring human abilities* (37–58). San Francisco: Jossey-Bass.

HIERONYMOUS, A. N., LINDQUIST, E. F., & HOOVER, H. D. 1980. *Iowa tests of basic skills: Teacher's guide* (Early Primary Battery, Form 7). Iowa City, IA: The University of Iowa, Iowa Testing Programs.

HILLS, J. R. & GLADNEY M. B. 1968. Predicting grades from below chance test scores. *Journal of Educational Measurement,* 5, 45–53.

HIRST, P. H. 1972. Liberal education and the nature of knowledge. In DEARDEN, R. F., HIRST, P. H., & PETERS, R. S. *Education and the development of reason.* London: Routledge and Kegan Paul.

HIVELY, W. 1974. Introduction to domain-referenced testing. In W. HIVELY (Ed.), *Domain-referenced testing* (5–15). Englewood Cliffs, NJ: Educational Technology Publications.

Hobson v. Hansen. 1967. 269 F. Supp. 406 (D.D.C.).

HOEL, P. G. 1947. *Introduction to mathematical statistics.* New York: Wiley.

HOGAN, T. P. 1981. *Relationship between free-response and choice-type tests of achievement: A review of the literature* (ERIC Document Reproduction Service No. ED 224 811).

HOOVER, H. D. 1983. *The most appropriate scores for measuring educational development in the elementary schools: GE's.* Invited paper presented at the meeting of the American Educational Research Association, Montreal.

HOYT, D. P. 1965. *The relationship between college grades and adult achievement: A review of the literature* (Research Report No. 7). Iowa City, IA: American College Testing Program.

HSU, L. M. 1979. Ordering power of separate versus grouped true-false tests: Interaction of type of test with knowledge level of examinees. *Applied Psychological Measurement,* 3, 529–36.

HSU, T. & NITKO, A. J. 1983. Microcomputer testing software that teachers can use. *Educational Measurement: Issues and Practice,* 2, 15–18, 23–30.

JACKSON, R. 1970. *Developing criterion-referenced tests* (TM Report No. 1). Princeton, NJ: ERIC Clearinghouse on Tests, Measurement, and Evaluation.

JENSEN, A. R. 1969. How much can we boost I.Q. and scholastic achievement? *Harvard Educational Review,* 34, 1–123.

JOHNSON, A. P. 1951. Notes on a suggested index of item validity: The U-L index. *Journal of Educational Psychology,* 62, 499–504.

JOHNSON, O. G. 1976. *Tests and measurements in child development: Handbook II.* San Francisco: Jossey-Bass.

Joint Technical Standards for Educational and Psychological Testing, 4th Draft. 1984. Unpublished manuscript, Joint Committee of the American Psychological Association, American Educational Research Association, and the National Council on Measurement in Education.

JOYCE, B. R. & WEIL, M. 1980. *Models of teaching* (2nd ed.). Englewood Cliffs, NJ: Prentice-Hall.

JUNG, C. G. 1959. *Psychological types: Or the psychology of individuation.* London: Routledge.

KALISH, R. A. 1958. An experimental evaluation of the open-book examination. *Journal of Educational Psychology,* 49, 200–204.

KANE, M. T. 1982. A sampling model for validity. *Applied Psychological Measurement,* 6, 125–60.

———— & BRENNAN, R. L. 1980. Agreement coefficients as indices of dependability for domain-referenced tests. *Applied Psychological Measurement,* 4, 105–26.

KELLER, F. 1968. Good-bye, teacher . . . . *Journal of Applied Behavioral Analysis,* 1, 79–89.

KELLEY, E. C. 1962. The fully functioning self. In *Perceiving, behaving, becoming.* Washington, D.C.: Association for Supervision and Curriculum Development, 1962 Yearbook.

KELLEY, T. L. 1939. The selection of upper and lower groups for the validation of test items. *Journal of Educational Psychology,* 30, 17–24.

KIBLER, R. J., CEGALA, D. J., WATSON, K. W., BARKER, L. L., & MILES, D. T. 1981. *Objectives for instruction and evaluation* (2nd ed.). Boston: Allyn and Bacon, Inc.

KLAUER, K. J. 1984. Intentional and incidental learning with instructional texts: A meta-analysis for 1970–1980. *American Educational Research Journal*, 21, 323–39.

KRATHWOHL, D. R., BLOOM, B. S., & MASIA, B. B. 1964. *Taxonomy of educational objectives. Handbook II: The affective domain.* New York: David McKay Co.

KRETSCHMER, E. 1936. *Physique and character: An investigation of the nature of constitution and the theory of temperament.* London: Routledge.

KUDER, G. F. 1939. The stability of preference items. *The Journal of Social Psychology*, 10, 41–50.

————— & RICHARDSON, M. W. 1937. The theory of the estimation of test reliability. *Psychometrika*, 2, 151–60.

Larry P. v. *Wilson Riles.* 1979. 495 F. Supp. 926 (N. D. Cal.).

LAZARSFELD, P. F. 1959. Latent structure analysis. In S. KOCH (Ed.), *Psychology: A study of a science*, Vol. III. New York: McGraw-Hill Book Co.

LEVINE, M. 1976. The academic achievement test: Its historical context and social functions. *American Psychologist*, 31, 228–38.

LIGON, E. M. 1961. Education for moral character. In P. H. PHENIX (Ed.), *Philosophies of education.* New York: John Wiley & Sons.

LIKERT, R. 1932. A technique for the measurement of attitude. *Archives of Psychology*, 22 (140), 1–55.

LINDQUIST, E. F. 1960. The Iowa Testing Programs—a retrospective review. *Education*, 81, 7–23.

LINN, R. L. 1983. Testing and instruction: Links and distinctions. *Journal of Educational Measurement*, 20, 179–89.

LIVINGSTON, S. A. & ZIEKY, M. J. 1982. *Passing scores.* Princeton, NJ: Educational Testing Service.

LORD, F. M. & NOVICK, M. R. 1968. *Statistical theories of mental test scores.* Reading, MA: Addison-Wesley.

LOREE, M. R. 1948. *A study of a technique for improving tests.* Unpublished doctoral dissertation, University of Chicago, Chicago.

McCALL, W. A. 1939. *Measurement.* New York: Macmillan.

McMORRIS, R. F., BROWN, J. A., SNYDER, G. W., & PRUZEK, R. M. 1972. Effects of violating test construction principles. *Journal of Educational Measurement*, 9, 287–95.

MAGER, R. F. 1962. *Preparing instructional objectives.* Palo Alto, CA: Fearon Publishers, Inc.

MEHRENS, W. A. & LEHMANN, I. J. 1984. *Measurement and evaluation in education and psychology* (3rd ed.). New York: Holt, Rinehart and Winston.

MERWIN, J. C. & WOMER, F. B. 1969. Evaluation in assessing the progress of education to provide bases of public understanding and public policy. In R. W. TYLER (Ed.), *Educational evaluation: New roles, new means* (305–34). Chicago: National Society for the Study of Education.

MESSICK, S., BEATON, A., & LORD, F. M. 1983. *National assessment of educational progress reconsidered: A new design for a new era* (NAEP Report 83-1). Princeton, NJ: Educational Testing Service.

MEYER, G. 1935. An experimental study of the old and new types of examinations: II, methods of the study. *Journal of Educational Psychology*, 26, 30–40.

—————. 1939. The choice of questions on essay examinations. *Journal of Educational Psychology*, 30, 161–71.

MILLMAN, J. 1974a. Program assessment, criterion-referenced tests, and things like that. *Educational Horizons*, 32, 188–92.

—————. 1974b. Criterion-referenced measurement. In W. J. POPHAM (Ed.), *Evaluation in education.* Berkeley, CA: McCutchan.

—————, BISHOP, C. H., & EBEL, R. L. 1965. An analysis of testwiseness. *Educational and Psychological Measurement*, 25, 707–26.

MILLMAN, J. & PAUK, W. 1969. *How to take tests.* New York: McGraw-Hill Book Co.

MINIUM, E. W. & CLARKE, R. B. 1982. *Elements of statistical reasoning.* New York: Wiley.

MITCHELL, J. V., JR. (Ed.). 1983. *Tests in print III.* Lincoln, NE: University of Nebraska Press.

MUELLER, D. J. & WASSER, V. 1977. Implications of changing answers on objective test items. *Journal of Educational Measurement*, 14, 9–14.

MULLIS, I.V.S. 1984. Scoring direct writing assessments: What are the alternatives? *Educational Measurement: Issues and Practice*, 3, 16–18.

NATIONAL ASSESSMENT OF EDUCATIONAL PROGRESS. 1970. *Citizenship: National results.* Denver: Author.

NATIONAL COMMISSION ON EXCELLENCE IN EDUCATION. 1983. *A nation at risk: The imperative for educational reform.* Washington, D.C.: Author.

NITKO, A. J. 1970. Criterion-referenced testing in the context of instruction. In *Testing in turmoil: A conference on problems and issues in educational measurement* (37–40). Greenwich, CN: Educational Records Bureau.

—————. 1983. *Educational tests and measurement: An introduction.* New York: Harcourt Brace Jovanovich, Inc.

NOLL, V. H., SCANNELL, D. P., & CRAIG, R. C. 1979. *Introduction to educational measurement* (4th ed.). Boston: Houghton Mifflin.

ODELL, C. W. 1927. *Scales for rating pupils' answers to nine types of thought questions in English literature.* Urbana, IL: University of Illinois, Bureau of Educational Research.

—————. 1950. Marks and marking systems. In W. S. MONROE (Ed.), *Encyclopedia of Educational Research.* New York: The Macmillan Co.

OWENS, R. E., HANNA, G. S., & COPPEDGE, F. L. 1970. Comparison of multiple-choice tests using different types of distracter selection techniques. *Journal of Educational Measurement*, 7, 87–90.

PALMER, O. 1962. Seven classic ways of grading dishonestly. *The English Journal*, 51, 464–67.

PATTERSON, D. G. 1926. Do new and old type examinations measure different mental functions? *School and Society*, 24, 246–48.

PIPHO, C. 1980. *State activity: Minimum competency testing.* Denver: Education Commission of the States.

POLANYI, M. 1964. *Personal knowledge.* Chicago: University of Chicago Press.

POPHAM, W. J. & HUSEK, T. R. 1969. Implications of criterion-referenced measurement. *Journal of Educational Measurement*, 6, 1–9.

POSEY, C. 1932. Luck and examination grades. *Journal of Engineering Education*, 23, 292–96.

POWELL, M. 1981. Uses of state assessment information. In D. CARLSON (Ed.), *New directions for testing and measurement: Testing in the states: Beyond accountability* (13–29). San Francisco: Jossey-Bass.

PYRCZAK, F. 1973. Validity of the discrimination index as a measure of item quality. *Journal of Educational Measurement*, 10, 227–31.

QUELLMALZ, E. S., CAPELL, F. J., & CHOU, C. 1980. Effects of discourse and response mode on the measurement of writing competence. *Journal of Educational Measurement*, 19, 241–58.

RICHARDSON, M. W. & STALNAKER, J. M. 1935. Comments on achievement examinations. *Journal of Educational Research*, 28, 425–32.

ROEBER, E. 1980. *Summer 1980 survey results of state assessment programs.* Lansing MI: Michigan Department of Education.

ROKEACH, M. 1968. *Beliefs, attitudes, and values: A theory of organization and change.* San Francisco: Jossey-Bass.

ROSS, C. C. 1947. *Measurement in today's schools* (2nd ed.). Englewood Cliffs, NJ: Prentice-Hall.

ROWLEY, G. L. & TRAUB, R. E. 1977. Formula scoring, number-right scoring and test-taking strategy. *Journal of Educational Measurement*, 14, 15–22.

RUCH, G. M. 1929. *The objective or new-type examination.* Glenview, IL: Scott, Foresman and Co.

RUMMEL, J. F. 1950. *The modification of a test to reduce errors in the classification of examinees.* Unpublished doctoral dissertation, University of Iowa, Iowa City.

RYLE, G. 1949. *The concept of mind.* London: Hutchinson and Co., Ltd.

SABERS, D. L. & WHITE, G. W. 1969. The effect of differential weighting of individual item responses on the predictive validity and reliability of an aptitude test. *Journal of Educational Measurement*, 6, 93–96.

SADLER, D. R. 1983. Evaluation and the improvement of learning. *Journal of Higher Education*, 54, 60–79.

SARNACKI, R. E. 1979, An examination of test-wiseness in the cognitive test domain. *Review of Educational Research*, 49, 252–79.

SATO, T. 1980. *The S-P chart and the caution index* (NEC Educational Informatics Bulletin). Tokyo: Nippon Electric Co., Ltd.

SAX, G. & COLLET, L. S. 1968. The effects of differing instructions and guessing formulas on reliability and validity. *Educational and Psychological Measurement*, 28, 1127–36.

SAX, G. & CROMACK, T. R. 1966. The effects of various forms of item arrangements on test performance. *Journal of Educational Measurement*, 3, 309–11.

SCRIVEN, M. 1967. The methodology of evaluation. In R. TYLER (Ed.), *Perspectives of Curriculum Evaluation. AERA Monograph Series on Curriculum Evaluation* (No. 1). Skokie, IL: Rand McNally.

SHAVELSON, R., BLOCK, J. H., & RAVITCH, M. M. 1972. Criterion-referenced testing: Comments on reliability. *Journal of Educational Measurement*, 9, 133–37.

SHAW, M. E. & WRIGHT, J. M. 1967. *Scales for the measurement of attitudes.* New York: McGraw-Hill Book Co.

SMITH, K. 1958. An investigation of the use of "double choice" items in testing achievement. *Journal of Educational Research*, 51, 387–89.

SPEARMAN, C. E. 1927. *The abilities of man.* New York: The Macmillan Co.

SPENCE, J. T., COTTON, J., UNDERWOOD, B., & DUNCAN, C. *Elementary statistics* (4th ed.). Englewood Cliffs, NJ: Prentice-Hall.

STALNAKER, J. M. 1937. Essay examinations reliably read. *School and Society*, 46, 671–72.

———. 1951. The essay type of examination. In E. F. LINDQUIST (Ed.), *Educational measurement.* Washington, D. C.: American Council on Education.

STANLEY, J. C. 1971. Reliability. In R. L. THORNDIKE (Ed.), *Educational measurement* (2nd ed.). Washington, D.C.: American Council on Education.

STARCH, D. & ELLIOTT, E. C. 1912. Reliability of grading high school work in English. *School Review*, 20, 442–57.

———. 1913a. Reliability of grading high school work in history. *School Review*, 21, 676–81.

———. 1913b. Reliability of grading high school work in mathematics. *School Review*, 21, 254–59.

Stell v. Savannah. 1964. 379 U.S. 933.

STERN, W. 1914. *The psychological methods of testing intelligence* (G. M. WHIPPLE, Trans.). Baltimore: Warwick.

STRONG, E. K. 1943. *Vocational interests of men and women.* Stanford, CA: Stanford University Press.

STROUD, J. B. 1946. *Psychology in education.* New York: David McKay Co., Inc.

SWIFT, J. 1948. On poetry, a rhapsody. In *The portable Swift.* New York: The Viking Press, Inc.

TAYLOR, H. 1980. *Contract grading* (ERIC/TM Report No. 75). Princeton, NJ: ERIC Clearinghouse on Tests, Measurement and Evaluation. (ERIC Document Reproduction Service No. ED 198 152).

TERRY, P. W. 1933. How students review for objective and essay tests. *Elementary School Journal,* 33, 592–603.

TERWILLINGER, J. S. 1971. *Assigning grades to students.* Glenview, IL: Scott, Foresman and Co.

THORNDIKE, E. L. 1918. *The seventeenth yearbook of the National Society for Study of Education* (Part II). Bloomington, IL: Public School Publishing Co.

THORNDIKE, R. L. 1951. Reliability. In E. F. LINDQUIST (Ed.), *Educational measurement.* Washington, D.C.: American Council on Education.

————. 1963. *The concepts of over- and under-achievement.* New York: Teacher's College Press.

THURSTONE, L. L. 1938. Primary mental abilities. *Psychometric Monographs,* No. 1.

———— & CHAVE, E. J. 1929. *The measurement of attitude.* Chicago: University of Chicago Press.

TORGERSON, W. S. 1958. *Theory and methods of scaling.* New York: Wiley.

TRYON, G. S. 1980. The measurement and treatment of test anxiety. *Review of Educational Research,* 50, 343–72.

TURNBULL, W. W. 1956. A normalized graphic method of item analysis. *Journal of Educational Psychology,* 37, 129–41.

TYLER, R. W. 1974. Assessing educational achievement in the affective domain. *Measurement in Education,* 4(1).

————. 1981. Foreword. In D. CARLSON (Ed.), *New directions for testing and measurement: Testing in the states: Beyond accountability* (ix–xi). San Francisco: Jossey-Bass.

U.S. OFFICE OF EDUCATION. 1951. Life adjustment education for every youth. Washington, D.C.: U.S. Government Printing Office.

VERNON, P. E. 1971. *The structure of human abilities.* London: Methuen.

———— & MILLICAN, G. D. 1954. A further study of the reliability of English essays. *British Journal of Statistical Psychology,* 7, 65–74.

WAGNER, R. K. & STERNBERG, R. J. 1984. Alternative conceptions of intelligence and their implications for education. *Review of Educational Research,* 54, 179–223.

WARD, W. C. 1982. A comparison of free-response and multiple-choice forms of verbal aptitude tests. *Applied Psychological Measurement,* 6, 1–11.

WESMAN, A. G. 1971. Writing the test item. In R. L. THORNDIKE (Ed.), *Educational measurement* (2nd ed.). Washington, D.C.: American Council on Education.

WILEY, D. E. 1981. Improving policy development. In D. CARLSON (Ed.), *New directions in testing and measurement: Testing in the states: Beyond accountability.* San Francisco: Jossey-Bass.

WILLIAMS, B. J. & EBEL, R. L. 1957. The effect of varying the number of alternatives per item on multiple-choice vocabulary test items. *The 14th yearbook of the National Council on Measurements Used in Education.* East Lansing, MI: Michigan State University.

WILSON, P. A., DOWNING, S. M., & EBEL, R. L. 1977. *An empirical adjustment of the Kuder-Richardson 21 reliability coefficient to better estimate the Kuder-Richardson 20 coefficient.* Unpublished manuscript.

WOMER, F. B. 1981. State level testing: Where we have been may not tell us where we are going. In D. CARLSON (Ed.), *New directions in testing and measurement: Testing in the states: Beyond accountability* (1–12). San Francisco: Jossey-Bass.

WOOD, R. 1976. Inhibiting blind guessing: The effect of instructions. *Journal of Educational Measurement,* 13, 297–308.

WRIGHT, B. D. 1977. Solving measurement problems with the Rasch model. *Journal of Educational Measurement,* 14, 97–116.

YERKES, R. M. (Ed.). 1921. Psychological examining in the United States army. *Memoirs of the National Academy of Sciences* (Vol. 15). Washington, D.C.: U.S. Government Printing Office.

GLOSSARY OF TERMS USED IN EDUCATIONAL MEASUREMENT

This glossary of terms used in educational measurement is intended primarily to aid the reader who encounters an unfamiliar term. An effort has been made to make the descriptions conform to usage in the text and to general usage by specialists in educational measurement.

Absolute Grades are based on teacher judgment of the adequacy of a student's achievement, without reference to the achievements of other students in the group.

An Achievement Test is one designed to measure a student's grasp of some body of knowledge or proficiency in certain skills.

Affective outcomes of education involve feelings more than understandings. A person's likes and dislikes, pleasures and annoyances, satisfactions and discontents, confidence and diffidence, pride and humility, ideals and values are some of the affective outcomes that education may develop.

Analytic Scoring requires preparation of a scoring guide which lists elements of quality or defects that may appear in the product to be scored. The guide may also indicate how many points to award or subtract for each degree of quality or deficiency.

An **Aptitude Test** is one given to determine the potential of an individual for development along a special line or the extent to which he or she is likely to profit from instruction along that line.

The **Basic Teaching Model** is a conceptual description of the major activities in the teaching process and of the relationship between these activities.

A **Battery of Tests** is a set of several tests intended to be administered in succession to the same examinees.

In a **Bimodel Distribution** the measures tend to concentrate or pile up at two distinct points or regions along the score scale.

A **Biserial Correlation Coefficient,** frequently used as an item discrimination index, shows the relationship between score on the item and total test score for a group.

Blind Guessing characterizes any response to

an objective test item that was not determined in any way by the content of the item, and which reflects a purely random selection among the alternatives offered.

The **Central Tendency** of a set of scores is some average value, such as the mean, median, or mode.

Comparable Scores are expressed on the same scale and have the same relative meaning within some common reference group. If scores on different tests are comparable, a particular numerical score represents the same level of proficiency or deficiency regardless of the subject matter of the test.

Construct-Related Validity evidence is comprised of judgmental and statistical information that shows what behaviors a particular test does and does not measure.

A **Content-Referenced** score interpretation involves comparing a test score to a set of scores, each of which represents a different absolute level of performance in a domain.

Content-Related Validity evidence is judgmental information gathered by a test user to demonstrate that the tasks in a particular test are appropriate measures of the abilities the user wishes to measure.

A **Correlation Coefficient,** limited by the values plus 1 and minus 1, expresses the degree of relationship between two sets of test scores or other measurements of each of the individuals in a group.

A **Criterion** is a standard of judging. In test development it usually refers to a characteristic or a combination of characteristics used as a basis for judging the validity of a test or some other measurement procedure.

A **Criterion-Referenced** score interpretation involves comparing a test score to a cutoff score that represents a performance standard.

Criterion-Related Validity evidence shows how scores on a test correlate with scores on an appropriate criterion measure.

A **Cumulative Frequency** is a number that shows, for any given score interval, the number of the scores in the distribution that lie below the midpoint of that interval.

A **Diagnostic Test** is designed to reveal specific weaknesses or failures to learn in some subject of study, such as reading or arithmetic.

The **Difficulty Index** of a test item is the proportion of examinees in a group who answer the test item correctly.

A **Discrimination Index** is a measure of the extent to which students who are judged to be good in terms of some standard succeed on the item and those who are judged to be poor on the same standard fail it. A commonly used index of discrimination is simply the difference in a proportion of correct responses between the group of those scoring in the top 27 percent on the total test and the group scoring in the bottom 27 percent on the same test.

A **Distracter** is any of the incorrect answer options in multiple-choice test items.

A **Distribution of Scores** is a tabulation or enumeration of the frequency of occurrence of each score in a given set of scores.

A **Domain-Referenced** score interpretation involves comparing a test score with the maximum possible score to estimate the proportion of content in the universe of interest known by the examinee.

The items in **Equivalent Forms** of a test are the same in type, cover the same content, have the same distribution of difficulty values, and yield scores having the same mean, variability, and reliability.

An **Error of Measurement** is the difference between an obtained score and the corresponding true score.

The **Error Variance** in a set of test scores is the mean of the squared errors of measurement for each score in the set.

An **Essay Test** presents one or more questions or other tasks that require extended written responses from the person being tested.

Evaluation is the process of judging the quality or worth of an object or activity, or it may be regarded as the outcome of such a process.

In an **Expectancy Table** the rows ordinarily correspond to score intervals on some predicter of achievement, and the columns correspond to score intervals on some measure of actual achievement. The figures in each cell of such a double-entry table indicate the relative frequency with which an individual having a given score on the predicter will receive a given score on the criterion of achievement.

Factor Analysis seeks to identify a small number of hypothetical characteristics that will account for the correlations between scores on a much larger number of tests for the individuals in a particular group.

A **Free-Response Test** requires the examinee to provide an answer to each question rather than to choose among several suggested alternatives.

A **Frequency Distribution** consists of a sequence of score intervals, opposite each of which is recorded the number of scores in the total group falling in that interval.

Global Quality Scaling of a student's answer to an essay test question is based on the reader's general, overall estimate of its quality. This kind of scaling is an alternative to analytic scoring.

A **Grade-Equivalent Score** is a developmental score that indicates the school grade level for which the examinee's performance is typical.

A **Grading System** in a school or college lists the grade symbols a teacher may use and describes what each symbol is intended to mean.

A **Group-Referenced** score interpretation uses the scores of a reference group of individuals (norm-referenced) or groups (treatment-referenced) to derive meaning from a score.

A **Guessing Correction** is a factor that is added to or subtracted from the number of items correctly answered. The purpose of this correction is to make the score a student could expect to get by guessing blindly on certain questions no higher than the score of a student who omits those items in preference to guessing blindly on them.

Halo Effect describes a bias in ratings arising from the tendency of a rater to be influenced in his or her rating of specific traits by his or her general positive impression of the person being rated.

Intelligence is the capacity to apprehend facts and propositions and their relationships, and to reason about them.

Methods of **Internal Analysis** use a single test administration and component subtest data to provide estimates of test reliability.

IQ stands for "intelligence quotient," originally a ratio of the individual's mental age to chronological age. On modern intelligence tests it may be a standard score whose mean is 100 and standard deviation 16 in the appropriate reference population.

Item Analysis involves the counting of responses to objective test items to determine the difficulty and discriminating power of the items.

The **Item Stem** of a multiple-choice test item is the introductory question or incomplete statement. The examinee chooses an answer to or a completion of the item stem from among the options provided in the remainder of the item.

The **Keyed Response** is the correct answer on a choice-type test item.

Knowledge is a structure of concepts and relations built by reflective thought out of information received. Any experience of participation, observation, reading, or thinking *can* become part of a person's knowledge. It *will* become part of that knowledge if he or she thinks about it, makes sense of it, understands it.

The **Kurtosis** of a frequency polygon is that characteristic that describes the relative flatness or peakedness of the curve.

A **Mastery Test** is not intended to indicate how much a student has achieved relative to other students, but only whether or not he or she has achieved enough to satisfy the minimum requirements of the teacher or the examining agency.

A **Matching Exercise** consists of two lists of statements, terms, or symbols. The examinee's task is to match an item in one list with the one most closely associated with it in the other.

The **Mean** is a measure of the average numerical value of a set of scores. It is calculated by adding all of the scores and dividing the sum by the number of scores.

Measurement is a process of assigning numbers to the individual members of a set of objects or persons for the purpose of indicating differences among them in the degree to which they possess the characteristic being measured.

The **Median** is the point in a score distribution that divides it into two parts containing equal numbers of scores.

Mental Age is an examinee's score on a test of mental ability expressed in terms of the chronological age of persons whose median score is the same as the examinee's.

A test of **Minimum Competence** contains tasks that represent the abilities examinees must display to be classified as "competent" or "passing" on the basis of their score.

The **Mode** is the most frequently occurring value in a frequency distribution.

A **Multiple-Choice Item** has two parts: the stem, consisting of a direct question or an incomplete statement, and two or more options, consisting of answers to the question or completions of the statement.

A **Normal-Curve Equivalent** is a normalized standard score ranging in value from 1 to 99 and having a mean of 50.

A **Normal Distribution** is a theoretical frequency polygon represented by a symmetrical, bell-shaped curve and characterized by scores concentrated near the middle and tapering toward each extreme.

Normalized Standard Scores are derived in a way that makes the distribution of scores approximately normal, regardless of the shape of the distribution of raw scores on which they were based.

A **Norm-Referenced** score interpretation involves comparing a test score with the scores of individuals in some appropriate reference group.

The **Norms** for a test indicate how the members of a particular reference group or groups scored on the test.

An **Objectives-Referenced** score interpretation involves comparing a test score with the maximum possible score to determine if a specific instructional objective or a related cluster of objectives have been mastered by the examinee.

An **Objective Test** is one that can be provided with a simple predetermined list of correct answers, so that subjective opinion or judgment in the scoring procedure is eliminated.

Objectivity is characteristic of statements that can be verified by an independent observer or judge.

Pass-Fail grades indicate only whether a student did or did not complete a course of study satisfactorily.

A **Percentile Band** is a range of percentile ranks within which a particular student's true percentile rank on the test is likely to fall.

The **Percentile Rank** of a particular score in a given distribution of scores is a number indicating the percentage of scores in the whole distribution that falls below the point at which the given score lies.

In a **Performance Test** the subject is required to demonstrate his or her skill by manipulating objects or instruments.

Personality refers to the complex of characteristics that gives a particular person identity, distinguishing him or her from other persons. A person's appearance, habits, attitudes, interests, values, and knowledge all contribute to personality. How that personality is perceived by others depends mainly on the individual's behavior in social situations.

A **Point-Biserial Correlation Coefficient,** frequently used as an item-discrimination index, shows the relationship between score on the item and total test score for a group.

A **Population** of persons, test items, or other objects is the whole number of all who belong to a particular set or collection. Some part of a population becomes a sample.

The **Predictive Validity** evidence for a test indicates how accurately some earlier measure of ability can forecast some later measure of performance.

A **Profile** is a graphic representation of the relative magnitude of a student's scores on several tests. In order for such a profile to be meaningful, the scores on all of the tests must be comparable scores, based on the same standard scale.

A **Proposition** is a sentence that can be said to be either true of false.

A **Quartile** is one of three points along the score scale of a frequency distribution that divide the distribution into four parts of equal frequency.

A **Random Sample** is selected in such a way as to guarantee equal probability of selection to all possible samples of this size that could be formed from the members of the universe involved.

A **Range of Scores** is the smallest interval on the score scale that will include all the measures in the distribution.

A **Raw Score** is the number first obtained in scoring the test, before any transformation to a standard score or other derived score.

In a **Rectangular Distribution** successive equal intervals along the score scale include the same number of scores.

The **Relevance** of a task in a test is the extent to which it contributes to the purposes of the test by virtue of the abilities it calls into play.

The **Reliability Coefficient** is the estimate of the coefficient of correlation between the scores for students in a particular group on two equivalent forms of the same test. Reliability is sometimes defined also as the proportion of total score variance that is not error variance.

A **Response Count** for an objective-test item indicates the frequency with which one or more of the answer options were chosen by examinees in a particular group.

A **Response Set** is a predisposition on the part of an examinee to resolve uncertainty in answering a test question in a particular way. Willingness or unwillingness to guess may be a response set.

Rote Learning is memorization of a sequence of words or other symbols by repeated utterance or observation. Rote learning does not rely on meaningfulness as an aid to learning.

A **Sample** is some part of a population, often used to provide a convenient estimate of some characteristic of the entire population.

A **Sampling Error** is the difference between the sample value of some statistic and the value obtained when calculated on the basis of the entire population.

A **Scatter Diagram** is a device for displaying the relationship between scores on two tests for the individuals in a group. Scores on one test are represented on the vertical dimension, those on the other along the horizontal dimension.

A **Score** is a number assigned to an examinee to provide a quantitative description of his or her performance on a particular measure.

A **Scoring Formula** indicates how the raw score on the test is to be obtained from the number of correct, incorrect, or omitted responses. The simplest scoring formula is "Score equals number right." Other formulas provide corrections for guessing.

A **Scoring Key** indicates the correct answer to each item.

A **Short-Answer Test** requires the examinee to produce a word, phrase, or number that answers the test question.

A **Skewed Distribution** is an asymmetrical distribution in which most of the scores are closer to one end of the distribution than they are to the other. If the longer tail of the distribution extends toward the lower end of the score scale, the distribution is said

to be negatively skewed. If the longer tail extends to the higher end of the score scale, the distribution is said to be positively skewed.

The **Spearman-Brown Formula** is used to predict the reliability of a lengthened test, assuming that the material added to the test is highly similar to that already present in it.

A **Specific Determiner** is some characteristic in the statement of a true-false test item that supplies an unintended clue to the correct answer. For example, statements including the words "every," "always," "entirely," "absolutely," and "never" are more likely to be false than true. Similarly, statements containing the words "sometimes," "usually," "often," and "ordinarily" are more likely to be true than false.

Speededness of a test is the extent to which an examinee's score on it depends on quickness in working through it. It is sometimes measured by the proportion of examinees who *do not* reach and answer the last item in the test.

A **Split-Halves Reliability Coefficent** is obtained by using half the items on the test, sometimes the odd-numbered items, to yield one score for an examinee and the other half of the items to yield another, independent score. The correlation between the scores on these two half-tests, corrected with the aid of the Spearman-Brown formula, provides an estimate of the reliability of the total test.

The **Standard Deviation** is a measure of variability, dispersion, or spread of a set of scores around their mean value. Mathematically, the standard deviation is the square root of the mean of the squared deviations of the scores from the mean of the distribution of scores.

The **Standard Error of Measurement** is an estimate of the standard deviation of the errors of measurement associated with the test scores in a given set. The standard error of measurement is estimated by multiplying the standard deviation of the scores by the square root of one minus the reliability coefficient.

A **Standard Score** is one derived from a raw score so that it can be expressed on a uniform standard scale without seriously altering its relationship to other scores in the distribution.

A **Standardized Test** is one that has been constructed in accord with detailed specifications, one for which the items have been selected after tryout for appropriateness in difficulty and discriminating power, one which is accompanied by a manual giving definite directions for uniform administration and scoring, and one which is provided with relevant and dependable norms for score interpretation.

A **Stanine Score** (from *stand*ard *nine*) is a single-digit standard score on a nine-unit scale. The distribution of stanine scores in the population from which they were derived has a mean of 5 and standard deviation of 2.

A **Statistic** is a number used to describe or characterize some aspect of a sample. For example, the number of cases in the sample, the mean value of the measures in the sample, the standard deviation of those measures, and the correlation between two sets of measures for the members of the sample are statistics.

A **Table of Specifications** or test blueprint is a content outline that specifies what proportion of the items should deal with each content area and each type of ability.

A **Taxonomy** is an orderly classification, originally of plants and animals, arranged according to their presumed natural relationships. Taxonomies of cognitive and affective educational objectives have been prepared.

A **Test** is a measure containing a set of questions, each of which can be said to have a correct answer.

Test Bias is a general term that represents a variety of factors or conditions that might give unfair advantage or disadvantage to individual examinees or groups of examinees. These influencing conditions may be present in the test itself, in the test administration, in the interpretation of scores, or in the use of the scores.

A **Test Item** is the smallest independent unit of a test. Each statement to be judged true or false, each question to which an answer is to be selected, each incomplete statement to which a completion is to be selected, each blank in a sentence or paragraph to be filled in is a separate test item.

Test-Retest Reliability is calculated by correlating scores for the same students on two administrations of the same test.

Testwiseness enables an examinee to do full justice to himself, or to outwit an inept examiner.

A **Trait** is any attribute of a person that is possessed in differing amounts by different members of a group or class. It is a physical characteristic or a relatively stable mode of behavior. Such things as height, intelligence, quality of handwriting, or understanding of chemical principles are traits.

A **Treatment-Referenced** score interpretation involves comparing the score or mean score of a group with the scores of some relevant set of groups.

A **True Score** is an idealized error-free score for a specific person on a specific test. It may also be defined as the mean of an infinite number of independent measurements of the same trait, using equivalent forms of the test.

A **T-Score** is a standard score obtained by transforming raw scores to a scale having a mean of 50 and a standard deviation of 10.

The **Validity** of a test refers to the extent to which a test is a precise measure of whatever the test user intended to measure. Evidence sometimes furnished to support the appropriateness of making specific inferences on the basis of scores from a test is categorized as content-related, criterion-related, or construct-related.

The **Variance** is a measure of the dispersion of scores about their mean. The variance is the mean of the squared deviations of the scores from their mean.

In **Weighted Scoring** the number of points awarded for a correct response is not the same for all items in the test. In some cases, weighted scoring involves the award of different numbers of points for the choice of different responses to the same item.

A **z-Score** is a standard score. Raw scores are converted into z-scores by subtracting the mean from the raw score and dividing the difference by the standard deviation. Thus, a z-score represents a raw score in standard-deviation units.

AUTHOR INDEX

SUBJECT INDEX